Understanding Second Language Acquisition

Understanding Second Language Acquisition

Rod Ellis

Oxford University Press

OXFORD
UNIVERSITY PRESS

Great Clarendon Street, Oxford OX2 6DP

Oxford University Press is a department of the University of Oxford.
It furthers the University's objective of excellence in research, scholarship,
and education by publishing worldwide in

Oxford New York

Auckland Bangkok Buenos Aires Cape Town Chennai
Dar es Salaam Delhi Hong Kong Istanbul Karachi Kolkata
Kuala Lumpur Madrid Melbourne Mexico City Mumbai
Nairobi São Paulo Shanghai Taipei Tokyo Toronto

OXFORD and OXFORD ENGLISH are registered trade marks of
Oxford University Press in the UK and in certain other countries

© Rod Ellis 1985

The moral rights of the author have been asserted

Database right Oxford University Press (maker)

First published 1985
2008 2007 2006 2005 2004
20 19 18 17 16

ISBN 0 19 437081 X

Typeset by Hope Services, Abingdon, Oxfordshire, UK

Printed in China

To my father

To my father

Contents

Acknowledgements

Acknowledgements are made to the following publisher from whose text the extract below has been taken:

Newbury House, for figure 5.1 by K. Bailey, published in *Classroom-oriented Research in Second Language Acquisition*, edited by H. Seliger and M. Long (1983).

Introduction

The aim of this book is to provide a thorough account of what is known about second language acquisition (SLA). As far as possible the book will describe, rather than prescribe; that is, it will not consciously project any single approach or theory of SLA as received opinion. Indeed, this is not possible at the moment, as the study of SLA is still in its infancy and there are still more questions than answers. Of course, it is impossible to separate description from interpretation entirely, so my own views on what second language (L2) learners do and why they do it will necessarily colour the account I provide, if only in the research and theories which I choose to report.

The book has been written for two kinds of readers: students taking an initial course in SLA who want an overview of the current state of the art in SLA studies, and teachers who want to improve their understanding of how learners learn a second language.

For students taking an initial course in SLA the book offers a review of the main aspects of SLA. These are outlined in Chapter 1. Each of the subsequent chapters tackles a particular issue. Chapter 10 then attempts to pull all the threads together in a survey of different theories of SLA. At the end of each chapter there are suggestions for further reading. These are designed to guide the student into the rapidly developing area of published SLA research.

It is envisaged, however, that many readers will be teachers of second or foreign languages and so the book has been written to give them a clear idea of what happens in SLA, both inside and outside the classroom.

Teachers traditionally decide both what classroom learners will learn and what order they will learn it in. A language textbook, for instance, imposes an organization of content on the learner. It assumes that the order in which features of the language are presented will correspond to the order in which the learner is capable of acquiring them. Likewise, a teacher who draws up his or her own scheme of work does so in the belief that a careful selection and ordering of the teaching material will facilitate learning. However, unless we know for certain that the teacher's scheme really does match the learner's own way of going about things, we cannot be sure that the teaching content will contribute directly to language learning.

Teachers do more than decide on the content and structure of teaching. They also decide on how the L2 will be taught. They provide a methodology. They decide whether to drill or not to drill, how much to drill, whether to correct or not correct, when and how much to correct, etc. It is by means of their chosen methodology that teachers seek to manage the process of language learning. Again, however, there is no guarantee that the methodological principles which the teacher chooses to follow will conform to the way in which the learner learns the language. For instance, the teacher may decide to focus on grammatical correctness, whereas the learner may focus on trying to get his meaning across, irrespective of how grammatical his utterances are. The teacher may concentrate on instilling mastery of the language item by item, whereas the learner may tackle the learning problem globally, gradually gaining the ability to handle a whole range of items at one and the same time. If learning does take place, it may not be in the manner in which the teacher's methodology envisaged. In order to discover how the learner utilizes the language data made available to him, it is necessary to consider the strategies that the learner uses. In this way we can try to explain why learners learn in the way they do.

All teachers have a theory of language learning. That is, they act in accordance with a set of principles about the way language learners behave. This theory, however, may not be explicit. In many cases the teacher's views about language learning will be covert and will only be implicit in what he does. For instance, he may decide to start teaching a class of complete beginners the Present Continuous Tense. In so doing, he may have consciously decided that grammar should take precedence over other aspects of language such as pronunciation or vocabulary in the early stages because he believes that this corresponds to the learner's order of priorities. Or he may simply have assumed this without conscious enquiry. The decision to begin with the Present Continuous Tense has further implications. One is that learning can and should begin with verbs, rather than nouns or some other part of speech. Another is that out of all the verb tenses the Present Continuous is the one the learner will need to learn first. The teacher may be aware of these implications or he may not. He may have intuitions which he has never made explicit. Language teaching cannot take place without a theory of language learning, but this may exist only as a set of covert beliefs.

This book seeks to help teachers make their theory of language learning *explicit* through an examination of language-learner language and the processes that produce it. It is based on the conviction that teachers will be better off with an explicit set of ideas about language learning. This conviction needs some justification.

It is only when principles are made explicit that they can be examined with a view to amending or replacing them. Teachers who operate in accordance with implicit beliefs may be not only uncritical but also resistant to change. Alternatively they may shift and change in an unprincipled way, following blindly the latest fashion in language teaching. Teachers who make explicit the principles by which they teach are able to examine those principles critically.

This book is based on the belief that teachers will do better to operate with a theory of language learning that is explicit and therefore open to revision, than with an implicit theory that may ignore what learners actually do. Greater consciousness of the complex process of language learning will not guarantee more effective teaching—arguably our state of knowledge is insufficient to warrant firm pedagogical applications—but it will stimulate critical thought, challenge old principles, and maybe suggest a few new ones. A conscious understanding of SLA is a basis for modifying and improving teaching.

Whether the reader is a student of SLA or a teacher keen to know more about the process of language learning, there is a need for him to develop his own theory of SLA. This book seeks to provide the necessary background knowledge on which to base this theory. In Chapter 10 I develop a framework and a set of hypotheses to account for what is known about SLA.

This book could not have been written without the support and guidance of a number of people. In particular I would like to acknowledge the assistance of Henry Widdowson and Keith Johnson. Their help has been instrumental in shaping and revising the manuscript of the book. Needless to say, any faults the book may have are of my own doing.

In this book the pronouns used to refer to 'learner' and 'teacher' are 'he', 'his', and 'him'. They have been chosen as a stylistic convenience and are intended as unmarked forms. To those readers for whom this convention is not acceptable, I extend my apologies.

1 Key issues in Second Language Acquisition

Introduction

Second language acquisition (SLA) is a complex process, involving many interrelated factors. This chapter will examine the main issues that have arisen in the study of this process. It will begin by considering what is meant by 'second language acquisition' and then go on to discuss briefly the issues that have preoccupied SLA researchers. Finally, a framework will be set up for the discussion of these issues in the rest of the book.

What is second language acquisition?

In order to investigate SLA, it is important to establish clearly what is meant by the term. A number of key questions need to be addressed so that the reader is clear what positions researchers have taken up in order to study how a second language (L2) is learnt. The points considered below are all central to an understanding of how researchers have set about examining SLA. They underlie the various perspectives that inform the subsequent chapters of this book.

SLA as a uniform phenomenon

SLA is not a uniform and predictable phenomenon. There is no single way in which learners acquire a knowledge of a second language (L2). SLA is the product of many factors pertaining to the learner on the one hand and the learning situation on the other. It is important, therefore, to start by recognizing the complexity and diversity that results from the interaction of these two sets of factors. Different learners in different situations learn a L2 in different ways. Nevertheless, although the variability and individuality of language learning need to be emphasized, the study of SLA assumes interest only if it is possible to identify aspects that are relatively stable and hence generalizable, if not to all learners, then, at least, to large groups of learners. The term 'second language acquisition' is used to refer to these general aspects. This book will examine both what seems to be invariable and what is apparently variable about the process of acquisition.

Second language acquisition vs first language acquisition

Second language acquisition stands in contrast to *first* language acquisition. It is the study of how learners learn an additional language after they have acquired their mother tongue. The study of language-learner language began with the study of first language (L1) acquisition. SLA research has tended to follow in the footsteps of L1 acquisition research, both in its methodology and in many of the issues that it has treated. It is not surprising that a key issue has been the extent to which SLA and L1 acquisition are similar or different processes.

Second language acquisition vs foreign language acquisition

Second language acquisition is not intended to contrast with *foreign* language acquisition. SLA is used as a general term that embraces both untutored (or 'naturalistic') acquisition and tutored (or 'classroom') acquisition. It is, however, an open question whether the way in which acquisition proceeds in these different situations is the same or different.

The centrality of syntax and morphology

Second *language* acquisition refers to all the aspects of language that the language learner needs to master. However, the focus has been on how L2 learners acquire grammatical sub-systems, such as negatives or interrogatives, or grammatical morphemes such as the plural {s} or the definite and indefinite articles. Research has tended to ignore other levels of language. A little is known about L2 phonology, but almost nothing about the acquisition of lexis. SLA researchers have only recently turned their attention to how learners acquire the ability to communicate and started to examine how learners use their knowledge to communicate their ideas and intentions (i.e. pragmatic knowledge). This book, therefore, will be largely confined to what is known about the SLA of syntax and morphology. It must be acknowledged from the start that this constitutes a limitation. Many researchers would now accept that not only is it important to know about other aspects of SLA (in particular how the ability to participate in discourse is acquired), but also that these other aspects need to be studied in order to find out about the acquisition of grammar.

Competence vs performance

A distinction is often made between *competence* and *performance* in the study of language. According to Chomsky (1965), competence consists of the mental representation of linguistic rules which constitute the speaker-hearer's internalized grammar. Performance consists of the comprehension and production of language. Language acquisition studies—both first and second—are interested in how competence is developed. However, because the rules the learner has internalized are not open to direct inspection, it has been necessary to examine how the learner performs, mainly in production. The utterances that the learner produces are treated as windows through which the internalized rule system can be viewed. In one sense, therefore, SLA research is about performance; it looks at actual utterances. But these are treated as evidence for what is going on inside the learner's head. One of the major problems of SLA research has been precisely to what extent competence can be inferred from performance.

Acquisition vs learning

Second language *acquisition* is sometimes contrasted with second lanugage *learning* on the assumption that these are different processes. The term 'acquisition' is used to refer to picking up a second language through exposure, whereas the term 'learning' is used to refer to the conscious study of a second language. However, I wish to keep an open mind about whether this is a real distinction or not, so I shall use 'acquisition' and 'learning' interchangeably, irrespective of whether conscious or subconscious processes are involved. If I wish to use either of these terms with a more specific meaning, they will be italicized and their reference made explicit.

To summarize, the term 'second language acquisition' refers to the subconscious or conscious processes by which a language other than the mother tongue is learnt in a natural or a tutored setting. It covers the development of phonology, lexis, grammar, and pragmatic knowledge, but has been largely confined to morphosyntax. The process manifests both variable and invariable features. The study of SLA is directed at accounting for the learner's competence, but in order to do so has set out to investigate empirically how a learner performs when he or she uses a second language.

The sections of this chapter that follow will consider a number of key issues in the study of second language acquisition.

The role of the first language

Beginning in the post-war years and carrying on into the 1960s, there was a strong assumption that most of the difficulties facing the L2 learner were imposed by his or her first language. It was assumed that where there were differences between the L1 and L2, the learner's L1 knowledge would interfere with the L2, and where the L1 and L2 were similar, the L1 would actively aid L2 learning. The process that was held responsible for this was called *language transfer*. In the case of similarities between the L1 and L2 it functioned positively, while in the case of differences it functioned negatively. Teachers were encouraged (e.g. by Brooks 1960 and Lado 1964) to focus their teaching on the areas of difficulty created by negative transfer. They were exhorted to apply massive practice to overcome these difficulties.

In order to identify the areas of difficulty, a procedure called Contrastive Analysis was developed. This was founded on the belief that it was possible, by establishing the linguistic differences between the learner's L1 and L2, to predict what problems the learner of a particular L2 would face. To this end, descriptions of the two languages were obtained and an interlingual comparison carried out. This resulted in a list of features of the L2 which, being different from those of the L1, were presumed to constitute the problem areas and which were given focal attention in the teaching syllabus.

It was not until the late 1960s that the Contrastive Analysis hypothesis was submitted to empirical investigation. Were learners' errors traceable to the effects of the L1? The findings of researchers such as Dulay and Burt (1973;1974a) raised grave doubts about negative transfer as a major factor in the process of SLA. A large proportion of grammatical errors (although precisely what proportion was a controversial issue) could not be explained by L1 interference. As a result of such studies, the role of the L1 was played down and Contrastive Analysis became less fashionable.

There were, however, many questions left unanswered by the early empirical studies. In particular no consideration was given to the possibility that the effects of the L1 operated in ways other than through transfer. The theory of transfer was linked to a particular view of language learning as a series of habits which could be developed only through practice and reinforcement. In order to challenge this view of language learning, it was necessary to demonstrate that the 'old' habits of the L1 did not get in the way of learning the 'new' habits of the L2. Hence the attempt to show that L2 errors were not predominantly the result of interference. However, the L1 may contribute to learning in entirely different ways. For instance, learners may not *transfer* L1 rules into the L2, but may *avoid* using those rules that are absent in their L1 system. Or there may be linguistic constraints on which differences between the L1 and the L2 constitute difficulties so that transfer occurs only under certain linguistic conditions. Or learners may use the L1 as a resource from which they consciously *borrow* in order to improve their performance (i.e. they 'translate'). If a more cognitive perspective on the role of the L1 is adopted, it remains an issue which is very much alive.

Chapter 2 examines the Contrastive Analysis hypothesis and its rejection as a result of studies of learner errors. Chapters 2 and 8 look at more recent research in which a positive role for the L1 in SLA is once again advanced.

The 'natural' route of development

One of the assumptions of the Contrastive Analysis hypothesis was that learners with different L1s would learn a L2 in different ways, as a result of negative transfer imposing different kinds of difficulty. Challenging the Contrastive Analysis hypothesis led to a consideration of the possibility that L2 learners followed a universal route in acquiring a L2. This possibility was encouraged by research in L1 acquisition which showed that children learning their mother tongue followed a highly predictable route in the acquisition of structures such as negatives and interrogatives (Klima and Bellugi 1966) and a range of grammatical morphemes (R. Brown 1973). If this was true for L1 acquisition and if, as the studies of L2 learner errors showed, negative transfer was not the major factor in SLA that it was once assumed to be, then it was not unreasonable to hypothesize that SLA followed a 'natural' sequence of development. That is, that all learners, irrespective of their L1, learnt the grammar of the L2 in a fixed order.

A key issue, then, was whether there was a 'natural' route of development and if so, what it consisted of. A related issue was whether the route of development in L1 acquisition matched that of SLA. This issue became known as the L2 = L1 hypothesis. This states that the processes of SLA and L1 acquisition are very similar as a result of the strategies learners employ. The task of 'cracking the code', which every language learner faces, is met through the application of a common set of mechanisms which have their origin in the special characteristics of the human language faculty.

The L2 = L1 hypothesis was investigated in two different ways. One was through the analysis of learner errors. Samples of language-learner language were collected and then examined in order to discover the different types of error that learners made. The errors were classified according to whether they could be predicted by contrastive analysis or whether they resembled the developmental errors that occurred in L1 acquisition. A large proportion of developmental-type errors was evidence that the processes of L1 acquisition and SLA were similar. Error analysis was also used in another way to examine the L2 = L1 hypothesis. If it was assumed that structures in which errors were very common were learnt later than structures containing few errors, then it was possible to work out an order of development based on error frequencies. For instance, if a larger proportion of errors occurred in the use of plurals than in the use of pronouns, then it could be assumed that plurals were acquired later than pronouns. By equating the order of difficulty with the order of acquisition, a developmental route could be established and the L2 = L1 hypothesis tested.

The second way in which the L2 = L1 hypothesis was examined was in longitudinal studies of L2 learners. A number of longitudinal studies of L1 acquisition had already taken place, so there was a basis for comparison. The 1970s saw a remarkable growth in the number of longitudinal studies of SLA, many of them originating in the University of California, Los Angeles, under the supervision of Evelyn Hatch (see Hatch 1978a).

Both Error Analysis and the longitudinal studies show that there are striking similarities in the ways in which different L2 learners learn a L2. Strong claims have been made that these amount to a 'natural' sequence of development. This route resembles that reported for L1 acquisition but is not identical with it. Chapter 3 examines the 'natural' route and the L2 = L1 hypothesis.

Contextual variation in language-learner language

Language-learner language contains errors. That is, some of the utterances produced by learners are not well formed according to the rules of the adult grammar. Errors are an important source of information about SLA, because they demonstrate conclusively that learners do not simply memorize target language rules and then reproduce them in their own utterances. They indicate that learners construct their own rules on the basis of input data, and that in some instances at least these rules differ from those of the target language.

The existence of errors in language-learner language, however, is only of interest if they can be shown to be systematic – that is, that their occurrence is in some way regular. One of the major problems of investigating SLA is that learner errors are not systematic in any simple way. It is rare that a learner produces the same error in all contexts of use. It is much more likely that a learner produces an error in some contexts but not in others. However, accepting that errors are variable does not mean rejecting the notion that they are in some way regular and therefore rule-based. If it is accepted that learners perform differently in different situations, but that it is possible to predict how they will behave in specific situations, then the systematicity of their behaviour can be captured by means of *variable rules*. These are 'if . . . then' rules. They state that if x conditions apply, then y language forms will occur. For instance, we may find that subject–verb inversion in WH questions occurs in some questions but not in others. The learner's performance may seem entirely haphazard, but on closer inspection it may be possible to specify when subject–verb inversion occurs and when it does not. A variable rule might be constructed to show that inversion occurs in 'what' and 'who' questions but not in 'where' and 'when' questions. Although 'if . . . then' rules are much more complex than simple invariable rules, they are necessary if the true systematicity of language-learner language is to be understood.

There are two types of contextual variation. Language-learner language varies according to the *situational* context. That is, learners use their knowledge of the L2 differently in different situations. For example, when learners are under pressure to communicate instantly, they will not have time to maximize their existing knowledge and are likely to produce errors that would not occur in situations when they have the opportunity to monitor their output more carefully. Language-learner language also varies according to the *linguistic* context. That is, learners produce errors in one type of sentence but not in another. For example, errors in the third person singular of the English Present Simple Tense may not occur in sentences consisting of a single clause (e.g. 'He *buys* her a bunch of flowers'), but may occur regularly in the second clause of complex sentences (e.g. 'He visits her every day and *buy* her a bunch of flowers'). A full account of contextual variability needs to consider both types.

The notion of a 'natural' route of development and the notion of contextual variation need to be reconciled. If learners vary in their use of a L2, in what sense is it possible to talk about a general developmental route? How can there be an invariable route if language-learner language is inherently variable? In many respects this is the single most important issue in SLA research. It is considered in Chapter 4.

Individual learner differences

Variability in language-learner language is the result not only of contextual factors. It also occurs because of individual differences in the way learners learn a L2 and the way they use their L2 knowledge. It is probably accurate to say that no two learners learn a L2 in exactly the same way.

The learner factors that can influence the course of development are potentially infinite and very difficult to classify in a reliable manner. SLA research has examined five general factors that contribute to individual learner differences in some depth. These are age, aptitude, cognitive style, motivation, and personality.

A question that has aroused considerable interest is whether adults learn a L2 in the same way as children. A common-sense approach to this issue suggests that adult and child SLA are not the same. Adults have a greater memory capacity and are also able to focus more easily on the purely formal features of a language. However, these differences need not lead to differences in the route through which learners pass, which may be the product of a language faculty that does not change with age. The comparison of child and adult SLA needs to be undertaken in two parts. First it needs to be shown whether the learning route differs. Is there a 'natural' route for adults and a different one for children? Second, the *rate* at which adults and children learn needs to be investigated. The commonly held view that children are more successful learners than adults may not be substantiated by empirical research. It is possible, therefore, that differences exist with regard to both route and rate of learning. It is also possible that differences exist in rate (but not necessarily with children as the more successful learners) but not in route. Finally, it is possible that no significant differences exist in either route or rate.

Aptitude is to be contrasted with intelligence. The latter refers to the general ability that governs how well we master a whole range of skills, linguistic and non-linguistic. Aptitude refers to the special ability involved in language learning. The effects of aptitude have been measured in terms of proficiency scores achieved by classroom learners. A number of studies (e.g. Gardner 1980) have reported that aptitude is a major factor determining the level of success of classroom language learning, but doubts remain about the value of such studies, mainly because it is not entirely clear what cognitive abilities constitute aptitude.

Learner motivation and needs have always had a central place in theories of SLA. Learners who are interested in the social and cultural customs of native speakers of the language they are learning are likely to be successful. Similarly when learners have a strong instrumental need to learn a L2 (e.g. in order to study through the medium of the L2), they will probably prosper. Conversely, learners with little interest in the way of life of native speakers of the L2 or with low instrumental motivation can be expected to learn slowly and to stop learning some way short of native speaker competence. The role of motivation has been extensively examined in the work of Gardner and Lambert (1972) in the context of bilingual education in Canada and elsewhere.

A full explanation of the role played by motivation and needs requires an account of *how* these affect the process of learning. Such an explanation has been provided by Dulay and Burt (1977). They propose that the learner has a 'socioaffective filter' which governs how much of the input gets through to the language processing mechanisms. As a result of conscious or unconscious motives or needs, attitudes or emotional states, the learner is 'open' or 'closed' to the L2. Thus once learners have obtained sufficient L2 knowledge to meet their communicative and emotional needs, they may stop learning. This results in what Selinker (1972) has called *fossilization*. No matter how much input and no matter in what form the input is provided, the learner does not learn.

Little is known about how personality and cognitive style influence SLA, although there is a general conviction that both are potentially extremely important. What kind of personality is most successful in learning a L2? Are extroverts more successful than introverts because they are prepared to take more risks and try to get more exposure to the L2? What role does inhibition play in SLA? There are few clear answers.

Similarly research has not been able to show that cognitive style ('the way we learn things in general and the particular attack we make on a problem'—Brown 1980a: 89) affects learning in any definite way. One of the major problems of investigating both personality and cognitive style is the lack of testing instruments that can reliably measure different types.

Chapter 5 considers individual learning approaches and also the role of age, aptitude, cognitive style, motivation, and personality.

The role of the input

It is self-evident that SLA can take place only when the learner has access to L2 input. This input may be in the form of exposure in natural settings or formal instruction. It may be spoken or written. A central issue in SLA is what role the input plays.

Early theories of SLA, based on the notion of habit formation through practice and reinforcement, emphasized the importance of the input. The whole process of learning could be controlled by presenting the L2 in the right-sized doses and ensuring that the learner continued to practise until each feature was 'overlearned' (i.e. became automatic). Learning a L2 was like any other kind of learning. It consisted of building up chains of stimulus–response links which could be controlled and shaped by reinforcement. In this Behaviourist view of learning there was little room for any active processing by the learner. Language learning—first or second—was an external not an internal phenomenon.

In the 1960s this view of learning was challenged, most notably by Chomsky. It was pointed out that in many instances there was no match between the kind of language to be observed in the input and the language that learners produced. This could best be explained by hypothesizing a set of mental processes inside the learner's mind which were responsible for working on the input and converting it into a form that the learner could store and handle in production. Chomsky's mentalist view of language learning emphasized what he called the learner's 'language acquisition device' and played down the role of the linguistic environment. Input served merely as a trigger to activate the device.

A major issue in SLA, therefore, is whether the input shapes and controls learning or is just a trigger. Currently, there is considerable interest in the input, which is directed both at discovering how native speakers talk to L2 learners and what part is played in SLA by the way they talk. The research is beginning to show that mere exposure to the L2 is not enough. Learners appear to need L2 data that are specially suited to whatever stage of development they are at. There is somewhat less agreement, however, about precisely what constitutes an optimal input. Is it, as teachers assume, an input selected and graded according to formal and logical criteria, or is it, as Krashen (1981a) argues, simply a matter of 'comprehensible input', providing learners with language that they can understand? The role of input in the process of SLA remains one of the most controversial issues in current research.

Chapter 6 discusses these issues in greater depth and also seeks to show that it is not so much 'input' (i.e. getting L2 data) as 'interaction' (i.e. taking part in communicative activities) that is important for SLA.

Learner processes

Learners need to sift the input they receive and relate it to their existing knowledge. How do they do this? There are two possible explanations. They may use general cognitive strategies which are part of their procedural knowledge and which are used in other forms of learning. These strategies are often referred to as *learner strategies*. Alternatively they may possess a special linguistic faculty that enables them to operate on the input data in order to discover the L2 rules in maximally efficient ways. This linguistic faculty is referred to as *Universal Grammar*.

Tarone (1980) distinguishes three sets of learner strategies. There are *learning strategies*. These are the means by which the learner processes the L2 input in order to develop linguistic knowledge. Learning strategies can be conscious and behavioural (e.g. memorization or repetition with the purpose of remembering), or they can be subconscious and psycholinguistic (e.g. inferencing or overgeneralization). The second type consists of *production strategies*. These involve learners' attempts to use the L2 knowledge they have already acquired efficiently, clearly, and with minimum effort. Examples are the rehearsal of what should be said and discourse planning, working out a way of structuring a series of utterances. The third type is *communication strategies*. Like production strategies, these are strategies of use rather than of learning, although they can contribute indirectly to learning by helping the learner to obtain more input. Communication strategies consist of learners' attempts to communicate meanings for which they lack the requisite linguistic knowledge. Learners, particularly in natural settings, constantly need to express ideas which are beyond their linguistic resources. They can either give up and so avoid the problem, or try to find some way around it. Typical communication strategies are requests for assistance (e.g. 'What d'you call ____?') and paraphrase (e.g. 'wow wow' for 'bark'). Communication strategies involve compensating for non-existent knowledge by improvising with existing L2 knowledge in incorrect and inappropriate ways.

The investigation of learner strategies has a central place in SLA. The current reconsideration of the importance of the linguistic environment has not meant a return to Behaviourist views. Rather, it emphasizes the relationship between the input and internal processing in order to discover how each affects the other. An optimal input is one that learners can handle by means of learning strategies. Learners adjust the strategies they use to suit the type of input they are getting. Learners can also attempt to control the type of input they are exposed to through the use of production and communication strategies. Input, learner strategies, and output are all interrelated in a highly complex manner.

Learner strategies cannot be observed directly. They can only be inferred from language-learner behaviour. Inevitably the literature on learner strategies is speculative and rather theoretical. It is a bit like trying to work out the classification system of a library when the only evidence to go on consists of the few books you have been allowed to take out. Early studies of learner strategies were based on Error Analysis. The data were isolated learner utterances. Later research recognized the importance of using continuous stretches of discourse in order to identify how the learner negotiates meaning in collaboration with his or her interlocutor. In this way the interrelationship between input, internal processing, and output can be more clearly witnessed.

The alternative view of learner processing is that proposed by Chomsky (1965,1980). It has already been noted that Chomsky's view of language learning is mentalist; that is, he emphasizes the contribution of the learner, rather than that of the environment. Chomsky is also specific about the nature of the learner's contribution. Although he does not rule out the possibility that the language processing of the young child may ultimately be explained in terms of general cognitive development, he believes that it can be best explained in terms of an independent language faculty. That is, Chomsky claims that language acquisition is primarily the result of mental mechanisms that are specifically linguistic.

What does this linguistic faculty consist of? Chomsky describes it as a 'language acquisition device' that contains a knowledge of linguistic universals. These are innate and provide the child with a starting point for acquiring the grammar of the language he or she is exposed to. Chomsky believes that natural languages are governed by highly abstract and complex rules that are not immediately evident in actual utterances or, as Chomsky calls it, 'surface structure'. If the child were totally reliant on the data available in the input, he would not be able to acquire these rules. Therefore, the child must possess a set of innate principles which guide language processing. These principles comprise Universal Grammar—the linguistic features and processes which are common to all natural languages and all language learners.

Chomsky's 'language acquisition device' operates in L1 acquisition. However, the idea that there is an independent linguistic faculty which determines SLA is tenable. Recently it has been explored as the *Universal Hypothesis*. This is based on the notion of 'core' rules that are to be found in all natural languages. There are also rules that are language-specific; that is, they are found in only one or two languages. The Universal Hypothesis states that L2 learners find it easier to learn 'core' rules than language-specific rules. It has also been suggested that the effects of L1 transfer may be restricted to non-core features. That is, if learners discover that a L2 rule is not in agreement with a universal rule, they will seek to interpret that rule in terms of the equivalent rule in their L1.

Learner strategies are examined in Chapter 7. Chapter 3 discusses Chomsky's 'language acquisition device', while Chapter 8 looks at the Universal Hypothesis in SLA.

The role of formal instruction

From the teacher's point of view, the role that formal instruction plays in SLA is of central importance. It has been left to the end because it is an issue that is related to many of the issues discussed in the previous sections. It must be considered in two parts – the effect that instruction has on the *route* of learning and the effect that it has on *rate* of learning. There has been little direct study of either of these aspects, largely because of the pedagogic assumption that it is possible to determine both route and rate through teaching.

Earlier it has been pointed out that learners may pass through a relatively invariable route in acquiring linguistic competence in a L2. This may be the result of the operation of universal learning strategies which are part of the human faculty for language. Alternatively it may be the result of exposure to particular kinds of input which models at different stages of development just those features which the learner is ready to acquire. If SLA is the result of some kind of 'language acquisition device', which is triggered off only by the linguistic environment, then the learner must be credited with his or her own 'syllabus' which is more or less immune to influence from the outside. If, however, SLA is the result of attending to those features that are frequent and salient in the input, then the possibility arises that there is more than one 'syllabus' for SLA and that a specially constructed input, such as that provided by formal instruction, can influence the order in which the grammar of a L2 is acquired.

The few studies of the effects of formal instruction on the developmental route suggest that the 'natural' route cannot be changed. These are not conclusive, however. Formal instruction can take many different forms and it is possible that the route of development is amenable to influence by certain methods but not by others. The research undertaken so far may not have investigated the right methods in the right conditions. It is also possible that the 'natural' route reflects a particular type of language use—free, spontaneous conversation—and will be found whenever this is investigated. Formal instruction may not easily influence this type of language use, but it may aid other types, for example those associated with planned speech or writing. Such a view is in accordance with what is known about contextual variability in SLA. Formal instruction may help learners to perform in some types of situation but not in others.

Irrespective of whether formal instruction affects the order of learning, it may enhance SLA by accelerating the whole process. Learners who receive formal instruction may learn more rapidly than those who do not. The experience of countless classroom learners testifies to this. Even if the L2 knowledge derived from formal instruction is not immediately available for use in spontaneous conversation (a common enough experience), it soon becomes serviceable once the learner has the opportunity to use the L2 in this kind of communication. Formal instruction can have a powerful delayed effect. There is also some research that suggests that formal instruction speeds up SLA.

The role of instruction in SLA, a controversial area subject to much speculation, is considered in Chapter 9.

Conclusion: a framework for investigating SLA

Having considered the key issues in SLA research, I shall conclude this chapter by outlining a framework for investigating SLA. This serves to draw together the various components considered in the discussion of the key areas.

The framework posits a number of interrelated factors. These are:

1 Situational factors
2 Input
3 Learner differences
4 Learner processes
5 Linguistic output.

Each of these factors is considered briefly below, together with some ideas on how they interrelate.

1 Situational factors

Situational factors influence both the nature of the linguistic input and the strategies used by the learner. The situation and the input together constitute the linguistic environment in which learning takes place.

Two major types of acquisition can be identified in respect of environmental factors—naturalistic SLA and classroom SLA. A key issue is the extent to which the process of SLA is similar or different in the two environments.

Within each general situational type a host of 'micro' situations can be identified, according to who the interlocutors are, the context of interaction (e.g. a supermarket or a crowded classroom), and the topic of communication. The linguistic product is likely to vary situationally.

2 Linguistic input

The central issue here is the extent to which the input determines the process of SLA. Does it merely activate the learning process or does it structure it?

There is now considerable research to show that native-speakers adapt their speech to suit the level of the L2 learners they are talking to. Another important issue, then, is what part these adaptations play in facilitating learning.

3 Learner differences

There is a whole range of learner factors that potentially influence the way in which a L2 is acquired. The key ones are age, aptitude and intelligence, motivation and needs, personality and cognitive style.

Another type of difference lies in the learner's L1. The role that the L1 plays in SLA was a dominant issue in much of the research that took place in the late 1960s and early 1970s. It was motivated by the need to submit the Contrastive Analysis hypothesis to an empirical test.

4 Learner processes

Learner processes may be cognitive or linguistic. Cognitive learner processes can be divided into three categories – learning strategies are used to internalize new L2 knowledge; production strategies are the means by which the learner utilizes his or her existing L2 knowledge; and communication strategies are employed when there is a hiatus caused by the need to communicate a message for which the learner lacks L2 resources. These strategies are general in nature and mediate between the linguistic input and the language the learner produces. Linguistic processes involve universal principles of grammar with which the learner is innately endowed. They provide the learner with a starting point. The task is then to scan the input to discover which rules of the target language are universal and which are specific.

5 The linguistic output

Language-learner language is highly variable, but it is also systematic. The learner uses his or her knowledge of the L2 in predictable ways, but not in the same way in every context.

The linguistic output is developmental. It changes as the learner gains more experience of the language. One possibility that has received a lot of attention is that there is a 'natural' order of acquisition. That is, that all learners pass along a more or less invariable route.

The linguistic output is the main source of information about how a learner acquires a L2. In particular the errors that learners make give clues concerning the strategies they employ to handle the joint tasks of learning and using a L2.

In order to account for the complexity of SLA, it is necessary to consider all the factors discussed above. For the sake of convenience the issues reflected in the overall framework will be treated separately in the chapters that follow. They are all interrelated, however. A theory of SLA is an attempt to show how input, internal processing, and linguistic output are related. Chapter 10 examines a number of different theories of SLA and concludes with a series of hypotheses about the five factors that comprise the overall framework.

Further reading

Most of the published work on second language acquisition is addressed to highly specific issues, or alternatively it projects a particular view of the process of acquisition. There are few overviews written from an objective standpoint.

A good starting point is an article by J. Richards and G. Kennedy: 'Interlanguage: a review and a preview', *RELC Journal* 8/1 (1977). The authors examine seven basic questions about SLA, which cover much of the same ground as this chapter. Another helpful overview article is 'Second language learning: a psycholinguistic perspective', by V. Cook, in *Language Teaching and Linguistics: Abstracts* 11/2 (1978). Cook considers how the learner develops a knowledge of a L2, and then examines the contribution of learner and situational factors.

A rather different overview is presented by H. Brown in the first chapter of *Principles of Language Learning and Teaching* (Prentice Hall, 1980). Brown places SLA in a wider context by examining what language is and the different schools of linguistics, psychology, and education which have influenced SLA enquiry. This would be useful for readers who approach SLA without a background in these other areas.

2 The role of the first language

Introduction

It is a popular belief that second language acquisition (SLA) is strongly influenced by the learner's first language (L1). The clearest support for this belief comes from 'foreign' accents in the second language (L2) speech of learners. When a Frenchman speaks English, his English sounds French. The learner's L1 also affects the other language levels — vocabulary and grammar. This is perhaps less immediately evident, but most language learners and teachers would testify to it.

It is also a popular belief that the role of the L1 in SLA is a negative one. That is, the L1 gets in the way or interferes with the learning of the L2, such that features of the L1 are transferred into the L2. In fact, the process of SLA is often characterized in popular opinion as that of overcoming the effects of L1, of slowly replacing the features of the L1 that intrude into the L2 with those of the target language and so of approximating ever closer to native-speaker speech. Corder (1978a) has referred to this view of SLA as a 'restructuring process'. It is a view that is based on a theory of general learning, as will be explained in the next section.

If in popular opinion the L1 interferes with the acquisition of the new language system, how does SLA research characterize the role of the mother tongue? The research literature reveals considerable disagreement about how pervasive the L1 is in SLA. On the one hand the popular belief is given support:

> Taking a psychological point of view, we can say that there is never peaceful co-existence between two language systems in the learner, but rather constant warfare, and that warfare is not limited to the moment of cognition, but continues during the period of storing newly learnt ideas in memory. (Marton 1981: 150)

On the other hand, the popular belief is rejected and the role of the L1, if not denied totally, is at least minimized:

> . . . our data on L2 acquisition of syntactic structures in a natural environment suggest that interference does not constitute a major strategy in this area . . . it seems necessary to me to abandon the notion of interference as a natural and inevitable phenomenon in L2 acquisition. (Felix 1980b: 107)

In order to understand why there is such disparity regarding the role of the L1, it is necessary to examine the evolution of 'the notion of interference' that Felix talks about. This will involve tracing its origins in behaviourist learning theory, its development in terms of the Contrastive Analysis hypothesis, and the theoretical and empirical attack on this hypothesis which followed. This chapter will follow these developments, reflecting the historical shifts of direction that have taken place over the last thirty years or so. It will conclude with an account of the current reappraisal of 'interference', which once again seeks to allocate an important role in the L1 in SLA. Current developments will be considered further in Chapter 8.

Behaviourist learning theory

In order to understand the early importance that was attached to the role of the first language, it is necessary to understand the main tenets of behaviourist learning theory. Up to the end of the 1960s, views of language learning were derived from a theory of learning in general. There were few studies of SLA based on the actual language that learners produced, and few attempts to examine the process of SLA empirically before this. The dominant school in psychology, which informed most discussions of language learning, was behaviourism. Two key notions can be identified in these discussions: 'habits' and 'errors'.

Habits

Behaviourist psychology set out to explain behaviour by observing the responses that took place when particular stimuli were present. Different stimuli produced different responses from a learner. These responses could be haphazard (in the sense that they could not be predicted), or they could be regular. The association of a particular response with a particular stimulus constituted a *habit*, and it was this type of regular behaviour that psychologists such as Watson (1924) or Skinner (1957) set out to investigate. They wanted to know how habits were established.

Behaviourist psychologists attributed two important characteristics to habits. The first was that they were observable. As Watson argued, the true basis for psychological enquiry existed only in objects that could be touched and actions that could be observed. Watson denied the existence of internal mental processes, dismissing them as 'superstition' and 'magic'. The second noteworthy characteristic was that habits were automatic. That is, they were performed spontaneously without awareness and were difficult to eradicate unless environmental changes led to the extinction of the stimuli upon which they were built.

A habit was formed when a particular stimulus became regularly linked with a particular response. There were various theories about how this association could take place. In the classical behaviourism of Watson, the stimulus was said to 'elicit' the response. That is, the presence of the stimulus called forth a response. If the stimulus occurred sufficiently frequently, the response became practised and therefore automatic. In the neo-behaviourism of Skinner a rather different account of how habits developed can be found. Skinner played down the importance of the stimulus, on the grounds that it was not always possible to state what stimulus was responsible for a particular response. Instead he emphasized the consequences of the response. He argued that it was the behaviour that followed a response which reinforced it and thus helped to strengthen the association. The learning of a habit, then, could occur through *imitation* (i.e. the learner copies the stimulus behaviour sufficiently often for it to become automatic) or through *reinforcement* (i.e. the response of the learner is rewarded or punished depending on whether it is appropriate or otherwise, until only appropriate responses are given).

Theories of habit formation were theories of learning in general. They could be and were applied to language learning. In L1 acquisition children were said to master their mother tongue by imitating utterances produced by adults and having their efforts at using language either rewarded or corrected. In this way children were supposed to build up a knowledge of the patterns or habits that constituted the language they were trying to learn. It was also believed that SLA could proceed in a similar way. Imitation and reinforcement were the means by which the learner identified the stimulus–response associations that constituted the habits of the L2. Language learning, first and second, was most successful when the task was broken down into a number of stimulus–response links, which could be systematically practised and mastered one at a time.

Irrespective of whether the type of learning behaviour described by psychologists working within the frameworks provided by Watson and Skinner actually occurred, habit-formation theory dominated discussion of both first and second language acquisition up to the 1960s. One of its major attractions was that it provided a theoretical account of how the learner's L1 intruded into the process of SLA. In other words, in addition to offering a general picture of SLA as habit-formation, it also explained why the L2 learner made errors.

Errors

According to behaviourist learning theory, old habits get in the way of learning new habits. Where SLA is concerned, therefore, 'the grammatical apparatus programmed into the mind as the first language interferes with the smooth acquisition of the second' (Bright and McGregor 1970: 236). The notion of *interference* has a central place in behaviourist accounts of SLA.

Interference was the result of what was called *proactive inhibition*. This is concerned with the way in which previous learning prevents or inhibits the learning of new habits. In SLA it works as follows. Where the first and second language share a meaning but express it in different ways, an error is likely to arise in the L2 because the learner will transfer the realization device from his first language into the second. For example, a French speaker may express the idea of being cold (= meaning common to first and second language) as 'I have cold' in L2 English, as a result of the way this meaning is expressed in L1 French, 'J'ai froid'. Learning a L2 involves developing new habits wherever the stimulus–response links of the L2 differ from those of the L1. In order to develop these new habits, the learner has to overcome proactive inhibition.

Of course, not all the patterns or habits of the L1 are different from those of the L2. It is quite possible that the means for expressing a shared meaning are the same in the first and second language. For example, when referring to age, German and English employ the same formal devices—'Ich bin zwanzig Jahre alt' is analogous with 'I am twenty years old'. In cases such as this it is possible to transfer the means used to realize a given meaning in the L1 into the L2. When this is possible, the only learning that has to take place is the discovery that the realization devices are the same in the two languages. The learner does not need to overcome proactive inhibition by mastering a different realization device.

Behaviourist learning theory predicts that *transfer* will take place from the first to the second language. Transfer will be *negative* when there is proactive inhibition. In this case errors will result. Transfer will be *positive* when the first and second language habits are the same. In this case no errors will occur. Thus differences between the first and second language create learning difficulty which results in errors, while the similarities between the first and second language facilitate rapid and easy learning.

In behaviourist accounts of SLA, errors were considered undesirable. They were evidence of non-learning, of the failure to overcome proactive inhibition. Some language teaching theorists even suggested that there was a danger of errors becoming habits in their own right if they were tolerated. Brooks (1960), for instance, wrote: 'Like sin, error is to be avoided and its influence overcome. . .'. However, as errors were the result of the negative transfer of first language habits (i.e. were habits already), it is difficult to see how they could become habits simply by tolerating them. Errors, according to behaviourist theory, were the result of non-learning, rather than wrong learning. But in either case there was almost total agreement that errors should be avoided. To this end attempts were made to predict when they would occur. By comparing the learner's native language with the target language, differences could be identified and used to predict areas of potential error. In this way classroom practice could be directed on the problem areas in order to help the learner overcome the negative effects of first language transfer.

Having examined the main principles of behaviourist learning theory as it was applied to SLA, it is time to consider the means that were used to predict potential errors. These were contained in the procedure known as *Contrastive Analysis*.

Contrastive Analysis

Contrastive Analysis was rooted in the practical need to teach a L2 in the most efficient way possible. As Lado (1957), one of the prime movers of Contrastive Analysis, makes clear, 'The teacher who has made a comparison of the foreign language with the native language of the students will know better what the real problems are and can provide for teaching them'. The origins of Contrastive Analysis, therefore, were pedagogic. This was reflected in comparisons of several pairs of languages by scholars in the United States, all directed at establishing the areas of learning difficulty that were likely to be experienced by English speakers learning other languages. In addition to these pedagogically oriented studies, there have been a number of more theoretical contrastive studies carried out in Europe, some of which have not been concerned with SLA at all. Clearly Contrastive Analysis is an area of considerable theoretical interest for general linguistics, but I shall concern myself only with those studies that are concerned with SLA.

Contrastive Analysis had both a psychological aspect and a linguistic aspect. The psychological aspect was based on behaviourist learning theory, and the linguistic aspect, in the first place at least, on structuralist linguistics.

The psychological aspect of Contrastive Analysis

The psychological rationale takes the form of the *Contrastive Analysis Hypothesis*. This exists in a strong and a weak form (Wardhaugh 1970). The *strong* form claims that all L2 errors can be *predicted* by identifying the differences between the target language and the learner's first language. As Lee (1968:180) notes, it stipulates that 'the prime cause, or even the sole cause, of difficulty and error in foreign language learning is interference coming from the learner's native language'. The strong form of the hypothesis was common before research began to show that many of the errors produced by L2 learners could not be traced to the L1 (see next section).

The *weak* form of the hypothesis claims only to be diagnostic. A constrastive analysis can be used to *identify* which errors are the result of interference. Thus according to the weak hypothesis, Contrastive Analysis needs to work hand in hand with an Error Analysis. First actual errors must be identified by analysing a corpus of learner language. Then a contrastive analysis can be used to establish which errors in the corpus can be put down to differences between the first and second language. Implicit in the weak version is the assumption that not all errors are the result of interference. The weak form claims a less powerful role for the L1 than the strong form of the hypothesis.

The strong form of the hypothesis has few supporters today. It is now evident that the L1 is not the sole and probably not even the prime cause of grammatical errors. Nevertheless, the weak form is not very satisfying. It makes little sense to undertake a lengthy comparison of two languages simply to confirm that errors suspected of being interference errors are indeed so. As James (1980) points out, this is a 'pseudo procedure'. In order to hypothesize that the errors in a corpus are interference errors, a *de facto* contrastive analysis must have taken place. It makes little sense to conduct a complicated contrastive analysis simply to confirm what a *de facto* analysis suggested. If Contrastive Analysis is to be worth while, it should be predictive. Diagnosis will then remain the job of Error Analysis.

Ideally the psychological aspect of Contrastive Analysis should deal with the conditions under which interference takes place. That is, it should account for instances when linguistic differences between the first and second languages lead to transfer errors and instances when they do not. It is because it is not possible to predict or explain the presence or absence of transfer errors solely in terms of linguistic differences between the first and second languages that a psychological explanation is necessary. What are the non-linguistic variables that help to determine whether and when interference occurs?

One possible variable is the setting in which SLA takes place. Marton (1980) argues that whereas interference need not be a major factor in naturalistic SLA, it will always be present in classroom or foreign language learning. In naturalistic SLA learners have the chance of extensive and intensive contacts with the target language, but in classroom SLA learners will always use their L1 between classes, and this strengthens proactive inhibition. The difference of opinion represented in the two quotations in the introduction to this chapter can be explained in terms of this variable. Whereas Marton is writing about classroom SLA, Felix is writing about naturalistic SLA.

Another variable may be the learner's stage of development. Taylor (1975) argues that there are quantitative differences in errors produced by elementary and intermediate students. Whereas the former rely on transfer, the latter rely to a greater extent on overgeneralization of target language rules (e.g. they overgeneralize the use of the regular past suffix -ed to irregular verbs, as in 'goed').

There is, however, no clearly articulated theory that explains how such variables as type of learning and stage of development affect the mechanisms of transfer. A major failing of Contrastive Analysis has been the lack of a well-developed psychological theory. This has been one of the major sources of criticism of contrastive analysis.

The linguistic aspect of Contrastive Analysis

A comparison of two languages can be carried out using any of several different models of grammar. Initially the model used was that of structuralist linguists (e.g. Bloomfield 1933; Fries 1952). This emphasized the importance of detailed 'scientific description' of languages based on a description of the different categories that make up the patterns of a language. These categories were defined in formal terms and they were established inductively. The differences among languages were emphasized:

> The differences (among languages) are great enough to prevent our setting up any system of classification that would fit all languages. (Bloomfield 1933)

It is clear that Contrastive Analysis and structuralist linguistics made strange bedfellows. How can an effective comparison be executed if languages do not have any categories in common?

This problem was ignored, however, in the spate of contrastive studies that were carried out in the United States (e.g. Stockwell and Bowen 1965; Stockwell, Bowen and Martin 1965). These studies compared languages from within the same language family (e.g. English and Spanish), so the problem of identifying a set of categories which were common to both languages was not acute. However, although for practical purposes the problem of establishing the linguistic basis for comparison could be overlooked, the theoretical problem remained. Ideally Contrastive Analysis needs to be based on universal categories (i.e. categories that can be found in all natural languages), which differ in the way they are linguistically realized from one language to another. Chomsky's (1965) theory of grammar proposed just such a model and as such offered a sounder theoretical basis for contrastive analysis (see van Buren 1974 for a fuller discussion of this point).

However, most of the contrastive studies carried out have been based on surface structure characteristics, such as those described by the structuralists. The procedure followed was (1) *description* (i.e. a formal description of the two languages is made); (2) *selection* (i.e. certain items, which may be entire subsystems such as the auxiliary system or areas known through error analysis to present difficulty, are selected for comparison); (3) *comparison* (i.e. the identification of areas of difference and similarity); and (4) *prediction* (i.e. identifying which areas are likely to cause errors).

In (3), *comparison*, the simplest procedure was to identify which aspects of the two languages were similar and which were different. However, contrastive analysts soon realized that there were *degrees* of similarity and difference. Here are some of the possibilities that a comparison might reveal:

1 No difference between a feature of the first and second language
   e.g. The contracted form 'J'ai' in French is mirrored by the contracted form 'I've' in English.
2 'Convergent phenomena' (i.e. two items in the first language become coalesced into one in the L2)
   e.g. Where the L2 is English, German 'kennen' and 'wissen' coalesce into 'know'.
3 An item in the first language is absent in the target language
   e.g. In German, subordinate clauses require a different word order from main clauses, whereas in English the word order is the same in both clause types.
4 An item in the first language has a different distribution from the equivalent item in the target language
   e.g. In many African languages [ŋ] occurs word-initially, but in English it only occurs word medially or finally (e.g. si*ng*er or thi*ng*).
5 No similarity between first language feature and target language feature
   e.g. In Spanish, negation is preverbal ('No se'), whereas in English it is postverbal ('I don't know'). In addition English negation involves the use of the auxiliary system, whereas Spanish negation does not.
6 'Divergent phenomena' (i.e. one item in the first language becomes two items in the target language)
   e.g. Where the L2 is French, English 'the' diverges into 'le' and 'la'.

It is one thing to develop categories, such as (1) to (6) above, for classifying the ways in which two languages differ. It is quite another, however, to relate these linguistic *differences* to learning *difficulty*. Differences can be identified linguistically, but difficulty involves psychological considerations. Stockwell, Bowen and Martin (1965) and Prator (1967) have proposed that linguistic differences can be arranged in a 'hierarchy of difficulty'. Prator, for example, suggests that (1) to (6) above are ordered from zero to greatest difficulty. This claim is not based, however, either on a psycholinguistic theory which explains why some differences create more learning difficulty than others, or on empirical research. It is based only on the conviction that the degree of linguistic difference corresponds to the degree of learning difficulty.

Most contrastive analyses have compared phonological systems, probably as a recognition of the role that the L1 plays in 'foreign' accents. However, the Contrastive Structure Series (Stockwell, Bowen and Martin) provided full-length studies of the contrastive syntax of the major European languages and English, while the 1970s saw a number of studies in Europe (see James 1980: 205 for a list). As Sridhar (1981) notes, there have been relatively few studies of vocabulary, while Lado's (1957) suggestion that contrastive studies of cultures should be carried out has not been taken up.

There are several problems concerning the linguistic aspect of Constrastive Analysis. One of these—the descriptive basis of the comparison—has already been briefly considered. Other problems are considered in the next section. However, if the problems with Constrastive Analysis were only linguistic, they would be amenable to a linguistic solution. As the tools of contrastive linguistics grow more refined, the problems would recede. The major problems, however, have to do with the relationship between the psychological and the linguistic aspects of Contrastive Analysis. There is little point in comparing languages if learners make only limited use of their first languages in SLA. The accuracy of prediction will always be open to doubt if Contrastive Analysis fails to specify the conditions that determine if and when interference takes place. The 'hierarchy of difficulty' was an attempt to solve this problem linguistically, but unless the solution has psychological validity (i.e. corresponds to what learners actually *do*), it will be inadequate. Contrastive Analysis constituted a hypothesis, and like all hypotheses was open to empirical investigation. The real failure of the 1960s was to rely on extrapolation from a general learning theory instead of getting down to the business of testing out theory by examining the language that learners produce.

Criticisms of the Contrastive Analysis hypothesis

The criticisms that gathered force in the early 1970s were of three major types. First, there were the doubts concerning the ability of Contrastive Analysis to predict errors. These doubts arose when researchers began to examine language-learner language in depth. Second, there were a number of theoretical criticisms regarding the feasibility of comparing languages and the methodology of Contrastive Analysis. Third, there were reservations about whether Contrastive Analysis had anything relevant to offer to language teaching. The 'crisis' in Contrastive Analysis was the result, therefore, of empirical, theoretical, and practical considerations. I shall consider the major criticisms under these three headings.

Empirical research and the predictability of errors

The existence of non-interference errors was always recognized, except by the staunchest of supporters of the Contrastive Analysis Hypothesis. Brooks (1960), for instance, gives four causes of learner error. (1) The learner does not know the structural pattern and so makes a random response. (2) The correct model has been insufficiently practised. (3) Distortion may be induced by the first language. (4) The student may follow a general rule which is not applicable in a particular instance. The issue was not, therefore, whether interference could account for *all* errors, but whether it could account for *most*.

Dulay and Burt (1973, 1974a) set out to examine this issue empirically. They identified four types of error according to their psycholinguistic origins:

1 Interference-like errors, i.e. those errors that reflect native language structure *and* are not found in first language acquisition data.
2 First language developmental errors, i.e. those that do not reflect native language structure but are found in first language acquisition data.
3 Ambiguous errors, i.e. those that cannot be categorized as either interference-like or developmental.
4 Unique errors, i.e. those that do not reflect first language structure and also are not found in first language acquisition data.

Dulay and Burt (1973) calculated the frequencies of these error types in the speech data of Spanish-speaking children learning English. They examined morphological features like past tense inflections. After eliminating ambiguous errors they claimed that 85 per cent were developmental, 12 per cent unique, and only 3 per cent interference. On the basis of this and similar studies, Dulay and Burt argued that children do not organize a L2 on the basis of transfer or comparison with their L1, but rely on their ability to construct the L2 as an independent system, in much the same way as in L1 acquisition. They suggested that interference may be a major factor only in phonology.

Dulay and Burt's research constituted a powerful attack on the Contrastive Analysis Hypothesis. Clearly, if only 3 per cent of all learners' errors were the result of interference, then a comparison of the learner's native and target languages could not help to predict or explain very much about the process of SLA. However, other research does not bear out Dulay and Burt's findings and there has been little agreement as to exactly what proportion of errors can be put down to transfer. Table 2.1 lists the percentage of interference errors reported in different studies since the early 1970s. Two points are worth making about Table 2.1. The first is that there is very considerable discrepancy. This is likely to be the result of a number of variables (age of learner; degree of contrast between the first and second language; type of data collected), but it is probably inevitable given the difficulty of coding errors in terms of their psycholinguistic source (see below). The second point is that Dulay and Burt's 3 per cent is conspicuously below the percentages reported by the other researchers. The mean percentage is more like 33 per cent.

Study	% of interference errors	Type of learner
Grauberg (1971)	36%	First language German – adult, advanced
George (1972)	33% (approx)	Mixed first languages – adult, graduate
Dulay and Burt (1973)	3%	First language Spanish – children, mixed level
Tran-Chi-Chau (1974)	51%	First language Chinese – adult, mixed level
Mukattash (1977)	23%	First language Arabic – adult
Flick (1980)	31%	First language Spanish – adult, mixed level
Lott (1983)	50% (approx)	First language Italian – adult, university

Table 2.1 Percentage of interference errors reported by various studies of L2 English grammar

The major difficulty in attempts at empirically validating the Contrastive Analysis Hypothesis has been the lack of well-defined and broadly-accepted criteria for establishing which grammatical utterances are the result of language transfer. In particular, interference errors are difficult to distinguish from developmental errors. Felix (1980b) draws attention to this problem. He points out that omission of the subject in 'be' sentences, which Butterworth (1978) put down to L1 interference in his Spanish-speaking subject, is common in the L1 acquisition of English and is best considered developmental. Similar examples abound in the literature. Jackson (1981) argues that non-inverted WH questions (e.g. 'How I do this?') are indicative of the influence of the first language in Punjabi-speaking learners of English. But this ignores the well-attested fact that non-inversion is a universal characteristic of both first and second language acquisition. However, the presence of the same error in the speech of learners with a variety of first languages cannot be taken as fool-proof evidence that the error is developmental. As James (1980) points out, it is possible that all the first languages sampled contrast with the target language with respect to the structure involved. Given the practical problems of assigning errors to categories such as those employed by Dulay and Burt, it is hardly surprising that the results of research do not agree.

Even allowing for the problems of identifying the causes of errors, the results reflected in Table 2·1 indicate that L1 interference is probably not the prime cause of learner errors. The Contrastive Analysis Hypothesis together with habit-formation theory is not capable of providing an adequate explanation of SLA. It was this conclusion that lay at the root of the 'crisis' in Contrastive Analysis.

Theoretical criticisms

A number of rather different issues will be considered under this heading. These are: (1) the attack on behaviourist accounts of language learning which was given impetus by Chomsky's (1959) review of Skinner's *Verbal Behaviour*; (2) the nature of the relationship between the notion of 'difficulty', as predicted by a contrastive analysis, and 'error'; (3) the problems concerning the linguistic basis of a contrastive analysis, in particular 'translation equivalence' and the need to accommodate the variability of learner performance when predicting errors.

Chomsky's attack on behaviourism struck at the psychological basis of theories of language learning. It was argued by Chomsky and others that extrapolating from studies of animal behaviour in laboratory conditions, as Skinner did, could show nothing about how human beings learn language in natural conditions. The terms 'stimulus' and 'response' were dismissed as vacuous when applied to language learning, because it was not possible to tell what constituted the stimulus for a given speaker response. The concept of 'analogy', which Skinner had evoked to account for the language user's ability to generate novel sentences, was ridiculed as far too crude a notion to capture the creative use of language that lay within each individual's competence. Also the concepts of 'imitation' and 'reinforcement' were rejected as inadequate, both because they could not account for the creativity of language and because it was shown in L1 acquisition that parents rarely corrected formal errors or rewarded correct utterances, and that children were only able to imitate utterances which lay within their existing competence and could not, therefore, learn new habits in this way.

These criticisms of behaviourist learning theory were directed to begin with at L1 acquisition. However, they soon spread to SLA. If language learning could not be explained in terms of habit-formation, then clearly the central notion of interference was bound to be challenged. This notion, as previously explained, rested on the assumption that L1 habits intrude into the L2 system. The question arose, therefore, as to what exactly interference consisted of if it did not involve habit transfer.

In addition to these criticisms of behaviourist learning theory, there were objections to other aspects of the Contrastive Analysis Hypothesis, in particular the validity of equating 'difference' with 'difficulty' on the one hand and 'difficulty' with 'error' on the other. The problem with the first of these equations has already been considered. Briefly, 'difference' is a linguistic concept, whereas 'difficulty' is a psychological concept. Therefore, the level of learning difficulty cannot be inferred directly from the degree of linguistic difference between two language systems. It may, for instance, be possible to argue that the absence in the target language of a different word order rule for main and subordinate clauses constitutes a smaller degree of difference than a totally distinct rule for negatives, but this is no basis for arguing that the former is easier to learn than the latter.

The second of the two equations (i.e. that difficulty led to error) was also shown to be of doubtful validity. The empirical research referred to earlier demonstrated that items predicted to be difficult on the basis of a contrastive analysis did not in fact produce errors. Theoretical arguments were also put forward to suggest that there was no necessary relationship between difficulty and error. A sentence which contained several errors might have caused the learner no difficulty at all. Indeed, one of the reasons why the errors occurred might have been because they contained forms which were easy for the learner to process. Conversely, a well-formed sentence might have been produced at the cost of considerable difficulty on the learner's part. One of the reasons why it was well formed might have been the difficulty experienced. These theoretical objections gave support to the empirical studies. Difficulty and error were shown to be not significantly related (e.g. Jackson and Whitnam 1971). Thus the central claim of the Contrastive Analysis Hypothesis, namely that linguistic difference between first and second language led to error as a result of learning difficulty, was called into question.

The linguistic basis of Contrastive Analysis was also challenged, on the grounds that there was no theoretical basis for 'translation equivalence'. The usual practice in Contrastive Analysis was to compare the formal features of translationally paired sentences. One problem that has already been pointed out concerned the categories which served as the basis for the comparison. Ideally these needed to be 'universal', in the sense that they can be found in all natural languages. However, the problem does not end there. For two sentences to be truly equivalent, they would have to perform similar communicative functions as well as to share structural similarities. For example, 'si' + conditional clause in French can be used to perform a number of communicative functions— hypothesizing, requesting, suggesting—whereas 'if' + conditional clause in English is restricted to the first of these functions (Riley 1981). A fully adequate Contrastive Analysis needs to compare pragmatic as well as linguistic aspects of the two languages. It needs to account for *appropriate language* use as well as *correct language usage*.

Another problem to do with the linguistic aspect of contrastive analysis is that of accounting for learner variability. It has already been pointed out that language-learner language is characterized by considerable contextual and situational variability. Theoretically, then, contrastive analysis needs to incorporate the variability of language use into its framework. It needs to predict the particular non-linguistic and linguistic contexts in which transfer errors are likely to occur. Categorical error predictions are bound to be unreliable, because they run contrary to the way learners perform in a L2. Sridhar (1981), however, comments that none of the current models of Contrastive Analysis incorporates variability analysis.

These various theoretical criticisms of Contrastive Analysis have important practical repercussions, because they suggest that it is not clear how a comprehensive and valid comparison of two languages can be achieved and, more importantly, because they suggest that even if such a comparison is achieved, it may serve little purpose, since SLA cannot be adequately explained by behaviouristic accounts of interference from the first language. In addition, there are a number of other objections based more directly on practical considerations.

Practical criticisms

The final set of criticisms concerns whether Contrastive Analysis is of any practical worth to language teachers. Clearly, if a majority of learner errors are not caused by interference, then Contrastive Analysis is of limited value, far less than was thought to be the case when Contrastive Analysis first started. There are other doubts as well. Many of the predictions made by Contrastive Analyses proved to be superficial, in the sense that they did no more than confirm the average teacher's practical experience of where errors were likely to occur. Also, if, as was later claimed by Sanders (1981), it was necessary to present learners with items which were similar to their first language and which were not, therefore, predicted to cause difficulty, as well as with items that were different from their L1, the whole rationale of Contrastive Analysis appears less certain. Why bother to carry out a contrastive analysis if every item, easy or difficult, needs to be presented and practised? The argument that Contrastive Analysis will show which items should receive greater *weight* in teaching is less strong than the original argument that it would show which items to select for teaching.

However, the main doubt about Contrastive Analysis from a pedagogic point of view has arisen from changing attitudes to the role of error in language learning. Contrastive Analysis was predicated on the need to *avoid* error, but if error is seen as a positive aspect – evidence of continued hypothesis testing (see next chapter) – then the importance of devising a teaching programme geared to its prevention becomes less obvious. Is it worthwhile, then, doing a contrastive analysis? The answer is that it is only worthwhile if it is considered important to explain why some errors occur. It may not be necessary, however, to undertake a formal contrastive analysis to identify instances of L1 interference, and, in any case, identification is a much weaker use of Contrastive Analysis than prediction.

Reappraisal

Although the 'crisis' in Contrastive Analysis has not been entirely resolved, in recent years there has been a successful reappraisal of the role of the L1 in SLA. This reappraisal took two forms. The nature of language transfer was re-examined in order to state more precisely the conditions under which interference took place and the type of L1 knowledge that was utilized. Also the contribution made by the L1 was recast in a more cognitive framework to make it more acceptable to the mentalist views which dominated discussion of language acquisition following Chomsky's attack on Skinner's neo-behaviourist theory. The key concept in this new framework was that of 'strategy'.

Language transfer re-examined

There were three noteworthy developments of the Contrastive Analysis hypothesis. First, it was recognized that the difficulty predicted by Contrastive Analysis might be realized as avoidance instead of error. Second, empirical evidence was forthcoming to show that interference was more likely to take place when there was some similarity between the first and second language items than when there was total difference. Third, and perhaps most important, it was recognized that error was a multi-factor phenomenon and that interference, as one of the factors, interacted in complex ways with other factors.

Avoidance

The evidence for avoidance induced by the first language was first provided in a now famous study by Schachter (1974). Schachter investigated the relative clauses produced by adult L2 learners from different language backgrounds. She found that Chinese and Japanese learners, whose first languages do not contain English-like relative clauses, made few errors, while Persian and Arabic learners, whose first languages resemble English in relative clause structure, made far more. On the face of it, this contradicts the Contrastive Analysis hypothesis, but Schachter also observed that the Chinese and Japanese students made fewer attempts at using relative clauses in the first place. The learners' L1, therefore, predicted the extent to which the learners avoided using relative clauses. Bertkau (1974) also found that Japanese students scored lower on the comprehension of relative clauses than Spanish learners. Here, then, was evidence to suggest that the learner's L1 played a definite role in both production and reception of a L2 without the 'difficulty' predicted by contrastive analysis being realized as 'errors'. The studies by Schachter and Bertkau (and others that followed, e.g. Kleinmann 1978) indicated that the criticisms of the Contrastive Analysis hypothesis advanced by Dulay and Burt on the basis of observed error frequencies were not fool-proof. Although Contrastive Analysis might fail to predict *production* errors, it might still be successful in predicting *comprehension* errors and *avoidance* of structures.

Degree of similarity

The Contrastive Analysis Hypothesis was founded on transfer theory, which stated that learning difficulty was the result of interference from old habits in the learning of new habits. It should follow, therefore, that difficulty (and therefore errors) will correlate positively with the magnitude of the distance between languages. The greater the difference, the greater the difficulty and the more numerous errors will be. This did not always prove to be the case, however. Lee (1968) reported that he experienced little interference from his mother tongue, English, when learning Chinese, and suggests that this was because the structures of the two languages were so different.

Interference, in fact, appears to be more likely when there is 'a crucial similarity measure' (Wode, 1976) between the first and second languages. Thus, for instance, Wode (1976; 1978) noted that interference from L1 German in the L2 acquisition of English negatives and interrogatives occurs only at particular developmental points. He observed examples of post-verb negation (e.g. 'John go not to school') and of inverted full verb interrogatives (e.g. 'Catch Johnny fish today?'), both of which mirrored the structure of German. In other respects, however, the development of both L2 English negatives and interrogatives parallelled that observed in L1 acquisition. That is, in general, transfer did not appear to be a major factor. Wode (1976: 27) concluded that 'certain conditions have to be met for what is commonly called interference to take place at all'. He argued that the notion of interference had to be developmentalized if it was to provide any fruitful insights.

Wode's observations have been repeated elsewhere. Jackson (1981), for instance, compared English and Punjabi and found that if the comparison was a gross one (e.g. related to the position of a preposition or of the verb in a sentence), errors did not usually occur. Errors appeared when there were some similarities and some contrasts between equivalent items or structures in the two languages (e.g. in possessive constructions involving 'of'). Zobl (1983a) argues that contrastive grammars will tend to overpredict unless account is taken of the nature of the L2 rule. For example, Zobl observes that French learners of L2 English make errors in the use of infinitive markers, as in 'He do that *for to* help the Indians'. The use of 'for to' can be traced to the French 'pour' + infinitive construction. But Zobl suggests that transfer occurs only because there is a 'structural predisposition' in the English infinitive construction. This predisposition is evident in the existence of 'for to' in a number of English dialects, in the L1 acquisition of English, and in Old and Middle English.

The need for 'relative similarity' between items for interference to take place is not, in fact, contrary to transfer theory. James (1980) notes that the Skaggs and Robinson hypothesis, framed in 1927, states that interference is greatest when there is a certain degree of similarity, and eases when the learning tasks have what has been called 'neutral resemblance'.

It is now clear that L1 interference occurs in certain contexts, but not in others. The task facing SLA research is to specify precisely what the 'crucial similarity measures' consist of in order to predict, or explain, with greater accuracy, when interference takes place. This is a complex task, because it requires balancing psychological and linguistic factors, a task which traditional Contrastive Analysis never attempted.

A multi-factor approach

The early research that sought to challenge the role played by the L1 in SLA (e.g. Dulay and Burt 1973) was conducted on the basis that an error was *either* the result of interference *or* of some other factor such as developmental processing. It is now clear that this is a naive view. Any particular error may be the result of one factor on one occasion and another factor on another. There is no logical or psycholinguistic reason why a given error should have a single, invariable cause.

Hatch (1983a) explores in some depth the extent to which 'natural-ness' factors and interference can account for what is known about SLA. Naturalness factors are determinants of SLA, such as how salient a feature of the L2 is to the learner or how clear the relationship between a given form and its meaning is. Such factors are independent of the L1, but can cause learning difficulty. Hatch concludes that in the case of phonology and morphology both naturalness factors and L1 interference are at work, often in such a way that errors are doubly determined. In the case of the higher levels of language—syntax and discourse—natural-ness factors may predominate.

An interesting suggestion of how 'doubly determined' errors can occur has been made by Cazden *et al.* (1975). In their study of Spanish learners' acquisition of L2 English they noted that the same developmental route in negatives was followed by all the learners. The first negatives consisted of 'no + V'. On the face of it this appeared an example of L1 interference, as Spanish has an identical pattern. However, 'no + V' utterances occur in both the L1 acquisition of English and in the SLA of learners whose mother tongues do not have this pattern. It is more likely, therefore, to be a developmental feature of acquisition induced by 'naturalness' factors. Cazden *et al.*, however, noted that the 'no + V' stage lasted much longer in their Spanish learners than was the case with learners whose L1s had different negative patterns. They concluded that the presence of a developmental pattern in the learner's L1 can serve to lengthen the stage of development characterized by the use of the pattern. They outlined how this takes place. The L2 learner begins by attending to L2 input and hears 'no'. He checks this against his L1 knowledge and finds the form is similar. In this way the 'no + V' pattern is confirmed and is maintained for a longer period of time than would otherwise be the case. Later, the confirmed pattern is replaced by a developmentally later structure as a result of the learner's continued attention to the input data. If, after checking against L1 knowledge, the learner finds his initial hypothesis is not confirmed, he is more ready to attend to the input data and consequently to modify his initial rule.

It is likely that three sets of factors are involved in SLA:

1 universal factors, i.e. factors relating to the universal way in which natural languages are organized (see Chapter 8 for a fuller discussion of these);
2 specific factors about the learner's L1;
3 specific factors about the L2.

A multi-factor approach to SLA requires identifying the relationships that exist between these three sets of factors in the acquisition of various L2 items. As a result of a study of the acquisition of relative clauses by learners from different language backgrounds, Gass (1980:180) proposes the following:

> Universal factors determine the general outline of learning. Language-specific considerations (of either the native or the target language) can come into play only where universal factors underdetermine the result.

The role of the first language proposed by researchers such as Gass is a highly complex one. Interference is a relevant factor if its operation is related to that of other non-interference factors.

L1 interference as a learner strategy

The Contrastive Analysis hypothesis fell into disfavour because it was apparent that large numbers of errors could not be predicted or explained by it. It is not surprising that researchers turned to other explanations of SLA. In particular the behaviourist view of language learning as habit-formation was rejected in favour of a more mentalist approach which took into account the active contribution of the learner. This alternative interpretation of SLA is examined in detail in Chapter 3.

Viewing SLA as a process in which the learner is actively engaged involves attributing to the learner *strategies* for both sorting the L2 data into a form in which it can be stored and for making use of knowledge already in store. The notion of 'strategy' is incompatible with the behaviourist psychologist's insistence on examining only observable events. It is, however, part and parcel of a cognitive view of language learning and use. The point at issue, therefore, became to what extent and in what way the behaviourist notion of 'interference' could be reframed as a learner 'strategy'. As Sridhar (1981) points out, the notions of 'interference' and 'strategy' are not incompatible. The learner's first language knowledge can serve as one of the inputs into the process of hypothesis generation.

Corder (1978b) outlines one way in which 'interference' can be recast as a learner 'strategy'. He suggests that the learner's L1 may facilitate the developmental process of learning a L2, by helping him to progress more rapidly along the 'universal' route when the L1 is similar to the L2. 'Interference' errors result not from negative transfer but from 'borrowing'. That is, when learners experience difficulty in communicating an idea because they lack the necessary target language resources, they will resort to their L1 to make up the insufficiency. This explains why the L1 is relied on more at the beginning of the learning process than later—the learner has greater insufficiency of target language resources to surmount. In effect Corder's proposal reframes the concept of 'interference' as 'intercession'. Whereas interference has been traditionally seen as a feature of *learning*, intercession is to be considered as a strategy of *communication*. A rather similar proposal is made by Krashen (1981a), when he suggests that learners can use the L1 to initiate utterances when they do not have sufficient acquired knowledge of the target language for this purpose. Both Corder's and Krashen's proposals view the L1 as a resource which learners can use for *ad hoc* translation to overcome their limitations.

'Strategies' have as their input existing knowledge. One type of existing knowledge is L1 knowledge. A cognitive view of SLA, therefore, does not preclude a contribution from the L1. Rather, as McLaughlin (1978a) and Taylor (1975) have argued, the use of the L1 is merely one manifestation of a very general psychological process—that of relying on prior knowledge to facilitate new learning. Thus, while the notion of 'interference', with its behaviouristic connotations, may need to be rejected, the notion of 'intercession', based as it is on a view of the learner as an active contributor to SLA, is an important part of any general theory of SLA.

Contrastive pragmatics

It has already been noted in the discussion of 'translation equivalence' that Contrastive Analysis needs to consider not only linguistic contrasts but also pragmatic contrasts such as the similarities and differences in the stylistic uses of items in the first and second language and in form–function relationships. Contrastive Pragmatics is a fairly recent development, although arguably it has its origins in Lado's (1957) *Linguistics Across Cultures*, which sought to provide a framework for comparing cultural differences in the ways in which languages are used.

Sajavaara (1981b) argues that the basic idea of contrasting languages is a correct one. The problem lies not in the idea, but in the way in which the contrast has been carried out. He argues that Contrastive Analysis needs to be undertaken with reference to communicative networks, rather than purely linguistic parameters. Riley (1981) suggests how this might be undertaken. One way is to take a particular function (e.g. suggesting) and then contrast its linguistic realizations in two or more languages. Another approach is to examine the different functions served by the same linguistic structure in two languages. Yet another, more ambitious, possibility is to compare the discourse structure of representative interactions in the two languages.

These proposals raise some important questions. One of these is, to what extent are the communicative parameters of language universal or language-specific? If they are language-specific, to what extent are the rules of language use transferable from the first to the second language? James (1981) notes that Widdowson (1975a) makes strong claims about the universality of specialized communicative functions such as those associated with scientific and technical discourse. If this is the case, James argues, there can be no such thing as 'Contrastive Pragmatics', because there are no differences among languages at the level of use.

However, Contrastive Pragmatics is not just about comparing the communicative functions of different languages. It is also about comparing how different languages express the same communicative functions. The universality of communication systems does not preclude the existence of obvious differences in the ways in which languages realize the same functions. It is highly probably that all languages have some way of making polite requests (e.g. 'Could you help me, please?' in English), but they are likely to differ in the formal ways in which this function is expressed. There is a need, therefore, to discover whether and under what conditions learners transfer the realizations of a given function in their L1 to their use of the L2.

There has been little empirical research on this issue. One interesting study, however, has been carried out by Schachter and Rutherford (1979). They observed these errors in the English of Chinese and Japanese learners:

1 Most of the food which is served in such restaurants have cooked already.
2 Irrational emotions are bad but rational emotions must use for judging.
3 Chiang's food must make in the kitchen of the restaurant but Marty's food could make in the house.

They showed these errors to a random selection of American teachers who diagnosed them as confusion between active and passive voice. Schachter and Rutherford, however, argue, that these sentences are a direct reflection of the sentence structure of Chinese and Japanese, which consists of stating a 'topic'—the first information in the sentence, which is 'given' in the sense that it has already been previously mentioned or can be taken for granted by the speakers—and then carrying on to make a 'comment', which contains the 'new' information. Thus the learners in Schachter and Rutherford's study can be seen to transfer the means of realizing the topic/comment structure of their L1 into English.

It is likely that Contrastive Analysis will increasingly turn to pragmatic issues in the future. In this new formulation it is possible that Contrastive Analysis will recover not only its theoretical bearings (which arguably it never entirely lost), but its practical worth to language teachers.

Summary and Conclusion

This chapter began by showing that although in popular belief SLA is strongly influenced by the learner's L1, there is considerable disagreement among researchers about the extent and nature of role of the L1. The explanation for this lies mainly in the changes that have taken place in the psychological base for examining SLA. The role of L1 was first seen in terms of transfer theory and was closely linked to behaviourism, which saw SLA as a process of habit-formation. Errors, according to this theory, were the result of interference from the entrenched habits of the L1. Contrastive Analysis was developed in order to predict the areas of difficulty that learners with specific L1s would experience, so that teaching could provide massive practice to eliminate the chance of errors induced by the first language. Up to this point, however, there were few empirical studies of SLA. Contrastive Analysis was based on an extrapolation from general learning theory. The beginnings of the 1970s saw a number of attempts to validate the Contrastive Analysis Hypothesis. These showed that many of the errors predicted by Contrastive Analysis did not in fact arise. Also many errors which were not predicted did occur. As a result of this research, the importance of L1 interference was questioned and fell into disfavour. Theoretical attacks on the validity of behaviourist accounts of language learning also helped to create a 'crisis' in Contrastive Analysis. Gradually, however, the role of the L1 was reappraised rather than rejected out of hand. The reappraisal took two forms. The Contrastive Analysis Hypothesis was modified to take account of avoidance, the need for there to be a 'degree of similarity' between the first and second language items for interference to take place, and the multi-factor nature of learner error. Also the Contrastive Analysis Hypothesis was incorporated into a cognitive framework by reinterpreting 'interference' as 'intercession', a strategy for communicating when there were insufficient L2 resources. More recently, interest in Contrastive Analysis has shifted to reflect current developments in linguistics which emphasize the communicative uses of language. This development is known as 'Contrastive Pragmatics'.

The learner's L1 is an important determinant of SLA. It is not the only determinant, however, and may not be the most important. But it is theoretically unsound to attempt a precise specification of its contribution or even to try to compare its contribution with that of other factors. The L1 is a resource of knowledge which learners will use both consciously and subconsciously to help them sift the L2 data in the input and to perform as best as they can in the L2. Precisely when and how this resource is put to use depends on a whole host of factors to do with the formal and pragmatic features of the native and target languages (i.e. linguistic factors) on the one hand, and the learner's stage of development and type of language use (i.e. psycho and sociolinguistic factors) on the other hand. The influence of the L1 is likely to be most evident in L2 phonology—the 'foreign' accent is ubiquitous—but it will occur in all aspects of the L2. Perhaps the most unsatisfactory aspect of traditional Contrastive Analysis was the assumption that this influence was a negative one. If SLA is viewed as a developmental process, as suggested in the next chapter, then the L1 can be viewed as a contributing factor to this development, which in the course of time, as the learner's proficiency grows, will become less powerful.

Further reading

It is a good idea to start by reading some of the early literature dealing with Contrastive Analysis. *Linguistics Across Cultures* by R. Lado (University of Michigan, 1957) provides a detailed account of both the procedures and theory of Contrastive Analysis. *The Sounds of English and Spanish* by R. Stockwell and J. Bowen (University of Chicago, 1965) is a good example of an actual contrastive analysis. Extracts from both of these books, together with a number of other useful articles on Contrastive Analysis, can be found in *Second Language Learning*, edited by B. Robinett and J. Schachter (University of Michigan, 1983).

Contrastive Analysis was closely linked to pedagogical considerations. *Language and Language Learning* by N. Brooks (Harcourt Brace and World, 1960) is representative of these pedagogical links.

One of the first articles to question the validity of the Contrastive Analysis hypothesis was that by R. Wardhaugh (see *TESOL Quarterly* 4/2:123–30). A paper by H. Dulay and M. Burt, 'You can't learn without goofing' in *Error Analysis*, edited by J. Richards (Longman, 1974) provides a strong attack, together with empirical evidence.

Probably the best all-round and balanced account of Contrastive Analysis is *Contrastive Analysis* by C. James (Longman, 1980).

Recent collections of articles which illustrate current developments are *Contrastive Analysis and the Language Teacher,* edited by J. Fisiak (Pergamon, 1981) (see in particular articles by Sajavaara and Riley) and *Language Transfer in Language Learning*, edited by S. Gass and L. Selinker (Newbury House, 1983).

3   Interlanguage and the 'natural' route of development

Introduction

The principal goal of this chapter is to examine the claims that second language (L2) learners acquire a knowledge of a L2 in a fixed order as a result of a predisposition to process language data in highly specific ways. These claims stand in stark contrast to behaviourist accounts of second language acquisition (SLA), which emphasized the importance of environmental factors and first language (L1) interference. The claims about a fixed order are based on a theory of learning that stresses the learner-internal factors which contribute to acquisition. This theory was first developed with regard to L1 acquisition, which also saw the first attempts to examine empirically how a learner builds up knowledge of a language. The starting point for this chapter, therefore, will also be L1 acquisition. Where SLA was concerned, the key concept in the revised thinking about the process of learning was that of *interlanguage*. This was used to refer to the systematic knowledge of language which is independent of both the learner's L1 and the L2 system he is trying to learn. Interlanguage was the theoretical construct which underlay the attempts of SLA researchers to identify the stages of development through which L2 learners pass on their way to L2 (or near-L2) proficiency. This research indicated that there were strong similarities in the developmental route followed by different L2 learners. As a result of this research, it was suggested that SLA followed a 'universal' route that was largely uninfluenced by such factors as the age of the learner, the context in which learning took place, or the learner's L1 background. According to this view of SLA, the controlling factor was the faculty for language that all human beings possess and which was also responsible for L1 acquisition. Inevitably the question arose as to what extent the order of development in SLA paralleled that in L1 acquisition. The validity of the L2 = L1 hypothesis has been a recurrent issue in SLA research. However, although learner-internal factors are powerful determinants of SLA, the conviction that they are capable of accounting for the entire process, which in some circles at least has been suggested, is not warranted. This chapter will conclude with an examination of some of the problems of explanations of SLA that rely extensively on internal learner factors.

To begin with, then, this chapter will briefly consider the background theory and research in L1 acquisition. It will then examine the notion of interlanguage, before reviewing in some detail the research upon which claims about a 'natural' route of development have rested. This leads into a discussion of the L2 = L1 hypothesis. Finally, a number of caveats regarding the centrality of learner-internal processes in accounts of SLA will be considered.

Mentalist accounts of first language acquisition

I do not intend to examine mentalist theories of L1 acquisition in detail here (but see Chapter 8). I wish only to sketch in broad outline the principal tenets in order to provide a context for the discussion of interlanguage and the L2 = L1 acquisition hypothesis. This sketch will consist of a composite picture drawn from the work of a number of psychologists and linguists. Two figures dominate, however—Chomsky and Lenneberg—and their claims and observations serve as a framework. The mentalist account of L1 acquisition is put most strongly in the work of McNeill (1966; 1970).

Chomsky's (1959) attack on Skinner's theory of language learning led to a reassertion of mentalist views of first language acquisition (FLA) in place of the empiricist approach of behaviourists. Chomsky stressed the active contribution of the child and minimized the importance of imitation and reinforcement. He claimed that the child's knowledge of his mother tongue was derived from a *Universal Grammar* which specified the essential form that any natural language could take. As McNeill (1970: 2) put it:

> The facts of language acquisition could not be as they are unless the concept of a sentence is available to children at the start of their learning. The concept of a sentence is the main guiding principle in a child's attempt to organize and interpret the linguistic evidence that fluent speakers make available to him.

The Universal Grammar, then, existed as a set of innate linguistic principles which comprised the 'initial state' and which controlled the form which the sentences of any given language could take. Also part of the Universal Grammar was a set of discovery procedures for relating the universal principles to the data provided by exposure to a natural language. This view of FLA was represented in the form of a model (e.g. Chomsky 1966):

primary linguistic data → AD → G

For the '*Acquisition Device*' (AD), which contained the 'Universal Grammar', to work, the learner required access to 'primary linguistic data' (i.e. input). However, this served only as a trigger for activating the device. It did not shape the process of acquisition, which was solely the task of the acquisition device. For Chomsky the task of the linguist (or psychologist) was to specify the properties of the AD that were responsible for the grammar (G) of a particular language.

Lenneberg (1967) emphasized the biological prerequisites of language. Only homo sapiens was capable of learning language. Thus, whereas even severely retarded human beings were able to develop the rudiments of language, even the most socially and intellectually advanced of the primates, chimpanzees, were incapable of mastering the creativity of language. Lenneberg argued that the child's brain was specially adapted to the process of language acquisition, but that this innate propensity was lost as maturation took place. Using as evidence studies of aphasia (i.e. loss of language function as a result of brain damage) which showed that total recovery of language functions was not possible once puberty had been reached, Lenneberg argued that there was an 'age of resonance', during which language acquisition took place as a genetic heritage. Lenneberg's work provided empirical and theoretical support for the concept of a built-in capacity for language as part of every human being's biological endowment.

One further feature of mentalist accounts of SLA needs mentioning. The child built up his knowledge of his mother tongue by means of *hypothesis testing*. The child's task was that of connecting his innate knowledge of basic grammatical relations to the surface structure of sentences in the language he was learning. According to McNeill (1966), he did this by forming a series of hypotheses about the 'transformations' that were necessary to convert innate knowledge into the surface forms of his mother tongue. These hypotheses were then tested out against primary linguistic data and modified accordingly. The result was that the child appeared to build up his competence by 'successive approximations, passing through several steps that are not yet English. . .' (McNeill 1966: 61).

In summary, therefore, mentalist views of L1 acquisition posited the following:

1 Language is a human-specific faculty.
2 Language exists as an independent faculty in the human mind i.e. although it is part of the learner's total cognitive apparatus, it is separate from the general cognitive mechanisms responsible for intellectual development.
3 The primary determinant of L1 acquisition is the child's 'acquisition device', which is genetically endowed and provides the child with a set of principles about grammar.
4 The 'acquisition device' atrophies with age.
5 The process of acquisition consists of hypothesis-testing, by which means the grammar of the learner's mother tongue is related to the principles of the 'universal grammar'.

The 1960s was also a period of intensive empirical research into L1 acquisition. Three similar projects (at Harvard, Berkeley, and Maryland) were started up in the United States to study the child's acquisition of grammar. When the first findings were made public, it was clear that the projects had independently arrived at very similar descriptions. To begin with, these descriptions were based on the techniques of structuralist linguists, but later they moved to consider the transformations required to derive the grammar of the target language from the universal grammar. From an early point onwards, then, the empirical research was closely tied to theoretical developments in syntax, initiated by Chomsky's *Syntactic Structures* (1957) and also the mentalist views of SLA described above. By the end of the 1960s, however, studies of L1 acquisition began to query whether a syntactical framework was the most appropriate way of characterizing the child's linguistic knowledge in the early stages, and proposals were made for describing the child's underlying semantic intentions.

These studies were longitudinal. They involved collecting samples of actual speech data by tape-recording samples of mother–child discourse in play situations at regular intervals over several years. The children's utterances were transcribed and submitted to grammatical—and later semantic—analysis. The aim was to describe the child's emerging linguistic competence as he gradually 'cracked the code'. In addition to the 'naturalistic' data collected, there were also attempts to elicit speech from children. One of the favourite means employed was imitation i.e. children were asked to imitate sentences that were just beyond their short term memory (Ervin 1964).

It is not possible to provide an adequate summary of a decade's research into L1 acquisition in the context of this book. It is sufficient, however, to draw attention to two major aspects. The first is that many of the children's early utterances were unique, in the sense that no native-speaking adult could have produced them. The second is that development was continuous and incremental, but could be characterized as a series of stages.

The uniqueness of children's early utterances is a universal feature of L1 acquisition. Utterances similar to the following observed in the L1 acquisition of English:

Mommy sock.
No the sun shining.
What the dollie have?
Want pussy Lwindi.

occurred in the child acquisition of any L1. That is, utterances different in form from adult utterances were attested in the L1 acquisition of all languages. This finding was important, because it provided a strong argument for rejecting behaviourist accounts of L1 acquisition on empirical grounds. It could not be argued that L1 acquisition consisted of stimulus–response connections learnt through imitation and reinforcement, if a large number of the utterances which children actually produced bore no resemblance to the kind of utterances modelled by an adult. Utterances such as those above can be explained only in terms of the child operating his own system, consisting of rules which were not part of the adult code. If the child's linguistic output does not match the input, the explanation must lie in the internal processing that has taken place.

The incremental nature of L1 acquisition is evident in two ways. First, the length of children's utterances gradually increases. Initially the utterances consist of one word. Later two-word, then three- and four-word utterances follow. Second, knowledge of the grammatical system is built up in steps. Inflections such as the 'ing' of the Present Continuous Tense or the auxiliary 'do' are not acquired at the same time, but in sequence. Similarly, complex grammatical systems such as negatives or interrogatives are learnt slowly in piecemeal fashion and involve rules quite unlike those in the target language. For example, early negatives typically consist of 'no' + statement (e.g. 'No the sun shining'). The gradual increase in utterance length and the constant revision of the rules required to generate structures such as negatives are together reflected in the growth in *mean length of utterance* (MLU), which is frequently used as an index of development. This is usually calculated by counting the number of morphemes in a given corpus of utterances and dividing by the total number of utterances. As the child develops memory capacity and acquires grammatical information, so his mean length of utterance increases. Crystal (1976), for example, provides an account of first language acquisition in terms of six stages, each defined with reference to mean length of utterance.

According to mentalist accounts of L1 acquisition, language acquisition is a universal process. The term *process*, which is common in acquisitional studies, is used with two related meanings. It refers both to the sequence of development (i.e. to the incremental nature of acquisition) and to the factors that determine how acquisition takes place. The vast bulk of L1 acquisition research that took place in the 1960s and which has continued up to the present moment indicates that there is a more or less fixed sequence of development through which children pass on the way to achieving adult competence in their L1. 'Process', then, is used to refer to the stages of development that characterize the route the child follows; it is a *descriptive* term. The second sense of 'process' concerns how the child constructs internal rules and how he adjusts them from stage to stage; it is an explanatory term. The natural sequence also suggests that there must be underlying mechanisms which are common to all learners and which are responsible for the route taken. There is, however, somewhat less agreement about precisely what these mechanisms consist of. The mentalist claim that the processes are internal and operate largely independently of environmental influences is no longer entirely defensible, as we shall see. First, however, it is necessary to consider the impact that mentalist theories and empirical research had on accounts of SLA.

Interlanguage

In this section I shall consider early interlanguage theory and shall not attempt to trace how interlanguage theory has evolved. Later developments require a consideration of the nature of variability in language-learner language and also a much fuller specification of the internal strategies which are responsible for the learner's output. These are important developments and so are considered separately in Chapters 4 and 6 respectively. In this chapter I wish to concentrate on relating the concept of interlanguage to its background in mentalist views on language acquisition and then to show how early interlanguage theory provided an impetus for empirical research into both the nature of L2 errors and the sequence of development in SLA.

The term *interlanguage* was first used by Selinker (1972). Various alternative terms have been used by different researchers to refer to the same phenomenon; Nemser (1971) refers to *approximative systems*, and Corder (1971) to *idiosyncratic dialects* and *transitional competence*.

These terms reflect two related but different concepts. First, interlanguage refers to the structured system which the learner constructs at any given stage in his development (i.e. *an interlanguage*). Second, the term refers to the series of interlocking systems which form what Corder (1967) called the learner's 'built-in syllabus' (i.e. the *interlanguage continuum*).

The assumptions underlying interlanguage theory were stated clearly by Nemser (1971). They were: (1) at any given time the approximative system is distinct from the L1 and L2; (2) the approximative systems form an evolving series; and (3) that in a given contact situation, the approximative systems of learners at the same stage of proficiency roughly coincide.

The concept of 'hypothesis-testing' was used to explain how the L2 learner progressed along the interlanguage continuum, in much the same way as it was used to explain L1 acquisition. Corder (1967) made this comparison explicit by proposing that at least some of the strategies used by the L2 learner were the same as those by which L1 acquisition takes place. In particular, Corder suggested that both L1 and L2 learners make errors in order to test out certain hypotheses about the nature of the language they are learning. Corder saw the making of errors as a strategy, evidence of learner-internal processing. This view was (and was intended to be) in opposition to the view of the SLA presented in the

Contrastive Analysis Hypothesis. 'Hypothesis-testing' was a mentalist notion and had no place in behaviourist accounts of learning.

However, the notion of L1 interference was not rejected entirely. As discussed in the previous chapter, it was reconstituted as one factor among many of the cognitive processes responsible for SLA. Selinker (1972) suggested that five principal processes operated in interlanguage. These were (1) language transfer (this was listed first, perhaps in deference to the contemporary importance attached to L1 interference); (2) overgeneralization of target language rules; (3) transfer of training (i.e. a rule enters the learner's system as a result of instruction); (4) strategies of L2 learning (i.e. 'an identifiable approach by the learner to the material to be learned' (1972:37); and (5) strategies of L2 communication (i.e. 'an identifiable approach by the learner to communication with native speakers' (1972: 37). Interference, then, was seen as one of several processes responsible for interlanguage. The five processes together constitute the ways in which the learner tries to internalize the L2 system. They are the means by which the learner tries to reduce the learning burden to manageable proportions and, as such, it has been suggested by Widdowson (1975b) that they can be subsumed under the general process of 'simplification'. Learners have limited processing space and, therefore, cannot cope with the total complexity of a language system, so they limit the number of hypotheses they test at any one point in time. This concept of 'simplification' is explored more fully in Chapter 6.

Selinker also noted that many L2 learners (perhaps as many as 95 per cent) fail to reach target language competence. That is, they do not reach the end of the interlanguage continuum. They stop learning when their interlanguage contains at least some rules different from those of the target language system. He referred to this as *fossilization*. Fossilization occurs in most language learners and cannot be remedied by further instruction. Fossilized structures can be realized as errors or as correct target language forms. If, when fossilization occurs, the learner has reached a stage of development in which feature x in his interlanguage has assumed the same form as in the target language, then fossilization of the correct form will occur. If, however, the learner has reached a stage in which feature y still does not have the same form as the target language, the fossilization will manifest itself as error. Common fossilized errors cited by Selinker (1972) are French uvular /r/ in English interlanguage and German time–place order after the verb, also in English interlanguage. Fossilized structures may not be persistent, however. On occasions the learner may succeed in producing the correct target language form, but when the learner is focused on meaning—especially if the subject matter is difficult—he will 'backslide' towards his true interlanguage norm. Selinker and Lamendella (1978a) argue that the causes of fossilization are both internal and external. It can occur both because the learner believes that he does not need to develop his interlanguage any further in order to communicate effectively whatever he wants to, or it can occur because changes in the neural structure of his brain as a result of age restrict the operation of the hypothesis-testing mechanisms. Fossilization is discussed further in Chapter 10 when Schumann's (1978a) views on the role of acculturation in SLA are considered. The role of age is considered in greater depth in Chapter 5.

So far the account of interlanguage theory has closely followed the principles of mentalist theories of language acquisition. The emphasis on hypothesis-testing and internal processes, together with the insistence on the notion of a continuum of learning involving successive restructuring of an internal system, are direct borrowings from L1 acquisition theory. In one respect, however, mentalist theorizing cannot be easily carried over into SLA research. According to Chomsky and others, the true determinant of L1 acquisition was the child's 'acquisition device', but this changed with age such that automatic, genetically-endowed language acquisition was not possible after puberty. The question for SLA, then, was this: how did adults succeed in learning a L2 at all if recourse to the 'acquisition device' responsible for L1 acquisition was not possible? This question raised what is the central issue in mentalist accounts of SLA—the psycholinguistic basis of learning.

Selinker set out to address this issue. He suggested that those adults who successfully achieve native-speaker proficiency in the TL do so because they continue to make use of the 'acquisition device', or, as Lenneberg (to whom Selinker specifically refers) put it, *latent language structure*. Thus, like the child in L1 acquisition, the successful adult L2 learner is able to transform the universal grammar into the structure of the grammar of the target language. This takes place by *reactivating* the 'latent language structure'. However, as Selinker noted, relatively few adult L2 learners reach native-speaker competence. The vast majority fossilize some way short. It follows that for some reason they are unable to reactivate the 'latent language structure'. Selinker explained this by suggesting that these adult L2 learners fall back on a more general cognitive mechanism, which he labelled *latent psychological structure*. This is still genetically-determined, but does not involve recourse to universal grammar. It is responsible for the central processes described above. According to Selinker, therefore, SLA can proceed in two different ways. It can utilize the same mechanisms as L1 acquisition, or it can make use of alternative mechanisms, which are presumably responsible for other types of learning apart from language. The term that eventually became popular to describe the mechanisms responsible for the second type of learning was *cognitive organizer* (Dulay and Burt 1977). The process of SLA that resulted from its operation was called *creative construction*.

Selinker's 1972 paper was seminal. It provided the theoretical framework for interpreting SLA as a mentalistic process and for the empirical investigation of language-learner language. Subsequent discussions of interlanguage focused on its three principal features, all of which were raised by Selinker in one way or another. I shall examine each feature separately as a way of focusing attention on the essential characteristics.

Language-learner language is *permeable*

The L2 learner's interlanguage system is permeable, in the sense that rules that constitute the learner's knowledge at any one stage are not fixed, but are open to amendment. In many respects this is a general feature of natural languages, which evolve over time in ways not dissimilar to the developments that take place in language-learner language. For example, in Chaucer's English the standard negative construction involved using 'not' after the main verb (e.g. N'apoplexie shente nat hir heed); the present-day English pattern, where 'not' is positioned between the auxiliary and main verb, evolved only gradually over several centuries. In a similar way some L2 learners of English (e.g. those with German or Norwegian as a L1) pass through a stage involving main verb negation before introducing an auxiliary into their interlanguage system. In this way the historical development of English resembles the SLA of English. All language systems are permeable. Interlanguage differs from other language systems only in the degree of permeability, and, if the idea of fossilization is accepted, in the loss of permeability that prevents native-speaker competence being achieved by most learners (Adjemian 1976).

Language-learner language is *dynamic*

The L2 learner's interlanguage is constantly changing. However, he does not jump from one stage to the next, but rather slowly revises the interim systems to accommodate new hypotheses about the target language system. This takes place by the introduction of a new rule, first in one context and then in another, and so on. A new rule *spreads* in the sense that its coverage gradually extends over a range of linguistic contexts. For example, early WH questions are typically non-inverted (e.g. 'What you want?'), but when the learner acquires the subject-inversion rule, he does not apply it immediately to all WH questions. To begin with he restricts the rule to a limited number of verbs and to particular WH pronouns (e.g. 'who' and 'what'). Later he extends the rule, by making it apply both to an increasing range of verbs and to other WH pronouns. This process of constant revision and extension of rules is a feature of the inherent instability of interlanguage and its built-in propensity for change.

Language-learner language is *systematic*

Despite the variability of interlanguage, it is possible to detect the rule-based nature of the learner's use of the L2. He does not select haphazardly from his store of interlanguage rules, but in predictable ways. He bases his performance plans on his existing rule system in much the same way as the native speaker bases his plans on his internalized knowledge of the L1 system. It has often been pointed out (e.g. Jakobovits 1970; Cook 1971) that evaluating L2 performance in terms of the target language grammar is unsatisfactory, because the learner behaves 'grammatically' in the sense that he draws systematically on his interlanguage rules. The term 'error' itself is, therefore, doubtful. A learner utterance can be classified as erroneous only with reference to the norms of the target language. For the L2 learner, however, the true norms are contained in the interlanguage system he has constructed.

Interlanguage theory was based on 'behavioural events'. As Selinker acknowledged, the behavioural events that have aroused the greatest interest in discussions of SLA have been 'errors'. However, whereas the Contrastive Analysis Hypothesis was devised to justify procedures for predicting errors, interlanguage theory constitutes an attempt to explain errors. Early interlanguage theory, then, was closely associated with Error Analysis. As this served as one of the main devices for examining the processes of interlanguage, the principles and methodology of Error Analysis will be considered briefly.

Error Analysis

Sridhar (1981) points out that Error Analysis has a long tradition. Prior to the early 1970s, however, Error Analysis consisted of little more than impressionistic collections of 'common' errors and their linguistic classification (e.g. French 1949). The goals of traditional Error Analysis were pedagogic—errors provided information which could be used to sequence items for teaching or to devise remedial lessons. The absence of any theoretical framework for explaining the role played by errors in the process of SLA led to no serious attempt to define 'error' or to account for it in psychological terms. Also as the enthusiasm for Contrastive Analysis grew, so the interest in Error Analysis declined. In accordance with Behaviourist learning theory, the prevention of errors (the goal of Contrastive Analysis) was more important than the identification of errors. It was not until the late 1960s that there was a resurgence of interest in Error Analysis. A series of articles by Corder (e.g. 1967; 1971; 1974) both traced this resurgence and helped to give it direction.

The procedure for Error Analysis is spelled out in Corder (1974). It is as follows. (1) A corpus of language is selected. This involves deciding on the size of the sample, the medium to be sampled, and the homogeneity of the sample (with regard to the learners' ages, L1 background, stage of development, etc). (2) The errors in the corpus are identified. Corder (1971) points out the need to distinguish 'lapses' (i.e. deviant sentences that are the result of processing limitations rather than lack of competence) from 'errors' (i.e. deviant sentences that are the result of lack of competence). He also points out that sentences can be 'overtly idiosyncratic' (i.e. they are ill formed in terms of target language rules) and 'covertly idiosyncratic' (i.e. sentences that are superficially well formed but when their context of use is examined are clearly ungrammatical). (3) The errors are classified. This involves assigning a grammatical description to each error. (4) The errors are explained. In this stage of the procedure an attempt is made to identify the psycholinguistic cause of the errors. For example, an attempt could be made to establish which of the five processes described by Selinker (1972) (as discussed earlier in this chapter) is responsible for each error. (5) The errors are evaluated. This stage involves assessing the serious-ness of each error in order to take principled teaching decisions. Error evaluation is necessary only if the purpose of the Error Analysis is pedagogic. It is redundant if the Error Analysis is carried out in order to research SLA.

The context for the new interest in errors was the recognition that they provided information about the *process* of acquisition. As I pointed out earlier, this term has two meanings. Two questions can be asked, therefore. What light can the study of learner errors throw on the sequence of development—the interlanguage continuum—through which learners pass? What light can errors shed on the strategies that the learner uses to assimilate the rules of L2? Both of these questions are of central importance to the main theme of this chapter—the 'natural' order of development.

Error Analysis provides two kinds of information about interlanguage. The first—which is relevant to the first of the two questions posed above—concerns the *linguistic type* of errors produced by L2 learners. Richards (1974), for instance, provides a list of the different types of errors involving verbs (e.g. 'be' + verb stem instead of verb stem alone—'They are speak French'). However, this type of information is not very helpful when it comes to understanding the learner's developmental sequence. Error Analysis must necessarily present a very incomplete picture of SLA, because it focuses on only part of the language L2 learners produce—that part containing idiosyncratic forms. Describing interlanguage requires identifying what the learner can do *in toto* by examining both idiosyncratic and non-idiosyncratic forms. Also because SLA is a continuous process of development, it is doubtful whether much insight can be gained about the route learners take from a procedure that examines language-learner language at a single point in time. Error Analysis provides a *synchronic* description of learner errors, but this can be misleading. A sentence may appear to be non-idiosyncratic (even in context), but may have been derived by means of an 'interim' rule in the interlanguage. An example might be a sentence like 'What's he doing?' which is well formed but may have been learnt as a ready-made chunk. Later, the learner might start producing sentences of the kind 'What he is doing?', which is overtly idiosyncratic but may represent a step along the interlanguage continuum. For these reasons an analysis of the *linguistic types of errors* produced by learners does not tell us much about the sequence of development.

The second type of information—which is relevant to the question about the strategies used in interlanguage—concerns the *psycholinguistic type of errors* produced by L2 learners. Here Error Analysis is on stronger ground. Although there are considerable problems about coding errors in terms of categories such as 'developmental' or 'interference', a study of errors reveals conclusively that there is no single or prime cause of errors (as claimed by the Contrastive Analysis hypothesis) and provides clues about the kinds of strategies learners employ to simplify the task of learning a L2. Richards (1974) identifies various strategies associated with developmental or, as he calls them, 'intralingual' errors. *Overgeneralization* is a device used when the items do not carry any obvious contrast for the learner. For example, the past tense marker, '-ed', often carries no meaning in context, since pastness can be indicated lexically (e.g. 'yesterday'). *Ignorance of rule restrictions* occurs when rules are extended to contexts where in target language usage they do not apply. This can result from analogical extension or the rote learning of rules. *Incomplete application of rules* involves a failure to learn the more complex types of structure because the learner finds he can achieve effective communication by using relatively simple rules. *False concepts hypothesized* refers to errors derived from faulty understanding of target language distinctions (e.g. 'is' may be treated as a general marker of the present tense as in 'He is speaks French'). Perhaps the most ambitious attempt to explain SLA by analysing the psycho-linguistic origins of errors, however, is to be found in George (1972). George argues that errors derive from the learner's need to exploit the redundancy of language by omitting elements that are non-essential for the communication of meaning. Implicit in the types of analysis provided by both Richards and George is the assumption that at least some of the causes of errors are universal. Error Analysis can be used to investigate the various processes that contribute to interlanguage development.

The most significant contribution of Error Analysis, apart from the role it played in the reassessment of the Contrastive Analysis Hypothesis, lies in its success in elevating the status of errors from undesirability to that of a guide to the inner workings of the language learning process.

As a result of interlanguage theory and the evidence accumulated from Error Analysis, errors were no longer seen as 'unwanted forms' (George 1972), but as evidence of the learner's active contribution to SLA. This contribution appeared to be broadly the same irrespective of differences in learners' backgrounds, suggesting that the human faculty for language may structure and define the learning task in such a way that SLA, like L1 acquisition, was universal in nature. However, the conclusive evidence—proof that there was a natural route of development—was not forthcoming from Error Analysis, although, as the next section will show, with a number of methodological developments the cross-sectional analysis of language-learner language could provide such evidence.

Empirical evidence for the interlanguage hypothesis

So far the case for an interlanguage continuum has been largely theoretical. There were questions, however, that could only really be settled by empirical research. In particular, empirical research was required to decide on the nature of the interlanguage continuum. Was the continuum to be conceived as stretching from the learner's mother tongue to the target language? Corder (1978a) refers to this view of the continuum as a *restructuring continuum*. Alternatively, was the continuum to be conceived as the gradual complexification of interlanguage knowledge? Corder refers to this as the *recreation continuum*. In the former view the learner is seen as gradually replacing features of his mother tongue as he acquires features of the target language. In the latter view the learner is seen as slowly creating the rule system of the target language in a manner very similar to the child's acquisition of his first language. Early statements of the interlanguage hypothesis tended to assume that the continuum was mainly a restructuring one (see for instance Nemser 1971). However, as the role of the L1 began to be questioned, this view fell out of favour and interlanguage was viewed as a recreation continuum (see, for instance, Dulay and Burt 1977). Empirical research played an important part in this shift of viewpoint. The purpose of this section, therefore, is to consider the strength of the empirical evidence in favour of a 'creative construction' interpretation of the interlanguage continuum, by examining the claims that SLA follows a 'natural' route of development.

This section will first examine the evidence supplied by cross-sectional and longitudinal studies of SLA. In the light of this evidence a distinction between the *sequence* of acquisition and the *order* of acquisition will be proposed, to reflect the fact that although there are broad similarities in the route taken by all L2 learners, there is also some variation.

Cross-sectional research

A number of studies, commonly referred to as the *morpheme studies*, were carried out to investigate the order of acquisition of a range of grammatical functors in the speech of L2 learners. They were motivated by the hypothesis that there was an invariant order in SLA which was the result of universal processing strategies similar to those observed in L1 acquisition.

These studies were conducted according to a more or less fixed procedure. Data (oral and later written) were elicited from a sample of L2 learners, using some kind of elicitation device such as the Bilingual Syntax Measure (Burt *et al.* 1973). This consisted of a series of pictures which the learners were asked to describe. The authors claimed that the corpus they collected in this way reflected natural speech. The next step was to identify the grammatical items which were the target of the investigation. The procedure followed here involved identifying the *obligatory occasions* for each item in the speech corpus. An 'obligatory occasion' was defined as a context in which use of the item under consideration was obligatory in correct native-speaker speech. Each item was scored according to whether it was correctly used in each context, and an accuracy score of its total use by all the learners in the study was calculated. It was then possible to rank all the items in order of their accuracy scores. This produced an *accuracy order*, which was equated with *acquisition order* on the grounds that the more accurately an item was used, the earlier it was acquired. There have been a number of criticisms of this procedure, which will be considered later.

Two early studies (Dulay and Burt 1973, 1974b) claimed that the vast majority of errors produced by child L2 learners were developmental (i.e. not subject to L1 interference) and that the 'acquisition orders' of child learners remained the same, irrespective of their L1s or of the methods used to score the accuracy of use of the morphemes. These studies were replicated with adult subjects by N. Bailey *et al.* (1974), and similar results achieved. All these studies used the Bilingual Syntax Measure to collect speech data. Larsen-Freeman (1976), however, found that the accuracy orders of adult learners varied according to the elicitation instrument used. The orders on oral production tasks agreed with Burt and Dulay's order, but those on listening, reading, and writing tasks produced different orders. Krashen *et al.* (1978), however, calculated the acquisition order using written data collected under two different conditions. One set of data consisted of 'fast' writing (i.e. the adult subjects were given a fixed time) and another set consisted of 'careful' writing (i.e. the subjects were given as much time as they wanted). The results showed that these conditions did not affect the morpheme order, which correlated significantly with Dulay and Burt's order. These studies are just a sample of all the morpheme studies carried out, but they illustrate the nature of the variables that were investigated. The studies are summarized in Table 3.1.

The general picture that emerges is that the 'acquisition order' for various grammatical functors is more or less the same, irrespective of the subjects' language backgrounds, of their age, and of whether the medium is speech or writing. The only time that a different order occurs is when the elicitation instrument required the subjects to focus specifically on the form rather than the meaning of their utterances, as in some of the tasks in Larsen-Freeman's study. But as Krashen (1977: 148) puts it, where the data represented a focus on meaning there is 'an amazing amount of uniformity across all studies'. It should be noted, however, that the standard order that was reported was different from the order of morpheme acquisition reported for L1 acquisition.

The order was not entirely invariable across studies. Even in those studies that reported significant statistical correlations in the rank orders of the morphemes studied, there were some differences. Also the ranking procedure used disguised the fact that some of the morpheme scores differed narrowly, while others were far apart. For these reasons Dulay and Burt (1975) proposed that rather than list the morphemes in order of accuracy, it was better to group them together. Each group would then reflect a clear developmental stage, with the morphemes within each group being 'acquired' at more or less the same time. These groupings were presented as a 'hierarchy' (see Figure 3.1). Each box represents a group of morphemes acquired concurrently. Thus, for example, the case distinction between subject and object pronouns is acquired at the same time as basic subject-verb-object word order and together they constitute the first stage of development. In this way the minor differences between the studies could be ironed out.

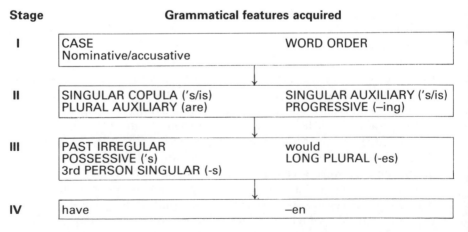

Stage	Grammatical features acquired	
I	CASE Nominative/accusative	WORD ORDER
II	SINGULAR COPULA ('s/is) PLURAL AUXILIARY (are)	SINGULAR AUXILIARY ('s/is) PROGRESSIVE (–ing)
III	PAST IRREGULAR POSSESSIVE ('s) 3rd PERSON SINGULAR (-s)	would LONG PLURAL (-es)
IV	have	–en

Figure 3.1   The acquisition hierarchy (based on Dulay and Burt 1975)

Study	Subjects	Data collection	Results	Conclusion
Dulay and Burt (1973)	3 separate groups of 6–8 yr. old Spanish-speaking children; total 151	Oral data from Bilingual Syntax Measure	1 85% of errors were developmental. 2 The 'acquisition orders' for the three groups were strikingly similar, but different from L1 order. 8 morphemes investigated.	1 There may be 'a universal or natural order' in which L2 children acquire certain morphemes. 2 Exposing a child to a natural communication situation is sufficient for SLA to take place.
Dulay and Burt (1974b)	60 Spanish-speaking children; 55 Chinese-speaking children; both groups 6–8 years	Oral data from Bilingual Syntax Measure	1 The 'acquisition orders' for both groups of children were basically the same. 11 morphemes investigated. 2 The orders obtained by different scoring methods were the same.	1 The learner's L1 does not affect the order of development in child SLA. 2 'Universal cognitive mechanisms' are the basis for the child's organization of the target language.
Bailey, Madden and Krashen (1974)	73 adults aged 17–55 yrs; classified as Spanish and non-Spanish-speaking; members of 8 ESL classes	Oral data from Bilingual Syntax Measure	1 The 'acquisition orders' for both Spanish and non-Spanish groups were very similar. 2 The adult orders of this study were very similar to those reported for all but one of Dulay and Burt's (1973) groups. 3 The adult orders were different from L1 order.	1 Adults use common strategies independent of L1 for SLA. 2 Adults process linguistic data in similar ways to children. 3 The most effective instruction is that which follows observed order of difficulty.
Larsen-Freeman (1976)	24 adults (L1s = Arabic, Japanese, Persian, Spanish); learning English at University of Michigan	Battery of 5 different tests of reading, writing, listening, speaking, and imitating	1 L1 did not have a significant effect on way adults learn English morphemes. 2 Differences in morpheme orders occurred on different tasks but orders on production tasks (speech and imitation) agreed with Dulay and Burt's order. 3 Accuracy orders correlate with frequency orders for production of morphemes.	1 There is a standard morpheme order for production tasks. 2 The frequency counts for morphemes on speaking task reflect the actual occurrence in real communication. Frequency in native-speaker speech is main determinant of accuracy orders.
Krashen, Butler, Birnbaum, and Robertson (1978)	70 adult students from 4 language backgrounds; at University of Southern California	Free compositions, with (1) time limit; (2) no time limit and chance for self-correction.	1 The 'acquisition' order for the 'fast' writing was the same as that for the 'careful'. 2 The orders obtained in both written tasks were very similar to those reported for adults in the Bailey, Madden, and Krashen study.	1 The students were focused on communication in both tasks, hence a 'natural order' was obtained. 2 The processes involved in SLA underlie both the oral and the and the written mode.

Table 3.1 A summary of key morpheme studies

On the face of it, the morpheme studies provided strong evidence of a 'natural' sequence of development in SLA. Irrespective of learner differences, L2 learners appear to progress along the interlanguage continuum in a very similar way. The main hypothesis of interlanguage theory, therefore, was supported. Even the difference between L1 and L2 orders was interpretable in terms of the hypothesized differences in the pyschological basis of the two types of acquisition. However, the evidence of the morpheme studies was not accepted uncritically. Attempts to test the validity of the studies against case studies of individual learners (Hakuta 1974; Rosansky 1976) suggested that 'accuracy order' was not the same as 'acquisition order'. The evidence of these longitudinal studies ran counter to that of the morpheme studies.

Longitudinal studies

Although longitudinal studies have examined the acquisition of grammatical morphemes, in general they have also focused on other aspects of development. They have tried to account for the gradual growth of competence in terms of the strategies used by a learner at different developmental points. Examples of such studies are Itoh and Hatch (1978), who emphasize the extensive use their child learner makes of ready-made chunks or patterns in the early stages, and Wagner-Gough (1975), who illustrates how her learner builds utterances by imitating parts of the previous discourse. Perhaps the fullest account of the developmental nature of the learner's strategies, however, can be found in Fillmore (1976; 1979), in her account of the SLA of English of five Spanish-speaking children. These studies are in many ways the most interesting and revealing, but a full discussion of their findings will be postponed to Chapters 5 and 6, when learner strategies are examined in detail. The longitudinal studies that will be discussed in this section are those that focus on the acquisition of particular grammatical subsystems—negatives, interrogatives, and relative clauses. It is from these studies that the strongest evidence for a natural route of development comes.

Longitudinal studies of SLA have one major advantage over both Error Analysis and the cross-sectional studies. They provide data from different points of time and therefore enable a reliable profile of the SLA of individual learners to be constructed. The disadvantage, of course, lies in the difficulty of making generalizations based on the profiles of one or two learners. However, the evidence provided by the studies is accumulative, and the case for a natural sequence in the acquisition of negatives, interrogatives, and relative clauses is based on the high degree of similarity in the profiles of many individual learners. The studies on which the discussion of developmental sequences below has been based are all of L2 English. The vast majority took place in the United States.

Studies of other L2s—e.g. the Heidelberg Project which has investigated the SLA of German by immigrant workers (Dittmar 1980)—give support to the general finding of the American studies, namely that the acquisition of L2 syntax involves a series of transitional stages which are more or less universal.

The grammatical sub-systems of negation, interrogation, and relative clause modification are all examples of *transitional constructions* in SLA. Transitional constructions are defined by Dulay *et al.* (1982: 121) as 'the language forms learners use while they are still learning the grammar of a language'. L2 learners do not progress from zero knowledge of a target language rule to perfect knowledge of the rule. They progress through a series of interim or developmental stages on their way to target language competence. This is probably true for all grammatical structures, including functors such as articles and verb inflections, but is most clearly evident in the acquisition of grammatical sub-systems. For this reason negation, interrogation, and to a lesser extent relative clauses in SLA provide the best indicators of the progression which, according to interlanguage theory, is the basis of SLA.

Negation

The development of negatives that is outlined below is based on several studies (Ravem 1968; Milon 1974; Cazden *et al.* 1975; Wode 1976 and 1980a; Adams 1978; Butterworth and Hatch 1978). These studies cover learners of English with Japanese, Spanish, German, and Norwegian as their L1 and also children, adolescents, and adults. Schumann (1979) provides an excellent overview of a range of studies of SLA negation. The type of acquisition involved was either 'naturalistic' or 'mixed' (i.e. involving both instruction and natural exposure to the target language).

Initially, negative utterances are characterized by external negation. That is, the negative particle (usually 'no') is attached to a declarative nucleus:

e.g. No very good.
No you playing here.

A little later internal negation develops; that is, the negative particle is moved inside the utterance. This often coincides with the use of 'not' and/or 'don't', which is used variably with 'no' as the negative particle. 'Don't' at this stage, however, is an unanalysed unit and so cannot be described as 'do + not'.

e.g. Mariana not coming today.
I no can swim.
I don't see nothing mop.

A third step involves negative attachment to modal verbs, although this may again occur in unanalysed units initially.

e.g. I can't play this one.
    I won't go.

In the final stage of negation the target language rule is reached. The learner develops an auxiliary system and uses 'not' regularly as the negative particle (i.e. 'no + V' is eliminated). Negative utterances, like positive utterances, are marked for tense and number, although not necessarily always correctly.

e.g. He doesn't know anything.
    I didn't said it.
    She didn't believe me.

The way along this route is a gradual one, which for some learners can take longer than two years. The stages are not clearly defined. They overlap, so that development does not consist of sudden jumps, but of the gradual reordering of early rules in favour of later ones. There are also some differences among learners. Those with German or Norwegian as a L1 go through an additional stage involving main verb negation, while those with Spanish as a L1 seem to spend longer on the external negation stage. There are also individual preferences in the choice of negative particle, for, whereas all learners appear to start off with 'no', some add 'not' and others 'don't' in the next stage.

Interrogation

Studies drawn on for the description of interrogation are Ravem (1974), Cazden *et al.* (1975), Gillis and Weber (1976), Wode (1978), Shapira (1978), Adams (1978), and Butterworth and Hatch (1978). These studies involved types of learners similar to those described for negation above. Two types of interrogatives—yes/no questions and Wh-questions —have been considered.

There appears to be an early 'non-communicative' stage during which the learner is not able to produce any spontaneous interrogatives, but just repeats a question someone has asked him. This is more common with children than with adults. The first productive questions are intonation questions, i.e. utterances with declarative word order but spoken with a rising intonation. At this stage there are also some Wh-questions, but these appear to have been learnt as ready-made chunks.

e.g. I am colouring?
    Sir plays football today?
    I writing on this book?
    What's this?

The next development sees the appearance of productive Wh–questions. There is no subject–verb inversion to start off with, and the auxiliary verb is often omitted.

e.g. What you are doing?
　　　What 'tub' mean?
　　　What the time?
　　　Where you work?

Somewhat later, inversion occurs in yes/no questions and in Wh-questions. Inversion with 'be' tends to occur before inversion with 'do'.

e.g. Are you a nurse?
　　　Where is the girl?
　　　Do you work in the television?
　　　What is she's doing here?

Embedded questions are the last to develop. When they first appear, they have a subject–verb inversion, as in ordinary Wh-questions:

e.g. I tell you what did happen.
　　　I don't know where do you live.

and only later does the learner successfully differentiate the word order of ordinary and embedded Wh-questions:

e.g. I don't know what he had.

As with negatives, development of the rules of interrogation is gradual, involving overlapping stages and the slow replacement of transitional forms. There are also differences which can be attributed to the learner's language background (e.g. German speakers pass through a stage where they invert the main verb—'Like you ice-cream?') and individual preferences (e.g. some learners make much more extensive early use of formulaic Wh-questions than others).

Relative clauses

Interest in the SLA of relative clauses is more recent. Apart from a number of early experimental studies (e.g. Cook 1973), some of the major studies to date are Schumann (1980) and Gass (1980). Only Schumann's study, however, is truly longitudinal.

　　Schumann examined the development of relative clauses in five Spanish-speaking learners of English. They were of different ages. He found that relative clauses used to modify the object of a sentence were acquired first:

e.g. And she said all the bad things that he do.
　　　Joshua's a boy who is silly.

while relative clauses modifying the subject of a sentence appeared later:

e.g. But the one you gonna go it don't have ice.
The boys who doesn't have anybody to live, they take care of the dogs.

With regard to the use of relative pronouns, Schumann found evidence to suggest (although not conclusively) that initially the relative pronoun was typically omitted (e.g. 'I got a friend speaks Spanish'), next an ordinary personal pronoun was substituted for the relative pronoun (e.g. 'I got a friend he speaks Spanish'), and finally the relative pronoun proper was used (e.g. 'I got a friend who speaks Spanish'). The first two of these stages co-occurred with the external negation stage.

There is, as yet, insufficient evidence to argue that there is a definite natural sequence of development for relative clauses. Schumann's study, however, is suggestive. Cross-sectional studies of the order of development of relative pronouns serving different grammatical functions (subject, object, etc.) are considered in Chapter 8.

A composite longitudinal picture

In addition to the study of how specific grammatical sub-systems evolve, there have been attempts to paint a composite picture of the interlanguage continuum based on longitudinal research. Schumann (1978a) and Andersen (1981) have suggested that the developmental continuum closely resembles that of the pidginization–depidginization continuum. That is, in the early stages SLA is characterized by interlanguage forms which are the same as those observed in pidgin languages, while in the later stages interlanguage rules become more complex in much the same way as pidgin languages do when they are required to serve a wider range of functions. This analogy between interlanguage and pidgins has been presented as a theory of SLA which is considered in detail in Chapter 10.

Ellis (1984a) attempts to summarize the developmental progression which has been observed in longitudinal studies. He identifies four broad stages of development. The first stage is characterized by a standard word order, irrespective of whether or not this is the word order of the target language structure. Thus, for instance, learners first operate with rules that lead to external negation and to non-inverted interrogatives. Another characteristic of this stage is that utterances are propositionally reduced—that is, sentence constituents are omitted (e.g. 'Me house' for 'I live in a house'). In the second stage of development the learner expands his propositions to include all or most of the constituents required, and also begins to vary the word order of utterances in accordance with the word order patterns of the target language. For example, internal negation and inverted interrogatives begin to appear. During the first two stages some grammatical morphemes will have appeared in the learner's utterances, but these will be erratic and will not be used to perform the same functions as in native speaker speech. In the third stage grammatical morphemes begin to be used systematically and meaningfully. The fourth stage consists of the acquisition of complex sentence structures such as embedded Wh-clauses and relative clauses modifying the subject of a sentence. Right from the beginning and throughout the four stages, the learner also acquires and uses unanalysed units such as 'I don't know'. He may slowly analyse these and so release the grammatical elements for use in creative speech. This may fuel the process of grammatical development. The process of unpackaging units that are initially unanalysed is considered in Chapter 7. This composite picture is displayed schematically in Figure 3.2. The numbers represent the four basic stages of development, with 1 as the starting point. The arrows coming from the segment marked 'U' are intended to represent the unpackaging of unanalysed units and the contribution to the various stages of development which this constitutes. It should be emphasized that these stages are not clear cut, but rather blend into each other.

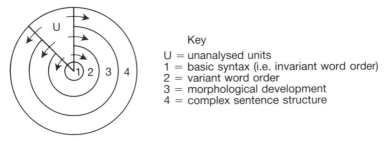

Key
U = unanalysed units
1 = basic syntax (i.e. invariant word order)
2 = variant word order
3 = morphological development
4 = complex sentence structure

Figure 3.2   A composite picture of the interlanguage continuum

Summary

The longitudinal research has provided strong evidence in favour of a natural developmental route in SLA. There is evidence to show considerable similarity in the way that negation and interrogatives develop in learners with different L1s, including those that belong to different language types (e.g. German and Japanese). There is some evidence to show that advanced grammatical structures such as relative clauses may also follow a universal course. Attempts have also been made to describe the overall course of development in SLA as a series of overlapping stages, and so create a composite picture. However, the universality of the interlanguage continuum needs to be tempered by the recognition that there are differences traceable both to the learner's L1 and also to individual preferences.

Interpreting the empirical evidence

It is easy to overstate the case for a natural route of development. The sequence is not universal in the sense that all learners acquire every item in exactly the same order. There are differences which can be attributed to factors such as the L1. Also there can be broad differences in the approach that learners adopt. Hatch (1974) distinguishes 'data gatherers' and 'rule formers'. The first type of learner is not bothered very much with formal accuracy and concentrates instead on fluency. This can be achieved through the adroit use of ready-made chunks and the juxtaposition of nouns. Vocabulary, therefore, is much more important than sorting out rules. The second type, however, attends closely to the input in the attempt to identify the target language forms, and then tries to use them accurately.

How can the claims for the universality of the interlanguage continuum and those emphasizing the differences be reconciled? One way is to make a distinction between the *sequence* of development and the *order* of development. The sequence refers to the overall developmental profile as outlined in Figure 3.2. This is universal, the product of the process of creative construction. All learners pass through the four stages, and this will be reflected in a basic sequence for such transitional structures as negatives and interrogatives. Thus, for instance, external negation will always precede internal negation, and intonation questions will precede inverted questions. However, learners will still vary in when and if specific grammatical features appear in their interlanguage. For example, some learners will build into their interlanguage a step involving main-verb negation or main-verb inversion, perhaps as a result of the influence of their L1. Learners may also leave out a small step within a general stage. Thus some individual differences in the order of specific morphosyntactic features will be evident within the natural sequence of development. To put it another way, learners take the same road but they do not necessarily drive along it the same way. They follow a standard sequence but vary in the order in which specific features are acquired.

The existence of a universal *sequence* of development and the emphasis on interlanguage as the product of creative construction rather than the restructuring of L1 knowledge leads to a consideration of the extent to which SLA is similar to L1 acquisition, which, as discussed earlier, has also been seen as a creative process of discovery.

The L2 = L1 hypothesis

The L2 = L1 hypothesis is not easy to investigate. The problem is that age is a confounding factor, particularly when the comparison is between first language acquisition in children, and second language acquisition in adults. As Brown (1980a) points out, age brings about differences in the physical, cognitive, and affective domains of learners. For example, if it is discovered that an adult learns a L2 differently from a child learning a L1, this may simply reflect a difference in mental capacity, which changes with age and which interacts with the language learning process. In other words, any difference between L1 acquisition and SLA may not be the result of the L2 learner's prior knowledge of his L1, but of other factors to do with the ageing process.

A study by Cook (1977) gives some idea of how cognitive—as opposed to linguistic—processes produce differences between L1 acquisition and SLA. Cook distinguishes 'speech processing memory' and 'primary (or short term) memory'. He found that when the load on memory was too great in the processing of relative clauses, native-speaking children, native-speaking adults, and adult foreign-language learners used the same strategy of treating the first noun phrase in the sentence as the subject and the first noun phrase after the verb as the object, irrespective of whether this was in fact the case. In another experiment, designed to establish the maximum number of digits that foreign-language learners could repeat in a L2, Cook was able to show that an adult learner behaved like a native-speaking adult rather than like a child. On the basis of these experiments Cook concludes that when the memory process depends on features of syntax, the same restrictions apply to the L1 and adult L2 learner, but where the memory process is minimally dependent on language, the adult L2 learner exploits his general memory capacity. The general point is that the L2 = L1 hypothesis is only justified 'to the extent that other attributes of the mind are not involved' (Cook 1977). Unfortunately, however, we do not have a very precise idea about which aspects of language learning are influenced by general cognitive processes and which ones are dependent on the language-learning faculty.

What evidence is there to suggest that L1 acquisition and SLA are similar? In answering this question it is useful once again to distinguish the two meanings of *process*. Is the order of acquisition similar in L1 acquisition and SLA? Are the strategies used by L1 and L2 learners the same? I shall look at each of these two questions.

Order of acquisition comparisons have been common as a result of the close links between theoretical and methodological approaches in L1 acquisition and SLA research. These links have already been examined in the early sections of this chapter. The morpheme studies provided one basis for comparison. Dulay and Burt (1974b) compared the 'acquisition order' they obtained from speech data collected from 6–8 year old Spanish- and Chinese-speaking children with the 'acquisition order' obtained in both longitudinal studies of L1 English (e.g. Brown 1973) and cross-sectional studies of L1 English (e.g. de Villiers and de Villiers, 1973). They found that the orders were different. However, the L2 order they obtained did correlate with the L1 order obtained by Porter (1977). Results such as these are indicative of the kinds of contradictions that exist in SLA research, but one possible explanation is that the 'acquisition order' achieved for SLA is the result of the instrument they used to collect data—the Bilingual Syntax Measure—as this was also the instrument used by Porter. If the 'acquisition order' is only an artefact of this measure, then comparisons between L1 acquisition and SLA based on studies in which it has been used are of doubtful validity. In short, the morpheme studies do not provide a reliable basis for comparison.

A sounder basis for examining the L2 = L1 acquisition hypothesis exists in the longitudinal studies. The evidence from studies of negatives and interrogatives in L1 acquisition and SLA suggests that where transitional constructions are concerned, there is a high level of similarity. Cazden's (1972) summary of the order of development for interrogatives in L1 acquisition is strikingly similar to that in SLA. Here are the main stages Cazden identifies:

1 One-word utterances are used as questions.
2 Intonation questions appear on a regular basis and there are some Wh-questions learnt as ready-made chunks.
3 Intonation questions become more complicated, and productive Wh-questions without inversion occur.
4 Inversion involving auxiliary verbs occurs in yes/no questions, but not in Wh-questions.
5 Inversion occurs in Wh-questions.
6 Embedded Wh-questions develop.

However, although in general the features of L1 interrogatives are the same as in SLA (in particular, the fact that productive interrogatives without subject–verb inversion appear first in both), there are also differences. For instance, in SLA a one-word stage for questions does not appear common, and there is no clear evidence that subject–verb inversion occurs in yes/no questions before Wh-questions.

Felix's (1978) comparison of the acquisition of sentence types in L1 acquisition and SLA of German also points to clear differences. Felix found that in SLA the children produced only three different multi-word utterance types, and argues that this contrasts with L1 acquisition, where learners have been shown to produce a multitude of different structures in the two-word stage onwards. Thus in comparison with L1 acquisition the sentence patterns of the two L2 learners were 'amazingly restricted'. Felix suggests that this might be because L2 learners' utterances are organized syntactically right from the beginning, whereas L1 learners' utterances express conceptual rather than grammatical relations. However, Ervin-Tripp (1974) in a study of thirty-one English-speaking children's acquisition of French found that both L1 acquisition and SLA were characterized by a similar attention to word order.

In conclusion, then, the evidence from the comparisons of the L1 and L2 acquisitional routes is mixed. There is some evidence to suggest that SLA proceeds in more or less the same way as L1 acquisition, but there is also evidence that points to differences. It is not clear whether these differences are the result of L1 transfer or of other factors to do with the learner's more advanced cognitive development. Most likely they are the result of both.

When it comes to examining the kinds of strategies used in the two types of acquisition, the similarity is more evident. Slobin (1973) suggested that the way children process language in L1 acquisition can be explained in terms of a series of *Operating Principles*:

A. Pay attention to the ends of words.
B. The phonological forms of words can be systematically modified.
C. Pay attention to the order of words and morphemes.
D. Avoid interruption and rearrangement of linguistic units.
E. Underlying semantic relations should be marked overtly and clearly.
F. Avoid exceptions.
G. The use of grammatical markers should make semantic sense.

It is not difficult to find evidence of these Operating Principles in SLA. Operating Principle D, for instance, is evident in external negation, where interruption of the standard declarative word order is prevented by attaching the negative particle to the utterance nucleus. It is also evident in non-inverted Wh-questions. Operating Principle B can be observed in the free variation of alternative negative particles—'no', 'not', 'don't'—early on. Principle C occurs in the early attention that the SLA learner pays to word order. Ervin-Tripp (1974), for instance, observed that her subjects interpreted utterances consisting of noun + verb + noun as subject–verb–object sentences, irrespective of morphological information denoting the passive. However, it is Principle F that is lent the strongest support in SLA research. Over-generalization of target language rules is widely commented on in the Error Analysis literature. Avoiding exceptions is one of the main ways in which the learner tries to simplify the learning task. It might be argued, therefore, that Slobin's operating principles apply equally to L1 acquisition and to SLA. However, it is not clear whether all of Slobin's Principles can be found in SLA. Wode (1980a) notes that in SLA free morphemes such as articles and prepositions tend to be learnt before bound morphemes such as tense inflections, and this casts doubt on Principle A. Also it is not clear how the learner's L1 affects the nature and the working of the Operating Principles in SLA. Yet another problem is that one Principle often seems to contradict another; D, for example, seems to be in opposition to C. Only if some means is found of ordering and delimiting the application of the various Principles will there be a truly sound basis for comparing L1 acquisition and SLA.

The mentalist view of the language learner's knowledge of language as an internal system which is gradually revised in the direction of the target language system underlies both the notions of 'Aquisition Device' and 'interlanguage'. SLA and L1 acquisition both involve transitional competence and, as might be expected, this is reflected in similarities, which are not total but nevertheless are strong, between both the acquisitional routes and the strategies that are responsible for them. It is this aspect of language learning which the notion of creative construction has been used to describe. The nature of the rules that learners construct is determined by the mental mechanisms responsible for language acquisition and use. In so far as these mechanisms are innate, L1 acquisition and SLA will proceed in the same way.

It is now time to consider in greater detail some of the caveats about this mentalist interpretation of language learning.

Some outstanding issues

In this final section of the chapter, I wish to consider a number of methodological and theoretical difficulties of the interlanguage construct and the claims for a natural sequence of development.

Methodological problems

The empirical research of the 1970s was of three types—Error Analysis, cross-sectional studies (e.g. the morpheme studies), and longitudinal case studies. The evidence supplied by this research has been used to make claims about a natural sequence of development which is the result of innate internal processes. However, there are problems with each type of research, which must necessarily detract from the strength of the claims.

Error Analysis

Error Analysis is a limited tool for investigating SLA. It can provide only a partial picture, because it focuses on only part of the language that L2 learners produce, i.e. the idiosyncratic forms. Also because it examines language-learner language at a single point in time, it does not cast much light on the developmental route learners take. There are also practical difficulties about identifying what an 'error' is. Corder's (1971) proposal that 'errors' need to be distinguished from 'lapses' is probably unworkable in practice.

Morpheme studies

The morpheme studies instigated by Dulay and Burt were an ingenious attempt to overcome the principal limitation of cross-sectional research —its inability to inform about the sequence of SLA. However, more than perhaps any other area of SLA research, these studies are controversial. In particular it has been argued that there is not a sufficient theoretical base for assuming that the accuracy with which learners use morphemes corresponds to the order in which they are acquired. The case studies have shown that learners may begin by using a grammatical form correctly, only to regress at a later stage, which makes a mockery of attempts to equate accuracy and acquisition. Other doubts about the studies include the suspicion that the orders obtained are an artefact of the Bilingual Syntax Measure; and criticisms concerning the choice of morphemes for investigation and the methods used to 'score' each morpheme. Also Rosansky (1975) has argued that the rank correlation statistics used to compare the orders achieved in different studies disguise much of the variability in the data. Hatch (1978b; 1983a) provides an excellent account of the main objections.

Longitudinal studies

The most convincing evidence comes from the longitudinal studies, but there are problems here, too. The major one is that it has not proved possible to build a profile of development for L2 learners in the same way as in L1 research. L1 researchers have been able to use mean length of utterance as a reliable index of development, but as Larsen-Freeman (1978) notes, mean length of utterance cannot be used in SLA because so many of the L2 learner's earliest utterances consist of rote-learnt chunks which lack internal structure. Various alternative indices have been suggested, but none has become widely accepted. The result is that it is difficult to make reliable comparisons between learners. Each study has chosen its own method for analysing the data. Another limitation of the case studies is that relatively few areas of grammar have been investigated—negatives, interrogatives, and basic sentence types are the favourites, and complex structures have begun to receive attention only recently (e.g. Ioup 1983).

The focus on grammar

It was pointed out in Chapter 1 that probably the major limiting factor in the empirical research in SLA to date has been its preoccupation with grammar. This can be seen as a direct result of the close links between mentalist accounts of language acquisition and the theories of syntax associated with Chomsky. Acquiring a language was understood as the construction of *linguistic competence*. However, whereas research into first language acquisition rapidly broadened the scope of its enquiry to consider how the child's ability to *communicate* developed, SLA research has continued to neglect the study of how communicative competence is acquired and how it contributes to grammatical develop-ment. There have been few studies of the relationship between form and meaning in SLA. A number of recent studies (e.g. Huebner 1979; Eisenstein *et al.* 1982), however, suggest that this relationship is central in understanding how SLA progresses. It has been shown, for instance, that a learner may use a particular grammatical form (e.g. the progressive '-ing' inflection) to express a range of meanings. Acquisition involves gradually sorting out which meanings can be realized by a particular form in the target language. Any analysis based only on form will be acquired long before the process of sorting out the form–function relationships has been concluded. The acquisition of form–function relationships is considered in greater detail in Chapter 4.

The major theoretical issues concern (1) the starting point of the interlanguage continuum; (2) the extent to which an adequate explanation of SLA requires a consideration of factors external to the learner as well as internal factors; and (3) the problems posed for interlanguage theory and the natural sequence by the variability inherent in language-learner language. Each of these issues will be considered separately below.

Origins of interlanguage

The starting point of interlanguage becomes a major issue when SLA is seen as a recreation continuum rather than a restructuring continuum. If the learner builds up his interlanguage by gradually increasing the complexity of the system, what is his starting point? Corder (1981) considers two possibilities. One is that the learner starts from scratch in the same way as the infant acquiring his mother tongue. But Corder considers this possibility unlikely, as it is highly implausible that entire processes of language acquisition will be replicated. The second possibility is that the learner starts from 'some basic simple grammar' (Corder 1981: 150). Corder suggests that language learners regress to an earlier stage in their own linguistic development before starting the process of elaboration. Ellis (1982a), however, argues that there is no need to posit that the learner remembers early acquisitional stages. The starting point consists of the early vocabulary that the learner has acquired. This is used in non-grammatical utterances, and conveys the learner's meaning with the help of information supplied to the listener by the context of situation. In other words, the starting point is the learner's knowledge of how to get a message across without the help of grammar. This is part of any language user's capacity and can be called upon whenever there is a need to create 'simple' messages. The same process is evident in the speech that mothers address to children, and that native-speakers address to L2 learners to facilitate communication. In general, however, the question of the origins of interlanguage is still an open one, subject to speculation. There have been very few empirical studies of the initial stage of the interlanguage continuum.

Neglect of external factors

Mentalist accounts of language acquisition originated in the rejection of behaviourist explanations of how language was learnt. They sought to play down the contribution of the environment by emphasizing instead the centrality of mental processes, and in particular the innate human propensity for language. The input functioned only as a trigger for setting in motion the internal processing mechanisms. It was for this reason that considerable importance was attached to demonstrating the universality of both L1 acquisition and SLA. If it could be shown that despite differences in the situational context of learning, the sequence of development was invariable, then this would be strong evidence in favour of a language acquisition device. Chomsky went so far as to label the linguistic input as 'degenerate'. He argued that it was logically impossible for a child to develop a competence that generated well-formed sentences from exposure to data consisting of sentence fragments, deviations from rules, and false starts. Chomsky's claims about the nature of the input, however, were conjectural and have proved to be ill founded. The speech addressed to young children and also to L2 learners is generally well formed. As a result of the adaptations on the part of those who communicate with language learners, the input that is provided may be specially suited for language acquisition. By minimizing the role of the environment, early interlanguage theory ignored what may be the most important factor in SLA, namely the relationship that exists between the input and the learner's internal processing mechanisms. The concept of strategy, for instance, needs to be understood not just as a hidden mental process but as a device for relating the input to existing knowledge on the one hand, and for relating existing knowledge to output on the other. This can be achieved only if the basis of investigation becomes the interactions involving the learner and his interlocutors, rather than disembodied learner utterances which have served as the data in the bulk of the research referred to in the previous sections. There needs to be a shift from an intra-organism to an inter-organism perspective. This will be the concern of Chapter 6.

The problem of variability

One of the main principles of interlanguage theory is that language-learner language is systematic. At any one stage in his development, the learner operates in accordance with the system of rules he has constructed up to that point. A crucial issue, then, is why his performance is so variable. On one occasion he uses one rule, on another he uses a different rule. Each developmental stage, therefore, is characterized not by a system of categorical rules which are invariably applied, but by a system of alternative rules. It is for this reason that the natural sequence of development is so fuzzy. Not only do the stages overlap, but also the amount of overlapping is variable (Hatch 1974). The only explanation for this phenomenon offered by early interlanguage theory was 'backsliding'. But variability does not take place only when 'fossilization' has set in; it is common throughout the interlanguage continuum. Interlanguage theory does not cope easily with learner variability—it struggles to explain why or when variability takes place. It has, however, adapted to try to account for contextual variability. Chapter 4 examines how.

The natural route of development also ignores another type of variability, that which derives from individual learner differences. The case-study literature indicates that there are considerable differences in the ways in which learners orient to the task of learning. The extent to which this is reflected in modifications of the natural sequence of transitional constructions such as negatives and interrogatives is not clear. But there is plenty of evidence to show that it can affect the *rate* of SLA and also the point at which cessation of learning occurs. Mentalist accounts of language acquisition pay scant attention to individual learner differences. They are an important explanatory factor, however. Chapter 5 considers the role they play.

Summary and conclusion

This chapter has explored the case for a mentalist interpretation of SLA. In order to do so, it has considered mentalist accounts of L1 acquisition, the interlanguage construct in SLA, the empirical evidence for a natural developmental route, and the extent to which this route is the same in L1 acquisition and SLA.

As a result of theoretical attacks on the behaviourist view of language acquisition as habit-formation, it was hypothesized that L1 acquisition was the product of an 'acquisition device' by which means the child related a set of universal grammatical rules to the surface structure of the language he was learning. The counterpart of the 'acquisition device' in SLA was 'creative construction'. That is, SLA was seen as a series of evolving systems which comprised the interlanguage continuum. Each system was considered to be internally consistent, in the sense that it was rule-governed. It was, however, also permeable to new rules, and, therefore, dynamic. The continuum was initially viewed primarily as a restructuring continuum stretching from the learner's L1 to the target language. Later it was viewed as a recreation continuum in which the learner gradually added to the complexity of interim systems. Most learners never reached the final stage of the continuum; their interlanguage fossilized some way short of target language competence.

Interlanguage theory both generated and fed off empirical research into SLA. This research initially took the form of Error Analysis. This helped to demonstrate that many of the errors that L2 learners made were not traceable to the L1. It also helped to identify some of the processes that were responsible for interlanguage development. Increasingly, however, SLA research focused on identifying the developmental route along which learners passed. Both cross-sectional and longitudinal studies sought answers to two questions: (1) was there a natural route of development?; and (2) was this route the same or different from that reported in L1 acquisition? The answer to the first question was that there was evidence to show that learners followed broadly similar routes, although minor differences could also be observed as a result of the learner's L1 and other factors. SLA is characterized by a natural *sequence* of development (i.e. there are certain broad stages that they pass through), but the *order* of development varies in details (i.e. some steps are left out, or specific morphological features are learnt in a different order). It may well be that the sequence of development is common to both L1 acquisition and SLA, whereas the order of development is different. Certainly the L2 = L1 acquisition hypothesis has not been proven in its strong form, although similar processes appear to operate in both types of acquisition. In SLA both the L1 and also maturational factors, which affect the use of at least some cognitive processes, play a part.

Both interlanguage theory and the empirical studies that supported it have had a major impact on our thinking about the nature of SLA. The switch from a behaviourist to a mentalist framework proved a source a great insight into both L1 acquisition and SLA. It has become generally accepted that the human language faculty is a potent force in language acquisition. But internal processing and innate mechanisms are not the full story. It is also necessary to consider how the linguistic input contributes to the process of acquisition. This has been one of the chief ways in which more recent research has redirected its attention. Chapter 6 looks in detail at the role of the linguistic environment. In other respects, interlanguage theory has been able to accommodate to new thinking, in particular by attending to the inherent variability of language-learner language (see Chapter 4).

One of the most important effects of mentalist interpretations of SLA has been the reassessment of errors. Whereas in behaviourist accounts errors were treated as evidence of non-learning, in mentalist theory they serve as evidence of the learner's active contribution to acquisition. It is doubtful, in fact, whether learners ever do completely fossilize. Some revision of the interlanguage system always carries on. Errors are the external manifestation of the hypothesis-testing process which is responsible for the continual revision of the interlanguage system. This alternative view of error has had important pedagogical repercussions.

Further reading

Child Language and Linguistics by D. Crystal (Edward Arnold, 1976), provides a sound and fairly brief summary of the route followed by children in L1 acquisition.

The reader who wants a more thorough theoretical foundation in L1 research, together with a summary of the key empirical research, is strongly recommended to consult Chapters 8, 9, and 10 of *Psychology and Language: An Introduction to Psycholinguistics* by H. Clark and E. Clark (Harcourt Brace Jovanovich, 1977).

All the important papers relating to early interlanguage theory are to be found in *Error Analysis*, edited by J. Richards (Longman, 1974). The two papers by Corder and the one by Selinker are perhaps the most important.

A very useful article by E. Hatch ('Second language learning—universals') in *Working Papers on Bilingualism* 3: 1–17, 1974) summarizes the findings of several research projects and puts the case for 'universals' into perspective.

There is no substitute in the final analysis for reading some of the reports of empirical studies. *Second Language Acquisition*, edited by E. Hatch (Newbury House, 1978), contains a collection of papers. The ones relevant to this chapter and worth looking at are those by Itoh and Hatch, Wode, Huang and Hatch, Cancino *et al.*, Butterworth and Hatch, Adams, and Dulay and Burt. The book is probably the single most important publication in SLA, and other articles contained in it will be recommended later in this volume.

It is also worth looking at *Second Language Development*, edited by S. Felix (Gunter Narr Verlag, 1980). This contains reports of German projects in SLA and makes a change from a diet of American-based research.

More recent collections of SLA studies are to be found in *Research in Second Language Acquisition*, edited by R. Scarcella and S. Krashen (Newbury House, 1980), and in *Second Language Acquisition Studies*, edited by K. Bailey, M. Long, and S. Peck (Newbury House, 1983). These are best read after looking at the earlier research in the books mentioned above.

4 Variability in interlanguage

Introduction: types of variability

The last chapter looked at evidence in favour of a natural route of development. It was noted that interlanguage theory needs to take into account the variability inherent in language-learner language. The natural route does not manifest itself in a series of clearly delineated stages. Rather each stage overlaps with the one that precedes and follows it. Each new rule is slowly extended over a range of linguistic contexts. Therefore, at any given stage of development, the learner's interlanguage system will contain a number of competing rules, with one rule guiding performance on one occasion and another rule on a different occasion. In addition, each interlanguage system contains linguistic forms that are in free variation; that is, forms that are not guided by rules and whose use is not systematic at all. These types of variability pose both practical and theoretical problems for SLA research. The practical problems concern how to collect data in order to study language-learner language. If the learner's performance varies from one task to another, how can the researcher evaluate the particular data he has collected? The theoretical problems concern how to reconcile the inherent variability of the learner's performance with claims that interlanguage is systematic, and how to account for non-systematic variability.

This chapter will examine the nature of *contextual variability* in language-learner language. That is, it will concern itself with the variable performance that can be explained with reference to either the *linguistic* or the *situational context* of use. Contextual variability contrasts with *individual variability*. This consists of the variability that can be explained in terms of individual differences to do with such factors as age, motivation, and personality. Individual variability is considered separately in Chapter 5.

This chapter will also consider one type of non-systematic variability. This is the variation apparent in the haphazard use of two or more alternate forms which exist within the learner's interlanguage. This type of variability will be referred to as *free variability*. It will be argued later that this type of variability serves as an important mechanism of development in interlanguage. Not all non-systematic variability, however, involves free variation. Psycholinguistic factors to do with the learner's emotional or physical condition can lead to slips, hesitations, and repetitions. This type of variability can be called *performance variability*. It will not be considered in this chapter, because it does not shed any light on how acquisition takes place.

These different types of variability are summarized in Figure 4.1 below.

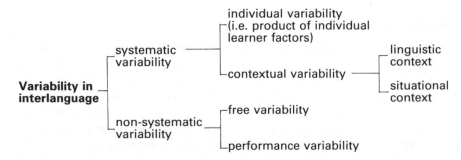

Figure 4.1   Types of variability in language-learner language

Variability is, of course, not only a characteristic of language-learner language. It occurs in all language use. Before we turn to variability in interlanguage, therefore, the general nature of variability in language use will be considered.

Variability in language use

In accordance with Figure 4.1, it is possible to identify two basic types of variability: systematic and non-systematic variability. Each of these will be described separately.

Systematic variability

The status of the variability in the language use of native speakers has been viewed very differently by linguists, depending on whether they approach it in terms of a *homogeneous competence* model or a *heterogeneous competence* model. In a homogeneous competence model all variability is classified as non-systematic variability. That is, the language user is credited with a system of rules (his 'competence') which is homogeneous. This underlies all his efforts at performance, and the fact that he does not always manifest the ideal system in the way he speaks or writes is dismissed as irrelevant to an understanding of the ideal system (Chomsky 1965). In the competence model, linguistic knowledge is separated from non-linguistic knowledge, even though this may be called upon when linguistic knowledge is put to use. Thus even if non-linguistic knowledge (or, as Chomsky, currently calls it, pragmatic knowledge) is systematic, it does not need to be taken into account when explaining linguistic competence. The homogeneous competence model, therefore, discounts stylistic variability, or rather treats it only as an aspect of performance.

Figure 4.1 is very clearly not derived from a homogeneous competence model. It distinguishes non-systematic variability on the one hand and systematic contextual and individual variability on the other. Figure 4.1 is representative of a heterogeneous competence model of language use. It posits that although some of the variability observed is the result of relatively unpredictable factors to do with the state of the mind or emotions of the user, other variability, particularly that deriving from the user's knowledge of how to use language *appropriately*, is systematic, and, more importantly, constitutes an integral part of the user's communicative competence (Hymes 1971). According to the heterogeneous competence model, therefore, the user's knowledge of language rules is interlocked with his knowledge of when, where, and with whom to use them. According to this view of language, the user's ability to perform needs to be understood in terms of *communicative* rather than *linguistic* competence. In a heterogeneous competence model, therefore, stylistic variability is viewed as an integral part of competence, not performance.

Labov (1970) operates within a heterogeneous competence model. He lists five axioms about how to study language use. Because these are of central importance for understanding the nature of user variability, they are summarized below.

1 All speakers possess several 'styles'. That is, they adapt their speech to make it fit the social context.
2 'Styles can be ranged along a single dimension, measured by the amount of attention paid to speech.' A language user varies in the degree to which he is able to monitor his speech in different situations.
3 The *vernacular* is the style in which minimum attention is given to monitoring speech. It is the style associated with informal, everyday speech. It provides 'the most systematic data' for linguistic study.
4 It is not possible to tap the vernacular style of the user by systematic observation of how he performs in a formal context (such as an experiment).
5 The only way to obtain good data on the speech of a language user is through systematic observation.

The conflict between the fourth and fifth axioms leads to what Labov calls the 'Observer's Paradox'. Good data require systematic observation, but this prevents access to the user's vernacular style, which, because it is the most systematic style, is the principal goal of linguistic enquiry.

As an example of how a sociolinguistic model deals with variability caused by situational factors, let us consider one of Labov's studies.

Labov (1970) examined the speech patterns of New Yorkers. He collected data in various ways in order to sample a range of speech styles. These he classified as (1) casual speech, (2) careful speech, (3) reading, (4) word lists, and (5) minimal pairs. These styles were spread along a continuum according to the amount of attention paid by the speakers to their own speech. Thus in (1) very little attention was paid, while in (5) careful monitoring occurred. Labov examined the frequency of certain socially marked sounds as they occurred in each speech style. For instance, |Θ| (the first sound in '*th*ing') is a prestige sound in New York English, but there are also a number of non-prestige variants e.g. /t/. Labov found that the degree to which |Θ| was replaced by less socially prestigious forms varied according to the degree of attention the users paid to their speech in different contexts. Thus the more attention given, the more instances of |Θ| there were, and correspondingly fewer instances of non-prestigious variants. It was possible, therefore, to characterize the different styles in terms of the variable use of sounds such as |Θ|. The important point was that language behaviour was predictable. Style-shifting took place systematically.

Labov also deals with variability determined by linguistic factors. He examined the use of the copula ('be') in utterances produced by speakers of Black English Vernacular in New York and found that the presence or absence of the copula was largely systematic. Its use depended on the specific linguistic context provided by an utterance. For instance, the copula was more likely to be used when the preceding syntactic environment constituted a noun phrase rather than when it was a pronoun. Similarly, it was more likely to occur when the following grammatical structure was 'gonna' than when it was a noun phrase. It is important to note, however, that the syntactic environment did not determine the absolute occurrence of the copula, only its relative frequency. Thus 'be' was variable in all contexts, but certain contexts predisposed the speaker to use it more frequently than other contexts.

Both a homogeneous and heterogeneous competence model account for the variable nature of a language user's performance. But whereas a homogeneous competence model does so by excluding those factors that are responsible for variability, a heterogeneous competence model, such as that proposed by Labov, views contextual factors as an integral part of the user's ability to use his linguistic knowledge. The user not only knows what is *correct*, but also what is *appropriate* for each context of use. The user's ability is not that of an 'ideal speaker-hearer'; it is heterogeneous. A heterogeneous competence model, however, still seeks to characterize the user's underlying knowledge, and not just his performance.

Whereas a homogeneous competence model accounts for a homogeneous linguistic competence in terms of *invariant rules*, a heterogeneous competence model such as Labov's accounts for communicative competence in terms of *variable rules*. Invariant rules are categorical statements which specify the set of well-formed sentences in the grammar of a language. Variable rules are statements which give the probability of certain grammatical forms occurring in particular situational and linguistic contexts. If the variable nature of language use is allocated a constitutive role in the user's competence, it will be necessary to account for this ability, and one way of doing so is in terms of variable rules.

An alternative way of accounting for variability is by means of *implicational analysis* (Decamp 1971; Bickerton 1975). This approach involves viewing language as an intersecting set of idiolects. Any one speaker will have access to a number of such idiolects, but is unlikely to be capable of the full range. But within a language community, the full range of idiolects will be observed. The competence of the speech community can be viewed as a continuum. At one end of this continuum is an idiolect (usually the standard dialect) which contains all of a number of specified linguistic features, while at the other end of this continuum is an idiolect which contains few or even none of these features. Furthermore, these features can be seen to be hierarchically ordered, such that the presence of one feature in an idiolect entails the co-occurrence of one or more other features. For example, a language user whose speech manifested the uncontracted 'I am' would also employ the contracted 'I'm', but a language user who used 'I'm' might not necessarily also use 'I am'. Language users shift along this continuum of styles, varying their choice of idiolect in accordance with social factors.

Implicational analysis has been used extensively in pidgin and creole studies. For example Bickerton (1975) used it to study variation in the language of speakers of the creole continuum in Guyana. Bickerton identified three segments in this continuum. The *basilect* was the creole variety most distinct from the standard form of the language. The *mesolect* is an intervening variety, and the *acrolect* the variety closest to the standard. Bickerton was able to classify the speakers as basilect, mesolect, or acrolect on the basis of the frequency with which they used certain forms. All the creole speakers were likely to use a range of linguistic forms, but certain of these could be specifically associated with the basilect, etc. Bickerton found that some linguistic features implicated the presence of others. For example, where the acrolect contained features F1, F2, and F3, the mesolect would contain only F1 and F2, and the basilect only F1 or none of the features. Thus the presence of F3 implicated the presence of F2 and F1, and the presence of F2 implicated the presence of F1 (but not F3). Bickerton also found that the presence of features in the creole was governed by the linguistic environments in which they occurred. Creole studies such as that of Bickerton have been of considerable interest to SLA research, because the creole continuum corresponds in many respects to the developmental route followed by L2 learners.

The advantages and disadvantages of different ways of accounting for the variability of language use have been debated at length (see Dittmar 1976: 132ff.). These, however, do not concern us here. The important points are that variation is systematic, governed by both situational and linguistic factors, and that the user's linguistic knowledge is organized in such a way that the existence of one linguistic form presupposes the presence of one or more other forms. In so far as interlanguage is a natural language, it can be expected that these points will also hold true in SLA. Also, as will be shown later, the descriptive methods for handling variability have proved useful in SLA research.

Non-systematic variability

Native-speaker language use is also characterized by non-systematic variability. As discussed earlier, this is of two types. Performance variability, however, is not part of the user's competence. It occurs when the language user is unable to perform his competence. It is the second type of non-systematic variability—free variability—which is of greater interest for understanding SLA and which will, therefore, be discussed here.

It is not difficult to find examples of free variation, although the examples are likely to be idiosyncratic. For example, I sometimes say /ɔfn/ and sometimes /ɔftn/. In this chapter I have used 'variation' and 'variability' interchangeably, as far as I can tell. I alternate haphazardly between 'who' and 'that' as subject relative pronouns in non-restrictive relative clauses. In native-speaker speech, however, such free variability is circumscribed; it is unlikely to be observed in more than a few instances. Interlanguage, in contrast, is marked by a high level of free variability, a characteristic that is important for explaining how interlanguage evolves.

In general, non-systematic variability has not received much attention from linguists, who have preferred to explore systematic variability. Bickerton (1975), however, has disputed the prevailing 'contextual theory' of linguistic variation. He observes

> While with the help of a little hindsight, a plausible contextual explanation can be given for many stylistic shifts, there are many more that operate in quite unpredictable ways. (Bickerton 1975: 183).

Bickerton points to Labov's famous example of phonological change in the speech of Martha's Vineyarders. They attempted to maintain their own group identity in the face of an influx of outsiders by their choice of a specific sound. However, the sound they used was not specially introduced, but rather a sound that already existed in their speech and which they intensified. In other words, a sound which began its existence in free variation with other sounds came to be used systematically to convey social meaning. This process of exploiting a form in free variation is a key feature of interlanguage development.

Summary

Language use is characterized by systematic and non-systematic variation. Systematic variation can be explained with reference to both situational and linguistic factors, which determine which variants are used where, when, and how. The language user can be credited with a competence that comprises a continuum of idiolects, as is most clearly evident in the creole continuum. This continuum is composed of a number of varieties, or lects, which vary in their level of complexity and which can therefore be ordered hierarchically. One type of non-systematic variation is free variation. Linguistic forms which are initially used in free variation may later be used systematically to convey different meanings.

Variability in interlanguage

The same types of variability are evident in interlanguage as in natural languages. However, although there is no difference in kind, there is difference in degree; variability is extensive in interlanguage. The following account will first consider contextual variability and then free variability.

Contextual variability

It has been pointed out that contextual variability is of two kinds: that which is determined by situational context and that which is determined by linguistic context.

Variability that is the result of situational context is analagous to the stylistic variability observed in native-speaker usage and described in the previous section with reference to Labov's work. Dickerson (1975) examined the occurrence of /z/ in the speech of ten Japanese speakers studying English at university level. She collected data on three separate occasions in a nine-month period, using a three-part test involving (1) free speaking, (2) reading dialogues aloud, and (3) reading word lists aloud. Dickerson found that the correct target language variant was used most frequently in (3) and least frequently in (1), with the frequency in (2) in between. This order was maintained over the three occasions. The same order was observed for other variants that were closest in form to the target language sound. In other words, Dickerson found that L2 learners employed multiple variants (one of which might be the correct target language form, but need not be). They used the target language variants or those variants linguistically closest to it in situations where they were able to audio-monitor their speech, and those variants linguistically distant from the correct target language form in situations where audio-monitoring was not possible. Development over time involved an increase in the proportion of the target and target-like sounds.

Other studies of phonological development have come up with observations similar to those of Dickerson. Schmidt (1977), for instance, noted that Arabic-speaking students of English became more accurate in their use of English 'th' sounds in a formal task than in an informal task. Also Schmidt noted that these learners did exactly the same in L2 English as they did in L1 Arabic, where they also style-shifted from relative low to high frequency in the use of 'th' sounds, depending on whether they were speaking colloquial Arabic (associated with informal situations) or classical Arabic (associated with formal situations). In other words, the patterns of style-shifting were the same in L1 and L2. Beebe (1980) also found evidence of the direct transfer of a formal feature of the L1 into the L2 when the situation demanded a formal style. Her Thai subjects actually produced fewer instances of the target sound (in this case /r/) in formal than in informal occasions. This was because they used the prestige Thai [r] variant, which they associated with formal use in their own language, in their formal English. The studies by Schmidt and Beebe, while reinforcing the overall picture provided by Dickerson's study, make it clear that when a learner is able to attend closely to his speech (i.e. in a careful style), he may produce not only a higher incidence of target language forms, but also a higher incidence of L1 forms, if these are associated with formal use in the L1. Language transfer, therefore, is also a variable phenomenon.

The studies referred to above all concern interlanguage phonology. Similar results, however, have been obtained for grammatical features. Schmidt (1980) investigated second-verb ellipsis in sentences like

Mary is eating an apple and Sue ø a pear.

Learners from a variety of language backgrounds always included the second verb in such sentences in free oral production, but increasingly omitted it in proportion to the degree of monitoring permitted by different tasks (i.e. elicited imitation, written sentence-combining, and grammatical judgement). Lococo (1976) found that twenty-eight university students enrolled in an elementary Spanish course produced systematically fewer errors in adjectives, determiners, and verbs when the task was translation than when it was free composition, with the scores for the picture description task intermediary. Thus it is seen once again that when the learner is able to monitor his performance, he produces target language forms with greater regularity.

Tarone (1983) represents the effects of situational context as a continuum of interlanguage styles (see Figure 4.2). At one end of the continuum is the *vernacular style*, which is called upon when the learner is not attending to his speech. This is the style that is both most natural and most systematic. At the other end of the continuum is the *careful style*, which is most clearly evident in tasks that require the learner to make a grammatical judgement (e.g. to say whether a sentence is correct or incorrect). The careful style is called upon when the learner is attending closely to his speech. Thus the stylistic continuum is the product of differing degrees of attention reflected in a variety of performance tasks. It should be noted, however, that Tarone views the stylistic continuum as competence, not just as performance.

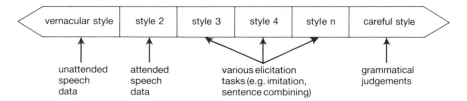

Figure 4.2   The interlanguage continuum (Tarone 1983: 152)

Variability as a result of the linguistic context occurs when two different linguistic contexts induce different forms even though in the target language they require the same form. For example, the learner might produce correct exemplars of the third person singular '-s' when the linguistic context consists of a single clause utterance as in:

Mr Smith *lives* in Gloucester.

but fail to do so when the linguistic context consists of a subordinate clause as in:

Mr Smith who *live* in Gloucester married my sister.

This variability may not involve a correct target language form at all. It may consist of the use of two (or more) deviant forms.

Dickerson's (1975) study also provides evidence of contextual variability according to linguistic context. She noticed that her subjects used a number of variants for English /z/ according to the linguistic environment. The phonetic quality of the sound they produced depended on what consonants and vowels were adjacent to /z/. Thus when /z/ was followed by a vowel, the learners used the correct target language form every time, even on the first occasion; but when /z/ was followed by silence, they used three variants, only one of which was /z/. Progress from one occasion to the next consisted of the increased use of /z/ in environments where initially it was little used, and also of increased use of variants that were phonetically closer to /z/. For instance in the dialogue-reading part of the first test, the subjects used /z/ fifty per cent of the time in environments where the target form was followed by silence (as in the word 'buzz'), but over eighty per cent of the time in the third test. Acquisition of /z/, therefore, consisted of the gradual mastery of its use in a range of linguistic contexts.

The effects of the linguistic and situational context interact to influence jointly the learner's use of interlanguage forms. If linguistic contexts are seen as a continuum ranging from 'simple' (e.g. single clause utterances for the third person singular '-s') to 'complex' (e.g. subordinate clauses for the third person singular '-s'), and if situational contexts are also viewed as a continuum (as shown in Figure 4.2), then the use of any particular interlanguage form can be plotted on the intersection of these two continua (see Figure 4.3).

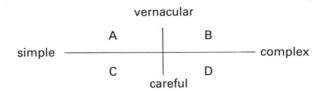

Figure 4.3   Interlanguage as the intersection of two continua

For example, it can be predicted that, to begin with, use of the third person singular will be most frequent when the linguistic context is simple and the style careful (i.e. section C of Figure 4.3). It will be least frequent when the linguistic context is complex and the style is vernacular (i.e. B). Whether A (i.e. simple linguistic context but vernacular style) or D (i.e. complex linguistic context but casual style) leads to greater regularity of use is not certain.

Free variability

Not all interlanguage variability is contextual. In the initial stages it is likely that a fair proportion of the variation is haphazard. That is, the learner possesses two or more forms which he uses to realize the same range of meanings. For example, Ellis (1984b) quotes two utterances produced by an eleven year old Portuguese boy learning English:

No look my card.
Don't look my card.

(The boy was playing a game of word bingo and wanted to stop other pupils looking at his card.) The utterances were produced within minutes of each other. In both cases the boy was focused on meaning and was not, therefore, audio-monitoring his speech. Also both utterances occurred discourse-initially and, therefore, shared the same linguistic context. The most likely explanation of these two utterances is that at this stage in his development, 'no + V' and 'don't + V' served as alternative negative rules which he drew on at will.

In order to detect free variation in interlanguage, it is necessary to look at form–function relationships, that is to investigate which forms are used to express which meanings. Unfortunately there are few SLA studies which have investigated these relationships. Those that have report considerable free variation. For instance, Wagner-Gough (1975) found that a six year old Iranian boy used the progressive '-ing' to realize ongoing activity, immediate intention, intention in the distant future, past reference, habitual activity, and imperative meanings. She also found that the simple verb form was used to express virtually the same range of language functions. Both forms were in semantic free variation. Eisenstein *et al.* (1982) also examined the use of the progressive and simple verb forms, this time in a cross-sectional study of adult L2 learners. The results they obtained were explained by hypothesizing that the simple and progressive forms were first stored as one form/function and only later differentiated. Further evidence comes from Huebner (1981). He investigated the use of two formulaic expressions in the speech of a Thai learner of English and found that the acquisition of the forms of the formulas preceded the acquisition of their functions. These studies provide evidence of what is probably a widespread phenomenon. When learners first internalize new linguistic items, they do not know precisely what functions they realize in the target language. The result is free variability.

Summary

This section has described and illustrated the presence of both systematic contextual variability and non-systematic free variability in interlanguage. It is clear that the process of acquisition is related to this variability. (1) The learner slowly extends the contextual range of the forms he has acquired, by mastering their use in additional stylistic and linguistic contexts. (2) The learner slowly resolves the free variability that exists in his interlanguage by developing clear form–function relationships. Both of the processes will be examined in detail. First, however, the different ways in which variability in language learner language is handled in SLA research will be considered.

Interlanguage variability and SLA research

The kinds of variability described in the previous section pose a number of problems for SLA research, and, therefore, for our understanding of language-learner language. These problems are:

1 What style is 'basic' or primary?
2 What are the best data to use in describing interlanguage?
3 How can the variable nature of the learner's interlanguage be accurately described?

These are related issues, but I shall consider each in turn.

The vernacular style is basic

Tarone (1982; 1983), following Labov, claims that the vernacular style of interlanguage is primary, as it is the most stable and consistent of all the styles. Because the vernacular style represents unmonitored capability, it contains fewer instances of either target language or L1 forms than other styles. It will, therefore, have greater internal consistency, because it is not subject to the variable influence of other knowledge sources. Whereas the interlanguage forms manifest in a careful style are likely to be highly variable, depending on the degree of monitoring and also which forms are focused on for close attention, the interlanguage forms manifest in the vernacular style are relatively invariable.

Tarone suggests that the forms characteristic of the vernacular style are internalized spontaneously. This is, presumably, because the learner is endowed with an innate disposition that governs the way he processes input and constructs an interlanguage system. This is the view of SLA as a process of 'creative construction', which is manifest in the natural route of development. The natural route, therefore, is a feature of the vernacular style. It can be expected to be observed only in studies which have examined spontaneous unmonitored language use. It is unlikely to emerge in studies based on data collected by imitation, translation, or other elicitation devices, which will reflect a careful interlanguage style. Evidence for these claims will be considered shortly.

The vernacular style can also be considered basic in another sense. We all find it easier and more natural to engage in 'unplanned discourse' than in 'planned discourse'. Ochs (1979) defines the former as discourse that lacks forethought and organizational preparation, and the latter as discourse that has been planned out and organized prior to expression. The difference between the two types of discourse is, again, to be seen as continuous. Ochs points out a number of formal differences in the language that occur in the two types (i.e. at the poles of the continuum). In unplanned discourse speakers tend to fall back on grammatical features that were learned in the early stages of first language acquisition and are, as a result, psycholinguistically 'deep'. Examples are the frequent use of demonstrative modifiers (e.g. 'this' and 'that'), the active voice, and present (rather than past) tenses. Unplanned discourse is the kind of communication that is likely to be found in untutored acquisitional contexts. It is also the type of discourse that most people participate in most frequently and with the greatest facility. When we talk about acquiring a second language, we normally mean acquiring the ability to communicate spontaneously in unplanned discourse. It is clear that Ochs's unplanned/planned continuum closely parallels Tarone's vernacular/careful continuum. Whereas Ochs's continuum refers to performance, Tarone's refers to competence (or 'capability', as she calls it). The primacy of the vernacular style is reflected in the centrality of unplanned discourse in most people's lives.

To summarize briefly, the vernacular style can be considered basic in IL because it is the most stable, it seems to reflect universal principles of language acquisition, and it is the style of unplanned discourse. It is the vernacular style in which the natural route of development in SLA is to be observed.

Collecting data for SLA research

It is evident that language users and language learners do not process their knowledge of language in the same way under all conditions. Their performance varies as a product of the stylistic norm they are drawing on, which in turn depends on whether they are participating in unplanned or planned discourse. In SLA research this variability is manifest in the type of task which the learners perform to supply the researcher with data. Just as Labov observed different kinds of regularities in the production of socially marked forms in native speaker speech depending on the task he gave them, likewise L2 learners can be observed to make different use of their interlanguage system in different tasks.

This variability as a product of the task is often commented on in social science research. It is axiomatic that performance in one set of circumstances does not guarantee an identical or even similar performance in a different situation. In particular, doubts have been expressed about the validity of examining human behaviour in experimental conditions (e.g. Cicourel *et al.* 1974), on the grounds that experimental tasks are not likely to elicit natural or normal behaviour. Butterworth (1980: 4) points out:

> Manipulating the stimuli and available responses is not the same as manipulating the person; even under tightly controlled conditions subjects can and will develop a strategy for dealing with the task, and not necessarily the strategy the experimenter intended.

There is considerable evidence in SLA research to show that the nature of the task influences the kind of language that is observed. Some of this research has already been mentioned in the discussion of styles in interlanguage. A further example is Fillmore (1976). She found that some of her subjects produced a high instance of one-word and fragmentary utterances in elicited data, while their spontaneous speech contained higher proportions of complex utterances. Burmeister and Ufert (1980) carried out a careful comparison of data collected from spontaneous speech and translation tasks in a longitudinal study of five German children's SLA of English. They identified four areas of difference in the two kinds of data:

1 In the elicited data there was a higher level of L1 interference than in spontaneous data.
2 Under experimental conditions the children often fell back on to structures that belonged to previous developmental stages.
3 The elicited data suggested that the children attempted to avoid certain structures such as complex negatives.
4 The elicited data were marked by quite a number of structures which never or rarely occurred in spontaneous speech. These unique structures may have been the result of experimental conditions inducing the children to exploit their linguistic knowledge to the utmost.

Burmeister and Ufert concluded that the experimental data arose from a special type of communicative behaviour. The experimental conditions presupposed knowledge of certain rules whether the learners possessed them or not, and so they were not free to choose their own means of communication. In contrast, the learners had a freer choice regarding both content and linguistic rules in spontaneous speech.

These observations are in line with Labov's and Tarone's claim that the most systematic style is the vernacular. In other styles, which are tapped in certain types of elicitation, the normal pattern of language is disturbed. The learner makes use of a variety of strategies which would not occur in natural conversation. These strategies lead to an erratic performance, with the transfer of L1 forms, primitive interlanguage forms, and more advanced interlanguage forms intermittently surfacing.

Another factor that may influence performance in different tasks is the cognitive complexity of the activity the learner is asked to perform. The cognitive operations involved in undertaking any task are multifarious, but one way of measuring the overall complexity is in terms of 'language perception distance' (Blank *et al.* 1978). This refers to the degree to which the language used relates to features of the situation that are perceptively salient. It has often been noted in L1 acquisition that in the early stages of development children use language to talk about objects and events that are part of their physical environment. It is obviously easier to do this than to talk about displaced activity. Blank *et al.* devised a test based on the language-perception continuum. The 'easiest' questions involved matching perception tasks (e.g. 'What things can you see on the table?') and the most 'difficult' involved reasoning about perception (e.g. 'What happens to the cookies when we put them in the oven?'). Ellis (1982b) devised a similar test for use with L2 learners. He found that the cognitive complexity of specific tasks influenced the success with which the L2 learners performed the tasks, and also the complexity and accuracy of their use of language. There is also evidence from the case studies (e.g. Hatch 1978c) to show that L2 learners benefit in much the same way as L1 learners from talking about the here-and-now.

The explanation for the differential effects of tasks in interlanguage performance lies in the amount of attention the learner is able to pay to what he is saying. In an elicitation task such as translation the learner is *required* to compare the target language with his L1, so it is not surprising that L1 interference is more evident. In a task which is cognitively complex (e.g. one with a wide language perception gap), the learner's attention is likely to be taken up with non-linguistic issues, with the result that he cannot focus on those interlanguage forms that are the most recent additions to his competence and that are therefore not fully automatized (except, of course, where the task requires attention to specific forms). The resulting speech is likely to be less target-like, less complex and more fragmentary than in easy tasks. Conversely, in a task that is cognitively simple (e.g. reading words from a list) the learner will be able to focus on his most advanced interlanguage forms and as a result to maximize his competence.

It is clear, therefore, that the nature of the task determines the kind of language-learner language that is observed. This raises an important question: what are the best data for studying SLA? An assumption is often made in SLA research that data are only valid if they reflect the learner's 'natural' performance, which in turn is equated with the kind of spontaneous communicative behaviour associated with unplanned discourse. This assumption is based on the belief that the vernacular style is in some way more basic than the other interlanguage styles. There are grounds for such an assumption, as discussed in the previous section. However, it could also be argued that what constitutes the best data for studying interlanguage is relative rather than absolute. That is, the best data are those that are representative of the specific interlanguage style which the researcher wishes to investigate. Thus if the researcher is interested in the vernacular style, he will need data from spontaneous speech, but if he is interested in a careful style, he will need elicited data that reflect monitored performance. If he is interested in interlanguage as a variable system, then he will need data from a range of tasks.

There are two dangers to be avoided in SLA research. The first is to avoid making false claims about the data used. It is, for instance, misleading to base statements about a 'natural' route on data that have been collected by means of an elicitation instrument. One of the criticisms that have been levelled at the morpheme studies is that the claimed 'natural' order is only an artefact of the elicitation instrument used (i.e. the Bilingual Syntax Measure). As already observed, Burt and Dulay (1980) claim that this measure taps the learner's vernacular style, as it leads to the type of communication found in natural settings. However, they do not give any examples of the kind of conversation that results from the measure, so this claim is difficult to evaluate. The available evidence suggests that elicited speech is likely to differ from naturally occurring speech, so the possibility that the 'natural' order is not so natural after all cannot be discounted. A study by Porter (1977) suggests this might indeed be the case. Porter used the Bilingual Syntax Measure on children learning their L1 and came up with a very similar order to that found by Dulay and Burt and others for SLA. This order, however, did not match the 'natural' order reported in interlanguage studies that made use of naturally occurring speech (e.g. de Villiers and de Villiers 1973; R. Brown 1973).

The second danger is that of mixing data from different sources, making it impossible to distinguish one interlanguage style from another. Larsen-Freeman (1976) found a different morpheme order according to whether the task was speaking, listening, reading, writing, or elicited imitation. If the data from such a range of tasks are not kept separate, the systematicity of interlanguage will be disguised. It is possible that much of the heterogeneity of language-learner language reported in some studies (e.g. Cazden *et al.* 1975) derives from pooling data which reflect differing degrees of attention on the part of the language user, although, as has already been noted, there is also considerable free variability in interlanguage.

Describing interlanguage variability

By keeping data from different tasks apart, it is possible to examine each style of the learner's variable system. However, as should be clear from the previous discussion of the different types of variability, the data will not be entirely homogeneous. There will be minor style fluctuations— each style represents a band on the continuum (see Figure 4.2)—there will be additional systematic variation as a response to linguistic context, and there will be free variability. The question arises, therefore, of how to describe interlanguage as a variable phenomenon.

One way is to make use of *variable rules*. These are rules which specify the probability of two or more variants occurring in different situational or linguistic contexts. For instance, learners sometimes produce WH questions which are inverted (as in native-speaker speech) and sometimes WH questions which are not inverted. A close analysis of a corpus of learner utterances may reveal that most (but not all) inverted WH questions contain the copula or auxiliary 'be'. Similarly it may reveal that most non-inverted WH questions (but again not all) contain auxiliaries other than 'be'. It is possible to capture this kind of regularity by writing a variable rule which shows the level of probability of inverted and non-inverted WH questions occurring when each linguistic condition prevails. Variable rules can also be devised to describe variable stylistic performance resulting from situational factors. Such rules are inevitably complex, but they are necessary if the true nature of the learner's interlanguage system is to be represented.

Variable rules are best used to describe systematic variability. They cannot handle free variability. Also, variable rules can reflect developmental changes only in a clumsy way, as it will be necessary to write new variable rules to represent the new pattern of variability at each stage of development.

Free variability and developmental changes can be dealt with more effectively using a *diffusion model* (Gatbonton 1978). The model posits two broad phases of development of an interlanguage rule. In the 'acquisition phase' the learner first uses a given form in his interlanguage in every situation or context and then introduces a second form. To begin with, this is used together with the first form in all environments. In other words, the two forms are used in free variation. In the replacement phase the learner first restricts one of the forms to a specific environment, while continuing to use both forms in all other environments. Later he restricts both forms to their respective environments. Gatbonton uses the diffusion model to describe phonological development, but it is applicable to all aspects of SLA. As will be argued in the next section, it provides an excellent account of interlanguage variability.

Another technique that has been used to represent the variation in L2 performance is *implicational scaling*. This technique was first used in creole studies (e.g. Decamp 1971). It is used to plot the variability that occurs at any point in time (i.e. the data are collected cross-sectionally), but an assumption is made that the observed horizontal variability matches the vertical development that takes place over time. Thus, the varieties are hierarchically ordered according to how complex they are, with the simple varieties taken to be developmentally prior to the more complex varieties. Implicational scaling, therefore, not only handles synchronic variation, but also provides a picture of the developmental route.

A good example of the use of implicational scaling is provided by Dittmar (1980). The procedure he followed was:

1 Identify the features to be investigated. Dittmar examined the verb phrase in the SLA of German and identified the following features:
   Verb
   Modal verb + verb
   Copular verb
   Auxiliary + verb
   Auxiliary + modal verb + modal verb
2 Count the number of instances in which each feature occurs in a fixed corpus (e.g. a hundred utterances) for each subject.
3 Form a matrix of the subjects' scores on each of the features so that:
   − the subjects are listed vertically according to the number of features they used. At the top of the list are those subjects whose speech contains fewest features and at the bottom those whose speech contains all or most of the features. Order each group of subjects with the same number of features according to the frequency with which the feature most common to all the subjects is used (i.e. verb, in this example);
   − the features are listed horizontally according to the number of subjects who have used each feature. Put the feature used by most of the subjects on the left and that used by the least on the right.
4 Distinguish different varieties (V1, V2, etc.) according to the different groups of subjects.
5 Draw a 'stair-case' to distinguish those groups of subjects who have acquired one, two, three features, etc.
6 Circle the exceptions, i.e. those instances which do not fit the implicational pattern.

Table 4.1 is the result of Dittmar's analysis.

The problem that faces SLA researchers is to discover a descriptive framework that is capable of handling the complex pattern of variability that changes from stage to stage in SLA. Variable rules can be used to describe the variability of language-learner language at various developmental points. The diffusion model handles both systematic and non-systematic variability and also the relationship between one variable system and the next in the process of development. Implicational scaling relates horizontal variability to vertical development. It is this relationship that is the key to understanding the role played by variability in SLA and to which I now turn.

Variety	Informant	Verb	Modal verb + verb	Copulative verb	Auxiliary + verb	Auxiliary + Modal verb + verb
V¹	01	15	-	-	-	-
	02	21	-	-	-	-
	03	31	-	-	-	-
	04	36	-	-	-	-
	05	40	-	-	-	-
	06	42	-	-	-	-
	07	49	-	-	-	-
	08	57	-	-	-	-
	09	65	-	-	-	-
	10	76	-	-	-	-
V²	11	71	3	-	-	-
	12	24	2	-	-	-
	13	45	1	-	-	-
	14	42	9	-	-	-
	15	68	5	-	-	-
	16	70	8	-	-	-
V³	17	51	⊙	3	-	-
	18	65	1	4	-	-
	19	66	1	2	-	-
	20	67	4	6	-	-
	21	60	2	4	-	-
	22	69	1	2	-	-
	23	55	10	1	-	-
	24	58	3	9	-	-
	25	48	2	23	-	-
	26	60	11	11	-	-
V⁴	27	57	14	⊙	1	-
	28	40	15	11	1	-
	29	58	1	6	3	-
	30	52	1	7	1	-
	31	66	4	8	1	-
	32	50	2	31	2	-
	33	54	1	5	6	-
	34	65	2	5	3	-
	35	55	6	15	11	-
	36	69	9	5	8	-
	37	26	9	39	5	-
	38	47	4	21	24	-
	39	50	7	23	8	-
	40	55	2	23	14	-
	41	40	15	18	27	-
	42	44	2	28	18	-
	43	52	5	20	15	-
	44	52	11	11	24	-
	45	43	9	21	27	-
	46	34	7	24	23	-
V⁵	47	11	3	24	59	3
	48	17	8	12	57	3

Table 4.1   The implicational scale-ordering of forty-eight adult learners on five verb phase rules (Dittmar 1980: 225)

The role of variability in SLA

So far I have concentrated on examining the nature of interlanguage variability, its determinants, and the various theoretical and descriptive problems which it poses for SLA research. It remains to consider the role that variability plays as a mechanism of development. I want to suggest that variability serves a dual purpose, depending on the nature of the variability. Contextual variability serves as a mirror for viewing the course that subsequent development will take. Free variability serves as the impetus for development, as the learner strives to make his interlanguage system more efficient.

Contextual variability

Widdowson (1975b: 195) comments: '. . . change is only the temporal consequence of current variation'. In what sense is this true? It has already been noted that the careful interlanguage style contains more target language forms than the vernacular style. One way in which SLA can proceed, therefore, is by forms which are initially part of the learner's careful style to spread to his vernacular style. Development does not consist of sudden jumps, but of the gradual extension of regularities from formal to progressively informal styles on the one hand, and from simple to increasingly complex linguistic contexts on the other. In this sense, then, SLA involves a gradual reduction in the degree of variability as non-target language variants are eliminated in a steadily growing range of environments. This reduction represents a shift to the norms of the careful style.

This is the explanation of SLA offered by Tarone (1982, 1983). Although there is only limited evidence available to support this explanation (e.g. Dickerson 1975), there are powerful theoretical arguments in its favour. The first of these has to do with the learner's motivation for developing his interlanguage system. It has often been pointed out (e.g. Schumann 1978) that it is possible to communicate effectively with very little grammar—a simple vernacular style will suffice for most everyday situations. However, such a system will not meet the demands of social appropriacy for which the norms of use associated with a careful style will be required. For those learners who seek to be socially acceptable, therefore, there is a need to transfer forms that are initially available in a formal style into the more informal styles. As Littlewood (1981: 156) puts it:

> This striving toward a norm will pull the learner's whole repertoire in the direction of the range of variation similar to that found in the native speaker's use of language. In this way it will provide the dynamism for the learning process.

This might be called the sociolinguistic argument.

The second argument in favour of Tarone's account of variability in SLA is a psycholinguistic one. It concerns the learner's capacity to attend to formal features in his speech. It has already been pointed out that in the vernacular style little or no monitoring takes place, while in the careful style close attention is needed. The reason for this lies in the differing degrees of automaticity of interlanguage forms. Whereas vernacular forms are instantaneously available, careful forms are not. However, as the careful forms are used, they are practised, with the result that they become more automatic, require less attention, and so are available for use in interlanguage styles nearer the vernacular end of the continuum. Thus styles of communication initially associated with planned discourse are eventually accessible in unplanned discourse, provided that sufficient practice has taken place.

Free variability

Free variability plays a rather different role. It is the major source of instability in interlanguage, because the learner will try to improve the efficiency of his interlanguage system by developing clear-cut form–function relationships. It is not efficient to operate a system in which two forms have total identity of function. The presence of two forms in free variation, therefore, is in conflict with the economy principle of linguistic organization. This states that ideally a linguistic system will contain enough and no more distinctive features than are required to perform whatever functions the user wishes to communicate. Although the economy principle does not determine what gets into interlanguage, it does determine what takes place once they are in. The economy principle sees to it that the new forms are either integrated into the system by putting them to work to distinguish meanings, or that they are eliminated.

SLA, therefore, consists of sorting out form–function correlations. Unless alternative forms can be justified by allocating them to different functions, redundant forms will be eliminated from the interlanguage. When new forms enter interlanguage, they are likely to be used in free variation. In subsequent stages the learner will progressively sort out forms into functional pigeon holes. It is likely that the first sorting out will not establish the form–function correlations of the target language. This may take several sortings, and many learners may never entirely achieve it. The sorting process is a continuous one only as long as new forms are assimilated, as each new form will require further functional reorganization in order to resolve the attendant free variability.

The diffusion model can be adapted to illustrate how this complex process of resolving free variability takes place. As an example, consider the following example based on these data:

Time 1	*Time 2*	*Time 3*	*Time 4*
I am no go	I am no go	I am no go	I am no go
No look	No look	Don't look	Don't go
I am no run	I am don't run	I am don't run	I am no run
No run	Don't run	Don't run	Don't run

This learner is using two negative rules:

1 no V
2 don't V

At Time 1 he uses rule (1), irrespective of whether the utterance is indicative or imperative. At Time 2 he uses rules (1) and (2) in both indicative and imperative utterances. At time 3 he uses (1) and (2), but only rule (2) is used in imperative utterances. At Time 4, (1) is used only in indicative utterances and (2) only in imperatives. Following Gatbonton, this development can be displayed in the form of a table.

	Environment	
	Indicative	*Imperative*
Acquisition phase		
Time 1	(1)	(1)
Time 2	(1), (2)	(1), (2)
Replacement phase		
Time 3	(1), (2)	(2)
Time 4	(1)	(2)

Table 4.2   Diffusion model for negatives

The data accounted for in Table 4.2 have been slightly idealized and they do not, of course, cover the entire acquisition of negatives, but the overall principles represented in the model could be applied to actual data covering the total span of acquisition.

To summarize, variability contributes to SLA in two ways. First, there is a spread of rules along the interlanguage continuum, from the careful towards the vernacular style and from simple to complex linguistic environments. This process is motivated by the learner's felt need to be socially acceptable and is helped by practice which automatizes rules that initially can be applied only when the learner is attending to his speech. Second, there is the need to make the interlanguage system more efficient by removing free variability. This involves the progressive reorganization of form–function relations and the eventual elimination of redundant forms.

Summary and conclusion

This chapter has looked at variation in interlanguage. In order to do so, it has looked at language-learner language from a sociolinguistic perspective; that is, the learner's competence has been described as heterogeneous, rather than homogeneous. This perspective not only enables a more accurate and reliable picture of interlanguage to be drawn, but also provides insights into the mechanisms by which the learner passes from one developmental stage to the next. It provides, therefore, a much more powerful account of SLA than early interlanguage theory.

Language-learner language, like native-speaker language, is variable. This variability is both systematic and non-systematic. Systematic variability is determined by both the situational and the linguistic contexts of use and is often referred to as contextual variability. Learners systematically vary their choice of interlanguage forms according to whether they call upon a vernacular style in unplanned discourse or a careful style in planned discourse. Their choice of forms is also influenced by the nature of the linguistic environment. The key to this pattern of variation is the extent to which the learner monitors his own language. Heavy monitoring is likely to result in the learner using his most advanced interlanguage forms or, alternatively, in the more extensive use of forms borrowed from the L1. A low level of monitoring will result in the vernacular style, which is both more natural and more systematic. It is characterized by the use of interlanguage forms that are 'deep' and fully automatized. Free (non-systematic) variability is prevalent in early SLA and continues throughout the course of development. It is evident when the learner uses two or more forms to express the same range of functions.

Interlanguage variability poses a number of problems for SLA research. One of these is to decide which variety is basic. In general the vernacular style is held to be basic, because it is both more natural and more systematic. Another problem is how to collect L2 data, as learner performance varies according to the nature of the task. Here it is important to operate with a research model that does not ignore the inherent variability, but gives explicit recognition to it. A third problem is how to describe interlanguage variability. The techniques that have been used include variable rules, the diffusion model, and implicational scaling.

Finally, this chapter has considered the role that variability plays in the process of development. It was emphasized that each stage of development consists of the rearrangement of a previous variable system into a new variable system. This takes place in two ways. First, forms that were to begin with available only in one style (e.g. the careful style) move along the continuum so that they can be used in another style (e.g.

the vernacular style). Second, there is a constant reshuffling of form–function relationships in order to maximize the communicative effectiveness of the interlanguage system; non-systematic variability slowly becomes systematic.

It should be clear from this account of variability in interlanguage that once it is acknowledged that the learner's competence is heterogeneous, it becomes very difficult to deal with SLA in terms of the acquisition of forms only. In order to study SLA it is necessary to examine the relationships between form and function that exist at each stage of development. However, with the exception of a few studies such as those referred to earlier in this chapter, this has not occurred in SLA research, where, as noted in Chapter 1, the focus has been confined largely to morphosyntax.

Further reading

A good starting point for understanding the nature of variability in language use is Labov's chapter 'The study of language in its social context' in his *Sociolinguistic Patterns* (Basil Blackwell, 1972).

Dickerson's article 'The learner's interlanguage as a system of variable rules' (*TESOL Quarterly* 9/4:401–7) reports on an important study of phonological variability and illustrates the sensitivity of the learner's interlanguage system to both situational and linguistic contexts.

Tarone deals more theoretically with interlanguage variability. Her article 'On the variability of interlanguage systems' (*Applied Linguistics* 4/2:142–63) discusses three different accounts of interlanguage variability (including those labelled the homogeneous and heterogeneous models in this chapter). She offers compelling reasons for adopting a sociolinguistic account.

For those interested in the methods that can be used to describe variability, a good account of the techniques available can be found in Chapter 5 of *Sociolinguistics*, by N. Dittmar (Edward Arnold, 1976). Dittmar, however, does not deal with L2 data. E. Hatch and H. Farhady, in *Research Design and Statistics for Applied Linguistics* (Newbury House, 1982), provide an excellent account of implicational scaling using L2 data.

5 Individual learner differences and Second Language Acquisition

Introduction

Second language (L2) learners vary on a number of dimensions to do with personality, motivation, learning style, aptitude, and age. The aim of this chapter is to examine the relationship between these factors and second language acquisition (SLA). First, however, it is important to consider two points about the nature of this relationship.

Aspects of SLA influenced by individual learner factors

There are two basic possibilities regarding which aspect of SLA is affected by individual learner factors. One is that differences in age, learning style, aptitude, motivation, and personality result in differences in the *route* along which learners pass in SLA. The other is that these factors influence only the *rate* and ultimate *success* of SLA. These are separate issues. To claim that individuals vary in the rate at which they learn or the level of competence they eventually attain is not controversial. Indeed, it is part of most language learners' and teachers' experience. However, to claim that individual differences influence the sequence or order in which linguistic knowledge is acquired is far more controversial. It runs counter to the arguments and evidence in favour of the 'natural' route of development (see Chapter 3).

As will be seen in the discussion of each individual learner factor, the effect on the route of SLA has not been seriously investigated. Nearly all the research into learner variables has involved either investigating their effect on the proficiency levels achieved by different learners, or describing how they affected an individual learner's response to the task of learning a L2. Neither proficiency nor learning response provides any insights about the route of acquisition.

There are stark disagreements about the role of individual differences in SLA. As Fillmore (1979) points out, on the one hand individual differences are seen as an all-important factor, while on the other they are treated as relatively insignificant. Research which has concentrated on accounting for differences in the proficiency levels of learners has tended to emphasize the importance of individual learner factors. Research which has tried to examine the process of SLA has tended to play down their importance.

Identification and classification of learner factors

The identification and classification of the different individual factors has proved to be problematic. The main difficulty is that it is not possible to observe directly qualities such as aptitude, motivation, or anxiety. These are merely labels for clusters of behaviours and, not surprisingly, different researchers have used these labels to describe different sets of behavioural traits. As a result, it is not easy to compare and evaluate the results of their investigations. Each factor is not a unitary construct but a complex of features which are manifest in a range of overlapping behaviours. It is, therefore, not surprising to find that a host of terms have been employed to describe the phenomena. Hawkey (1982) lists some of these: 'affective, cognitive, and social factors' (Tucker *et al.* 1976), 'affective and ability factors' (Chastain 1975), and 'attitudinal/motivational characteristics' (Gardner *et al.* 1979).

In an attempt to impose some order on this plethora of terms and concepts, I propose to make an initial distinction between *personal* and *general factors*. Personal factors are highly idiosyncratic features of each individual's approach to learning a L2. Some examples are provided by Schumann and Schumann (1977) in a report of their own language learning experiences. They include 'nesting patterns' (the need for a secure and orderly home base before learning can effectively begin), 'transition anxiety' (the stress generated by moving to a foreign place), and the desire to maintain a personal language learning agenda. The Schumanns found that such factors strongly influenced their SLA. The general factors are variables that are characteristic of all learners. They differ not in whether they are present in a particular individual's learning, but in the extent to which they are present, or the manner in which they are realized. General factors can be further divided into those that are modifiable (i.e. are likely to change during the course of SLA), such as motivation, and those that are unmodifiable (i.e. do not change in strength or nature as SLA takes place), such as aptitude.

Personal and general factors have social, cognitive, and affective aspects. Social aspects are external to the learner and concern the relationship between the learner and native speakers of the L2 and also between the learner and other speakers of his own language. Cognitive and affective aspects are internal to the learner. Cognitive factors concern the nature of the problem-solving strategies used by the learner, while affective factors concern the emotional responses aroused by the attempts to learn a L2. Different personal and general factors involve all three aspects in different degrees. Aptitude, for instance, is thought of as primarily cognitive in nature, but also involves affective and social aspects. Personality is primarily affective, but also has social and cognitive sides. Age is a factor that may involve all three aspects fairly equally. It is because the personal and general factors that make up an individual's language learning style are composed of social, cognitive, and affective features that they are so complex, and, as a result, often rather vaguely defined. Nevertheless, as the subsequent discussion will show, they play an important role in SLA.

Personal factors

Personal factors such as those identified by Schumann and Schumann are difficult to observe by a third person. This methodological problem has been solved in two ways. First, through the use of diary studies. In these, individual learners keep daily records of their experiences in learning a L2. When the learning period is over, the author of the diary can prepare a report, trying to highlight the 'significant trends'. Examples of published reports of diary studies are Schumann and Schumann (1977), F. Schumann (1980), and Bailey (1980 and 1983). (The last of these is a comprehensive review of a number of published and unpublished diary studies.) The second solution to the methodological problem is to use questionnaires and interviews with individual learners (e.g. Pickett 1978; Naiman *et al.* 1978). There are difficulties in collecting information about individual responses to SLA in this way. One is that subjects tend to say what they think the researcher wants to hear, or indulge in self-flattery. Another is that such techniques can reveal only those factors of which the learner is conscious. Nevertheless both the diary studies and the questionnaires/interviews have provided insights into the personal nature of language learning, particularly classroom language learning.

Personal factors are by definition heterogeneous. However, they can be grouped together under three headings: (1) group dynamics, (2) attitudes to the teacher and course materials, and (3) individual learning techniques. I shall consider each of these in turn.

Group dynamics

Group dynamics seem to be important in classroom SLA. Bailey (1983) records in some detail the anxiety and competitiveness experienced by a number of diarists. Some classroom learners make overt comparisons of themselves with other learners. In another kind of comparison, learners match how they think they are progressing against their expectations. Often these comparisons result in emotive responses to the language-learning experience. Competitiveness may be manifested in a desire to out-do other language learners by shouting out answers in class, or by racing through examinations to be the first to finish. McDonough (1978) in a review of reports on their own intensive language learning experiences by students on the M.A. in Applied Linguistics course at the University of Essex also pinpoints group dynamics as an important set of personal variables. He notes, however, that although rivalries can promote confusion, they can also serve as a stimulus for learning. McDonough also advances the interesting idea that group cohesiveness based on learners' collective rejection of pressure and acceptance of failure may depress performance.

As a result of her analysis of competitiveness in different language learners, Bailey (1983) proposes a model of how the learner's self-image in comparisons with other L2 learners can either impair or enhance SLA. Where the comparison results in an unsuccessful self-image, there may be debilitating or facilitating anxiety. In the case of the former, learners may reduce or abandon learning effort. In the case of the latter, learners increase their efforts in order to compare more favourably with other learners, and, as a result, learning is enhanced. Where the comparison results in a successful self-image, the learner experiences positive rewards and thus continues to display effort, so learning is also enhanced. Bailey's model provides an interesting generalization about how personal responses to the group situation can influence learning. It is summarized in Figure 5.1.

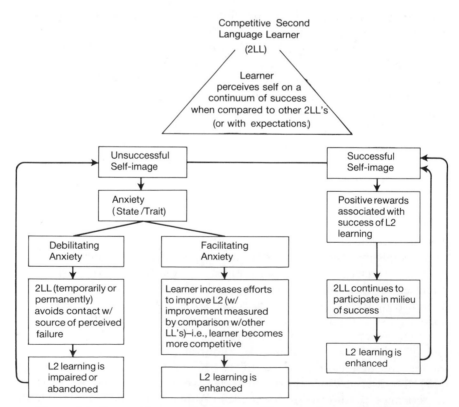

Figure 5.1 Competitiveness and the second language learner (Bailey, 1983)

Attitudes to the teacher and course materials

Students will inevitably have very different views about the kind of teacher they think is best for them. Some prefer a teacher who, in Stevick's (1980) term, creates 'space' for them to pursue their own learning paths. Others prefer a teacher who structures the learning tasks much more tightly. In general the diarists seem to prefer the former. Bailey (1980), for instance, states a definite preference for a democratic teaching style. She notes that student–student interaction in class rose sharply after a scene where the students had protested to the teacher about an unfair test. John Schumann also expresses a desire for a personal learning agenda in language learning. He observes: 'I discovered that I like to have my own agenda in second language learning . . . I like to do it my way. However, I found my agenda is often in conflict with my teacher's' (1978: 246). Many of McDonough's (1978) students also comment adversely on the problems of having to abide by someone else's teaching plan. However, Pickett's (1978) study of successful language learning reveals greater diversity in attitudes towards the role of the teacher. Some learners wanted the teacher to act as 'informant', but others praised teachers who were logical, clear, and systematic (i.e. who imposed a structure on the learner). The main generalization to emerge from Pickett's study is that learners need to feel sympathy for their teacher, and also want him or her to be predictable.

Learners also vary in their attitudes to teaching materials. In general, adult learners dislike having a coursebook imposed upon them in a rigid way. They prefer a variety of materials and the opportunity to use them in ways they choose for themselves. McDonough's students, for instance, often object to the pace and intensity of the short five-week courses they took part in. They report being unable to cope with external pressure, although some students, after closer reflection, express an appreciation of this pressure. However, all these studies dealt with the responses of teachers placed in a learning situation. Other learners may prove less critical than teacher-learners.

Individual learning techniques

There is tremendous variety in the techniques employed by different learners. They will be dealt with in two groups: those involved in studying the L2, and those involved in obtaining L2 input.

Naiman *et al.* (1978) and Pickett (1978) identify numerous study techniques. Here is a sample of those that learners reported they used to develop their vocabulary in the L2:

1 Preparing and memorizing vocabulary lists
   Individual learners appear to have highly idiosyncratic ways of coping with this. For instance, one of Pickett's subjects kept a notebook in

which he recorded first the English word, then the foreign word in phonetic transcription, and finally the orthographic version of the foreign word. He also reported having three vocabulary lists, which he kept going at the same time—one was arranged chronologically, the second alphabetically, and the third either grammatically or situationally.

2 Learning words in context
Some learners made no attempt to keep lists. They relied on picking out key vocabulary items from the contexts in which they were used.

3 Practising vocabulary
Various techniques fall under this heading: deliberately putting words into different structures in order to drill oneself, reading to reinforce vocabulary, playing games such as trying to think of words with the same ending, and repeating words to oneself.

Techniques similar to these have been identified for other aspects of language learning such as grammar and pronunciation. Vocabulary is the area that learners seem most conscious of.

The second group of learning techniques concerns the ways in which the learner gets into contact with the L2. Learners often seek out situations in which they can communicate with native-speakers, or they make use of the radio or cinema to get maximum exposure to the L2. Some learners even arrange their holidays so they visit a country where the L2 is used.

General factors

The general factors which I shall consider are (1) age, (2) aptitude, (3) cognitive style, (4) motivation, and (5) personality.

Age

Age is the variable that has been most frequently considered in discussions of individual differences in SLA. This is doubtlessly due in part to the ease with which it can be measured—unlike all the other general factors, it can be described reliably and precisely. Another reason, however, has been the need to submit to empirical investigation the commonly held belief that children are better language learners than adults. There are a number of comprehensive reviews of the SLA literature dealing with age and SLA (Hatch 1983a, Chapter 10; Stern 1983, Chapter 17; Dulay, Burt, and Krashen 1982, Chapter 4). There is a noticeable lack of agreement in the conclusions reached by these authors. This is a reflection of the complexity of the age issue. My main aim in this section is to highlight the key elements in this complex issue by first examining the effects of age and then looking at various explanations of these effects.

The effects of age

First, it is necessary to separate out the effects of age on the route of SLA from the effects of age on the rate or success of SLA. Most of the studies that have investigated the role of age have been concerned with the latter. That is, they have examined the extent of the correlation between measures of age or length of learning period and measures of proficiency achieved. However, there have been a number of both longitudinal and cross-sectional studies that have considered whether the 'natural' route varies with the age of the learner.

The available evidence suggests that age does not alter the route of acquisition. Bailey *et al.* (1974) investigated the order in which adults acquired the same set of grammatical morphemes studied by Dulay and Burt. They found an order similar to that found in the morpheme studies of children. Fathman (1975) found that the order of acquisition of twenty grammatical items remained constant in her sample of two hundred children aged from 6 to 15 years. In both of these studies, however, the method used was to equate accuracy and acquisition orders, so there are methodological doubts about the validity of the results. Longitudinal studies also indicate that age does not produce a different order of development in transitional structures such as negatives and interrogatives. Cazden *et al.* (1975) found that child, adolescent, and adult learners went through the same stages. Thus learners appear to process linguistic data in the same way, irrespective of how old they are.

Rate and success of SLA appear to be strongly influenced by the age of the learner. Where rate is concerned, there is evidence to suggest that older learners are better. That is, if learners at different ages are matched according to the amount of time they have been exposed to the L2, it is the older learners who reach higher levels of proficiency. This generalization, however, needs to be modified in two important ways. First, as Snow and Hoefnagel-Höhle (1978) have shown, the learners who progress most rapidly may be adolescents. In their study of Dutch L2 learners, they found that although the adults (15 years and older) outperformed the children (6 to 10 years), the teenagers (12 to 15 years) learnt more rapidly than both. It would appear that although age improves language learning capacity, performance may peak in the teens, after which performance declines. The second modification to the generalization concerns the aspect of language that is being investigated. The study by Snow and Hoefnagel-Höhle is also relevant here. They found that age was a factor only when it came to morphology and syntax. There were only very small differences on pronunciation tests. However, even where pronunciation is concerned, the common belief that children are superior was not upheld.

Where success of SLA is concerned, the general finding is, not surprisingly, that the longer the exposure to the L2, the more native-like

L2 proficiency becomes. Burstall (1975: 17), reviewing the results of the NFER project on the teaching of French in the primary school, concludes 'the achievement of skill in a foreign language is primarily a function of the amount of time spent studying that language. . .'. Thus those children who started French in the primary school tended to outperform those who did not start until the secondary school. However, Burstall also endorsed the results summarized in the previous paragraph, namely that older learners were more efficient. With the passage of time, the influence of the age of the learner begins to outweigh the length of the learning period, at least on listening and reading tests, but less clearly so on speaking and writing tests. This observation—that the effects of length of learning period are most strongly felt in productive rather than receptive skills—is lent support by Ekstrand (1975). He found that length of residence of immigrants learning Swedish in Sweden related to free oral production, but not to other aspects of proficiency. Thus it would appear that although number of years of exposure to the L2 leads to greater success, this may be restricted to overall communicative ability, rather than to grammatical or phonological accuracy (Hatch 1983a).

Success in SLA also appears to be strongly related to the age when SLA is commenced. This is particularly the case where pronunciation is concerned. Oyama (1976), for instance, found that the age of arrival of sixty Italian male immigrants in the USA was a far more potent determinant of the levels of pronunciation they achieved than was length of stay. In other words, as far as success in pronunciation is concerned, younger learners do better. In this respect, at least, popular opinion is substantiated. Oyama also investigated the effects of starting age on grammar, but the results were far less clear cut.

These results may appear confusing and contradictory, but a fairly clear pattern emerges if route, rate, and success are treated as separate, if due account is taken of the differential effects of age on pronunciation, vocabulary, and grammar, and if starting age is not confounded with the number of years' exposure to the L2. The pattern is:

1 *Starting age* does not affect the *route* of SLA. Although there may be differences in the acquisitional order, these are not the result of age.
2 *Starting age* affects the *rate* of learning. Where grammar and vocabulary are concerned, adolescent learners do better than either children or adults, when the length of exposure is held constant. Where pronunciation is concerned, there is no appreciable difference.
3 Both *number of years of exposure* and *starting age* affect the level of *success*. The number of years' exposure contributes greatly to the overall communicative fluency of the learners, but starting age determines the levels of accuracy achieved, particularly in pronunciation.

The only potential contradiction in this summary lies in the claim that starting young is likely to lead to more native-like pronunciation, but that younger learners do not acquire phonetic skills as rapidly as older learners. This can be resolved if it is hypothesized that although younger children only learn at the same rate or slower than older learners, they are more likely to go further (see Krashen *et al.* 1979).

Explaining the effects of age

In addition to the empirical research summarized above, there has been considerable theorizing about the effects of age on SLA. I shall examine a number of theories in the light of the summary of the empirical results.

The critical period hypothesis The critical period hypothesis states that there is a period when language acquisition takes place naturally and effortlessly. Penfield and and Roberts (1959) argued that the optimum age for language acquisition falls within the first ten years of life. During this period the brain retains plasticity, but with the onset of puberty this plasticity begins to disappear. They suggested that this was the result of the lateralization of the language function in the left hemisphere of the brain. That is, the neurological capacity for understanding and producing language, which initially involves both hemispheres of the brain, is slowly concentrated in the left hemisphere for most people. The increased difficulty which older learners supposedly experience was seen as a direct result of this neurological change.

Some evidence to support the critical period hypothesis was supplied by Lenneberg (1967). Lenneberg found that injuries to the right hemisphere caused more language problems in children than in adults. He also found that in cases of children who underwent surgery of the left hemisphere, no speech disorders resulted, whereas with adults almost total language loss occurred. Furthermore, Lenneberg provided evidence to show that whereas children rapidly recovered total language control after such operations, adults did not do so, but instead continued to display permanent linguistic impairment. This suggested that the neurological basis of language in children and adults was different.

Lenneberg's evidence, however, does not demonstrate that it is easier to acquire language before puberty. In fact Lenneberg *assumed* that language acquisition was easier for children. The critical period hypothesis is an inadequate account of the role played by age in SLA, because this assumption was only partially correct. Only where pronunciation is concerned is an early start an advantage, and even then only in terms of success, not rate of acquisition. The critical period hypothesis needs to be recast to account for why loss of plasticity affects pronunciation but not other levels of language. One possibility is that there are multiple critical periods (Seliger 1978). The process of the lateralization and localization of language functions is a gradual one, carrying on over many years. Different aspects of language are affected at different stages in this process. This explains why adolescents outperform adults in grammar acquisition—around sixteen a critical period affecting grammar may be reached. This explanation is, however, speculative. In general the evidence linking cerebral dominance and age differences in learners is not clear.

Cognitive explanations

One obvious difference between the young child and the adolescent or adult is the ability of the latter to comprehend language as a formal system. Older learners can learn *about* language by consciously studying linguistic rules. They can also apply these rules when they use the language. In contrast, younger children, while not totally lacking in meta-awareness, are not so prone to respond to language as form. For them language is a tool for expressing meaning. As Halliday (1973) pointed out, the young child responds not so much to what language *is* as to what it *does*. It is possible that age differences in SLA can be explained in terms of the different orientation to language of children and older learners.

Rosansky (1975) has argued that cognitive development accounts for the greater ease with which young children learn languages. She believes that L2 development can take place in two different ways, according to whether or not the learner is aware of what he is doing. The young child sees only similarities, lacks flexible thinking, and is self-centred. These are the pre-requisites of automatic language acquisition, because associated with them is an absence of meta-awareness. The young child does not know that he is acquiring language. Furthermore, the young child has not developed social attitudes towards the use of one language as opposed to another. For these reasons he is cognitively 'open' to another language. In contrast, the adult cannot learn a L2 automatically and naturally. The onset of abstract thinking that comes around the age of twelve with the final stage of cognitive development, as described by Piaget (i.e. Formal Operations), means that the learner is predisposed to recognize differences as well as similarities, to think flexibly, and to become increasingly de-centred. As a result he possesses a strong meta-awareness. Also he is likely to hold strong social attitudes towards the use of his own language and the target language. These may serve as blocks to natural language acquisition, forcing the learner to treat the acquisition task as 'a problem to be solved using his hypothetico-deductive logic' (ibid: 98). In Rosansky's view, then, it is the awareness that comes with age that inhibits natural learning and that leads to an alternative approach. It follows, as Rosansky recognizes, that even where the results of development appear to be very similar, they are, in fact, different.

The problem with Rosansky's arguments is the same as that with the neurological explanations. They are both based on the false assumption that post-puberty learners are less efficient and less successful than younger learners. However, although Rosansky's position cannot stand up to the empirical evidence, it is still possible that cognitive development is a factor. It can help to explain why adolescents learn more rapidly than children. The meta-awareness that comes with Formal Operations may facilitate more efficient learning. Not only can the adolescent 'pick up' language like a child, but he can supplement this process by conscious study. However, problems still remain. Why is no advantage in pronunciation seen in the adolescent learner? One possibility is that of all aspects of language it is pronunciation that is the least amenable to conscious manipulation. Another problem is why the adolescent outperforms the adult. It may be necessary to turn to another aspect of cognitive development—memory—to explain this. Adolescents may have better memories than adults.

Affective explanations

Another possibility that has been explored is that differences in the affective states of young and older learners account for age differences in SLA.

Brown (1980b) proposes that SLA is related to stages of acculturation (i.e. the ability of the learner to relate and respond easily to the foreign language culture). Brown identifies four stages of acculturation: (1) initial excitement and euphoria; (2) culture shock, leading to feelings of estrangement and hostility towards the target culture; (3) culture stress, involving a gradual and vacillating recovery; and (4) assimilation or adaptation to the new culture. Brown argues that stage (3) is the crucial phase. Young children are seen as socio-culturally resilient, because they are less culture-bound that adults. They move through the stages of acculturation more quickly and so acquire the L2 more quickly. The major problem with Brown's theory is once again the false assumption that children are the more rapid learners.

Neufeld (1978) offers a more convincing account of how affective factors are related to age differences in SLA. He distinguishes 'primary' and 'secondary' levels of language. Primary levels include a reasonably large functional vocabulary, and basic mastery of pronunciation and grammatical rules. Secondary levels include the ability to handle complex grammatical structures and different language styles. All learners, according to Neufeld, have an innate ability to acquire primary levels. However, children are more likely to achieve secondary levels than adults because they are much more strongly motivated by the need to be accepted by their peer groups. Whereas the adult is happy to maintain a foreign accent, for instance, the child who is exposed to the first language culture is anxious to achieve native-like pronunciation.

Conclusion

Neufeld's theory, supplemented by cognitive factors, can accommodate all the known facts about age differences in SLA. First, it explains why the route of acquisition is not influenced by age. If innate abilities account for the acquisition of primary levels, no differences in route between children and adults will be observed. Adults, however, will acquire primary levels more rapidly because of their greater cognitive abilities. The exception to this will be pronunciation, because of the difficulty of consciously manipulating this aspect of language. Children will prove the more successful learners, particularly when pronunciation is concerned, because they are strongly motivated to become part of the first language community and require a native-like accent to achieve this. It can also be predicted that they will achieve greater overall communicative fluency, both because they are likely to receive more years' exposure to the L2, and because of the importance of this aspect of proficiency in peer group interaction.

Intelligence and aptitude

Learning a L2 in a classroom involves two sets of intellectual abilities. It involves what might be called 'a general academic or reasoning ability' (Stern 1983: 368), often referred to as *intelligence*. This ability is involved in the learning of other school subjects as well as a L2. The other kind of ability consists of specific cognitive qualities needed for SLA, often referred to as *aptitude*.

Intelligence

Intelligence is the term used to refer to a hypothesized 'general factor' (often referred to as the 'g' factor), which underlies our ability to master and use a whole range of academic skills. As McDonough (1981: 126) emphasizes, it refers to 'capacity rather than contents of the mind'. That is, it is the underlying ability to learn, rather than the actual knowledge that is supposedly measured by intelligence tests. In practice, of course, it is extremely difficult to separate these.

To what extent does the 'g' factor influence SLA? Oller and Perkins (1978: 413) have argued that 'there exists a global language proficiency factor which accounts for the bulk of the reliable variance in a wide variety of language proficiency measures'. They claim that the 'g' factor of language proficiency is identical with the 'g' factor of intelligence.

One of the problems of this point of view is that the 'g' factor does not appear to be an essential factor in L1 acquisition. All children, except those who are severely mentally retarded, succeed in developing grammatical competence in their L1 (Lenneberg 1967). If intelligence is not a major determinant of L1 acquisition, it is possible that it is also not very important in SLA, particularly when this is acquired naturally.

Cummins (1979) provides a way of reconciling Oller's claims with the objection described above. He distinguishes two kinds of language ability. (1) Cognitive/academic language ability (CALP); this is the dimension of language proficiency which is strongly related to overall cognitive and academic skills and can be equated with Oller and Perkins's 'g' factor and general intelligence. (2) Basic interpersonal communication skills (BICS); these are the skills required for oral fluency and also include sociolinguistic aspects of competence. They are 'basic' in the sense that they are developed naturally. Cummins argues that CALP and BICS are independent and that both sets of abilities are to be found in first and second language acquisition. Different measures of language proficiency are likely to tap both abilities in varying proportions.

The distinction between CALP and BICS explains a number of research findings in studies that have investigated the effects of intelligence. For example, Genesee (1976) found that intelligence was strongly related to the development of academic L2 French language skills (reading, grammar, and vocabulary), but was in the main unrelated to ratings of oral productive skills by native speakers. Ekstrand (1977) also found only low-level correlations between intelligence and proficiency as measured on tests of listening comprehension and free oral production, but much higher correlations when proficiency was measured on tests of reading comprehension, dictation, and free writing. Chastain (1969) reported a significant correlation when students were taught by cognitive-code methods that emphasized deductive reasoning skills, but none when students were taught by audio-lingual methods that emphasized habit formation.

To conclude, intelligence may influence the acquisition of some skills associated with SLA, such as those utilized in the formal study of a L2, but it is much less likely to influence the acquisition of oral fluency skills. To put it another way, intelligence may be a powerful predictor of success in classroom SLA, particularly when this consists of formal teaching methods, but much less so in naturalistic SLA, when L2 knowledge is developed through learning how to communicate in the target language. It should also be noted that the effects of intelligence are limited to the rate and success of SLA; there is no evidence that intelligence affects the route of acquisition evident in spontaneous language use (i.e. unplanned discourse—see Chapter 4).

Aptitude

Aptitude is not easy to define. It is usually defined in terms of the tests that have been used to measure it (Carroll and Sapon's Modern Language Aptitude Test (1959) and Pimsleur's Language Aptitude Battery (1966)). These tests do not measure exactly the same behaviours. Both tests, however, seek to measure the abilities of learners to discriminate the meaningful sounds of a language, to associate sounds with written symbols, and to identify the grammatical regularities of a language. It is evident that this view of aptitude reflects the skills which the audio-lingual approach to language teaching, so popular in the post-war decades, emphasized.

Carroll and Sapon (1959) identify three major components of aptitude: (1) *phonetic coding ability*, which consists of the ability to perceive and memorize new sounds; (2) *grammatical sensitivity*, which is 'the individual's ability to demonstrate awareness of the syntactical patterning of sentences of a language' (ibid: 7); and (3) *inductive ability*, which consists of the ability to notice and identify similarities and differences in both grammatical form and meaning. In this view of aptitude, which is shared with Pimsleur's Language Aptitude Battery, the emphasis is on 'a composite of different characteristics' (Stern 1983: 369).

Most of the available research into the effects of aptitude have operated with such a 'composite' view. It should be noted, however, that this emphasizes the linguistic as opposed to the communicative aspects of aptitude. That is, aptitude as defined by Carroll corresponds to the kinds of skills Cummins identified as cognitive/academic language ability, rather than the kinds of skills involved in basic interpersonal communication.

The effects of aptitude on language learning have been measured in terms of the proficiency levels achieved by different classroom learners. The usual procedure is to obtain aptitude scores using one of the tests referred to above, and proficiency scores consisting of the results of a language test or teachers' grades. The two sets of scores are then statistically correlated (e.g. using the Pearson Product Moment Coefficient[1]). In this way it is possible to state the degree of variance in the proficiency scores that can be statistically accounted for by aptitude. For example, Gardner (1980) reports a median correlation of $r = 0.41$ between the Modern Language Aptitude Test Scores of English-speaking Canadian school children in different classes throughout Canada and their grade levels in French. This means that approximately 16 per cent of the total variance in the grade levels can be accounted for by aptitude. Gardner claims that this constitutes a strong relationship between aptitude and proficiency.

Although the results of studies such as Gardner's can be used to support claims about the importance of aptitude as a factor in SLA, many doubts remain. It is still not clear what cognitive processes are subsumed under the label of aptitude. The structural measures that have been used to obtain aptitude scores hardly seem adequate, as SLA involves not only an ability to learn sound and grammar systems, but also the ability to use these systems to communicate meanings. The concept of aptitude needs to be widened to take account of these communicative aspects of SLA. Also it is not clear to what extent intelligence and aptitude are separate concepts. As already commented on, Oller has argued that general intelligence and ability to use language in language tests are essentially the same. He disputes the existence of a separate purely linguistic ability. One set of doubts about aptitude, therefore, concerns whether it exists and, if it does, what it consists of.

Another set of doubts concerns what aspect of SLA is affected by aptitude. Krashen (1981a) distinguishes two aspects of SLA; *acquisition* and *learning* (see Chapter 10 for a fuller distinction of Krashen's theory of SLA). Acquisition is the subconscious internalization of L2 knowledge that occurs through using the L2 naturally and spontaneously. Learning is the conscious study of a L2 that results in knowledge about the rules of the language. Krashen argues that aptitude relates only to learning. That is, it is only an important factor in the type of formal language study associated with classrooms. He points out that the kinds of skills tested by the Modern Language Aptitude Test are just those associated with formal study. Cummins's distinction between cognitive/academic language proficiency and basic interpersonal and communicative skills is also relevant, as already noted. The former is associated with classroom language learning and the latter with naturalistic SLA. The kinds of tests that have been used in the correlation studies of the effects of aptitude typically measure cognitive/academic language proficiency. The results, therefore, do not demonstrate that aptitude plays a major role where basic interpersonal and communicative skills are concerned.

In assessing the role of aptitude in SLA, it is once again useful to separate out the question of the route of acquisition from those of its rate and success. There is no evidence to suggest that aptitude has any effect on the *route*. Just as all children acquire their first language according to a universal pattern, so too L2 learners operate the same basic cognitive processes in SLA. Aptitude, however, can be expected to influence the *rate* of development, particularly where formal classroom learning is concerned. Those learners with a gift for formal study are likely to learn more rapidly. This learning, however, may be of a particular kind: Krashen's 'learning' or Cummins's cognitive/academic language proficiency. Aptitude may be age-related. It may develop along with the general ability for abstract thinking. Aptitude is also likely to affect ultimate *success* in SLA, particularly if this is measured by formal tests of linguistic competence. In general, however, the nature of these effects on the rate and success of SLA will remain uncertain until we know more about the abilities that are supposed to constitute aptitude.

Conclusion

This discussion of the role of intelligence and aptitude in SLA indicates that there are several problems in establishing whether any effects can be traced to their influence and, if so, what the effects are. The main problem is one of definition. Is intelligence distinct from aptitude, or are they both aspects of a single general language faculty, as claimed by Oller? If they are separate, what is each one composed of? Is it possible to identify the discrete components of each, or do they exist as composites? Cummins's distinction between cognitive/academic language proficiency and basic interpersonal and communicative skills may provide a starting point for answering these questions. The former may be related to general intelligence, as Cummins suggests, while the latter may correspond to aptitude. If this is the case, however, new measures of aptitude need to be developed, as both the Modern Language Aptitude Test and the Language Aptitude Battery measure skills that appear to belong more to academic than to communicative proficiency.

Cognitive style

Cognitive style is a term used to refer to the manner in which people perceive, conceptualize, organize, and recall information. Each person is considered to have a more or less consistent mode of cognitive functioning.

Various dimensions of cognitive style have been identified. These are usually presented as dichotomies. The dichotomy which has received the greatest attention where SLA is concerned is that of *field dependence/independence*. The principal characteristics of field dependency and field independency are summarized in Table 5.1. The terms do not really represent alternatives, but poles on a continuum, with individuals varying in the extent to which they lean towards dependence or independence. The distinction is neutral as to which style is most facilitative of learning. It is assumed that whereas 'field independents' will perform some tasks more effectively than 'field dependents', the opposite will be true for other tasks.

There are a number of hypotheses about the role of field dependence/independence in SLA. One of the most interesting is the suggestion that field dependence will prove most facilitative in naturalistic SLA, but field independence will lead to greater success in classroom learning. The reasoning behind this is that in naturalistic learning the greater social skills of the field-dependent learner will lead to more frequent contact with native speakers and so to more input, whereas in classroom learning the greater ability to analyse the formal rules of the language will be important.

Field dependence	Field independence
1 *Personal orientation* i.e. reliance on external frame of reference in processing information	1 *Impersonal orientation* i.e. reliance on internal frame of reference in processing information
2 *Holistic* i.e. perceives a field as a whole; parts are fused with background	2 *Analytic* i.e. perceives a field in terms of its component parts; parts are distinguished from background
3 *Dependent* i.e. the self-view is derived from others	3 *Independent* i.e. sense of separate identity
4 *Socially sensitive* i.e. greater skill in interpersonal/ social relationships	4 *Not so socially aware* i.e. less skilled in interpersonal/social relationships

Table 5.1   Principal characteristics of a field-dependent and a field-independent cognitive style (based on Hawkey 1982)

The empirical research into the effects of cognitive style, however, has not addressed this hypothesis. The approach has been similar to that used to investigate aptitude. That is, measures of field dependence/independence are obtained using a test such as the Group Embedded Figures Test (Witkin *et al.* 1971), which requires the subject to perceive a simple geometric figure within a larger more complex design. These measures have then been correlated with various measures of proficiency (e.g. using imitation tasks, comprehension tests, or teacher grades). The learners investigated in this way have been invariably classroom learners. The results are not conclusive. Bialystok and Fröhlich (1977) found that field dependence/independence had little effect on the reading comprehension of Grade 9 and 10 learners of French in Canadian schools. Naiman *et al.* (1978), however, found that the cognitive style of some students—those in Grade 12—did influence performance on imitation and listening comprehension tests, with the field independents scoring more highly. However, Naiman *et al.* found that the proficiency of other students—those in Grades 8 and 10—was not influenced by cognitive style. One explanation of these results is that the effects of cognitive style are age-related; that is, field independency is facilitative in the case of late adolescence but not before. Such an interpretation, however, is in need of confirmation. In another study, Hansen and Stansfield (1981) found that field independence was related to three measures of proficiency of 253 students in a beginning-level university Spanish course, but the relationship was only a weak one. They concluded that cognitive style played only a minor role in the development of overall foreign language proficiency. In general, field dependence/independence does not appear to be an important factor in SLA.

These results run counter to intuitive expectations. The hypothesis that SLA is influenced by the way in which learners orient to the processing, storing, and retrieval of information is an appealing one. The problem may lie in the type of research that has taken place. Instead of large-scale quantitative studies, a more qualitative approach which focuses on the actual utterances produced by individual learners may be more relevant. Naiman *et al.* (1978) found some evidence to show that learners produce different kinds of errors, depending on their cognitive style. Analytic learners were more likely to omit small items than whole phrases in sentence imitation, whereas holistic learners were more likely to do the opposite. Cognitive style may interact with other learner factors. Fillmore (1980), for instance, suggests that there may be differences in the level of attention which learners from different ethnic backgrounds typically give to a task. She notes that whereas Mexican children had difficulty in concentrating for a long period of time, Chinese children were able to stay on task for a sustained period of time. Thus, although the relationship between cognitive style and proficiency has not been clearly demonstrated, there are a number of interesting possibilities which have not yet been explored fully.

It is premature to address the question of what aspect of SLA is influenced by cognitive style. The existing research does not conclusively show that it is a major factor where success is concerned. There has been no research into the effects of cognitive style on route of acquisition. Hatch's (1974) distinction between 'data gatherers' who become fluent but do not bother to sort out many rules and 'rule formers' who concentrate on accuracy, which seems to reflect the holistic/analytic distinction which is the principal characteristic of congitive style, suggests that cognitive style may eventually turn out to be an important factor determining rate of development.

Attitudes and motivation

The problems of defining attitudes and motivation are considerable. A common-sense view is that a person's behaviour is governed by certain needs and interests which influence how he actually performs. However, these cannot be directly observed. They have to be inferred from what he actually does. Not surprisingly, therefore, the study of attitudes and motivation in SLA has involved the development of concepts specific to language learning. The concepts have been derived from the behaviours of language learners and have been only loosely related to general theories of motivation in psychology.

It is not always clear in SLA research what the distinction is between *attitudes* and *motivation*. Schumann (1978) lists 'attitude' as a social factor on a par with variables such as 'size of learning group', and 'motivation' as an affective factor alongside 'culture shock'. Gardner and Lambert (1972) define 'motivation' in terms of the L2 learner's overall goal or orientation, and 'attitude' as the persistence shown by the learner in striving for a goal. They argue that there is no reason to expect a relationship between the two; the type of motivation is distinct from the attitudes displayed to different learning tasks. However, Gardner (1979) suggests that attitudes are related to motivation by serving as supports of the learner's overall orientation. Brown (1981) also distinguishes 'motivation' and 'attitudes'. He identifies three types of motivation: (1) *global motivation*, which consists of a general orientation to the goal of learning a L2; (2) *situational motivation*, which varies according to the situation in which learning takes place (the motivation associated with classroom learning is distinct from the motivation involved in naturalistic learning); (3) *task motivation*, which is the motivation for performing particular learning tasks. (1) clearly corresponds to Gardner and Lambert's sense of 'motivation', (2) is a new concept, and (3) seems to be the same as Gardner and Lambert's 'attitudes'. Brown uses the term 'attitudes' to refer to the set of beliefs that the learner holds towards members of the target language group (e.g. whether they are seen as 'interesting' or 'boring', 'honest', or 'dishonest', etc.) and also towards his own culture. These also figure in Gardner and Lambert's later use of the term 'attitudes'. It is clear that there is no general agreement about what precisely 'motivation' or 'attitudes' consist of, nor of the relationship between the two. This is entirely understandable given the abstractness of these concepts, but it makes it difficult to compare theoretical propositions.

The most extensive research into the role of attitudes and motivation in SLA has been conducted by Gardner and Lambert. Where 'motivation' is concerned, they draw a basic distinction between an *integrative* and an *instrumental* orientation to L2 learning. The former occurs when the learner wishes to identify with the culture of the L2 group. This type of motivation is an extension of Mowrer's (1960) account of motivation in first language learning. Mowrer argued that the child associates the language he hears with the satisfaction provided by the parents' presence. Thus, just as the child seeks to identify with his parents by learning their language, so the L2 learner may be motivated to identify with the L2 speech community by learning its language. Later, Gardner (1979) linked an integrative motivation to 'additive bilingualism'. That is, learners with an integrative motivation are seen as likely to maintain their mother tongue when they learn a L2. Instrumental motivation occurs when the learner's goals for learning the L2 are functional. For instance, learning directed at passing an examination, furthering career opportunities, or facilitating study of other subjects through the medium of the L2 are all examples of instrumentally motivated learning. Gardner proposes that instrumental motivation is more likely to be linked to 'subtractive bilingualism', where the learner either loses his mother tongue or fails to develop the ability to express certain kinds of functions (such as those associated with literacy) in it. In Britain it has been suggested by Fitzgerald (1978) that the motivational disposition of L2 learners among ethnic minorities is more likely to be instrumental. Gardner and Lambert, however, point out that the integrative/instrumental distinction reflects a continuum, rather than alternatives.

Gardner and Lambert have also investigated a number of different attitudes which they consider relevant to L2 learning. Stern (1983: 376–7) classifies these attitudes into three types: (1) attitudes towards the community and people who speak the L2 (i.e. 'group specific attitudes'); (2) attitudes towards learning the language concerned; and (3) attitudes towards languages and language learning in general. These attitudes are influenced by the kind of personality of the learner, for instance whether he is ethnocentric or authoritarian. They may also be influenced by the social milieu in which learning takes place. Different attitudes, for instance, may be found in monolingual and bilingual contexts.

The results of the empirical research based on Gardner and Lambert's theoretical framework are mixed and difficult to interpret. The following is a summary of the major findings:

1 Motivation and attitudes are important factors, which help to determine the level of proficiency achieved by different learners. For example, Gardner (1980) reports that a single index of attitude/motivation derived from various measures of affective responses to L2 learning is strongly related to measures of French proficiency in Canadian school leavers. Savignon (1976: 295) claims that 'attitude is the single most important factor in second language learning'.
2 The effects of motivation/attitudes appear to be separate from the effects of aptitude. The most successful learners will be those who have both a talent and a high level of motivation for learning.
3 In certain situations an integrative motivation may be more powerful in facilitating successful L2 learning, but in other situations instrumental motivations may count far more. For instance, Gardner and Lambert (1972) found that an integrative orientation was related to successful learning of French in schools in both Canada and USA, but that instrumental motivation was more important in the Philippines. They explained this in terms of the role the L2 plays in the learner's community. Where the L2 functions as a 'foreign language' (i.e. is not important outside the classroom for the learners), an integrative motivation helps; but where the L2 functions as a 'second language' (i.e. is used as means of wider communication outside the classroom), an instrumental motivation is more effective. Lukmani (1972) also

found that instrumental motivation could be more effective than integrative motivation. Non-westernized female learners of L2 English in Bombay, who were instrumentally motivated, achieved high scores on a Cloze test. The learning situation Lukmani investigated was very similar to that in the Philippines described by Lambert and Gardner. It has been pointed out, however, that the two types of motivation are not mutually exclusive. SLA rarely involves just an integrative or just an instrumental motivation. Burstall (1975) found that the pupils' achievement in the NFER primary French project was closely associated with both types of motivation. The pupils' progress was infuenced by both a desire to do well in French as a school subject, and by an interest in French people and their culture.

4 The level and type of motivation is strongly influenced by the social context in which learning takes place, as has already been noted.

There can be little doubt that motivation is a powerful factor in SLA. Its effects are to be seen on the rate and success of SLA, rather than on the route of acquisition. Precisely *how* motivation affects learning, however, is not clear. One of the problems of the correlational studies, which constitute the bulk of the available research, is that it is only possible to show a relationship, not the direction of this relationship. We do not know whether it is motivation that produces successful learning, or successful learning that enhances motivation. Burstall (1975) has addressed just this issue and concluded that achievement affected later attitudes and later achievement to a greater extent than early attitudes affected either later achievement or later attitudes. In other words, it was the motivation that was engendered by the learning process itself that seemed to matter most. A rather similar view is taken by MacNamara (1973). He argues that 'the really important part of motivation lies in the act of communication itself' rather than in any general orientation as implied by the integrative/instrumental distinction. It is the need to get meanings across and the pleasure experienced when this is achieved that motivates SLA. These are views which are encouraging to the language teacher. Motivation that is dependent on the learner's learning goal is far less amenable to influence by the teacher than motivation that derives from a sense of academic or communicative success. In the case of the latter, motivation can be developed by careful selection of learning tasks both to achieve the right level of complexity to create opportunities for success and to foster intrinsic interest.

Personality

In general psychology, personality has been explored in terms of a number of personal traits, which in aggregate are said to constitute the personality of an individual. Cattell (1970), for instance, attempts to measure personality using a series of dichotomies, seen as poles on continua, such as cool/warm, shy/venturesome, not assertive/dominant. Eysenck (1964) identifies two general traits, again represented as dichotomies—extrovert/introvert and neurotic/stable. However, with one or two exceptions (e.g. Hawkey 1982), SLA researchers have preferred to develop their own battery of personality traits, calling them anything from 'social styles' (Fillmore 1979; Strong 1983) to 'egocentric factors' (Brown 1981). Some researchers (e.g. Dulay, Burt and Krashen 1982) even include cognitive style as a personality trait. This confusion is the result of both the many-faceted nature of personality and the need that individual researchers have felt to investigate traits which intuitively strike them as important.

Extroversion/introversion

One of the intuitively appealing hypotheses that has been investigated is that extroverted learners learn more rapidly and are more successful than introverted learners. It has been suggested that extroverted learners will find it easier to make contact with other users of the L2 and therefore will obtain more input. Krashen (1981a), for instance, argues that an outgoing personality may contribute to 'acquisition'. The classroom learner may also benefit from being extroverted by getting more practice in using the L2. The research results, however, lend only partial support to this hypothesis. Naiman *et al.* (1978) found no significant relationship between extroversion/introversion and proficiency. Likewise Swain and Burnaby (1976) did not find the expected relationship between their measures of sociability and talkativeness on the one hand and proficiency on the other in early grade French immersion and French as a second language students. However, Rossier (1976) did find that his subjects' oral fluency correlated significantly with extroversion/introversion measured by Eysenck's Personality Inventory.

Social skills

Related to the extroversion/introversion distinction are the types of social skills involved in SLA. Fillmore (1979) in a longitudinal study of five Spanish-speaking children's acquisition of English argues that the social skills of the learner control the amount of exposure to the L2. Those children who found it easy to interact with English-speaking children progressed more rapidly than those who did not. However, Strong (1983) disputes the emphasis Fillmore places on social skills. The thirteen children in his study learnt English at markedly different rates. After one year the differences were so great that whereas some children had become comfortable communicators, others had hardly acquired any English at all. However, of the seven social styles Strong investigated, only 'talkativeness' and 'responsiveness' were significantly related to measures of language development (i.e. to structural knowledge, play vocabulary, and pronunciation). Strong concludes that it was not so much social skills which enabled the children to obtain more input as the ability to make more active use of the English they were exposed to that led to fast learning. What counted were those personality traits that controlled the *quality* of interaction in the L2, rather than those that led to *quantity* of input.

Inhibition

The other major aspect of personality that has been studied with regard to SLA is inhibition. It is hypothesized that the defensiveness associated with inhibition discourages the risk-taking which is necessary for rapid progress in a L2. Krashen (1981a) suggests that the onset of Formal Operations has a profound effect on the affective state of the learner. It induces egocentrism, which in turn leads to increased self-consciousness and greater inhibition. Thus adolescent learners tend to obtain less input and to make less effective use of the input they do obtain than younger learners. The research quoted in support of inhibition as a negative factor is that by Guiora *et al.* (1972a; 1972b). They designed an experiment aimed at studying the effects on pronunciation of a reduction in inhibition brought about by administering small doses of alcohol. The results were positive. Those subjects who received the alcohol treatment did better on pronunciation tests than those who did not. Guiora *et al.* concluded that inhibition had a negative effect on L2 pronunciation. Such experiments, while interesting, are not convincing. Alcohol-reduced inhibition in an experimental setting is far removed from the realities of most classroom or naturalistic learners. Also Krashen's arguments appear tenuous, given that adolescents in general perform better than younger learners (see the section on Age in this chapter), and even where pronunciation is concerned do not do significantly worse.

Conclusion

In general the available research does not show a clearly defined effect of personality on SLA. One reason why this is so may be because personality becomes a major factor only in the acquisition of communicative competence. Strong (1983) suggests that the rather confused picture presented by the research can be clarified if a distinction is made between those studies that measured 'natural communicative language' and those that measured 'linguistic task language'. Personality variables can be seen to be consistently related to the former, but only erratically to the latter. Certainly a relationship between personality and communicative skills seems more intuitively feasible than one between personality and pure linguistic ability. Or alternatively, different personality characteristics are involved in promoting communicative and linguistic abilities. Perhaps sociability is related to the former, and traits such as 'quickness in grasping new concepts' and 'perfectionist tendencies' (Swain and Burnaby 1976) to the latter. Other traits, such as a preparedness to be 'experimental', may be important in both (Hawkey 1982).

The major difficulty in investigating the effects of personality, however, remains that of identification and measurement. At the moment, a failure to find an expected relationship (e.g. between extroversion and proficiency) may be because the test used to measure the personality trait lacks validity. It follows that not only can such failure be explained away, but that positive relationships may also be an artefact of the measurement used.

The 'good language learner'

There have been a number of attempts to specify the qualities of the 'good language learner', based on studies of personal and general learner factors (Rubin 1975; Naiman *et al.* 1978). I shall draw on these in my own list of the characteristics of good language learning.

The good language learner will:

1 be able to respond to the group dynamics of the learning situation so as not to develop negative anxiety and inhibitions;
2 seek out all opportunities to use the target language;
3 make maximum use of the opportunities afforded to practise listening to and responding to speech in the L2 addressed to him and to others—this will involve attending to meaning rather than to form;
4 supplement the learning that derives from direct contact with speakers of the L2 with learning derived from the use of study techniques (such as making vocabulary lists)—this is likely to involve attention to form;
5 be an adolescent or an adult rather than a young child, at least as far as the early stages of grammatical development are concerned;
6 possess sufficient analytic skills to perceive, categorize, and store the linguistic features of the L2, and also to monitor errors;
7 possess a strong reason for learning the L2 (which may reflect an integrative or an instrumental motivation) and also develop a strong 'task motivation' (i.e. respond positively to the learning tasks chosen or provided);
8 be prepared to experiment by taking risks, even if this makes the learner appear foolish;
9 be capable of adapting to different learning conditions.

These characteristics are a mixed bunch. Some apply more to classroom learners than to naturalistic learners, e.g. (7). Some characteristics are beyond the learner's own control, e.g. (5). Other characteristics, however, are within his control. The learner can, for instance, make a conscious decision to seek out opportunities to use the target language or to supplement natural learning by conscious study. Taken together, the list of good learning characteristics reflects the social, cognitive, and affective factors that have been seen to be important in SLA.

Summary and conclusion

The study of individual learner variables is not easy, and the results of research not entirely satisfactory. This is partly because of the vagueness of many of the concepts that have been investigated. This is reflected in a common refrain in the research literature that the tests chosen to measure a particular concept may not have been valid. Another reason lies in the interrelatedness of the various factors. It is difficult to distinguish variables relating to cognitive style and personality, or even to age and motivation. However, some of the problems are the result of the quantitative research methods used. The observation by Naiman *et al.* that the interviews they conducted with individual learners provided more insight than the statistical analysis of test scores is revealing. Although quantitative studies are obviously needed to test hypotheses on large samples of learners, a more qualitative approach based on interviews and introspection may first be necessary in order to identify the relevant hypotheses. In this way some of the problems of the vagueness of the concepts may be overcome.

The purpose of studying individual learner variables is to see how they affect SLA. This involves two rather separate issues. The first is *what* the effects are. The second is *how* individual factors influence SLA.

In Chapter 3 it was shown that L2 learners follow a natural sequence of development. This sequence was established by examining how the learner performs in spontaneous language use. One of the questions which this chapter has sought to answer is whether the sequence evident in this kind of performance is affected by individual learner factors such as age, aptitude, or personality. The available evidence indicates that the natural sequence is not influenced by these variables. The basic interlanguage progression associated with a vernacular style (see Chapter 4) is universal.[2]

A second question which this chapter has addressed is whether individual factors contribute to the rate at which the learner progresses along the natural route and to the overall level of proficiency achieved. L2 learners vary considerably both in how quickly they learn and in how successful they are. The evidence suggests that the explanation for this lies in differences in personal and general factors. Age, aptitude, motivation, and personality (but less certainly cognitive style) account for a substantial amount of the variance in the learning rate and learning outcomes of different learners. It is also possible to hypothesize that different factors may be responsible for different types of L2 competence. One set may facilitate what Cummins calls cognitive/academic language ability and another set basic interpersonal communicative skills.

How learner factors come to influence the rate and success of SLA has not been considered in detail in this chapter. It has to do with the way they control the amount of input received by the learner and the way he or she handles this input. A full discussion of this issue will be postponed until Chapter 9, after the role of the input has been considered in greater detail (see Chapter 7).

Two other issues need a final comment. The first concerns the relationship between personal and general factors. The former are to be seen as a reflection of the latter. How the learner responds to the group dynamics of the learning situation or to the teacher and course materials, or how he selects study techniques are determined by age, aptitude, cognitive style, motivation, and personality. However, those general factors that are open to modification can also be influenced by a successful personal learning style. Personal and general factors have a joint effect on L2 proficiency. Schumann and Schumann (1978) describe the relationship between personal and general factors in terms of an analogy with a pin-ball machine. The knobs of the machine represent the various general factors, but the path of the ball (i.e. SLA) is determined by the personal characteristics of the individual learner.

The second issue concerns the direction of the relationship between the various learner factors on the one hand and proficiency on the other. Personality and motivation may be modified by the experience of learning a second language. Therefore, the relationship must be treated as two-way. As Burstall (1975) notes: 'In the language learning situation nothing succeeds like success'.

These conclusions about the role of learner factors in SLA can be summarized in the form of a model (see Figure 5.2).

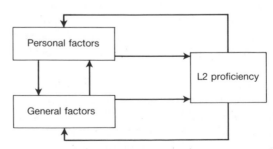

Figure 5.2   Facilitative personal and general learner factors in SLA

Notes

1 The Pearson Product Moment Correlation is a statistical procedure for establishing the degree of fit between two sets of measurements relating to two separate variables. It enables the researcher to establish whether increases or decreases in measurements of one variable are related to increases or decreases in measurements of the second variable. The procedure indicates the relationship between the two variables, but it does not indicate whether the relationship is a causative one.

2 The effects of individual variables on the developmental sequence require further investigation, as (with the exception of the age variable) there has been little research. The robustness of the findings regarding the natural route, however, suggests that it is unlikely that individual factors will disturb it. One aspect of L2 competence that individual factors are likely to contribute to is knowledge associated with a careful style. This knowledge, however, is not reflected in the natural route.

Further reading

The most detailed study of individual learner differences is *The Good Language Learner*, by N. Naiman, A. Fröhlich, and H. Stern (Ontario Institute for Studies in Education, 1978). This reports both on interviews with individual learners and on a classroom study. It investigates most of the general factors discussed in this chapter.

The 'diary studies' provide an interesting and refreshing view of personal variables. A sound overview of these studies can be found in 'Competitiveness and anxiety in adult second language learning: looking at and through the diary studies', by K. Bailey, in *Classroom Oriented Research in Second Language Acquisition*, edited by H. Seliger and M. Long (Newbury House, 1983).

Child-Adult Differences in Second Language Acquisition, edited by S. Krashen, R. Scarcella, and M. Long (Newbury House, 1982), is a collection of important articles dealing with the effects of age.

On intelligence, see 'Communicative competence: can it be tested?' by J. Oller, in *Research in Second Language Acquisition*, edited by R. Scarcella and S. Krashen (Newbury House, 1980), and 'Cognitive/academic language proficiency' by J. Cummins, in *Working Papers on Bilingualism* 19: 197–205. On aptitude, see the collection of papers in *Individual Differences: Universals in Language Learning Aptitude*, edited by K. Diller (Newbury House, 1981).

J. Hansen and C. Stansfield, in their article 'The relationship of field dependent–independent cognitive styles to foreign language achievement' (*Language Learning* 31/2: 349–67) provide a survey of research into the effects of cognitive stye, and a report of their own study.

On motivation, *Attitudes and Motivation in Second Language Acquisition* by R. Gardner and W. Lambert (Newbury House, 1972) is an important source, both of theory and of empirical research.

'Social styles and the second-language acquisition of Spanish-speaking kindergartners', by M. Strong (*TESOL Quarterly* 17/2: 241–158) is a useful article on the effects of personality, both because it provides a review of previous research, and because of the interesting study it describes.

6 Input, interaction, and Second Language Acquisition

Introduction

This chapter and the one following comprise a pair. Whereas this chapter considers what happens *outside* the learner and how this affects SLA, the next chapter investigates what happens *inside* the learner.

The starting point of this chapter is an account of three different views on the role of input in language acquisition: the behaviourist, the nativist, and the interactionist views. The contribution of studies of the input provided by mothers in L1 acquisition is then briefly considered. These are important for understanding the direction that SLA research has followed, as they have provided both a methodology for investigating input in SLA and the research questions. The next two sections look at input and interaction in natural and classroom settings respectively. Here the aim is descriptive—to identify the major features that characterize the linguistic environment that learners are exposed to. The subsequent section is explanatory: it considers the role that input and interaction plays in SLA, with regard both to the developmental route and to the rate of learning.

In this chapter the terms input, interaction, and intake will be used with specific meanings. *Input* is used to refer to the language that is addressed to the L2 learner either by a native speaker or by another L2 learner. *Interaction* consists of the discourse jointly constructed by the learner and his interlocutors; input, therefore, is the result of interaction. Not all the available input is processed by the learner, either because some of it is not understood or because some of it is not attended to. That part of the input that is processed or 'let in' will be referred to as *intake*.

Three views on input in language acquisition

It is axiomatic that in order for SLA to take place, there must be (1) some L2 data made available to the learner as input and (2) a set of internal learner mechanisms to account for how the L2 data are processed. A major issue in the study of SLA, however, has been to decide what weight to allot to (1) and (2). On the one hand it is possible to conceive of the learner as 'a language-producing machine' who automatically and effortlessly learns a L2, provided he gets the right input data. On the other hand, the learner can be seen as 'a grand initiator'; that is, he is equipped with just those abilities that are needed to discover the L2, no matter how impoverished the L2 data are. Also, of course, there are intermediate positions in which the learner is seen as actively contributing to SLA, but dependent on the provision of appropriate input.

Behaviourist accounts of SLA view the learner as 'a language-producing machine'. The linguistic environment is seen as the crucial determining factor. In this model of learning, input comprises the language made available to the learner in the form of *stimuli* and also that which occurs as *feedback*. In the case of the former, the learner's interlocutor models specific forms and patterns which are internalized by the learner imitating them. Thus the availability of suitable stimuli is an important determining factor in SLA. Behaviourist theories emphasize the need to regulate the stimuli by grading the input into a series of steps, so that each step constitutes the right level of difficulty for the level that the learner has reached. Feedback serves two purposes. It indicates when the L2 utterances produced by the learner are correct and so *reinforces* them, and it also indicates when the utterances are ill formed by *correcting* them. The regulation of the stimuli and the provision of feedback shape the learning that takes place and lead to the formation of habits.

Nativist accounts of SLA view the learner as 'a grand initiator'. They maintain that exposure to language cannot account satisfactorily for acquisition. Input is seen merely as a trigger which activates the internal mechanisms. Chomsky (1965) argued that the imperfect nature of the mother's speech input in first language acquisition made it unlikely that any child could successfully internalize the rule system of a language if he worked on this alone. 'Degenerate' input was inadequate for acquisition.

As a result of the pre-eminence of nativist views in the 1960s and early 1970s, research focused on the output of L2 learners, in particular the errors they manifested in speech and writing. This was because it was believed that the output would reveal the nature of the learning strategies involved. As Larsen-Freeman (1983a: 88) observes:

> . . . researchers all too often have confined the scope of their studies to examining the learner's linguistic product, thus overlooking an important source (i.e. input) of information which could prove elucidating in achieving a better understanding of the acquisition process.

In other words, nativist views precluded the possibility that at least some aspects of the learner's output could be explained in terms of the characteristics of the input.

Thus, whereas a behaviourist view of language acquisition seeks to explain progress purely in terms of what happens outside the learner, the nativist view emphasizes learner-internal factors. A third view, however, is tenable. This treats the acquisition of language as the result of an interaction between the learner's mental abilities and the linguistic environment. The learner's processing mechanisms both determine and are determined by the nature of the input. Similarly, the quality of the input affects and is affected by the nature of the internal mechanisms. The interaction between external and internal factors is manifest in the actual verbal interactions in which the learner and his interlocutor participate. It follows from this *interactionist* view of language acquisition that the important data are not just the utterances produced by the learner, but the discourse which learner and caretaker jointly construct.

Three different views regarding the role of input in language development have been discussed. The behaviourist view emphasizes the importance of the linguistic environment, which is treated in terms of stimuli and feedback. The nativist view minimizes the role of the input and explains language development primarily in terms of the learner's internal processing mechanisms. The interactionist view sees language development as the result both of input factors and of innate mechanisms. Language acquisition derives from the collaborative efforts of the learner and his interlocutors and involves a dynamic interplay between external and internal factors.

The discussion of the role of the linguistic environment in SLA which is the main purpose of this chapter is conducted largely within the interactionist framework. However, many of the early studies of input and interaction concerned the acquisition of a first language rather than a second language. The next section, therefore, looks at the way mothers talk to young children.

'Motherese' and L1 acquisition

The first challenge to the prevailing nativist views occurred in first language acquisition research. Gradually during the 1970s a considerable bulk of empirical research was built up which investigated how mothers talked to their children (e.g. Snow and Ferguson 1977; Waterson and Snow 1978). As this research served both as a model for similar research in SLA and has also been drawn on directly in justifying some theories of SLA (e.g. Krashen 1981a), it is important to consider the major findings. These are summarized below.

1 The nature of 'motherese'
   Much of the early research into the mother's language was concerned with identifying its linguistic properties in order to establish whether

it was in fact 'degenerate', as Chomsky claimed. Empirical studies were able to show that the mother's speech was remarkably well formed, containing few ungrammatical utterances or sentence fragments. Furthermore this speech was characterized by a number of formal adjustments in comparison to speech used in adult–adult conversations. Snow (1976) lists a number of these: a lower mean length of utterance, the use of sentences with a limited range of grammatical relations, few subordinate and co-ordinate constructions, more simple sentences, the occurrence of tutorial questions (i.e. questions to which the mother already knows the answer), and, overall, a high level of redundancy. There are also adjustments in pronunciation. Sachs (1977) shows that mothers tune the pitch, intonation, and rhythm to the perceptive sensitivity of the child. These adjustments were considered to constitute a special use of language or *register*, known as *motherese*.

2 The functions of 'motherese'
Given that mothers do tune their speech in the ways described above, the question arises of what purposes motherese serves. Ferguson (1977) suggests that there are three main functions: (1) an aid to communication, (2) a language teaching aid, and (3) a socialization function. It is the former, however, that motivates motherese. Mothers seek to communicate with their children, and this leads them to simplify their speech in order to facilitate the exchange of meanings. Mothers pay little attention to the formal correctness of their children's speech, but instead attend to the social appropriateness of their utterances. Brown (1977) describes the primary motivation as 'to communicate, to understand and to be understood, to keep two minds focused on the same topic'. Thus if motherese also serves to teach language and to socialize the child into the culture of the parents, it does so only indirectly as offshoots of the attempt to communicate.

3 The basis of adjustments made by mothers
Another question concerns how mothers determine the nature and the extent of the modifications which are needed. Gleason and Weintraub (1978) suggest that parents have a general idea of their children's linguistic ability, particularly their ability to understand, but they lack an accurate knowledge of what specific linguistic features their children have mastered. Parents may internalize a model of a 'typical' child of a given age and then adjust their speech upwards and downwards on the basis of feedback from an individual child. Of crucial importance, therefore, is the extent to which the child *comprehends* what is said to him and the extent to which he signals his comprehension or lack of comprehension to his caretaker. This conclusion is supported by Cross (1977), who found little evidence that mothers were able to monitor either their own or their children's

syntactic levels. They responded to the semantic elements of the interaction by evaluating the extent to which the children were able to demonstrate an understanding of the mother's previous utterance.

4 The effects of motherese

In discussing the ways in which the mother's speech adjustments affect first language acquisition, a distinction needs to be drawn between the *route* and the *rate* of acquisition. Little is known about the relationship between motherese and the route of development. Newport *et al.* (1977) suggest that input influences only language-specific features of the language being learnt (e.g. verb auxiliaries in English) and that universal aspects (e.g. basic sentence types) 'proceed in indifference to the details of varying individual environments'. However, other studies have produced rather different results. Furrow *et al.* (1979) found a large number of strong relationships between measures of mothers' input and formal measures of their children's speech. They conclude that 'the linguistic environment . . . must be considered a significant contributor to all aspects of the language learning process'. However, the results of Furrow *et al.* have not been replicated and may be a reflection of the methodological procedures they followed, as Gleitman *et al.* (1984) suggest. This latter study argues that although there are some environmental effects, these are regulated by the learner's own dispositions. In general the available evidence suggests that the route of L1 acquisition does not change in any significant way as a result of differences in the linguistic environment.

However, there is much stronger evidence for an effect on the rate of acquisition. There is now considerable evidence from studies conducted by Cross (1977; 1978), Ellis and Wells (1980), and Barnes *et al.* (1983), among others, to suggest that the way mothers talk to their children influences how rapidly they acquire the language. However, the key features of the input appear to be interactional rather than formal. That is, it is the mother's choice of discourse function (e.g. commands rather than questions) and the devices she uses to sustain conversation (e.g. requests for clarifications; expansions; acknowledgements) which provide the right kind of data to foster development.

5 Explaining the effects

How does the input affect first language acquisition? Wells (1981: 109) provides the following account:

> . . . the general principle involved seems to be one of constructing a linguistic representation on the basis of the speech signal that he (the child) hears, and comparing that with the conceptual representation of the situation to which he believes the spoken message applies, using any available cues to help him along with the task.

Thus, listening and being able to relate one sensory modality (the aural) to another (the visual) is of central importance. This process is facilitated by the interactional routines in which the mother and child participate. As Ferrier (1978) explains, the child finds himself in routine interactional contexts in which his mother produces a limited set of predictable utterances. The regularity and invariance of the caretaker's utterances, together with the accommodations of the caretaker whenever she observes the child in communicative difficulty create activities of shared attention which serve as the basis for the process of modality matching. In contrast, language heard but not addressed directly at the child does not appear to help.

Clark and Clark (1977) suggest that in the process of making their children understand, mothers provide three types of 'language lessons in miniature'. Conversational lessons occur when the adult helps the child to sustain a conversation by means of attention-getters and attention-holders, prompting questions, and expansions of the child's preceding utterance. Mapping lessons occur when the adult provides utterances which the child can decode with the help of context, or when the adult expands on what the child has said by using words for different aspects of the context. Segmentation lessons occur when the adult gives incidental clues as to how utterances can be divided up into words, phrases or clauses (e.g. by putting new words in familiar frames like 'There's a . . .'). These lessons are, of course, the result of attempts to communicate with the child, not to teach him.

Research into motherese, as reflected in the five issues discussed above, led to a reappraisal of the role of the linguistic environment in L1 acquisition. It came to be seen to serve as far more than just a trigger to activate innate processing mechanisms and led to an interactionist interpretation of development.

This brief summary of motherese research provides a basis for considering the role of input and interaction in SLA. It indicates the nature of the questions which need to be asked. In general, however, SLA research has not progressed as far as L1 research, particularly when it comes to considering the effects of input and interaction. The bulk of the research has been concerned with describing what adjustments occur in input and interaction directed at learners, and why and how these adjustments take place. The next two sections look at these issues first in natural settings and secondly in classroom settings.

Input and interaction in natural settings

The study of natural linguistic environments comprises two related approaches: (1) the study of *foreigner talk* (i.e. the register used by native speakers when they address non-native speakers), and (2) the study of *discourse* involving conversations between native speakers and L2 learners. These will be considered separately.

Foreigner talk studies

Studies of foreigner talk were stimulated by Ferguson's (1971) account of simplified registers. This pinpointed the linguistic similarities among motherese, foreigner talk, and also fossilized forms of interlanguage. As in the case of motherese, research and discussion have centred on describing and explaining foreigner talk and, more recently, speculating what role it plays in SLA. In this section I shall concern myself with the description and explanation of foreigner talk, delaying a consideration of its role in SLA until later.

The description of foreigner talk

In order to describe foreigner talk, it is necessary to collect and analyse samples of speech addressed by native speakers to non-native speakers. Long (1981a) points out that many of the studies have failed to obtain baseline data (i.e. speech between native speakers) to serve as the basis for comparison. Also some studies where baseline data have been collected have not taken care to ensure that both sets of data were derived from identical tasks. As with any other register, foreigner talk is likely to be influenced by a whole host of variables such as the topic of conversation, the age of the participants (i.e. whether they are children, adolescents, or adults), and, in particular, the proficiency of the learners. Therefore, foreigner talk is not to be thought of as a static, fixed set of features, but as dynamic, changing in accordance with various situational factors.

Foreigner talk has both formal and functional characteristics. Long (1981a) labels these *input* and *interactional* features respectively. The input features are of two types: (1) those that involve simplifications within the grammatical rule structure of the language, and (2) those that involve simplifications leading to ungrammatical speech. Interactional features consist of the specific discourse functions performed by native speakers. These do not differ in kind from those observed in conversations involving just native speakers, but there are differences in the frequency with which specific functions are used. The principal input and interactional adjustments which have been identified in a number of studies (e.g. Ferguson and Debose 1977; Hatch, Shapira, and Gough 1978; Long 1981a, 1981b, 1983a; Arthur *et al.* 1980; Hatch 1980a) are listed in Tables 6.1 and 6.2 respectively. It should be noted that not all the input and interactional features will be present in every conversation between a native speaker and a non-native speaker.

With reference to the distinctions between input and interaction features and between grammatical and ungrammatical simplifications, three types of foreigner talk can be identified:

1 foreigner talk consisting only of interactional adjustments (i.e. there are no formal simplifications);

2 foreigner talk consisting of interactional and grammatical input adjustments (i.e. there are no ungrammatical simplifications);
3 foreigner talk consisting of interactional adjustments as well as both grammatical and ungrammatical input adjustments.

Which type of foreigner talk occurs is the result of various factors concerned with the proficiency of the learner and the role relationships between the participants. In general (1) appears to be more common than (2), which in turn is more common than (3).

A number of studies have considered the factors that influence the degree to which input and interactional adjustments are present in foreigner talk. Scarcella and Higa (1981) have compared the foreigner talk addressed to child non-native speakers with that addressed to adolescents. They conclude that child non-native speakers receive a simpler input in a more supportive atmosphere. Thus the native speaker speech addressed to them contains shorter utterances, involving fewer complex grammatical structures and fewer disfluencies, more simplified vocabulary, more imperative directives, and more clarification requests. Scarcella and Higa suggest that 'simplification is triggered more by age than linguistic competence'. Another factor which influences the extent of the adjustments is whether the communication is two-way (as in conversation) or one-way (as in monologue). Long (1981a) and Varonis and Gass (1983) have found that native speaker modifications are more frequent in the former, presumably because conversation provides the native speaker with feedback from the learner and thereby enables him to gauge more accurately the amount of adjustment required.

Foreigner talk closely resembles motherese, but there are notable differences in both input and interactional features. Ungrammatical adjustments are very rare in motherese, but they can occur under certain conditions in foreigner talk. Also Freed (1980) found that the relative distribution of different language functions was not the same. Whereas motherese displays a high proportion of instructions and questions, foreigner talk has a higher proportion of statements. Freed suggests that whereas the main functional intent of motherese is to direct the child's behaviour, in foreigner talk it is to exchange information. This, however, may simply be a reflection of general differences between talking to a child and talking to an adult (as the Scarcella and Higa study suggests), rather than specific differences between motherese and foreigner talk.

Explaining foreigner talk

Explanations of foreigner talk need to consider both *why* adjustments occur and also *how* they take place.

Hatch (1983b) suggests that foreigner talk has the same basic functions as motherese. That is, (1) it promotes communication, (2) it

Level	Standard	Non-standard
Pronunciation	slowing down speech separate word/syllable articulation more careful pronunciation (e.g. final stops released) heavier stress increased volume on key words	addition of vowel to final consonant fewer reduced vowels exaggerated intonation
Lexis	restricted vocabulary size difficult items replaced with more frequently occurring items fewer pro forms (e.g. nouns preferred to 'he', 'she', 'it') repetition of words use of analytic paraphrases (e.g. hammer: 'tool for hitting with') use of gesture (e.g. ostensive definition)	special lexicon of quantifiers, intensifiers, and modal particles Use of foreign or foreign sounding words (e.g. 'savvy')
Grammar	fewer contractions overall shorter utterance length grammatical relations made explicit (e.g. He asked to go → He asked if he could go) co-ordination preferred to subordination less preverb modification topics moved to the beginnings of utterances (e.g. I like John → John, I like him) fewer WH questions and more yes/no questions more uninverted questions (e.g. You like John?) More 'or-choice' questions More tag questions More present (versus non-present) temporal markings	Omission of: – copula – 'it' – 'do' – verb inflections Use of interlanguage forms (e.g. 'no' + verb)

Table 6.1   Input modifications in foreigner talk

Type	Description	Example
More 'here-and-now' topics	Native-speaker refers to objects/events which are contiguous.	NS: What's that you are wearing?
More topic-initiating moves	Native speaker starts a conversational topic by asking a question or making a comment.	
More confirmation checks	Utterances designed to elicit confirmation that a learner utterance has been correctly heard or understood.	NNS: I went to cinema. NS: The cinema?
More comprehension checks	Attempts by the native speaker to establish that the learner is following what he is saying.	NS: It was raining cats and dogs. Do you follow?
More clarification requests	Utterances designed to get the learner to clarify an utterance which has not been heard or understood.	NNS: She very high. NS: Sorry?
More self-repetitions	The native speaker repeats part or the whole of his preceding utterance.	NS: He got stuck in the window trying to get in. He got stuck.
More other-repetitions	The native speaker repeats part or the whole of the learner's previous utterance without seeking confirmation.	NNS: I went to the cinema. NS: Yeah. You went to the cinema.
More expansions	The native speaker expands the learner's previous utterance by supplying missing formatives or by adding new semantic information.	NNS: I wear a sweater. NS: Yes, you're wearing a red sweater.
Shorter responses	The native speaker restricts the length of his response to a learner question or comment.	

Table 6.2   Interactional modifications in foreigner talk

establishes a special kind of affective bond between the native speaker and the non-native speaker, and (3) it serves as an implicit teaching mode. Of these, (1) is primary in that most adjustments are geared either to simplifying utterances in order to make them easier to perceive and understand, or to clarifying what the native speaker wishes to say (e.g. by repeating words or utterances), or to discovering what he has said (e.g. through confirmation checks or requests for clarification). Hatch suggests that (2) occurs because of the sense of fulfillment experienced when communication takes place, whereas (3) is only 'implicit', in the sense that foreigner talk does not serve any explicit pedagogic function, although it may have a pedagogic effect when successful communication takes place. However, Naro (1983) argues that foreigner talk can occur with an explicit teaching function i.e. be used specifically to help the learner learn.

A function that Hatch does not mention is the use of foreigner talk to mark the role relationship between the speakers—the 'talking down' function. This involves the use of ungrammatical simplifications such as the omission of grammatical functors and a special lexicon (e.g. 'savvy'). Long (1983b) suggests that the use of ungrammatical foreigner talk depends on four conditions: (1) the non-native speaker has very low proficiency in the L2; (2) the native speaker thinks he is of a higher status; (3) the native speaker has considerable prior experience of foreigner talk; (4) the conversation occurs spontaneously (i.e. is not part of a laboratory experiment). However, Hatch, Shapira, and Gough (1978) note frequent omission of functors and the imitation of interlanguage forms (e.g. 'no + V') in the speech addressed by an adult English native speaker to her Spanish-speaking friend. They record that the native speaker felt unable to stop herself from producing ungrammatical utterances. Thus, although ungrammatical adjustments may typically occur when the non-native speaker is considered to be of inferior status, this is not a necessary condition. It can occur between equals, perhaps as a way of cementing the affective bond that Hatch talks about.

Explanations of *how* native speakers are able to adjust their speech include (1) *regression* (i.e. the native speaker unconsciously moves back through the stages of development that characterized his own acquisition of the language until he reaches an appropriate level for the person he is addressing) in much the same way as Corder (1981) suggests the L2 learner regresses in the early stages of development; (2) *matching* (i.e. the native speaker assesses the learner's language system and then imitates the language forms he identifies in it); and (3) *negotiation* (i.e. the native speaker simplifies and clarifies in accordance with the feedback that he obtains from the learner). Hatch (1983b) considers all three explanations and concludes that (3) is the most convincing. She argues that regression is very unlikely and is not borne out by the observed features of foreigner talk. Matching is the explanation offered by Bloomfield (1933), but, as Hatch argues, it is asking a lot of the native speaker to measure simultaneously the learner's phonology, lexicon, syntax, and discourse with sufficient accuracy to adjust his own language output. Negotiation provides an interactional rather than a psycholinguistic explanation. It does not tell us what mental processes the native speaker operates in order to make adjustments to his speech. One feasible psycholinguistic account is given by Meisel (1980). He suggests that foreigner talk reflects universal strategies of simplification which are part of a speaker's competence to use a language. These strategies are evident in interlanguage production and occur also in the formation of pidgins.

The formal characteristics of interlanguage, pidgins, and foreigner talk are very similar (see, for instance, Ferguson and Debose 1977) and may therefore be the result of a single underlying process. Negotiation may be the crucial element in this process, as it provides the means by which the native speaker (in foreigner talk) or the learner (in SLA or a pidgin) obtains the evidence he requires to activate his strategies of simplification.

Discourse studies

L2 data are made available to the learner in the input he receives. However, this input is not determined solely by the native speaker. It is also determined by the learner himself. The feedback he provides affects the nature of the subsequent input from the native speaker. Also, as Sharwood-Smith (1981) notes, the learner's output serves as input to his own language processing mechanisms. It makes little sense, therefore, to consider the contribution of the native speaker independently of that of the learner. Because one affects the other, it is more fitting to consider the joint work done by native speaker and learner by looking at the *discourse* they construct together. The method for undertaking this is known as *discourse analysis*.

There is a further reason for investigating discourse, rather than just foreigner talk. It may shed light on *how* L2 learners learn. As Hatch (1978c: 403) argues:

It is not enough to look at input and to look at frequency; the important thing is to look at the corpus as a whole and examine the interactions that take place within conversations to see how interaction itself determines frequency of forms and how it shows language functions evolving.

In other words, Hatch proposes that we need to look at discourse in order to study how language learning evolves out of the strategies used to carry on conversations. Harder (1980: 168) makes a similar point when he states that 'extending one's action potential inevitably extends one's language'.

The types of discourse that learners take part in depend very much on who the learner is. In particular they depend on whether the learner is a child or an adult. Discourse involving children has been discussed by Hatch (1978c; 1978d), Peck (1978; 1980), and Wagner-Gough (1975). Discourse involving adult learners has been discussed by Hatch (1978c) and Schwartz (1980), among others.

Conversations involving child learners

Hatch shows that in child-learner discourse, conversations typically commence with attempts by the child to 'open the channel' by calling for the adult's attention (e.g. 'oh oh'; 'look it'). The adult then responds by identifying the object that appears to have attracted the child's attention and the child repeats the name of the object. The sequence may end there and a similar 'nominating' sequence be embarked upon. Alternatively the conversation might move into the development stage, stimulated by the adult demanding some comment on the nominated topic from the child. This may result in an attempt at elaboration by the child. Further developments can occur if the adult calls for further comments, or requests clarification. The entire discourse pattern is summarized in Figure 6.1. It is very similar to the pattern which has been observed in conversations between children and their mothers in L1 acquisition research (see, for instance, Clark and Clark 1977; Wells *et al.* 1979). This suggests that where child language learners are concerned, there may be general ways of going about building a conversation.

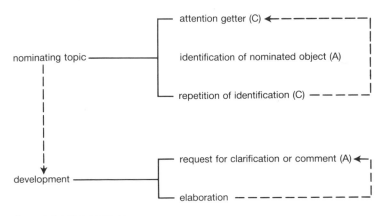

A = adult native speaker
C = child L2 learner

Figure 6.1   A schematic representation of adult–child L2 conversation as described by Hatch (1978b)

Whereas Hatch discusses the overall pattern of child–adult discourse, Wagner-Gough (1975) looks at the discourse strategies used by one child learner, Homer, when conversing with an adult. Homer frequently *imitates* the adult's previous utterance, either to provide a sense of participation in the conversation, or to tease, or for sheer fun. Homer also *incorporates* chunks of speech from the previous discourse into his own utterances. It is possible to explain apparently unique utterances like:

What this is Homer?
What is this is car?

in terms of the juxtaposition of the question 'What is this?' and the answer 'This is ____' with various deletions. For example, the first utterance above has 'is this' deleted from the combined question–answer pattern, and the second example just 'this'. Commenting in general on this kind of language behaviour, Hatch *et al.* write:

> The (child) learner's ability to use frequently heard formulae and to repeat large chunks of the input give him quick entry into the communicative aspect of language-learning, an advantage not shared by the adult second-language learner. (Hatch *et al.* 1979: 274–5)

Hatch and Wagner-Gough investigated child–adult conversations. Peck (1978; 1980) compares child–child and child–adult conversations. The former contain many examples of 'functions', which is the term Keenan (1974) uses to describe the modifications of both their own and another child's previous utterance which child learners make. There are both 'focus functions', where the whole or one of the constituent elements of the previous turn is repeated:

e.g. NS Child: You know why?
     L2 Child: You know why?

and 'substitution functions', where one of the constituents of a previous utterance is replaced by another of the same grammatical category:

e.g. NS Child: There one piece.
     L2 Child: There different piece.

Peck suggests that through performing such 'functions', the child may be able to explore and expand the limits of his L2 competence. In contrast, few functions appear in child–adult conversations. Adults tend to employ more questions and requests for clarification than child interlocutors. But the adults also give the L2 child more opportunity to nominate his own topic.

Conversations involving adult learners

Adult–adult conversations are described by Hatch (1978c). Whereas child–adult sequences follow the 'here-and-now' principle (i.e. they refer to objects that are physically present and to ongoing activity), adult conversations are more likely to be rooted in displaced activity. As a result, the adult learner has difficulty in identifying the topic. He resorts to the use of requests for clarification (e.g. 'huh?'), or to echoing part of the native speaker's question in order to establish the field of reference. Repair strategies are also common on the native speaker's part. These involve moving the topic to the beginning or end of the sentence where it is more salient (e.g. 'Holidays this summer—where are you going?'), simplifying lexis, adding gestures, and translating or switching to foreigner talk. Repair strategies are also found in adult–adult conversations where both of the speakers are L2 users (Schwartz 1980). In these cases conversation is organized in favour of self-repair. Schwartz also notes that negotiated repair often not only restores understanding, but at the same time helps to build a more syntactically complex unit. Hatch (1978c) notes that in adult–adult conversations with native speakers, there is often considerable cooperation as the native speakers try to help out by modelling what they think the learner wants to say.

The differences between adult–adolescent and adult–child learner discourse have also been examined by Scarcella and Higa (1981). They consider the work that both native speakers and non-native speakers do to sustain conversation. When speaking to children, the adult native speaker carries a greater responsibility and often dominates the conversation by using frequent rhetorical questions and repetition. In contrast, the adolescent learner is expected to play a much bigger part in keeping the conversation going. A number of learner strategies that contribute to this end are noted, such as 'stepping in sideways' (i.e. allowing the native speaker to introduce a topic and then trying to add some new and relevant information), repetition, changing the topic, and the use of conversation fillers like 'ya know'. These strategies were rarely used by the child learners. Krashen (1982) speculates that because older learners are more involved in keeping a conversation going, they may learn more rapidly than younger learners (see Chapter 5).

The negotiation of meaning

A major feature of conversations involving L2 learners is that the learner and native speaker together strive to overcome the communicative difficulties which are always likely to arise as a result of the learner's limited L2 resources. This has become known as the *negotiation of meaning*. On the part of the native speaker this involves the use of *strategies* and *tactics* (Long 1983a). Strategies are conversational devices used to avoid trouble; examples are relinquishing topic control, selecting salient topics, and checking comprehension. Tactics are devices for repairing trouble; examples are topic switching and requests for clarification. Other devices such as using a slow pace, repeating utterances, or stressing key words can serve as both tactics and strategies. The learner also needs to contribute to the negotiation of meaning, however, as it is a joint enterprise. He can do so by giving clear signals when he has understood or not understood and, most important, by refusing to give up. The result of the negotiation of meaning is that particular types of input and interaction result. In particular it has been hypothesized that negotiation makes input *comprehensible* and, as will be discussed later, in this way promotes SLA.

Summary

This section has looked at a number of studies of input (the contribution of the native speaker) and interaction (the joint contributions of native speaker and learner) in natural settings. Input has been considered in terms of foreigner talk. This involves a number of formal and interactional adjustments in native speaker speech. Some of these adjustments lead to ungrammatical speech. Foreigner talk adjustments are more frequent in discourse involving children than adults, and also in two-way as opposed to one-way communication. The primary function of foreigner talk is to promote effective communication, although it may indirectly serve a teaching function. Ungrammatical foreigner talk occurs under special conditions, such as when the native speaker considers he holds a superior status to the non-native speaker. Foreigner talk occurs because of the need to negotiate meaning and may be the result of universal processes of simplification also found in SLA and pidgins. Interaction has been considered in terms of the discourse that learner and native speaker participate in. Differences in the type of discourse involving child and adolescent/adult learners have been observed. Adults have to cope with topics that place greater communicative demands on them, but they are more likely to contribute to keeping the conversation going. Differences also occur according to whether the native speaker is a child or an adult. In the case of the child, there is more playing with language, whereas with adult native speakers, the learner gets the chance to nominate a topic which the adult helps to sustain. Studies of discourse involving L2 learners show that there is a negotiation of meaning when the participants struggle to avoid and overcome communicative breakdowns. This may be important for SLA.

Input/interaction in classroom settings

The last section examined the nature of the linguistic environment in natural settings. This section considers the classroom setting. It is necessary to distinguish these two setting types, because the kinds of communication that occur in each are in many respects very different.

Interest in the language of the classroom has grown steadily in the last twenty years. It has been motivated by the recognition that whether it is a subject lesson or a language lesson, successful outcomes may depend on the type of language used by the teacher and the type of interactions occurring in the classroom. In the case of the language classroom, the growth of interest in the analysis of teacher language and interaction has been stimulated by the rejection of language teaching method as the principal determinant of successful learning. Studies such as those by Scherer and Wertheimer (1964) and Smith (1970) investigated the comparative effectiveness of methods such as grammar-translation, audio-lingualism, and cognitive code, but were not able to demonstrate that one was more successful than another. One possible explanation for this is that, despite the apparent differences in methodological principles, the various methods led to very similar patterns of classroom communication, with the result that the language learning outcomes were also similar. In other words, it was hypothesized that classroom interaction was the major variable affecting SLA in formal settings. An offshoot of the comparative method studies, then, was to direct researchers' attention to the processes of classroom interaction by collecting language data from the classroom itself.

Classroom process research, as Gaies (1983) calls the study of communication in the classroom, has taken different forms. The earliest was *interaction analysis*, which consists of using sets of categories to code the kinds of language use which occur in classrooms. An alternative approach focused only on the language used by the teacher when addressing L2 learners. It sought to tabulate the adjustments which occur in *teacher talk*. Finally, the techniques of *discourse analysis* were applied to the classroom to help identify the different types of interaction which occur there. I shall consider each of these approaches in turn, before concluding with some general comments on the type of input/interaction found in classrooms in comparison to that found in natural settings.

Interaction analysis

Interaction analysis was initiated in subject classrooms. In the 1960s Flanders (see Flanders 1970) developed a category system for analysing the communicative uses of the teacher's and pupils' language. Later this system was adapted for use in language classrooms (e.g. Moskowitz 1971). More sophisticated systems have been devised by Fanselow (1977) and Allwright (1980). Allwright, for instance, proposes that classroom interaction be accounted for in terms of three types of analysis: (1) a turn-taking analysis, which consists of several categories grouped under the general headings of 'turn-getting' and 'turn-giving'; (2) a topic analysis, which makes use of such categories as instances of the target language intended primarily as 'models' (e.g. the teacher says something for the learner to imitate), and instances of communication concerned primarily with information about the target language;[1] and (3) a task analysis, which does not provide a detailed set of categories, but distinguishes tasks at the levels of turn-taking and topic management, and also at the cognitive level. Allwright's system requires the researcher to code each utterance in the interaction. He illustrates its use on an extract from a language lesson and shows that it is capable of revealing some interesting information about how learners and teachers use the target language.

Long (1980) provides a thorough critique of interaction analysis systems. The major problems lie in the choice of the variables to be examined (i.e. what features of classroom language to categorize). Long argues that the categories selected are no more than 'subjective hunches', as they are not verified by SLA research. For instance, with reference to Allwright's system described above, there is no basis in language learning theory for distinguishing the turn-getting category of 'accept' (i.e. a response to a question or instruction) and 'steal' (i.e. a response to a question or instruction addressed to another person). It may be a reasonable hypothesis that a classroom learner who frequently 'accepts' and 'steals' will progress more rapidly than one who does not, but it is not clear that one who 'accepts' can be expected to outperform one who 'steals' or vice versa. Another problem that Long draws attention to is that 'in general, interaction analysis systems code surface behaviour and so miss the communicative value of remarks' (op. cit.: 18). Thus although such systems may achieve reliability, their validity and relevance are in doubt.

It is difficult, if not impossible, to summarize what interaction analyses have revealed about the nature of input/interaction in language classrooms. This is largely because the proliferation of systems, each with their own sets of categories, precludes comparisons and therefore generalization. Many of the systems were developed for teacher training purposes, and as Allwright (1983) notes, these do not require highly refined and validated categories. However, the study of classroom input/interaction, as it relates to SLA, does require both valid and generally accepted categories so that cross-study comparisons can be made. One possibly fruitful approach is to employ interaction analysis systems within the framework of case studies of individual learners, so integrating the quantitative information made available by such analyses with the qualitative information of the case study approach. However, this has not yet been undertaken.

Teacher talk

The study of teacher talk parallels that of foreigner talk. The language that teachers address to L2 learners is treated as a register, with its own specific formal and interactional properties. Studies of teacher talk can be divided into those that investigate the type of language that teachers use in language classrooms and those that investigate the type of language they use in subject lessons (e.g. science) involving L2 learners.

Studies of the first type include those of Gaies (1977; 1979), Henzl (1979), Long (1983b), and Long and Sato (1983). The following is a summary of the main findings:

1 Formal adjustments occur at all language levels. Gaies found that teachers' utterances were simpler on a range of measures of syntactic complexity when they addressed pupils than when they were talking among themselves. Henzl compared the language that teachers used when teaching pupils of different levels of proficiency. He observed adjustments in pronunciation (e.g. with low-level students, the teachers used a more accurate, standard pronunciation), in lexis (e.g. they substituted items with a narrow semantic field like 'young gal' by more general words like 'woman'), and in grammar (e.g. they adjusted the mean length of their utterances). These modifications mirror those observed in foreigner talk (see Table 6.1).

2 In general, ungrammatical speech modifications do not occur. This is presumably because the conditions that permit deviations from the standard language do not arise in the classroom. However, extreme simplification involving deviant utterances can occur in certain types of classroom interaction such as those found in free discussion (see Hatch, Shapira, and Gough 1978).

3 Interactional adjustments occur. Gaies notes interactional devices in teachers' speech similar to those observed in motherese (e.g. repetition, prompting, prodding, and expansions). It is likely that many of the interactional adjustments found in other simplified registers will also occur in teacher talk. But there are likely to be differences also. Long (1983b) and Long and Sato (1983) note that in language classrooms, tutorial (or display) questions such as 'Are you a student?' and 'Is the clock on the wall?' are more frequent than in natural settings. The same researchers note that whereas comprehension checks are more frequent in the classroom, confirmation checks and requests for clarification are less so. They explain this by the predominance of one-way communication in classrooms. Confirmation checks and requests for clarification (unlike comprehension checks) are used as feedback after a learner utterance, but in classrooms teachers dominate the talk, with the result that pupils have few opportunities to speak. Thus by restricting the pupils' contributions, the teacher also delimits the range of discourse functions that they typically perform.

In summary, teacher talk in language lessons is broadly similar to foreigner talk. However, because special constraints operate in the classroom, there are both formal and interactional differences.

Studies of teacher talk in subject lessons involving L2 learners include Chaudron (1983a) and Wesche and Ready (1983). Both these studies looked at teacher talk in university classrooms. The studies showed a range of speech adaptations similar to those discussed above. For instance, the talk directed at L2 speakers (in comparison to native speaking students) was grammatically simpler (e.g. contained fewer words per clause), was slower, with more and longer pauses, and contained more repetition. It is possible, however, that fewer lexical adjustments occur, perhaps because the choice of vocabulary is determined by the subject content of the lessons. It should be noted that the adjustments in subject lessons are not motivated by attempts to teach the L2 (which is a possibility in language lessons), but by the attempt to share information.

An interesting issue in teacher talk is how the teacher determines what level of adjustment to make. Foreigner talk normally occurs in one-to-one interactions where there is plenty of feedback from the learner. Teacher talk occurs in one-to-many interactions, where the learners may vary in their level of proficiency and where there is likely to be only limited feedback from a few students. However, teachers do succeed in varying their adjustments to suit the linguistic competence of the class they are teaching, as Henzl showed. Adjustments are more frequent with beginners than with advanced students. Teachers must gauge the general level of proficiency of a class and then determine the nature and extent of the modifications to make. They may pitch these at what they take to be the 'average' level of the class. Consequently teacher talk is unlikely to be as finely tuned to the level of the learner as foreigner talk. This may have implications for its effect in promoting SLA.

Discourse analysis

Like interaction analysis (but unlike teacher talk studies), discourse analysis considers both the teacher's and the learner's contribution. It differs from interaction analysis in that it aims to describe not just the function of individual utterances, but how these utterances combine to form larger discoursal units. Also it seeks to account for all the data, avoiding a 'rag bag' category for coding awkward utterances which do not fit any of the other categories.

The analysis of classroom discourse has focused on one particular type—the three-phase discourse which is prevalent in teacher-centred classrooms. This focus owes much to the work in discourse analysis undertaken at the University of Birmingham (e.g. Sinclair and Coulthard 1975; Coulthard and Montgomery 1981; Sinclair and Brazil 1982).

Three-phase discourse consists of exchanges in which the teacher *initiates*, the pupil *responds*, and the teacher supplies *feedback*. For example:

T: Is the clock on the wall?   Initiates
P: Yes, the clock is on the wall.   Responds
T: Good. The clock is on the wall. Feedback

Known as IRF, exchanges of this type occur in both language and subject lessons where the teacher takes control of the lesson content and management. As Barnes (1976) has pointed out, they are associated with a 'transmission mode of education', in which the teacher seeks both to impart knowledge he possesses (and assumes the pupils do not) and to reinforce his social role as the arbiter of all classroom behaviour. The kind of discourse that results—illustrated above—is neatly summarized by Burton (1981: 63–4):

> Inside the classroom all parties are agreed that time will be spent in the transfer of information from teacher to pupils, with a ritualised structure of informatives, elicitations and directives etc. to be employed by the teacher to that end, and a set of appropriate reciprocal acts and moves to be employed by the pupils to assist in the attainment of the teacher's end.

The Birmingham research has looked at classroom discourse in general. However, other researchers, working within the same discourse framework, have examined discourse in the language classroom. McTear (1975) has shown that the IRF structure is often modified when the focus becomes the channel itself. For instance, he notes that an optional pupil response occurs after the teacher's feedback move. This produces the modified structure IRF(R):

T: What do you do every morning?   Initiates
P: I clean my teeth.   Responds
T: You clean your teeth every morning. Feedback
P: I clean my teeth every morning.   Responds

McTear suggests that this optional response occurs when the pupil believes the teacher is modelling an utterance that requires a further response. However, imitation is pervasive in language learner discourse outside the classroom (e.g. Huang and Hatch 1978), and the learner may simply be seizing the opportunity to practise.

McTear notes a number of other differences in the discourse of language classrooms. He identifies four types of language use: (1) mechanical, where no exchange of meaning is involved; (2) meaningful, where language usage is contextualized but still no real information is conveyed; (3) pseudo-communicative, where information is exchanged, but in a way that would be unlikely to occur outside the classroom; and

(4) real communication, which consists of spontaneous natural speech. Communicative breakdown can occur when the teacher and the pupils are in conflict about which type of language use is in operation. For example, the teacher may ask a question designed to practise a specific formal structure, and the pupil may respond as if it were a genuine question. McTear's analysis provides a number of insights about the special qualities of discourse in language classrooms.

To what extent does IRF discourse constitute a suitable source of input data for SLA? This issue has been addressed in a number of research publications emanating from the University of Nancy (e.g. Gremmo, Holec and Riley 1978; Riley 1977). The conclusion these researchers come to is that the kind of discourse which typically occurs in teacher-centred classrooms is distorted. Because the teacher adopts a central role, even communicative activity where one pupil is supposed to be talking to another is severely constrained. Gremmo, Holec and Riley believe that this distortion inhibits the opportunities for language learning:

> . . . when we analyze classroom discourse, it becomes clear that the very presence and participation of the teacher distorts the interaction to such an extent that it no longer provides even the basic raw materials from which a learner can construct his competence. (1978: 63).

They point out that the classroom only teaches pupils how to reply, and that this does not equip learners for interaction outside the classroom, where they have to initiate discourse.

It would be a mistake, however, to assume that IRF exchanges are the only kind which occur in classrooms. Ellis (1980; 1984a) examines a number of different types of classroom interaction. He proposes a framework for analysing the various possibilities. This is based on distinguishing three basic kinds of pedagogic goal: (1) core goals, which relate to the explicit pedagogic purpose of the lesson (e.g. to teach specific aspects of the L2, to impart specific subject content, to help the pupils make something); (2) framework goals, which relate to the organization requirements of the lesson (e.g. giving out materials, managing pupil behaviour); and (3) social goals, involving the use of language for more personal purposes (e.g. imparting private information; quarrelling). In addition Ellis distinguishes types of address (i.e. who functions as speaker, listener, hearer). Classroom discourse can be described in terms of the types of goal and address which occur. Ellis examines the discourse which occurs in elementary ESL classrooms, where English is both the pedagogic target and the medium of instruction. He demonstrates that a wide variety of interactions take place. Some of the interactions have a very different pattern from that discussed by Gremmo, Holec and Riley. For example, interactions with framework goals, where the teacher is engaged in organizing classroom activity, are characterized by the frequent use of directives, to which the pupils respond non-verbally.:

e.g. T: J . . . could you collect the scissors for me?
(The pupil picks up his own scissors only. The teacher goes to his table.)
T: In the box.
Go round and collect the scissors in the box.
(The teacher points at the box. The pupil picks up his scissors and pops them in.)
T: All right. Put the scissors in the box.
(The pupil starts to go round and collect the scissors.)

Interactions such as these may be ideally suited to the beginner learner in that they contain a lot of directives, which have been hypothesized to aid both first language acquisition (Ellis and Wells 1980) and SLA (Asher 1977), context-dependent language, and plenty of repetition. However, the frequency of this kind of discourse is likely to vary according to the type of classroom. For instance, it will be less common in foreign language classrooms, where the students' first language is used to accomplish framework goals.

The analysis of classroom discourse involving L2 learners illustrates the joint contributions of teacher and pupils, rather than focusing only on the teacher's language (as in the study of teacher talk). It can help to shed light on how meaning is negotiated in a classroom context, and on how the input is shaped to the requirements of the learner's language-processing mechanisms. However, doubts remain whether sufficient negotiation is possible in classrooms, particularly when IRF exchanges predominate. A one-to-many linguistic environment seems less well suited to promoting learning than a one-to-one environment.

A comparison of natural and classroom language environments

I began this section on the classroom environment by suggesting that input and interaction in the classroom setting is likely to be different from that in a natural setting. In this final part of the section I consider to what extent this is true, by making a direct comparison of the two settings.

There is often a general assumption that natural and classroom settings differ substantially, particularly when the classroom environment involves the formal teaching of a L2. Corder (1976: 68), for instance, writes:

. . . learners do not use their interlanguage very often in the classroom for what we may call 'normal' or 'authentic' communicative purposes. The greater part of interlanguage data in the classroom is produced as a result of formal exercises and bears the same relation to the spontaneous communicative use of language as the practising of tennis strokes does to playing tennis.

Corder is referring to the output of the learner, but his comments might be equally valid where the input is concerned. D'Anglejan (1978) notes that in classrooms where there is explicit teaching of the language, the communication that results rarely corresponds to any acceptable definition of communication outside the classroom. She argues that in such classrooms the input is of a reduced variety and affords limited opportunity for hypothesis formation and testing (see Chapter 7 for a discussion of these). This reduced input can be seen as the consequence of limited opportunities for the negotiation of meaning. The teacher is deprived of the feedback necessary to make appropriate adjustments to his speech, and the learner has forced on him discourse roles which limit the types of speech act he is able to perform. The differences between natural and classroom communication are also reflected in different motivational orientations. MacNamara (1973) suggests that the kind of motivation which occurs in classroom settings is completely different from that found in 'street' settings. It is rare that in the former either the teacher or the pupils has anything to say to each other that is so important they are willing to improvise and guess at each other's meanings. This is another reason why classrooms contain less negotiation of meaning.

However, although there are clear and obvious differences between natural and classroom environments, it would be wrong to overemphasize these differences. Natural environments themselves can vary enormously in the types of input they afford. Some learners may not be able to take part in the potentially facilitative interactions which have been described earlier. Also classrooms differ in the kinds of discourse they provide—as I have already shown. Rather than treat natural and classroom environments as opposites, it would be more accurate to see them as providing the same discourse types in different degrees. That is, the same kind of interactions can take place in both, but because of basic differences to do with the numbers of the participants and the physical arrangements, some types of these interactions are more frequent in one setting, and other types in the other setting. As Krashen (1976) comments, classrooms can afford opportunities for genuine communicative exchanges, while in natural settings learners can engage in formal study, or, as Corder puts it, the 'practising of tennis strokes'.

Thus the comparison between natural and classroom environments as sources of input for SLA will depend on the frequency of different types of interaction which occur in each setting. In particular, it will depend upon the type of educational setting in which the L2 learners find themselves. Table 6.3 summarizes the main characteristics of a number of these settings. From this it can be seen that the immersion classroom and in some cases also the bilingual classroom are more likely to closely resemble natural environments in that the kind of discourse observed there is more likely to be characterized by the negotiation of meaning. However, any classroom setting has the potential for this kind of discourse. In the final analysis, it is the style of teaching that counts, in particular whether it is teacher- or learner-centred.

Type of classroom setting	Principal characteristics	Comparison with natural setting
1 The foreign language classroom	Focus likely to be on language form, rather than meaning. L2 unlikely to be used for classroom management or for genuine social purposes.	Potentially least like a natural setting—little negotiation of meaning.
2 The second language classroom (e.g. ESL)	Many interactions will still focus on form, rather than meaning. L2 functions as a medium of instruction as well as goal—hence will be used for wider range of discourse functions than in (1).	More like a natural setting—some chance for negotiation of meaning.
3 The subject classroom (i.e. learner is placed in a class with native-speaking children)	The focus will be on meaning, rather than form. Input unlikely to be adjusted, unless numbers of L2 learners high. IRF exchanges likely to predominate.	Will resemble 'exposure' in natural settings (i.e. input which has not been modified)–but very little negotiation of meaning.
4 The bilingual classroom (i.e. where L2 learners receive instruction through both L1 and L2)	Mixed focus— sometimes on form, sometimes on meaning. No need for learners to attend to L2 if the same content is taught in L1 and L2—hence no input. Adjusted input will occur if L2 used to teach different subject content.	Potentially strong resemblance to natural setting—if learners have to attend to L2. Negotiation of meaning likely.
5 The immersion classroom (i.e. where a class of L2 learners are taught through medium of L2)	Focus will be on meaning in L2 subject lessons. Input likely to be simplified. IRF exchanges may still predominate.	Strongest resemblance to natural settings. Plenty of opportunity for negotiation of meaning, particularly if teaching is learner-centred.

Table 6.3 Input/interaction characteristics of different types of classroom setting

Summary

Input and interaction in classrooms have been investigated by means of interaction analysis, the study of teacher talk, and discourse analysis. Interaction analysis has spawned numerous category systems, some specifically designed for use in language classrooms. In general, however, it sheds little light on input and interaction in classrooms from the perspective of SLA. Studies of teacher talk indicate that similar kinds of modifications occur in the teacher's language as those observed in foreigner talk, although ungrammatical adjustments may be less common. Also teachers may not be able to tune their speech finely in the one-to-many classroom situation. Discourse analysis shows that many classroom interactions follow an IRF (initiate–response–feedback) pattern, which restricts the opportunity to negotiate meaning. However, other types of discourse also occur when the L2 is used for general classroom organization and management and for social purposes. Considerable differences between natural and classroom environments arise, particularly when the focus is on form in language lessons. These differences are not absolute; they vary in degree according to the type of classroom and also the type of teaching. Learner-centred teaching in subject or immersion classrooms can lead to examples of interaction similar to those found in natural settings.

The role of input and interaction in SLA

So far the discussion has focused on describing and explaining the different types of input and interaction. The key question, however, is whether SLA is significantly affected by the quality and quantity of the input and interaction and, if so, how. This section will consider this question. It will begin with an account of the different ways in which the question can be tackled. It will then consider how input and interaction affect the route of SLA and, following this, the rate of SLA.

Ways of investigating the effects of input and interaction

In order to demonstrate that input and interaction have an effect on SLA, it is necessary to establish a causal relationship between the L2 data made available to the learner and his output. A number of different approaches have been used to this.

1 The analysis of selected L2 input and interaction sequences
    This is the approach adopted by Hatch and Long for natural SLA and by Ellis for classroom SLA. For example, Hatch examines examples of native speaker–learner discourse and then speculates in what ways they constrain SLA. Although in this approach the relationship between input and output is not established empirically, it does offer many rich hypotheses.

2 Extrapolation from studies of the role of input and interaction in first language acquisition
This is Krashen's (1981a) approach. He lists those features of motherese which research has suggested are facilitative, and argues that similar features in the input and interaction involving L2 learners will foster SLA. This approach has the advantage of drawing on a substantial body of empirical research, but it is tenable only if the assumption is justified that the role of the environment is the same in first and second language acquisition. There are strong grounds for such an assumption.

3 Correlational studies
Correlational studies measure input features and output features, in order to establish to what extent the relationship between them is significant or a matter of chance. For example, the frequency of grammatical features of the input can be correlated with the frequency of the same features in the learner's output. This approach has been used by Hatch and Wagner-Gough (1975) and Snow and Hoefnagel-Höhle (1982). The main problem is that correlational statistics do not demonstrate a *causal* relationship. This can only be inferred from the results of the analysis.

4 Experimental studies
In an experimental study, the linguistic environment is carefully controlled in order to investigate the effects of specific features. Often a comparison is made between the effects of two different kinds of input on separate groups. In real-life situations, it is often neither possible nor ethical to manipulate the linguistic environment in this way. Naturally occurring environments do not usually afford the controlled input conditions to carry out this kind of study. One way out is to use miniature artificial languages consisting of a limited number of rules. Interesting studies of this kind have been carried out by Schachter and Kimmell (1983) and Zobl (1983b), but they are open to the commonly voiced objection that the language behaviour that is being examined is also artificial.

5 Indirect studies
Long (1983c) suggests that the effects of input and interaction can be investigated indirectly in terms of three steps:

Step 1: Show that (A) linguistic/conversational adjustments promote (B) comprehension.
Step 2: Show that (B) comprehensible input promotes (C) acquisition.
Step 3: Deduce that (A) linguistic/conversational adjustments promote (C) acquisition.

This is an attractive idea. It rests, however, on the view that comprehensible input is the causative variable in the input–output relationship. It is precisely this that requires demonstration.

In general there has been more theorizing about the effects of input and interaction in SLA than careful, empirical study. Of the approaches listed above, (1) and (2) have been most common. This should be borne in mind when considering the following discussion. As Hatch (1983b: 83) observes, the 'tremendous leaps we make in interpreting our findings' are 'disconcerting'.

The effects of input and interaction on the route of SLA

It has been shown earlier that there may be a 'natural' sequence for the development of grammatical knowledge in SLA (see Chapter 3). On the face of it, this suggests that the input is not the major determinant of the route of SLA. If it were a major factor, variations in the sequence of development would be expected to coincide with variations in the type of input available. Thus, it would appear at first sight that the 'natural' sequence can be more easily explained in terms of universal innate processing mechanisms. However, an explanation based on input is still tenable.

Hatch (1978c; 1978d) argues that the natural order is the product of the way in which conversations with learners are organized. As we have seen, the types of discourse in which L2 learners (particularly children) take part are predictable. It is possible, therefore, that the 'natural' sequence is the result of a more or less standard input derived from these predictable exchanges. Both the native speaker and the learner are concerned to establish and sustain a topic. The limited linguistic resources of the learner constrain how this is achieved, which in turn regulates the input the learner receives. Thus, indirectly, the natural sequence may be a reflection of conversational competence. As Hatch (1978c: 404) puts it:

> One learns how to do conversations, one learns how to interact verbally, and out of this interaction, syntactic structures develop.

However, as Hatch admits, there is a problem with this explanation in that, although the conversational topics seem to control the input for children, they do not seem to act in the same way for adults. Yet the general route of acquisition is the same for children and adults. Hatch suggests that the interactional negotiation that occurs in conversations with adult learners may lead to a similar kind of input to that derived from the topic constraints in the case of children, but it is not clear how.

If Hatch is right, and the order of acquisition is a reflection of conversation growth, it still remains to be shown in precisely what way. A number of explanations have been advanced. These are mutually compatible and together constitute the best current account of how input and interaction influences the route of SLA.

1 *Formulaic speech*

One way in which interaction can aid SLA is by providing the learner with ready-made chunks of speech which can be memorized as 'unanalysed wholes'. This is likely to occur when the learner participates in routinized interactions involving the use of invariant utterance types by the native speaker. Hatch (1983b) has referred to this type of input as 'canned speech'. She suggests that adult learners may be able to keep control of topics (i.e. avoid the risk of the conversation taking off into fields the learner is not linguistically competent to handle) by the adroit use of formulae. In this way they serve an immediate communicative purpose. Later on the learner breaks them down into their constituent parts, and in doing so augments his interlanguage system. Formulaic speech, therefore, contributes indirectly to the route of SLA by providing raw materials for the learner's internal mechanisms to work on. This process is examined in greater detail in Chapter 7.

2 *Vertical structures*

Vertical structures are learner utterances which are constructed by borrowing chunks of speech from the preceding discourse. Consider the following example from Ellis (1984a):

Teacher: Take a look at the next picture.
Pupil: Box.
Teacher: A box, yes.
Pupil: A box bananas.

The L2 pupil's final utterance can be seen to consist of a repetition of the teacher's preceding utterance (e.g. 'A box') plus an extra noun. It has been constructed 'vertically'. Scollon (1976) has observed large numbers of similar constructions in first language acquisition. He points out that they are one of the principal means by which the child overcomes the constraints on the length of his utterances imposed by processing limitations. They may serve a similar purpose in SLA. Wagner-Gough also found evidence of vertical structures in SLA. Her subject incorporated whole chunks of previous utterances into his speech:

NS child: Come here.
L2 child: No come here (= I won't come)

She notes that sometimes a pattern was not immediately incorporated, but stored for later use (i.e. it cropped up two or three turns later). Moreover, sometimes a pattern was imitated before it was combined with other words.

Long and Sato (1984) describe a rather different use that learners make of the discourse context. They show how they rely on the interlocutor's previous utterance as a means of establishing time reference. In other words, temporal reference is established by the interlocutor's utterance and assumed to 'carry over' to the learner's utterance, even though the latter is not linguistically marked for time. Long and Sato refer to this use of context as another example of the general process of *collaborative discourse*.

Collaborative discourse in the guise of vertical structures and context-dependency, as discussed above, offers a powerful explanation for familiar features of L2 output. The utterance 'A box bananas' looks as if it may have been the result of a strategy of simplification leading to the omission of the functor 'of', until its position in the discourse is considered. Also, vertical constructions can explain why the 'no + V' pattern is so common in early SLA. The learner simply adds 'no' to a previous chunk of language, as in the example above. The explanatory power of vertical constructions is increased by the notion of 'functions'. Not only does the learner add to previously occurring chunks, but he also deletes and substitutes. Many of the features of the output can be explained as the result of the learner working on preceding utterances (his own or the native speaker's) in various ways. It is for this reason that the output should never be considered in isolation, but always in context.

3 *Frequency*

Another way in which the structure of conversations can influence the route of SLA is by modelling specific grammatical forms which are then subconsciously acquired by the learner. In other words, the first structures the learner acquires are those to which he is exposed most frequently. Hatch and Wagner-Gough (1975) report a positive correlation between the frequency of various Wh-questions in the input and the order in which they are acquired. Larsen-Freeman (1976) compared the standard morpheme order for SLA with the frequency of the same morphemes in the parental speech examined by Brown in his study (1973) of first language acquisition. She found a significant correlation. Larsen-Freeman comments:

> Thus, the tentative conclusion is that morpheme frequency of occurrence in native-speaker speech is the principal determinant for the oral production morpheme accuracy order of ESL learners (1976: 378–9).

However, such conclusions must be treated with caution. Lightbown (1983) argues that the statistical methods used can mislead. She found that the frequency of verb morphemes in the speech of Grade 6 teachers in Canadian schools did not successfully predict the 'acquisition' order of the same morphemes in communicative speech. But Lightbown hypothesizes that the frequency of input forms can have a delayed impact. That is, the input frequency in Grade 6 is reflected in output frequency in Grade 7.

The relationship between input and output frequencies is an uncertain one. A significant correlation may simply reflect the fact that some structures naturally occur more frequently than others; thus the similarity between input and output frequencies may be coincidental and not indicative of any conscious teaching strategy. Moreover, it is not clear how input frequency can account for deviant utterance types in the output. It is possible that learners copy the ungrammaticalities they perceive in foreigner talk, but this has not been shown.

4 *Comprehensible input*

It is likely that simple 'exposure' to input data is not enough. Learners need *comprehensible input*. Krashen (1981a; 1982) and Long 1983b; 1983c) have argued strongly that SLA is dependent on the availability of comprehensible input before the learner's internal processing mechanism can work.

Krashen presents the case for comprehensible input in the form of the *input hypothesis*. He argues that for SLA to take place, the learner needs input that contains exemplars of the language forms which according to the natural order are due to be acquired next. Input must consist of 'i + 1'. Krashen (1982: 21) writes:

> . . .a necessary (but not sufficient) condition to move from stage 'i' to stage 'i + 1' is that the acquirer understand input that contains 'i + 1', where 'understand' means that the acquirer is focussed on the meaning and not the form of the message.

Thus acquisition takes place when the learner understands language containing 'i + 1'. This will automatically occur when communication is successful. Krashen emphasizes that input does not need to be 'finely tuned' in the sense that it is linguistically adjusted to contain 'i + 1'. It requires only rough tuning, which is automatic if the focus is on successful communication. Krashen talks of the input 'casting a net' in order to make certain that it is of an optimal size, providing a built-in review of language forms already acquired and guaranteeing that 'i + 1' is covered. 'Casting a net' requires that the focus is on meaning and not form.

Long (1983c) considers in some detail how input is made comprehensible. One way is by the use of structures and vocabulary which the learner already knows. However, this type of input cannot foster development, because it supplies no new linguistic material. Another way is by a 'here-and-now' orientation, which enables the learner to make use of the linguistic and extralinguistic contexts and his general knowledge to interpret language which he does not actually know (see Chapter 7 for a fuller discussion of this process). A third way is through the modification of the interactional structure of conversation. Long considers interactional adjustments to be the important ones for SLA and points out that these occur even when there are no formal modifications. A 'here-and-now' orientation, together with interactional adjustments, are the main source of comprehensible input. They ensure that communication proceeds, while exposing the learner to new linguistic material. Figure 6.2 provides a model to account for the way in which interactional adjustments in two-way communication aid SLA.

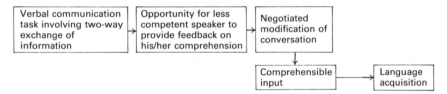

Figure 6.2   Model of the relationship between type of conversational task and language acquisition (Long 1983c: 214)

Krashen and Long's case for comprehensible input is a strong one. There are, however, problems. First, SLA can take place without two-way communication and hence without interactional modifications. As Larsen-Freeman (1983a) notes, there are cases of successful SLA when the only input is that obtained from reading or watching television. However, these counter-examples are anecdotal and it is not clear to what extent the learning that takes place from such input results in knowledge that is available for use in spontaneous communication. Another objection is that interactional adjustments do not always result in comprehensible input. Chaudron (1983a) notes that the kinds of input modifications which take place in teacher talk can lead to 'ambiguous over-simplification' and 'confusingly redundant over-elaboration'. However, Chaudron was investigating what Long refers to as one-way interaction (i.e. university lecturing), so there was probably little feedback from the students to help the teachers tune their input. It is less likely that such difficulties will arise in two-way communication, where there is fuller negotiation of meaning. A third and more serious objection to Long and Krashen's position is advanced by Swain (1983). She argues that the input hypothesis fails to recognize the importance of *comprehensible output.* Krashen (1982) specifically rejects the possibility that production (as opposed to comprehension) serves any purpose in SLA. Swain suggests that output is important in several ways: (1) the learner may be 'pushed' to use alternative means where there is communication breakdown, in order to express a message precisely, coherently, and appropriately; (2) using (as opposed to simply comprehending) the language may force the learner to move from semantic processing which is characteristic of the early stages of SLA to syntactic processing (i.e. whereas comprehension can take place by simply attending to the meaning of content words, production may trigger the focus on formal features); and (3) the learner has a chance to test out hypotheses about the L2 (see Chapter 7). The arguments of Larsen-Freeman, Chaudron, and above all Swain suggest that, although important, comprehensible input may not be either necessary or sufficient for SLA to take place.

5 Input and intake

Even if input is understood, it may not be processed by the learner's internal mechanisms. That is what Krashen meant when he stated that comprehensible input is not a *sufficient* condition for SLA. It is only when input becomes *intake* that SLA takes place. Input is the L2 data which the learner hears; intake is that portion of the L2 which is assimilated and fed into the interlanguage system.

We know very little about how the learner selects from the input data he receives. Is it to do with the way pieces of input data are presented? Is it to do with socio-affective factors such as motivation? Krashen argues that these act as a 'filter', controlling how much input is let in and how much is excluded. Is it to do with the nature of the internal processing mechanisms themselves? The crux of a nativist account of SLA is that it is these mechanisms which regulate the intake. It may be that learners do not respond to the available data on an all-or-nothing basis, either assimilating it or rejecting it. They may attend differentially to features of the input, using some to confirm or disconfirm existing hypotheses, others to form new hypotheses, and keeping others as 'savings' so that some 'trace' remains which can be worked on later (Hatch 1983b).

The discussion of how input becomes intake necessarily involves a consideration of the nature of the internal mechanisms. As such it belongs to Chapter 7.

Effects of input and interaction on the rate of SLA

Having considered in some detail the various ways in which input and interaction might influence the *route* of acquisition, I shall now turn to how it might affect the *rate* of development. It is entirely possible, of course, that even if the linguistic environment is not an important determinant of the learning sequence, it is a major factor in determining the speed at which learners learn.

There have been a number of studies which have sought to investigate the effect of input and interaction on the rate of SLA. As these have all been concerned with classroom SLA, they also serve to address the important question about the relationship between a classroom setting and SLA.

Snow and Hoefnagel-Höhle (1982) examined the classroom input to thirteen English-speaking learners of Dutch, aged three to eighteen. They found that although teachers and some native-speaking children (i.e. those in kindergarten and elementary schools but not those in secondary schools) modified their speech when addressing the L2 learners, neither the overall quantity of speech the learners were exposed to nor the quantity of the speech specifically directed at the learners predicted the subsequent improvement in language ability of the different learners. This study, therefore, suggests that the quantity of comprehensible input in the classroom does not determine the rate of SLA. However, as Snow and Hoefnagel-Höhle observe, this may be because the wrong measures of input were used. They examined the quantity of input, but it may be quality (i.e. specific kinds of interactionally adjusted input) that is important. However, Seliger (1977) in a study of adult classroom learners did find a significant correlation between the quantity of interaction and achievement scores at the end of the course. He hypothesizes that those students who were 'high input generators' in the classroom also capitalized on practice opportunities out of class. Thus, the evidence regarding the effects of quantity of input is mixed. There will need to be many further studies before a clear picture emerges.

Fillmore (1982) compared the progress of sixty L2 learners in kindergarten classrooms. She found that success in SLA occurred in (1) classes with high numbers of L2 learners where the classroom organization was teacher-directed, and (2) classes with mixed L2 learners and native-speaking children but with an open classroom organization. In contrast, little SLA took place in (3) classes with high numbers of L2 learners but with an open classroom organization, and (4) classes with mixed L2 learners and native-speaking children but teacher-directed organization. In other words, there was an interactive effect involving the composition of the classes and the type of organization. Fillmore explains these results in terms of the type of input which was received in the different classrooms. In (1) the teacher served as the main source of input, and because there were high numbers of L2 learners, she was able to ensure that the input was comprehensible. In (2) the L2 learners obtained negotiated input both from the teacher and also from the native-speaking children. But in (3) the pupils did not receive so much teacher input, and tended to use the L1 when talking among themselves; and in (4) the teachers found it difficult to tailor their language to suit the L2 learners, so that little comprehensible input was available. Fillmore's study suggests that both the quantity and the quality of input are infuential in determining the rate of SLA.

In addition to empirical studies of the effects of input and interaction, there have been several attempts to describe what constitutes an 'optimal learning environment' by drawing on research into the nature and effects of input in first and second language acquisition. Ellis (1984a) suggests that the following features are likely to facilitate rapid development:

1 A high quantity of input directed at the learner.
2 The learner's perceived need to communicate in the L2.
3 Independent control of the propositional content by the learner (e.g. control over topic choice).
4 Adherence to the 'here-and-now' principle, at least initially.
5 The performance of a range of speech acts by both native speaker/ teacher and the learner (i.e. the learner needs the opportunity to listen to and to produce language used to perform different language functions).
6 Exposure to a high quantity of directives.
7 Exposure to a high quantity of 'extending' utterances (e.g. requests for clarification and confirmation, paraphrases and expansions).
8 Opportunities for uninhibited 'practice' (which may provide opportunities to experiment using 'new' forms).

There are strong theoretical grounds for believing that a learning setting rich in these features will lead to successful SLA, but as yet there is little empirical proof.

Summary

A number of different ways exist for investigating the effects of input and interaction in SLA. Many of these, however, necessitate a leap from *description* of input language to *explanation* of its effects. There is little hard research showing whether input and interaction does affect SLA, what features of input and interaction are important, and what aspects of SLA are affected. With regard to the route of SLA, input may facilitate development by (1) providing the learner with ready-made chunks of language to memorize and later analyse, (2) helping the learner to build vertical constructions, (3) modelling specific grammatical forms with high frequency, (4) ensuring that the input is one step ahead of the learner's existing knowledge (by providing comprehensible input), and (5) providing the right affective climate to ensure that input becomes intake. With regard to the rate of SLA, a number of studies have investigated the effects of input and interaction, with mixed success. However, there are grounds for thinking that both the quantity and the quality of input are important. The characteristics of an optimal learning environment can be deduced from studies of input and interaction in both first and second language acquisition. A list of these characteristics is provided above.

Conclusion

The study of input and interaction in SLA seeks answers to the following questions:

1 What characteristics are displayed by input and interaction involving L2 learners?
2 Are the characteristics of input and interaction related to SLA, and if so in what way?
3 What are the differential contributions of input and interaction on the one hand and internal processing mechanisms to SLA on the other?

There are fairly clear answers to the first question. We know quite a lot about native speaker input and discourse between native speakers/ teachers and L2 learners. We know much less about the second question. Strong claims have been advanced that SLA is aided by two-way communication in which comprehensible input is provided by means of interactional adjustments. However, two-way communication is not a necessary condition for SLA. Nor is it sufficient. Where question (3) is concerned, we are even less sure. We do not know what proportion of responsibility to allocate to the linguistic environment, as opposed to the internal mechanisms. It may be that this question cannot be answered, because SLA is *jointly* determined by factors inside and outside the learner. As Hatch (1983a: 180) writes:

> While social interaction may give the learner the 'best' data to work with, the brain in turn must work out a fitting and relevant model of that input.

This being so, it is an interactionist view of SLA, rather than a behaviourist or nativist view, that may be most acceptable.

Notes

1 Allwright's use of the term 'topic' rightly reflects the importance of considering the purpose of an interaction as well as what is talked about. In language classrooms the 'topic' is often some item of language treated either inductively (i.e. as a 'model') or deductively (i.e. as a 'rule').

Further reading

A number of articles on motherese are collected together in *Talking to Children*, by C. Snow and C. Ferguson (Cambridge University Press, 1977). There is also a sound overview article on motherese by J. Gleason and S. Weintraub in *Children's Language*, Vol. 1, edited by K. Nelson (Gardner Press, 1978).

There are two general collections of articles dealing with input and second language acquisition: *Discourse Analysis in Second Language Research*, edited by D. Larsen-Freeman (Newbury House, 1980) deals primarily with non-classroom input/interaction. *Classroom Oriented Research in Second Language Acquisition*, edited by H. Seliger and M. Long (Newbury House, 1983) deals primarily with classroom input/ interaction (see articles by Long, Chaudron, Schinke-Llano, Gaies, Seliger, Long and Sato).

For the role of input/interaction in SLA there is E. Hatch's chapter 'Discourse analysis and second language acquisition' in *Second Language Acquisition*, edited by E. Hatch (Newbury House, 1978). 'Native speaker/non-native speaker conversation in the second language classroom', by M. Long, in *On TESOL '82: Pacific Perspectives on Language Learning and Teaching*, edited by M. Clarke and J. Handscombe (TESOL, 1983), reviews the comprehensible input hypothesis and considers it in relation to the classroom.

7   Learner strategies

Introduction

This chapter considers the internal processes which account for how the learner handles input data and how the learner utilizes L2 resources in the production of messages in the L2. It looks at the internal mechanisms, or the 'black box'. As such it complements the previous chapter. A complete account of SLA involves both showing how the input is shaped to make it learnable (an inter-organism perspective), and how the learner works on the input to turn it into intake (an intra-organism perspective).

The learner has two types of L2 knowledge: *declarative* and *procedural* (Faerch and Kasper 1983b). Declarative knowledge is 'knowing that'; it consists of internalized L2 rules and memorized chunks of language. Procedural knowledge is 'knowing how'; it consists of the strategies and procedures employed by the learner to process L2 data for acquisition and for use. When we talk about acquiring a L2, we normally mean declarative knowledge, as the learner is considered to have access already to a set of procedures for learning the L2. Declarative knowledge has been examined in Chapters 3 and 4. This chapter examines procedural knowledge. Whereas the earlier chapters were concerned largely with *describing* SLA, this chapter focuses on *explaining* it.

Procedural knowledge can be subdivided initially into *social* and *cognitive* components. The social component comprises the behavioural strategies used by the learner to manage interactional opportunities (i.e. the use of the L2 in face-to-face contact or in contact with L2 texts). Fillmore (1979) describes a number of general social strategies used by five Spanish-speaking children learning English in play situations with native-speaking children. To begin with, the children adopted the strategy of joining a group and acting as if they understood what was going on, even if they did not. Later, they sought to give the impression that they could speak the language by utilizing a few carefully chosen words. They also relied on their friends to help them out when they were in communicative difficulty. Other social strategies have been considered in Chapters 5 and 6. The focus of this chapter, therefore, will be cognitive strategies.

The cognitive component of procedural knowledge comprises the various mental processes involved in internalizing and automatizing new L2 knowledge and in using L2 knowledge in conjunction with other knowledge sources to communicate in the L2. These processes, therefore, involve both *learning* and *using* the L2. Learning processes account for how the learner accumulates new L2 rules and automatizes existing ones by attending to input and by simplifying through the use of existing knowledge. They can account for the 'natural' sequence of development described in Chapter 3. The processes involved in using L2 knowledge consist of *production* and *reception strategies* and also *communication strategies*. The former are defined by Tarone (1981) as attempts to use existing L2 knowledge efficiently and clearly with a minimum of effort. The latter occur when the speaker is not able to communicate his original communicative goal in the way he planned to, and so is forced to reduce the goal or to locate alternative means to express it. Communication strategies, then, are the result of an initial failure to implement a production plan. Language use, therefore, is characterized by both production and reception strategies, which operate when the learner utilizes available resources easily and subconsciously. It is also characterized by communication strategies, which operate when the learner needs to compensate for inadequate means and which, as a result, are likely to involve greater effort and to be closer to consciousness.

A framework of the different learner strategies is provided in Figure 7.1. It should be recognized that these strategies are not special to the learner. Native language speakers must be considered to use the same strategy *types*. What distinguishes learners and native speakers is the frequency with which the same strategies are called upon. Learners will manifest more strategy *tokens*.

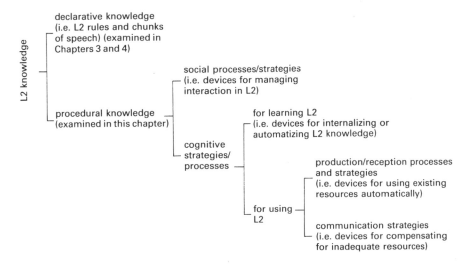

Figure 7.1 Types of L2 knowledge

Before examining the different types of procedural knowledge in detail, it is important to consider the metalanguage used to describe this kind of mental phenomenon. It is perhaps inevitable, given the abstractness of the concepts involved, that the metalanguage is often confusing and vague. In particular, researchers do not use terms like 'process', 'strategy', or 'principle' consistently. Sometimes they use them as synonyms for general mental operations, but sometimes they use them to differentiate operations involved in language processing. Faerch and Kasper (1980), for instance, make a clear distinction between 'strategy' and 'process'. They define the former as plans for controlling the order in which a sequence of operations is to be performed, and the latter as the operations involved either in the development of a plan (the planning process) or in the realization of a plan (the realization process)—see Figure 7.2.

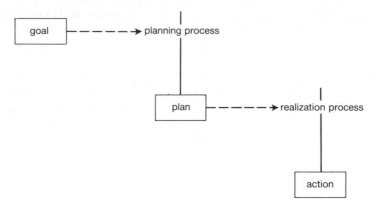

Figure 7.2   The planning and realization of intellectual behaviour
(Faerch and Kasper 1980)

A problem with such a distinction is that there is little consensus concerning which behaviours belong to 'processes', as opposed to 'strategies'. However, it makes good sense to distinguish the idea of a sequence of operations (as in 'the production/reception process') and the idea of a single operation as a feature of a process (as in 'a strategy of simplification'). Faerch and Kasper's distinction will be adhered to, therefore, as much as possible.

This chapter will begin by examining *learning strategies*. It will then look at the *production process*. Ideally it ought also to consider the reception process, but for reasons of space and also because this is an aspect of the 'black box' which has received little consideration (see, however, Faerch and Kasper 1980 and 1983b; Rivers 1971) it will be omitted. The final section will consider *communication strategies*.

Learning strategies

The proliferation of terms and concepts, so characteristic of accounts of every aspect of procedural knowledge, is perhaps most evident in discussions of learning strategies. Strategies as varied as memorization, overgeneralization, inferencing, and prefabricated patterns have all been treated under the general heading of 'learning strategies'. In addition there is constant reference to the process of hypothesis-testing, which underlies in a rather ill-defined way the operation of the more specific strategies. I shall attempt to impose some order on this heterogeneity, but do not seek to claim that the framework I offer represents psychological reality. Rather it is a heuristic device for coping with the lack of precision which characterizes discussions of learning strategies. The basis of the framework is a distinction between two types of linguistic product: formulaic speech and creative speech. These are defined below.

Formulaic speech

Formulaic speech has been considered briefly in Chapter 6. It consists of 'expressions which are learned as unanalysable wholes and employed on particular occasions. . .' (Lyons 1968: 177). It can be observed in the speech of native speakers as well as of learners. Krashen and Scarcella (1978) distinguish between *routines* and *patterns*, to refer respectively to whole utterances learnt as memorized chunks and to utterances that are only partially unanalysed and have one or more open slots (e.g. 'Can I have ____?'). Ellis (1984c) also suggests that formulaic speech can consist of entire *scripts*, such as greeting sequences, which the learner can memorize because they are more or less fixed and predictable.

Formulaic speech has been observed to be very common in SLA, particularly in the early stages of development. It figures frequently in the speech both of child learners (cf. Huang and Hatch 1978) and of adult learners (cf. Hellwig 1983) in naturalistic SLA, and also in some classroom learners (cf. Ellis 1984c). The particular unanalysed chunks which are learnt are likely to vary from learner to learner, but the following appear to be typical:

I don't know.
Can I have a ____?
There is no____.
What's this?
I wanna ____.
This is a ____.
How do you do?
I can't speak English.

Each formula is closely tied to a particular communicative goal. Ellis (1984a), for instance, notes that three classroom learners rapidly developed a number of formulas to meet the basic communicative needs in an ESL classroom where English functioned as the medium of communication. It has been suggested by Krashen and Scarcella (1978) that learners develop formulas as a response to communicative pressure. That is, they memorize a number of ready-made expressions to compensate for lack of sufficient L2 rules to construct creative speech. Krashen (1982) argues that formulaic speech occurs when the learner is forced to speak before he is ready. Left to his own devices, he will engage in a 'silent period' while he builds up sufficient L2 rules to speak creatively. The important point, however, is that formulaic speech is closely tied to the performance of specific meanings, and that it is common in early SLA because it reduces the learning burden while maximizing communicative ability.

What are the learning strategies involved in acquiring formulaic speech? It is very unlikely that these are the same as those involved in the acquisition of rules responsible for creative speech. One suggestion is that formulaic speech may involve the right hemisphere of the brain rather than the left hemisphere, which is responsible for the creative language function in most people. The right hemisphere is generally considered to involve holistic processing (Seliger 1982). That is, the learner subjugates the individual parts that make up an entity to the whole. The learner perceives the whole pattern as a *gestalt* rather than the elements that constitute it. In the case of formulaic speech, therefore, the learner may operate a strategy of *pattern memorization*. He attends to the input and, using mechanisms located in the right hemisphere, identifies a number of commonly occurring whole utterances in terms of the contexts in which they are used. He is aided in this by the facts that (1) the patterns are highly frequent, and (2) each pattern is linked to a communicative function which the learner is motivated to perform. The patterns are stored in the right hemisphere and are available for immediate processing in production and reception. The extent to which the strategy of pattern memorization is invoked is a product of the type of input the learner receives (i.e. how predictable and context-dependent it is) and the strength of the learner's need to communicate in the L2.

Pattern memorization is a psycholinguistic strategy. It occurs without the learner needing to activate it consciously and it has no overt manifestation. We cannot see or hear pattern memorization taking place. Some researchers refer to the use of prefabricated patterns as a learning strategy, but this is to confuse product and process. The patterns are the products of the process of pattern memorization.

The product—the patterns themselves—can also result from another, related strategy. *Pattern imitation* is the behavioural equivalent of pattern memorization. It is a behavioural strategy because it is usually consciously activated and because it can be observed when it takes place. Pattern imitation involves the deliberate and methodical copying of whole utterances or parts of utterances used in the speech of an interlocutor. It is common in classrooms where the audiolingual techniques of pattern practice are used. It can also occur in naturalistic SLA, when the learner imitates the previous utterance of a native speaker irrespective of its communicative appropriateness. This is very common, particularly with child learners (Itoh and Hatch 1978). Seliger (1982) considers that pattern imitation also involves right hemisphere abilities.

It has been suggested in both first and second language acquisition research that formulaic speech serves as the basis for creative speech. That is, the learner comes to realize that utterances initially understood and used as wholes consist of discrete constituents which can be combined with other constituents in a variety of rule-bound ways. Clark (1974) illustrates how in first language acquisition, new structures can result from the juxtaposition of two routines or from the embedding of one within another. Fillmore (1976) suggests that in SLA, formulas are slowly submitted to an analytical process that releases constituent elements for use in 'slots' other than those they initially occupied. Seliger (1982) proposes that patterns initially learnt through right hemisphere abilities are brought to the attention of left hemisphere abilities, which work on them in order to analyse out their parts. Ellis (1984c) shows how the 'I don't know' formula is built on, by combining it with other formulas:

e.g. That one I don't know.
    I don't know what's this.

and also broken down, so that 'don't' is used in similar but different expressions:

e.g. I don't understand.
    I don't like.

'Know' is used without 'don't':

e.g. I know this.

and subjects other than 'I' begin to occur:

e.g. You don't know where it is.

It is possible, therefore, that formulas are slowly unpackaged so that valuable information can be fed into the creative rule system.

The basis for this analysis must lie in the learner comparing utterances in order to identify which parts recur and which parts remain the same. The learner gradually notices variation in the formulaic structures according to the situation and also detects similarities in the parts of different formulas (Fillmore 1979). Thus earlier utterances, learnt and used as formulas, are often more grammatical in appearance than later utterances, which are constructed from rules. To account for this process, a strategy of *pattern analysis* can be posited. This works by comparing formulas and looking for similarities and differences. It ascribes to the learner something of the skills of a linguist seeking to identify the constituent structure of utterances.

There is not total agreement about pattern analysis. Krashen and Scarcella (1978) argue that formulaic speech and rule-created speech are unrelated. They claim that the learner does not unpackage the linguistic information contained in formulas, but internalizes L2 rules by attending to the input in accordance with the 'natural' sequence of development. They see the process of 'creative construction' of L2 rules as entirely separate.

Formulaic speech is an important factor in SLA, but is probably only a major factor in early SLA. The strategies of *pattern memorization*, *pattern imitation*, and (more controversially) *pattern analysis* are to be seen as minor learning strategies in comparison with those contributing directly to the creative rule system.

Creative speech

Creative speech is the product of L2 rules. These are 'creative' in the Chomskian sense that they permit the L2 learner to produce entirely novel sentences. They are the rules that constitute the learner's interlanguage system and which account for the 'natural' sequence of development (see Chapter 3). They are variable in that they permit the learner to vary his performance according to both the linguistic and the situational context (see Chapter 4).

A plethora of strategies have been proposed to account for the creative rule system. Faerch and Kasper (1980; 1983b) provide a framework which can be used to consider these strategies systematically. They distinguish strategies involved in *establishing* interlanguage rules, and strategies involved in *automatizing* interlanguage knowledge. In the former they also distinguish two basic and related processes: hypothesis formation and hypothesis testing. I shall use this framework in the following discussion, but will not limit myself to the specific strategies identified by Faerch and Kasper.

Hypothesis formation

Faerch and Kasper (1983b) suggest that hypotheses about interlanguage rules are formed in three ways:

1 by using prior linguistic knowledge (i.e. first language knowledge, existing L2 knowledge, or knowledge of other languages);

2 by inducing new rules from the input data;
3 by a combination of (1) and (2).

Underlying these general processes it is possible to identify two general strategies, each with a number of more specific strategies associated with them. The two general strategies are *simplification* and *inferencing*.

Simplification   Many of the early interlanguage publications recognized that learners seek to ease the burden of learning in various ways. Richards (1974) defines 'strategies of assimilation' as attempts to reduce the learning burden. As an example he quotes his own use of the equivalent of the 'going to' form in French to express future meaning, simply because he found it easier to learn. Simplification, then, consists of attempts by the learner to control the range of hypotheses he attempts to build at any single stage in his development by restricting hypothesis formation to those hypotheses which are relatively easy to form and will facilitate communication.

Simplification is evident in the use of a number of strategies. Widdowson (1975b) has suggested that Selinker's five interlanguage processes are tactical variations of the same underlying simplification strategy. Thus, for instance, *transfer* involves the use of the learner's L1 as a basis for forming hypotheses about the L2, while *overgeneralization* involves the use of existing L2 knowledge by extending it to new interlanguage forms. Both strategies can be seen as manifestations of the same basic strategy of relying on prior knowledge to facilitate new learning (Taylor 1975; McLaughlin 1978a). Which strategy is used may be partly a matter of individual preference, but is also likely to be governed by such factors as the learner's stage of development, the linguistic properties of the L2, and the learning context—Ervin-Tripp (1974), for example, proposes that transfer will be more common in a classroom than in a natural learning environment. Irrespective of which strategy is used, however, simplification takes place, in that the learner seeks to override the evidence of the input by positing interim rules which he finds easier to construct on the basis of existing knowledge. In this sense simplification serves as an alternative to inferencing by attending closely to input data (see below).

Not all researchers agree that simplification is a learning strategy. Faerch and Kasper (1980), for example, argue that strategies such as simplifying, regularizing, overgeneralizing, and redundancy reducing are, in fact, strategies of non-learning, as they prevent the formation of correct hypotheses. If, however, it is accepted that the formation of non-correct hypotheses is essential in the overall process of SLA, this argument appears tenuous. Learning does not only involve the formation of correct hypotheses; it also involves interim hypotheses which are systematically amended until the final correct hypothesis is arrived at.

Simplification plays a positive role in that it delimits the proportion of hypotheses which are formed by attending to input (i.e. through inferencing) at any one time.

Another objection to the notion of simplification is that it does not make sense to refer to the learner as simplifying what he does not possess. Corder (1981) has argued that SLA should be viewed as a process of 'complexification'. This, however, confuses product and process again. While Corder is right to claim that the learner cannot simplify L2 rules he has not acquired, it is perfectly feasible to argue that he simplifies the burden of learning by restricting hypothesis formation dependent on attending to input. Even if we accept that the product cannot be simplified—and this will be challenged in the next section—it is still viable to argue that the process is simplified. This is the position adopted by Meisel (1983). He uses the term 'elaborative simplification' to refer to the learner process of adjusting what has just been acquired to what has been acquired before, by forming approximations of the rule represented in the input.

Simplification is sometimes listed as a production strategy rather than a learning strategy (Tarone 1981). That is, the learner is attributed with L2 rules but is unable to utilize them because of language processing difficulties. He therefore simplifies them (e.g. by using some but omitting others). Meisel refers to this as 'restrictive simplification'. Simplification is clearly an important aspect of production and will be considered in the relevant section later. This does not preclude its contribution to learning in the ways discussed above. Simplification is both a learning strategy and a production strategy.

Inferencing Inferencing is the means by which the learner forms hypotheses by attending to input. That is, in cases where the appropriate L2 rules cannot be successfully derived by means of transfer or overgeneralization of existing interlanguage knowledge, the learner will need to induce the rule from the input. For example a Spanish learner of English will not succeed in acquiring the rule for negative sentences on the basis of simplification. A transfer strategy might lead to the 'no + V' rule (e.g. 'No like beer'). Such a rule might also be derived by overgeneralization (i.e. 'no' is overgeneralized as the negator of verbs as well as nouns). But in order to arrive at the correct rule for generating sentences like

I don't like beer

the Spanish learner will need to attend to L2 input and to form the appropriate hypothesis.

Existing treatments of inferencing do not entirely conform with the one I have just given. Carton (1971), for instance, discusses inferencing in terms of three types of cues: (1) intralingual (i.e. cues derived from the morphological and syntactic regularity of the L2); (2) interlingual (i.e. cues derived from loans between languages where similar forms are hypothesized); and (3) extralingual or contextual (i.e. cues based on regularities in the objective world which make predictions possible). Bialystok (1983a) also identifies three types of inferencing, but they are not the same as Carton's: (1) inferencing from implicit knowledge (i.e. making explicit L2 knowledge that is only intuitive to begin with); (2) inferencing from other knowledge (i.e. using knowledge of other languages, in particular the L1, and/or knowledge of the world), and (3) inferencing from context. In both Carton's and Bialystok's frameworks, however, inferencing is treated as a general process that incorporates both what I have called inferencing and simplification. I wish to restrict the notion to two types: intralingual inferencing and extralingual inferencing.

Intralingual inferencing involves a process similar to that of *pattern analysis* of formulaic speech, the difference being that in this case the learner operates on external L2 data rather than internal L2 data (i.e. stored formulas). Intralingual inferencing, then, is the result of *intake analysis*. The use of the strategy may be governed by innate linguistic or cognitive predispositions to attend to specific features of the input. If they are linguistic, they will resemble the 'universal grammar' which Chomsky believes the first language learner is endowed with (see Chapter 8). If they are cognitive, they will involve the use of general perceptual strategies such as those listed by Slobin as 'operating principles'. The detailed workings of intake analysis, however, have not yet been described, and our understanding of them is limited.

Extralingual inferencing is one of the most powerful devices available to the learner for building hypotheses from external input. It consists of paying attention to features of the physical environment and using these to make L2 input comprehensible. By observing the non-linguistic correlates of utterances, the learner can convert input that is beyond his competence into intake. MacNamara (1972) talks of the L1 learner using 'meaning as a clue to language rather than language as a clue to meaning'. The same must also hold true for the L2 learner, including the adult learner. The situational context of a speech act enables the learner to work out meanings right from the start of SLA. Extralingual inferencing, therefore, serves as the principal means that the beginner uses to formulate hypotheses from the external input. It continues to be important throughout SLA.

Hypothesis testing

The concept of hypothesis testing has already been introduced in Chapter 3. There it was pointed out that language learners may make errors in order to test out hypotheses about the L2 rule system. It remains to examine in some detail how this takes place and to consider some of the objections about hypothesis testing which have been raised.

Once the learner has developed a hypothesis, he can test it out in a variety of ways. Faerch and Kasper (1983b) list these ways:

1 receptively (i.e. the learner attends to L2 input and compares his hypotheses with the data provided—by means of *intake analysis*;
2 productively (i.e. the learner produces L2 utterances containing rules representing the hypotheses he has formed and assesses their correctness in terms of the feedback received);
3 metalingually (i.e. the learner consults a native speaker, teacher, grammar, or dictionary to establish the validity of a hypothesis);
4 interactionally (i.e. the learner elicits a repair from his interlocutor in the manner described in the previous chapter).

As a result of hypothesis testing carried out in one or more of these ways, the learner is in a position either to confirm or reject an initial hypothesis. The constant revision of interlanguage rules is the result of the learner responding to evidence that requires modification of hypotheses. SLA ceases either when the learner no longer receives contrary evidence, or when he stops testing out hypotheses (i.e. because he is satisfied with his existing competence).

There have been several criticisms of the hypothesis testing view of SLA. Most of these have to do with the role of feedback. It has been observed that the provision of negative feedback (i.e. corrections) does not appear to lead to more accurate performance, at least not immediately. Even when the negative feedback is provided in the course of ordinary conversation (e.g. in the form of expansions and paraphrases serving as confirmation checks and requests for clarification), there is still no evidence to suggest that the learner amends his hypothesis immediately. Moreover, as Long (1977) points out, it makes little sense to talk about learners actively seeking out negative feedback. The 'falsification idea' is not feasible.

Nevertheless, the hypothesis testing model is still viable. These criticisms relate to how hypotheses are rejected. The important process, however, may be hypothesis confirmation. The learner often builds two or more hypotheses relating to the form of a single rule. The role of feedback may be to enable him to decide which hypothesis to accept finally. He is unlikely to come to a conclusion until he has received substantial feedback to test each of the hypotheses fully. As a result, the alternative hypotheses are maintained for some time, with perhaps a gradual tendency to favour one rather than the other(s). Eventually one of the competing hypotheses wins through and becomes a permanent L2 rule. This view of hypothesis testing meets the objections described above and also gives due recognition to interlanguage as a variable phenomenon. The entire process is a subconscious one; that is, the learner does not carry out hypothesis testing in order to learn the L2, but as part of the process of communication. Thus different types of communication can hinder or facilitate the process, as suggested in Chapter 6.

The role of hypothesis testing is also considered in Chapter 8, when the 'universal hypothesis' in SLA is examined. This rests on the argument that inductive hypothesis formation cannot adequately explain how acquisition takes place.

Automatization processes

The variability of interlanguage phenomena is also a reflection of rules which have been differentially automatized. Competing hypotheses are held with varying degrees of certainty. The less certain a hypothesis is, the less accessible it is for use in L2 production. Part of the learning process, then, involves consolidating hypotheses by accumulating confirmatory evidence. Faerch and Kasper (1983b) suggest that this can be brought about by *practising* the L2 productively and receptively. They distinguish *formal* and *functional practice*, depending on whether the focus is on formal features of the L2 or communicative endeavour. Automatization involves both the practising of L2 rules which enter interlanguage at the formal end of the stylistic continuum and the practising of rules which are already in use in the 'vernacular'.

Summary

The processes and strategies responsible for creative speech are summarized in Table 7.1. They are typically subconscious procedures (i.e. they are spontaneously activated by the learner while he is focused on some communicative purpose), but they can also be conscious (i.e. deliberately activated by the learner with the intention of increasing his L2 knowledge). Some procedures—metalingual hypothesis testing and formal practice—are invariably conscious, however.

Process	Strategy

Hypothesis formation	Simplification
	  (1) overgeneralization
	  (2) transfer
	Inferencing
	  (1) intralingual (via intake analysis)
	  (2) extralingual

Hypothesis testing	Receptive (via intake analysis) Productive Metalingual Interactional
Automatization	Formal practice Functional practice

Table 7.1   Processes and strategies in creative language learning

Production strategies

It will be recalled that utilizing interlanguage rules involves both production/reception strategies and, when initial plans prove problematic, also communication strategies. This section considers the unproblematic use of L2 knowledge. It will present a basic model of production (reception is not considered, for reasons already stated), and then consider specific strategies associated with the planning and articulating components of this model.

A model of L2 production

It is hypothesized that L2 production follows the same pattern as native-speaker production. The model which is summarized below is that described by Clark and Clark (1977).

The starting point is the speaker's communicative goal. This might be to tell a story, to issue an instruction, or to answer a question. The communicative goal will determine the type of discourse plan the speaker needs to form. This plan will reflect whether the communicative goal needs to be realized through dialogue or through monologue. It will also reflect to what extent the discourse is conventional and therefore 'scriptal', or requires unique planning. Once the speaker has formed an appropriate discourse plan, he begins to construct sentence plans. These involve outlining the constituent structure of each utterance, after determining the general propositional content and illocutionary meaning. The discourse and sentence plans together constitute a 'skeleton'. The next stage leads into the execution component of the model. It consists of building plans for the structure of each constituent. However, the language user does not necessarily build plans for *all* the constituents of the proposed utterance. He is likely to alternate between the planning of individual constituents and their execution. Thus the constituent planning stage and the articulatory programme stages do not follow in linear fashion. Evidence that the user moves backwards and forwards from planning to execution can be found in the pauses which occur in speech. These are typically found at constituent boundaries and seem to be motivated by the learner's need for time to plan the next constituent. Clark and Clark suggest that the articulatory programme itself has five stages: (1) the selection of the meaning that each constituent is to have; (2) the selection of a syntactic outline for the constituent (i.e. specifying the actual word slots); (3) content word selection (i.e. choosing nouns, verbs, adjectives, and adverbs to fit into the appropriate slots); (4) affix and function word formation (i.e. slotting in form words and grammatical inflections); and (5) specification of the phonetic segments. The final component of the model is the motor programme i.e. the actual production of the utterance. Figure 7.3 provides a diagrammatical representation of Clark and Clark's 'skeleton and constituent' model.

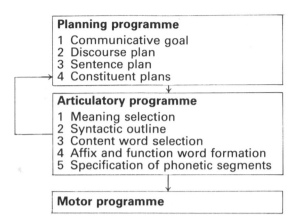

*Figure 7.3 The 'skeleton and constituent' model of language production
(based on Clark and Clark 1977)*

Littlewood (1979) proposes a production model specifically to account for L2 use. His model closely follows that of Clark and Clark. Littlewood distinguishes two sets of strategies based on the model: *minimal strategies* and *maximal strategies*. The former characterize production in the early stages of SLA. They involve the learner simplifying both the constituent planning and articulatory stages in a number of ways. The learner may not develop constituent plans for all the major constituents of the sentence. Instead he may plan for only the minimal number of unshared meaning elements, allowing the situational context to stand in for those missing. Ellis (1982a) describes this as a strategy of *semantic simplification*. Another type of simplification can occur in the articulatory programme when the learner chooses to encode only content words and to omit affix and function word formation. This may occur either because the learner has not yet constructed hypotheses for those aspects of the L2, or because of processing pressures which do not permit him time to make a thorough search of his linguistic resources. Thirdly, simplification may take place in the motor programme (i.e. sounds may be ellided). Maximal strategies occur when the learner has developed both sufficient L2 knowledge and adequate control over this knowledge to realize all constituents linguistically, thus removing the need to rely on shared knowledge. They also involve the ability to make linguistic selections of sufficient delicacy to encode stylistic markers such as those relating to politeness. Thus whereas early production is likely to be marked by *modality reduction* (Kasper 1979), later production will feature the use of those grammatical systems (e.g. modal verbs and adverbial expressions) associated with modality. Maximal strategies are reflected in the complexification of the inter-language system.

The skeleton and constituent model also provides a framework for interpreting Seliger's (1980) interesting distinction between planners and correctors. The planners are those who plan each constituent carefully before starting the articulatory programme. As a result, their performance is likely to be hesitant but correct, at least in terms of their current interlanguage system. In contrast, the correctors only partially plan each constituent before embarking on the articulatory programme, with the result that they produce fewer pauses, but are more prone to monitoring or to the use of communication strategies when they find they have not conformed to their interlanguage system or run into problems. The use of planning and correcting strategies is considered in greater detail below.

Planning strategies

Two basic planning strategies can be identified. These are *semantic simplification* and *linguistic simplification*. They are the procedures used by the learner in the early stages of SLA when he has minimal L2 resources and needs to employ them in a maximally easy and efficient manner.

Semantic simplification   Semantic simplification occurs when the learner simplifies the sentence plan by reducing the propositional elements that are linguistically coded. The learner selects specific constituents for encoding and leaves the others to be inferred by the listener from extralinguistic cues. The constituents deleted are not syntactic but semantic; that is, they consist of cases such as agent, object, dative, etc. (Fillmore 1968) which can be thought of as general conceptual categories, used in both the perception of real-life events and their linguistic representation. Imagine a situation in which Person A is hitting Person B. A full linguistic representation of this (from the viewpoint of Person B) might be:

He is hitting me.

which involves the case categories:

(Agent) (Action process) (Patient)

The learner may produce any one of the following abridged versions:

Hitting   (= Action process)
He hitting   (= Agent + Action process)
Hitting me   (= Action Process + Patient)
He me   (= Agent + Patient)

Which version the learner chooses will reflect (1) the linguistic resources he has available (e.g. he may not know the verb 'hit'), and (2) which constituents he feels will be maximally informative in terms of his communicative goal and the context of situation. Ellis (1982a; 1984a) has suggested that semantic simplification provides a powerful explanation of processes involved in both first and second language acquisition.

Linguistic simplification   Linguistic simplification involves the omission of form words and affixes. Unlike semantic simplification, it runs up against the logical objection that the learner cannot simplify what he does not possess. Thus if the learner produces an utterance like:

He hitting me.

where aux-be is omitted, this can only constitute linguistic simplification if the learner can be shown to possess an aux-be rule in his interlanguage. In fact there is plenty of evidence to suggest that learners do in fact omit functors such as aux-be, even though they have acquired the necessary forms. It is a common characteristic of the learner's variable use of his L2 knowledge. As Meisel (1983: 127) puts it: '. . . learners do produce utterances that are structurally simplified . . . although it can be assumed that their 'transitional competence' at this point contains rules that generate the corresponding nonsimplified structures'. Meisel argues that 'restrictive simplification' accounts not only for L2 production, but also for simplified registers such as motherese and foreigner talk. Linguistic simplification, therefore, is a very general language production strategy.

Correcting strategies: monitoring

The principal strategy responsible for correcting is *monitoring*. This has received considerable prominence in the form of Krashen's (1981) Monitor Model of L2 performance. Krashen argues that the learner possesses two kinds of knowledge, which are *implicit* or intuitive knowledge (referred to as 'acquisition' by Krashen), and *explicit* or metalinguistic knowledge (referred to as 'learning'). According to Krashen, the learner initiates utterances using only implicit knowledge, but is able to Monitor his performance using explicit knowledge either before or after articulation.

Krashen's theory has come under considerable attack (see Chapter 10). His notion of monitoring is seen as too narrow, in the sense that the learner is clearly able to edit his performance using implicit as well as explicit knowledge. Krashen, in fact, allows for this in his discussion of correction by 'feel', but this is allocated only a minor place in the overall theory. The kind of monitoring I wish to consider here is the broader kind, involving the use of any form of knowledge to correct incipient or actual output.

Morrison and Low (1983) propose a very similar production model to Clark and Clark's in order to discuss the role of monitoring. They distinguish post-articulatory monitoring, which occurs after the articulatory programme has been implemented, and pre-articulatory monitoring, which can occur at any stage during the articulatory programme. After the learner has begun the process of filling out constituent plans with linguistic forms, he can operate on the emerging utterance by substituting an initially selected form with another preferred form. This kind of monitoring can be carried out on lexis, syntax, morphology, and the phonetic realization. In other words, it can occur at any of the five stages in the articulation programme in Figure 7.3. It can also occur at higher levels, when it leads to an adjustment in communicative goal or discourse and sentence plans. But because monitoring can occur when no communicative or linguistic difficulty is experienced, it should be treated as a means of maximizing existing resources in an easy and efficient manner; it is, therefore, a production strategy rather than a communication strategy.

Summary

Production comprises a hierarchical process involving a planning, an articulation, and a motor programme. This process is common both to native speakers and to L2 users. Production strategies can be divided into those strategies involved in the planning of utterances, and those involved in the correction of utterances. Semantic simplification and linguistic simplification are 'minimal strategies' used to facilitate easy and effective use of the L2 system. They are planning strategies. Monitoring is a correcting strategy. It can occur before or after articulation and can utilize both implicit and explicit knowledge.

Strategies of communication

The term 'communication strategy' was coined by Selinker (1972) in his account of the processes responsible for interlanguage. There has been a steady increase of interest in the learner's communication strategies since then. Much of this interest, however, has been taken up with the problems of definition. It is to these that I first turn. Following this, a typology of communication strategies will be provided and a survey of empirical studies of their use by L2 learners undertaken. This section will conclude with some comments about the role of communication strategies in SLA.

Defining communication strategies

Two key concepts figure in most discussions of communication strategies. These are that they are conscious, and that they are problem-oriented.

Varadi (1973) points out that L2 errors may arise either inadvertently or deliberately. In the case of the former, they are the result of production strategies and reflect the transitional state of the learner's L2 knowledge. In the case of the latter, they are the result of communication strategies that are consciously employed by the learner in order to reduce or replace some element of meaning or form in the initial plan. Faerch and Kasper (1980) also consider consciousness to be a defining characteristic of communication strategies, but they recognize the difficulty of deciding empirically whether a strategy is conscious or otherwise. As learners may not always be aware of their use of communicative strategies, they suggest that a better definition is to refer to them as 'potentially conscious'.

Communication strategies are problem-oriented. That is, they are employed by the learner because he lacks or cannot gain access to the linguistic resources required to express an intended meaning. As Corder (1978c) puts it, there is a lack of balance between means and ends. Faerch and Kasper (1980) classify communication strategies as part of a particular kind of plan which is activated when the initial plan cannot be carried out. The learner is forced into substituting a 'strategic plan' for his original production plan, because he discovers he has insufficient means to implement the production plan. In terms of the model of speech production represented in Figure 7.3, this involves adding a loop, which starts from the source of the problem, which might lie at any point in the articulation process, and then leads into an alternative plan (which can be at discourse, sentence or constituent level) before feeding back into the articulation programme. However, communication strategies are not alone in being problem-oriented. Learner strategies can also be motivated by the learner's recognition that existing means are insufficient. But communication strategies differ from learning strategies in that the problem arises as a result of attempts to perform in the L2, and the strategies are needed to meet a pressing communicative need. If learning strategies are the long-term solution to a problem, communication strategies provide the short-term answer.

To begin with, communication strategies were discussed in *psycholinguistic* terms. That is, they were treated as the mental phenomena which underlay actual language behaviour. In some later discussions (e.g. Tarone 1981), an *interactional* perspective has been taken. In this, communication strategies are seen as attempts to bridge the gap between the linguistic knowledge of the L2 learner and the linguistic knowledge of the learner's interlocutor in real communication situations. They are characterized by the 'negotiation of an agreement on meaning' between interlocutors (Tarone 1981: 288). Tarone, therefore, sees communication strategies as the learner's contribution to the interactional work required to overcome a communication problem. However, as Faerch and Kasper (1983c; 1984) point out, there are several difficulties with this interactional definition. First, it is difficult to apply to monologue (e.g. writing), when the L2 learner's interlocutor is not present, and there is no overt negotiation of meaning. Communicative problems, however, occur in monologue just as much as in dialogue. Second, the application of a communicative strategy can take place without this becoming manifest in interaction. The learner may realize the inoperability of his initial production plan before he begins to execute it. The substitution of an alternative plan, therefore, can take place with no other signal than a pause, perhaps a slightly longer one than those characteristic of normal production. In Tarone's interactional definition, however, only those communicative strategies that are marked in performance by some form of appeal on the part of the learner are considered. In general, therefore, the psycholinguistic definition is to be preferred. The interactional perspective is best tackled by discourse analysis, which considers the joint contribution of learner and interlocutor, rather than singling out the learner's activity for separate analysis (see Chapter 6).

Communication strategies are employed by native speakers as well as by L2 learners. Most of the communicative strategies listed in the typology in the following section are common to both. They are to be seen as a part of communicative competence. Canale and Swain (1980: 25) identify 'strategic competence', defined as 'how to cope in an authentic communicative situation and how to keep the communicative channel open', as an integral part of the language user's overall communicative competence.

In the light of the foregoing discussion, communication strategies can be defined as follows:

> Communication strategies are psycholinguistic plans which exist as part of the language user's communicative competence. They are potentially conscious and serve as substitutes for production plans which the learner is unable to implement.

A typology of communication strategies

Perhaps because of the problems of definition, there is no generally agreed typology of communication strategies. Various typologies have been proposed by Varadi (1973), Tarone *et al.* (1976), Corder (1978c), and Faerch and Kasper (1980). In addition, typologies relating specifically to lexical problems are provided by Blum-Kulka and Levenston (1978), and Paribakht (1982). The typology provided in Table 7.2 is a summary of that given in Faerch and Kasper (1984). It should be noted that, once again, they refer to production and not reception.

Many of these strategies will be difficult to identify in actual data. Some (e.g. the retrieval strategies) will not be manifest in actual performance at all. Ideally, therefore, the identification of the use of communication strategies needs to make use of introspective research techniques as well as the analysis of speech data.

Empirical research

Theoretical discussion of communication strategies has predominated over empirical research into their use. This is a reflection of the uncertainties of their definition and the consequent problems of identification. Some empirical research has taken place, however, and is rapidly growing.

A number of rather different approaches have been followed. Early research (e.g. Varadi 1973; Tarone 1977) consisted of a comparison of learners' performance on story-telling tasks in their first and second languages. The comparison was motivated by the belief that L2 communication strategies can be identified only if base-line first language data are available. For example, avoidance cannot be said to have taken place if it is also evident in L1 performance. Another rather similar approach involves comparing the performance of a group of native speakers with that of L2 learners on an identical task (e.g. Hamayan and Tucker 1980; Ellis 1984d). A third approach consists of focusing on the use of specific lexical items. This can be done by embedding them in a picture story reconstruction task (Bialystok 1983b) or by asking subjects to label pictures or translate from the L1 (Paribakht 1982). Yet another approach involves the analysis of video-taped conversations between L2 and native speakers (Haastrup and Phillipson 1983).

The results of the available research are suggestive rather than definitive. They can be summarized in terms of the effects of different variables on the use of communication strategies.

1 Effects of proficiency level

The proficiency level of the learner influences his choice of strategy. Tarone (1977) notes that the less able students whom she investigated preferred reduction to achievement strategies. Ellis (1983) also found that one of the learners in his longitudinal study opted for reduction-type behaviour in the earlier stages, but increasingly turned to achievement-type behaviour as he progressed. Ellis (1984d), not surprisingly, found quantitative but not qualitative differences between the strategy use of ESL children and native-speaking English children. The former relied more on avoidance, and the latter more on paraphrase. Bialystok (1983b) found that advanced learners used

Type	Explanation	Example
A. Reduction strategies	These are attempts to do away with a problem. They involve the learner giving up part of his original communicative goal.	
1 Formal reduction strategies	These involve the avoidance of L2 rules of which the learner is not certain (i.e. tentative hypotheses) or which he cannot readily gain access to.	He made him to go ... → He asked him to go ...
2 Functional reduction strategies	These involve the learner avoiding certain speech acts or discourse functions, avoiding or abandoning or replacing certain topics, and avoiding modality markers.	He plays ... → He does sport
B. Achievement strategies	These are activated when the learner decides to keep to the original communicative goal but compensates for insufficient means or makes the effort to retrieve the required items.	
1 Compensatory strategies a) Non-cooperative strategies	These are compensatory strategies which do not call for the assistance of the interlocutor.	
i) L1/L3-based strategies	The learner makes use of a language other than the L2.	
– code-switching	The learner uses a form in the non-L2 language.	I don't have any Geschwester.
– foreignizing	The learner uses a non-L2 form but adapts it to make it appear like a L2 form.	Danish 'papirkurv' → 'papercurve'
– literal translation	The learner translates an L1/L3 form.	Danish 'grøntsager' (= vegetables) → 'green things'
ii) L2-based strategies	The learner makes use of alternative L2 forms.	
– substitution	The learner replaces one L2 form with another.	'rabbit' → 'animal'

Type	Explanation	Example
– paraphrase	The learner replaces an L2 item by describing or exemplifying it.	He cleaned the house with a . . → it sucks in air
– word coinage	The learner replaces an L2 item with an item made up from L2 forms.	'gallery' → 'picture place'
– restructuring	The learner develops an alternative constituent plan.	'I have two . . .' 'I have a brother and sister'
iii) Non-linguistic strategies	The learner compensates, using non-linguistic means such as mime or gesture.	
b) Co-operative strategies	These involve a joint problem-solving effort by the learner and his interlocutor.	
i) Direct appeal	The learner overtly requests assistance.	'What's this?'
ii) Indirect appeal	The learner does not request assistance, but indicates the need for help by means of a pause, eye gaze, etc.	
2 Retrieval strategies	These are used when the learner has a problem locating the required item but decides to persevere rather than use a compensatory strategy.	
a) Waiting	The learner waits for the item to come to him.	
b) Using semantic field	The learner identifies the semantic field to which the item belongs and runs through items belonging to this field until he locates the item.	
c) Using other languages	The learner thinks of the form of the item in another language and then translates it into the L2.	

Table 7.2   A typology of communication strategies

significantly more L2-based strategies and significantly fewer L1-based strategies than less advanced learners. In general, therefore, L2 learners of limited proficiency prefer either reduction strategies or L1-based achievement strategies while the more advanced learners prefer L2-based achievement strategies such as paraphrase.

2 Effects of the problem-source
There is less evidence to demonstrate that strategy choice is influenced by the specific nature of the problem, but this would seem likely. Tarone (1977) notes that code-switching is more likely when the first and second languages have close cognates. Hamayan and Tucker (1980) found that the extent to which L2 child learners displayed avoidance depended on the grammatical structures involved.

3 Effects of personality
Tarone (1977) observes definite differences in her learners' overall approach to story telling. One learner spoke quickly and provided little detail in either L1 or L2 performance, whereas another elaborated and frequently appealed for assistance. She suggests that personality factors may correlate highly with strategy preference.

4 Effects of the learning situation
It would seem probable that learners' use of communication strategies is affected by the situation of use. For instance, learners may use fewer strategies in a classroom environment than in a natural environment, particularly if the pedagogic focus is on correct L2 use, rather than on fluent communication. The situation may also influence the type of strategy used. Piranian (1979) found that American university students learning Russian relied more on avoidance, whereas learners with natural exposure used paraphrases too.

Of central importance in the study of communication strategies, however, is their effectiveness in promoting L2 communication. This has received little attention. Bialystok (1983b) suggests that the best strategy users are those with adequate formal proficiency who modify the strategy to suit the specific concept to be conveyed. Haastrup and Phillipson (1983) argue that L1-based strategies are the least effective and L2-based strategies the most effective. They found that L1-based strategies nearly always led to partial or absolute incomprehension and that non-linguistic strategies did not fare much better. They suggest that paraphrase is the strategy most likely to be successful. However, it may not be appropriate to argue about the relative merits of alternative strategies, as learners often use several communication strategies together, first trying one (e.g. a L1-based strategy) and then turning to another (e.g. a L2-based strategy) to supplement the first choice or to try again if it failed.

The role of communication strategies in SLA

Communication strategies, by definition, are concerned with L2 production. An important issue, however, is to what extent and in what ways they contribute to L2 learning.

Communication strategies have, in fact, been allocated a constitutive role in SLA. Corder (1978c), for instance, characterizes reduction strategies as 'risk-avoiding' and achievement strategies as 'risk-taking'. Faerch and Kasper (1980) argue that a basic condition for communication strategies to have a potential learning effect is that they belong to achievement behaviour rather than reduction behaviour. They base this view on the grounds that only achievement behaviour encourages hypothesis formation, and that risk is essential for automatization. Tarone (1980), however, challenges this view. She suggests that the conversational effect of communication strategies in general is to enable the native speaker to help the L2 learner use the right form to say what he wants. Thus all strategies can help to expand resources. Another argument to reinforce this point of view is that the main contribution of communication strategies is to keep the channel open. Thus even if the learner is not provided with the particular structure he needs, he will be exposed to a number of other structures, some of which may constitute a suitable intake for his learning strategies to operate on. As Hatch (1978c: 434) argues, the 'most important thing of all has to be "don't give up"'. Communication strategies are one of the main ways of keeping going.

It might also be argued, however, that the successful use of communication strategies will prevent acquisition. A learner may become so skilful in making up for lack of linguistic knowledge by the use of various communication strategies that the need for hypothesis formation or testing is obviated. Such learners are not unfamiliar in anecdotal accounts of SLA, but have not been investigated rigorously.

Another issue to do with the role of communication strategies in SLA is what aspect of interlanguage development is affected. In particular it is important to know whether the use of communication strategies facilitates the acquisition of lexis and/or grammatical rules. An argument can be presented for restricting their influence just to lexis. It has been observed that the strategies are common to both learner and native speaker performance. In the case of native speakers, it is feasible to argue that the strategies provide a means by which lexical knowledge can be expanded, but it would be counter-intuitive to argue that they lead to the acquisition of new grammatical rules. If, then, it were to be argued that L2 learners enhance both lexical *and* grammatical development through strategy deployment, it would be necessary to claim that communicative strategies have a different effect for learners than for native speakers. It may be, then, that communication strategies aid the acquisition of lexis rather than grammar.

This discussion of the role of communication strategies in SLA has necessarily been speculative, as there is little hard research. At the moment, therefore, it is difficult to come to any firm conclusions.

Summary

Communication strategies are used by L2 learners (and native speakers) when they are faced by a production problem. They consist of substitute plans and are potentially conscious. A typology of communication strategies distinguishes reduction strategies, which are used to avoid the problem altogether, and achievement strategies, which are used to overcome the problem. The latter can be further divided into compensatory strategies (including both L1 and L2 based strategies) and retrieval strategies. There has been only limited empirical study of communication strategies, but there is evidence to suggest that their use is influenced by the learner's proficiency level, the nature of the problem-source, the learner's personality, and the learning situation. It is not yet clear what effect, if any, communicative strategies have on linguistic development. The issues are (1) which strategies are facilitative (e.g. L2- or L1-based strategies) and (2) which aspects of SLA (e.g. lexis or grammar) are affected.

Conclusion

Peering into the 'black box' to identify the different learner strategies at work in SLA is rather like stumbling blindfold around a room to find a hidden object. There are, perhaps, two main consequences of the attempt. First, it is perhaps inevitable that the focus of attention has been on production rather than reception, as the researcher needs the support of the learner's actual utterances to guide his enquiry. The processes and strategies involved in reception have been neglected, therefore. Second, the mapping of strategies into a tight conceptual framework is bound to be arbitrary to some extent. It is doubtful whether learner strategies can be divided into learning, production, and communication as neatly as suggested in this chapter. This is evident in the discussion of simplification, which has been classified as both a general learning strategy and a strategy of production. It might also be counted as a communication strategy—semantic simplification, for instance, may occur when the learner has experienced a problem with his initial production plan. Researchers differ in the frameworks they provide, because of the problems of identifying and classifying the psycholinguistic events that underlie learning and use. They devote considerable effort to the problems of definition, for the same reason. Increasingly they are turning to introspective methods for studying SLA (see Chaudron 1983b) as one way of gaining greater insight. Understanding language-learner language, however, is not complete without an explanation of the 'black box'. This chapter has attempted to review the various psychological explanations of acquisition and use in order to provide an account of the learner's procedural knowledge.

Further reading

Strategies in Interlanguage Communication, edited by C. Faerch and G. Kasper (Longman, 1983), collects together some of the most important theoretical and empirical studies of strategies.

'Strategies in production and reception' by C. Faerch in *Interlanguage: Proceedings of the Seminar in Honour of S. Pit Corder*, edited by A. Davies and C. Criper (Edinburgh University Press, 1984), provides an excellent summary of empirical studies of the use of strategies.

'Monitoring and the second language learner', by D. Morrison and G. Low, in *Language and Communication*, edited by J. Richards and R. Schmidt (Longman, 1983), is an interesting discussion of one production strategy.

8 The Universal Hypothesis and Second Language Acquisition

Introduction

A number of possible determinants of second language acquisition (SLA) have now been considered—the learner's first language (L1), input/interaction, and learner strategies. One possibility that has not so far been considered is that SLA is governed by properties of the two languages involved—the target and the native languages. Wode (1980b), for instance, proposes that language acquisition manifests 'developmental principles', which he defines in terms of the linguistic properties of the target language. He argues that the order of development is determined by the nature of the linguistic rules that have to be acquired.

This proposal is very different from that discussed in the preceding chapter. There the process of development was explained as the result of inductive strategies operating on the input data. Although these strategies were defined with specific reference to SLA, they must nevertheless be seen as general cognitive procedures which will be involved in other kinds of development, quite apart from language. Wode, however, proposes that there is an independent linguistic faculty that is responsible for language acquisition. The developmental principles he discusses derive from *linguo-cognitive* abilities, rather than general inductive abilities. Wode (1984) makes this quite explicit:

> . . . the kind of cognition required to be able to learn languages must be different from the general cognition or the capacities underlying problem solving or the kind of operations crucial in Piagetian types of developmental psychology.

The claim that language acquisition—first or second—is dependent on a separate linguistic faculty which all human beings possess has already been discussed briefly in Chapter 3. The purpose of this discussion was to provide the background to the study of interlanguage universals. These universals, however, were explained by postulating a 'cognitive organizer' (Dulay and Burt 1977) rather than by considering the formal linguistic devices of the target language. That is, the regularities of SLA were seen as the product of inductive procedures rather than of an independent language faculty. The purpose of this chapter is to explore to what extent these regularities can be accounted for in terms of purely linguistic properties which influence how interlanguages can develop. The key concept in this chapter is that of *linguistic universals*.

The study of linguistic universals has contributed to explanations of SLA in two ways. First, it has been proposed that the linguistic properties of the target language vary in how difficult they are to acquire, according to whether they are universal or language-specific. That is, those properties of the target language which are common to many or all languages are easy to learn in comparison to those properties that are found in few languages, or only in the target language. This approach involves a consideration of just the target language. The second approach involves a comparison of the target and native languages. It has been suggested that the study of linguistic universals can help to overcome one of the major problems of the Contrastive Analysis hypothesis, namely that not all the linguistic differences between the native and target languages result in learning difficulty (see Chapter 2). Linguistic universals can be used to help predict which differences lead to difficulty and which ones do not. Thus, the study of linguistic universals has helped to revamp transfer theory.

This chapter will draw heavily on Chomsky's theory of Universal Grammar and also typological universals. These are explained in the section that follows. The next section considers the role of universals in L1 acquisition, as it is here where the pioneering research was done. Then the role of linguistic universals in SLA is examined, with regard to their effects on grammar formation and on L1 transfer. Finally some of the problems of the Universal Hypothesis are discussed.

Linguistic universals

Two rather different approaches to describing linguistic universals have been adopted. Chomsky (e.g. 1965, 1980, 1981) seeks to identify linguistic universals by the in-depth study of a single language. He argues that only in this way is it possible to discover the highly abstract principles of grammar that constrain the form of any specific grammar. He refers to these principles as Universal Grammar. In contrast, Greenberg (1966) and those following in his path (e.g. Comrie 1981) have set about identifying universals by examining a wide range of languages from different language families in order to discover what features they have in common. The universals established in this way are referred to as *typological universals.*

Universal Grammar

Cook (1985) in a lucid explication of the Chomskyan view of Universal Grammar writes:

> The language properties inherent in the human mind make up 'Universal Grammar', which consists not of particular rules or of a particular language, but a set of general principles that apply to all languages.

Two questions arise from this definition: (1) Why are these properties 'inherent in the human mind?', and (2) What exactly are the 'general principles that apply to all languages'?

Chomsky's explanation for the innateness of Universal Grammar is that without a set of innate principles it would not be possible for a child to learn the grammar of his mother tongue. This is because the data available from the input are insufficient to enable the child to discover certain rules. As those working in the Chomskyan tradition put it, the child's grammatical knowledge is necessarily undetermined by the input data. Felix (1984) gives three ways in which these data are inadequate. First, some structures are so rare and marginal that it would not be possible for the child to obtain sufficient exposure to them. Second, the only way in which wrong hypotheses could be discarded would be if the input were to provide negative feedback, which, in fact, it does not do. Third, the rules of any grammar are highly abstract and so do not reflect the surface properties of the language.

As an example of the kind of argument that is used to justify the existence of a genetically programmed Universal Grammar, consider the following two sentences:

1 We gave the book to the girl.
2 We explained the answer to the girl.

These sentences share the same surface structure, but whereas (1) contains an indirect object and can be rewritten as (3):

3 We gave the girl the book.

(2) contains a prepositional phrase and cannot be rewritten as (4):

4* We explained the girl the answer.

How does the child find out that 'give' takes an indirect object and 'explain' a prepositional phrase? How does the child discover that (4) is ungrammatical? One possible answer to these questions is that the child obtains negative evidence; that is, an adult tells him that (4) is ungrammatical and that this is because 'explain' can take only a prepositional phrase. But research has shown that parents do not provide this kind of information, nor do they correct children's errors very often. It seems logical to assume, therefore, that there must be some innate principle which prevents the child producing sentences like (4). The child must be constrained from wrongly categorizing verbs like 'give' and 'explain' as taking an indirect object or preposition phrase.

Universal Grammar is composed of different kinds of universals. Chomsky (1965) identifies two types: *substantive* and *formal*. Substantive universals consist of fixed features such as the distinctive phonetic features of which sounds are made, or syntactic categories such as noun, verb, subject, and object. Formal universals are more abstract. They are statements about what grammatical rules are possible. For example, it is possible to formulate principles constraining the way in which word order transformations are used to construct questions. Much of Chomskyan linguistics is taken up with the search for formal universals.

Universal Grammar constrains the form which the grammars of individual languages can take. However, it does not do this directly by providing the child with ready-made rules which he can incorporate into his grammar. Rather it sets parameters which must then be fixed according to the particular input data that the child obtains. In other words, formal and substantive universals constitute constraints on the kind of grammar that the child can develop. They delimit the number of options which the child needs to explore. The child, however, still has to discover which of the various options pertain in the target language. This is where the environment comes in: the child needs input data to fix the parameters by selecting the appropriate option.

Those rules that the child discovers with the aid of Universal Grammar form the *core* grammar of his language. However, not all rules are core rules. Every language also contains elements that are not constrained by Universal Grammar. These comprise the *periphery*. Cook (1985) gives some examples. Peripheral rules are those that are derived from the history of the language (e.g. structures like 'the more the merrier', which comes from Old English), that have been borrowed from other languages (e.g. the pronunciation of 'police' comes from French), or that have arisen accidentally. Thus, the child's knowledge of his mother tongue is made up of rules determined by Universal Grammar (the core) and those that have to be learnt without the help of Universal Grammar (the periphery).

Related to the concepts of core and periphery is Chomsky's theory of *markedness*. Core rules are *unmarked*; that is, they accord with the general tendencies of language. Periphery rules are *marked*; that is, they are exceptional in some way. However, marked and unmarked rules are at the opposite extremes of a continuum, and rules can be more or less marked. The relationship between core/periphery and unmarked/marked is shown diagrammatically in Figure 8.1. Rutherford (1982) provides a number of examples of unmarked and marked rules for English. The criterion of markedness that he applies is whether one of a pair of rules or features is more grammatically restricted that the other. Thus the adjectives 'big', 'long', and 'fast' are unmarked in relation to 'small', 'short', and 'slow', because they occur in both declarative and interrogative sentences, while the latter occur only in declarative sentences (i.e. they cannot be used in interrogative sentences like 'How slow can he run?'). Where syntax is concerned, another example is in declarative vs. interrogative sentences. The former are considered to be unmarked, because they can be used to form both statements and questions:

He can run fast.
He can run fast? (said with rising intonation)

while the latter can be used only to form questions. In general, unmarked rules are thought to be less complex than marked rules.

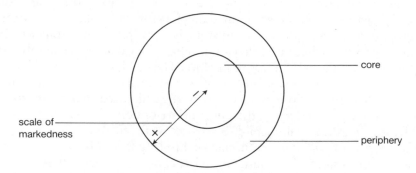

Figure 8.1   Core and peripheral grammar

To summarize, Universal Grammar consists of a set of principles which constrain the options from which a child must choose when learning his mother tongue. The rationale for Universal Grammar lies in what is known as 'the poverty of the stimulus'. That is, the child cannot possibly arrive at a grammar of the target language on the basis of input data alone. Universal Grammar is made up of formal and substantive universals. These help the child to build a core grammar consisting of unmarked rules. But there are also other rules that Universal Grammar does not determine. They form the periphery and are marked in varying degrees.

Typological universals

Typological universals are identified by examining a representative sample of natural languages, taking care to ensure that the sample is free from the bias that might result from concentrating on a single language or family of languages.

Three types of universals have been described; substantive, formal, and implicational. The first two correspond to the universals of Universal Grammar and have already been considered. *Implicational universals* relate the presence of one linguistic property to the presence of some other property or properties. That is, if property x is present in a given language, then it can be assumed that properties y, z . . . n are also present. Two rather different types of implicational universals arise, according to whether the properties concerned are clustered or hierarchical. In a *cluster* the properties are related in such a way that any one of them implies the existence of the others. A good example is the simple clustering of Verb–Subject–Object word order and post-noun adjectives. If a language has one of these properties, then it also has the other. In a *hierarchy* the related properties are ordered in such a way that the presence of one property implies the presence of all the properties higher—but not lower—in the hierarchy. A good example of a hierarchy is the *accessibility hierarchy* for relative clauses (see Comrie and Keenan 1979). This provides an ordering for relative clauses according to the grammatical function of the relative pronoun:

SU > DO > IO > OBL > GEN > O COMP

Table 8.1 gives a key to these symbols, together with examples of relative clauses where the pronouns take the various functions listed in the hierarchy. The hierarchy states that if a language permits relative pronouns with a given grammatical function (e.g. DO), then it will also permit relative clauses with all the pronoun functions higher in the hierarchy (e.g. SU). The languages of the world differ according to the lowest position where relativization can take place.

Symbol	Relative pronoun function	Example
SU	Subject	The man that kicked the dog . . .
DO	Direct object	The tree that the man cut down . . .
IO	Indirect object	The man that she cooked the cake for . . .
OBL	Oblique (in English = object of preposition)	The house that she lives in . . .
GEN	Genitive	The dog whose owner has died . . .
O COMP	Object of comparative	The man that I am richer than . . .

Table 8.1 Types of relative clauses

Universals are also differentiated according to whether they are *absolute* or *tendencies*.[1] Both of these categories apply to the three types of universals—substantive, formal, and implicational. Absolute universals have no exceptions: for example, any language that has verb–subject–object word order will also have prepositions. Tendencies occur when there is a statistical probability of a linguistic universal being found, but there are also exceptions: for example, most languages with subject–

object–verb basic word order have postpositions, but there are exceptions, such as Persian. A universal tendency can, of course, have varying strengths.

Whereas Chomsky claimed that language universals are innate, linguists investigating typological universals are prepared to consider a number of possible explanations. Comrie (1981: 23) writes:

> . . . in many instances, there seems to be no verifiable explanation for even well-established universals; in other instances, different universals seem to require different kinds of explanation, surely no surprise in examining a phenomenon like language which interacts so closely with many other facets of human cognition and behaviour.

Comrie goes on to consider a number of explanations. There may be a common genetic origin for all the world's languages (monogenesis); language universals may be innate (Chomsky's position); certain language universals may derive from the communicative uses to which language is put.

In summary, typological universals are derived from the study of a wide range of languages and language families. Substantive, formal, and implicational universals have been identified. The last mentioned involve examining how linguistic features form clusters or hierarchies such that one feature implicates all the others, or just those higher up the implicational order. Linguistic universals can be absolute, or just tendencies with varying degrees of probability. Various explanations for the existence of typological universals can be entertained.

Linguistic universals and L1 acquisition

The relationship between linguistic universals and L1 acquisition has been most thoroughly explored in terms of Universal Grammar. The relationship between Universal Grammar and L1 acquisition is, in fact, a necessary one, as Chomsky's primary justification for Universal Grammar is that it provides the only way of accounting for how children are able to learn their mother tongue.

Universal Grammar, then, is the solution to what is called 'the logical problem of language acquisition'. The child needs to be constrained from forming incorrect hypotheses. These constraints are not provided by the input data, so they must be part of the child's biologically determined endowment. As White (1981: 242) puts it:

> It is a reasonable working hypothesis that children's grammar construction is limited by the constraints of universal grammar so that they do not have to evaluate the full range of grammars that would be logically possible were they working from inductive principles alone.

Without Universal Grammar it would not be possible for a child to acquire a language successfully.

It follows from this position that the earlier view of L1 acquisition as a process of hypothesis testing (see Chapter 3) needs to be reconsidered. Cook (1985) discusses two interpretations of hypothesis testing. In the first, the child creates a hypothesis by means of inductive procedures and then amends this in the light of the feedback from the environment. Cook argues that this view of hypothesis testing is not tenable, because it would necessitate the child receiving negative as well as positive feedback, and this does not occur. The second interpretation is that the range of possible hypotheses is constrained by Universal Grammar. The child's task is to try out the options available to him and select the one that corresponds to the positive evidence provided by the environment. Cook concludes:

> Hypothesis-testing is a possible explanation for language acquisition only if it is recognised that the child's hypotheses are limited in number and that the environment contributes triggering rather than negative evidence.

As Cook goes on to point out, however, this view attributes a role to the environment that is not insignificant, as the possibility exists that the learner's task might be expedited by the provision of the right evidence at the right moment.

In addition to the logical problem of acquisition there is also the developmental problem. Felix (1984) identifies two related questions to do with this problem: (1) where do the unique constructions so characteristic of SLA come from? and (2) why do children move from one stage to the next? In order to consider these questions it is first important to examine the distinction that Chomsky makes between *acquisition* and *development*.

'Development' is real-time learning of a language. It is influenced not only by Universal Grammar but also by other non-linguistic factors such as memory capacity and general cognitive abilities (which together constitute *channel capacity*). 'Acquisition' is language learning unaffected by maturation and is dependent entirely on the learner's language faculty. To put it another way, if a child were not restricted by memory and processing limitations and by conceptual immaturity, the language he manifested would reflect pure acquisition. As it is, however, these restrictions do apply, with the result that the language he manifests is, so to speak, distorted. The terms 'acquisition' and 'development' correspond to the better-known pair of terms, 'competence' and 'performance'. Acquisition is the evolving linguistic competence of the child. Development is the product of maturation; as the child's cognitive abilities develop, so does his ability to perform his competence. Thus acquisition in Chomsky's view is an idealization. He argues that language is an independent mental organ, but that it is related to other mental organs which jointly determine the developmental order which L1 acquisition researchers have described. However, he maintains that the study of this developmental path sheds little light on 'acquisition'. For Chomsky, therefore, it is the logical rather than the developmental problem which is central, as the developmental problem is concerned, in part at least, with properties that do not belong to the language faculty.

The solution that White (1981) offers to the developmental problem accords with Chomsky's position. She suggests that the whole of Universal Grammar is available to the child from the start, but that there is an interaction between the universal principles and the child's developing perceptual abilities such that certain principles become relevant at different developmental points. The child's perception controls what features of the input data he is able to attend to. The child lets in different data at different stages of development in accordance with changes in his ability to perceive input signals. These data are then used to set different parameters of Universal Grammar. Each interim grammar that the child constructs is an optimal grammar in that it is the best grammar that can be built from the data he is able to perceive.

Felix (1984) offers a different solution of the developmental problem. He argues that White's account effectively excludes the stage-transition aspect of acquisition from the domain of grammatical theory, placing it instead in the domain of cognitive development. He argues that if White's basic premise is rejected (i.e. that the whole of Universal Grammar is immediately available to the child), development can be explained in terms of the linguistic faculty. Felix proposes that 'the principles of Universal Grammar are themselves subject to an innately specified developmental process'. That is, the principles of Universal Grammar gradually unfold over time in much the same way as teeth grow. Individual principles lie latent until the moment for their activation arrives. What makes the child restructure the grammar he has built is the emergence of a new principle which the existing grammar violates in some way.

White's view seems closer to that of Chomsky, who sees the language faculty as a mental organ analogous to other organs responsible for vision, hearing, motor co-ordination, etc. Language does not so much 'develop' as 'grow'. Thus although it is present from the start, the whole of Universal Grammar cannot manifest itself immediately. Non-linguistic factors limit the child's ability to perceive and to produce particular sentence-types. For example, to begin with the child does not have the channel capacity to produce complex sentences, and so the bulk of the principles which have been identified by linguists to date (the focus has been on complex sentence structure) are not applicable at this stage. Felix's view differs from Chomsky's in that he considers that the language faculty is not complete at the start; it develops along with other cognitive abilities.

It would be wrong, however, to suggest that those working in the Chomskyan tradition dismiss stage-transition features of acquisition as solely the product of channel-capacity constraints. They argue that they are in part determined by the language faculty itself. White (1981), for instance, argues that a less marked grammar is easier to acquire than a marked one, because it requires less elaborate triggering experience. In other words, the child finds it easier to acquire the unmarked rules comprising the core grammar of his mother tongue than the marked rules that form the periphery. This is because the unmarked rule is considered to be immediately available to the child, whereas more marked rules require varying amounts of positive evidence from the input. Cook (1985) relates the theory of markedness to acquisition in the following way:

> . . . the child prefers to learn unmarked rules that conform to Universal Grammar rather than marked rules that do not square with it . . . Core grammar and peripheral grammar are weighted differently in the child's mind.

Cook then suggests that there may in fact be two types of learning: core learning and peripheral learning. The former occurs in conformity with the principles of Universal Grammar. The latter involves other mental faculties and takes place when the universal principles are relaxed.

Although the learning sequence does not entirely follow the markedness scale, because maturational processes to do with 'development' interfere, it is nevertheless to be expected that at least some transition features can be explained by markedness theory. White (1981) points out that by recognizing degrees of markedness, predictions can be made about acquisition order. As an example she considers a number of sentences investigated by C. Chomsky (1969):

5 John told Bill to leave.
6 John promised Bill to leave.
7 John asked Bill to leave.
8 John asked Bill what to do.

These sentences are discussed with reference to the Minimal Distance Principle.[2] This states that the subject of an infinitival complement will be that noun phrase to the immediate left of the infinitive. In accordance with this principle, the subject of the infinitives in sentences (5) to (8) ought to be 'Bill' in each case. In fact the principle holds only for (5) and (7). In (6) and (8) the subject of the infinitive is the noun phrase 'John'. Markedness theory predicts that (5) and (7) will be acquired before (6) and (8) because they conform to a principle of Universal Grammar. C. Chomsky's study shows that this is in fact the case.

Related to the markedness scale is another interesting possibility. The acquisition of one universal rule may 'trigger' the automatic acquisition of other rules that are implicated by it. For example, it is conceivable that if a child discovers that the word order of the target language is verb–subject–object, then he will also 'know' that the language has prepositions. Zobl (1983c, 1984) has incorporated this idea of a triggering effect into the 'language acquisition device'. He proposes that this consists of two components. First there are the biologically specified constraints on the form that any natural language can take (i.e. Universal Grammar). Second, there is a *projection device*, consisting of a trigger that activates implicated rules once one rule in a cluster or hierarchy has been acquired.

Also part of the projection device according to Zobl is the ability to compute a new rule on the basis of input, even when the input does not provide any exemplars of the rule in question and the new rule is not actually implicated by another. Zobl argues that the child must possess a projection capacity, because the whole learning process would take too long if it had to rely on input as the source of all target language rules. Zobl's definition of unmarked rules is that they are rules which can be derived by the acquisition faculty without being directly represented in the input. A marked rule, in contrast, is one that requires data before it can be fixed in the child's grammar.

Zobl is interested primarily in SLA, but considers it important to take L1 acquisition as his starting point. Many of the claims made for language universals in L1 acquisition will hold true across acquisition types. A useful starting point for considering the role of universals in SLA, therefore, is to list the various points that have been raised in this discussion of L1 acquisition. These points are:

1 Grammar construction is constrained by the operation of Universal Grammar, which regulates the options the child has to choose from. That is, hypothesis formation is constrained by innate principles.
2 Regularities in the order of development can be explained only by considering both Universal Grammar and channel capacity. A distinction can be made between 'development' (actual progress) and 'acquisition' (the idealized learning that results from Universal Grammar).
3 Universal grammar may unfold as a maturational schedule, as suggested by Felix (1984), or it may be activated piecemeal in accordance with the data that the child perceives at different developmental stages, as suggested by White (1981).
4 The child is likely to learn unmarked rules before marked rules; he constructs a core grammar before a peripheral grammar.
5 The child possesses a projective capacity. This enables one rule to trigger off other rules with which it is implicationally linked, and also enables rules to be acquired when no direct evidence for them has been supplied by the input.

Linguistic universals and SLA

Chomsky has discussed the logical problem of acquisition almost entirely from the point of view of the child. There seems no reason, however, to assume that the language acquisition device atrophies with age. Only if it could be reliably shown that Universal Grammar is in some way 'used up' in the course of L1 acquisition would we be justified in restricting the Universal Hypothesis to children. The available evidence suggests that the Critical Period Hypothesis is not tenable (see Chapter 5). Adults seem to do as well, if not better, than children, and, more important, they manifest a similar developmental route in SLA. It must be assumed, therefore, that the principles of Universal Grammar are still available to the adult and are relevant to SLA. Thus Wode (1984) argues that the learnability axiom needs to be reconceptualized so that it is unrestricted with regard to age, acquisition type and situation. It must be assumed that there is 'a single mechanism for learning languages'.

The role of linguistic universals in SLA is more complicated than in L1 acquisition. This is because SLA involves two languages—the target language and the learner's native language. Thus the L2 learner brings two types of linguistic knowledge to the task of SLA: his knowledge of linguistic universals, and the specific grammar of his L1. Furthermore, he must presumably 'know' which rules in his L1 belong to the core and which to the periphery. It is possible, therefore, to ask two different but related questions. The first is: what use does the L2 learner make of his knowledge of linguistic universals? The second is: does the core/periphery distinction have any bearing on the use that the L2 learner makes of his L1 knowledge? These two questions will be considered separately.

Linguistic universals in interlanguage development

The purpose of this section is to consider how and to what extent linguistic universals contribute to interlanguage development. It will begin by examining a number of theoretical questions, and then review a number of empirical studies.

The first of the theoretical questions concerns the relationship between linguistic universals and channel capacity in SLA. It will be recalled that Chomsky argues that Universal Grammar interacts with other faculties responsible for channel capacity in L1 acquisition. In SLA, however, it is not clear whether the learner is subject to the same maturational constraints as the child. Gass and Ard (1980) suggest that whereas cognitive and perceptual development affect the young child's language abilities, this is not the case for the adult learning a L2:

> . . . patterns in first language acquisition may be much more modified by extra-linguistic exigencies than are patterns in second language acquisition. (1980: 445).

SLA, therefore, might be characterized as 'acquisition minus maturation' (Cook 1985), in that it reflects Universal Grammar in its pure form. The natural order of SLA may be closer to the true 'acquisition' order than the natural order of L1 acquisition. The lack of a significant correlation between the two orders can be explained as the result of the intrusive effect of maturational factors in L1 acquisition.

The assumption that cognitive processes are not involved in SLA, however, may not be justified. Channel capacity still seems to play a part in some aspects of SLA. For example, although L2 learners display the ability to produce fairly long utterances right from the beginning of SLA, they are still likely to resort to semantic simplification (Ellis 1982a: see Chapter 7), particularly in spontaneous conversation. Ellis has suggested that L1 and L2 learners produce very similar kinds of utterances in the early stages of development; the utterances of both types of learners are telegraphic as a result of both propositional and modality reduction. Cook (1975) provides further evidence that speech processing memory operates in SLA as well as in L1 acquisition in relative clauses, and that general linguistic principles apply only when the learner reaches a certain developmental point. Cook (1985) comments:

> The methodological problem is discovering which cognitive processes need to be re-established in a second language and which transferred.

It is not clear at the moment how this problem can be solved.

The second theoretical issue concerns hypothesis testing. In Chapters 3 and 7 hypothesis testing was seen as one of the central processes in interlanguage development. But, as Cook (1985) points out, this view is challenged by the Universal Hypothesis. The arguments against hypothesis testing in SLA are the same as in L1 acquisition. In natural environments the learner is not likely to encounter negative feedback and therefore will not be able to disconfirm certain hypotheses which he might have induced from the available data. Only in classroom settings will sufficient negative feedback be available, and even then it is likely to be erratic and inconsistent (see Allwright 1975 and Long 1977). However, the route of SLA appears to be the same in classroom contexts as in natural settings (see Chapter 9), suggesting that even if negative feedback is available, acquisition is not affected. Cook's conclusion is that hypothesis testing in SLA is acceptable only in the sense that the learner uses positive evidence to fix the parameters set by Universal Grammar.

Empirical studies have examined three related hypotheses to do with the effect of universals in interlanguage development. These are:

1 Interlanguage, like other natural languages, is subject to the constraints imposed by linguistic universals.
2 Implicational universals can be used to predict the order in which properties of the L2 appear in interlanguage.

3 L2 learners learn unmarked (or less marked) properties before marked (or more marked) properties of the target language.

It should be noted from the beginning, however, that there have been relatively few studies of how linguistic universals affect interlanguage. The results, therefore, should be treated circumspectly.

Schmidt (1980) set out to examine whether interlanguage was constrained by language universals. She looked at how L2 learners from five different language backgrounds deleted elements from co-ordinate structures in English. The basic types of deletion possible in English are shown in Table 8.2. Data were collected using four different tasks. None of the sentences produced by the learners exhibited an unnatural deletion pattern (i.e. one not found in the world's languages). The most difficult type of deletion proved to be (3). Schmidt argues that this is because object deletion is more marked than subject or verb deletion. Whereas no natural language permits subject or verb deletion from the main clause, natural languages do exist which permit main-clause object deletion (e.g. English) as well as languages that permit subordinate-clause object deletion (e.g. Chinese). Thus the learner has to discover which type of object deletion occurs in the target language and, until he does so, can be expected to make more errors. Schmidt's study provides evidence in favour of the first and third hypotheses listed above. That is, it suggests that interlanguages obey universal constraints and that more marked patterns are harder to acquire than less marked ones.

Type of deletion	Example
1 Subject deleted from co-ordinate clause	John sang a song and played a guitar.
2 Verb deleted from co-ordinate clause	John plays the piano and Mary the violin.
3 Object deleted from main clause	John typed and Mary mailed the letter.

Table 8.2   Types of deletion in English co-ordinate sentences

Gass (1979) investigated the acquisition of relative clauses by adult L2 learners of English. She compared the accuracy order for different relative pronoun functions with Comrie and Keenan's (1979) accessibility hierarchy and found a close correlation. That is, the easiest position to relativize was that of subject, the next easiest that of direct object, etc. The only exception was the genitive, which proved easier than predicted by its position in the hierarchy. Gass suggests that this may have been because 'whose' is a highly salient pronoun, or because 'whose + noun' was perceived and used as a unit. Gass's study lends support to the second hypothesis. The implicational ordering of rules predicts accuracy (and perhaps acquisition) orders for relative pronoun functions.[3]

It would be interesting to know if the acquisition of one feature low down on the hierarchy could trigger off the acquisition of other features higher up. Gass's (1979) study cannot report on this. However Gass (1982) carried out a study in an instructional setting to investigate this possibility. Students were given instruction on a universally more difficult position in the relative clause hierarchy and were then tested to see if they could generalize their knowledge to an easier position. The results showed they could. However, another group of students were not successful in generalizing instruction on an easy position to a more difficult one. Gass's study suggests that although it is not possible to change the order of difficulty, it may be possible to 'beat' it. However, many more studies are required before such a hypothesis can be accepted. These studies should examine not only the relationship between an implicational *hierarchy* and acquisition, but also that between an implicational *cluster* and acquisition. Ideally such studies should also involve longitudinal data to remove the problem of whether the accuracy/difficulty order is the same as the acquisition order.

There have been several studies that have investigated whether the markedness scale is able to predict the order of development in SLA. Rutherford (1982) and Gass (1984) review a number of these. I shall select one or two studies to illustrate the kind of research that has been undertaken and the claims that have been made.

Wode (1984) uses the acquisition of L2 negation to justify his claim that:

> The developmental sequences seem to reflect the internal complexity of the structure or the structural system to be learned, hence the degree of markedness. It seems that the unmarked or the less marked items are learned early, and the more marked ones later.

Wode claims that the pattern Subject + neg + verb phrase (i.e. preverbal negation) is the unmarked negative form or that its degree of markedness is very low. The principal ground for this claim is that preverbal negation is the most frequent and the geographically most widespread (see Dahl 1979 for an account of the universal properties of negation). Wode notes that preverbal negation appears in the developmental order even if it is not present in either the target language or the learner's native language, as, for example, in L2 English/L1 German. Thus strong typological universals like Subject + neg + verb phrase may occur in SLA irrespective of the formal characteristics of the languages involved.[4]

Rutherford (1982) provides an interesting illustration of how marked-ness factors can influence SLA. He shows that the following acquisitional order for Wh-questions, reported in Burt and Dulay (1980), can be explained by markedness theory:

9 What's that?
10 What are those?
11 I don't know what those are.
12 I don't know what this is.

Simple questions, i.e. (9) and (10), can be considered unmarked in relation to embedded questions i.e. (11) and (12), and are learnt first. Singular, i.e. (9), is unmarked in relation to plural, i.e. (10), and is learnt first. But plural embedded questions, i.e. (12), are learnt before singular embedded questions, i.e. (13), because the 'unlearning' of the inversion rule for simple questions occurs with the last learnt (i.e. plural) question type first.

There are also some interesting studies showing a markedness effect in the acquisition of L2 semantics. One of the best known of these is Kellerman (1979). This study examines to what extent the notion of core meanings in sentences like:

13 I broke the glass.
14 The bookcase broke by falling.

influences SLA. Kellerman found that learners from a variety of L1 backgrounds judged (13) to be more acceptable than (14). He argues that (13) reflects the core meaning of 'break' and is therefore more basic. Gass and Ard (1984) come to a similar conclusion in a study of the aspectual system involving sentences like:

15 I am driving a car now.
16 I am flying to New York tomorrow.

where (15) illustrates the core function of the progressive and (16) a more peripheral function. Once again learners judged sentences like (15) more acceptable than sentences like (16).[5]

All these studies show that language universals may influence how L2 grammars are formed. There is evidence to show that universals place constraints on interlanguage, that acquisition may follow the hierarchical ordering of features, and that unmarked or less marked features are acquired before marked or more marked features. However, it would be premature to draw definite conclusions, both because of the paucity of available research and also because there are a number of theoretical problems (discussed in the final section of this chapter). In addition, it is probably too simplistic to expect a straightforward correlation between linguistic universals and SLA. As Gass (1984) points out, we should not assume that the effect of linguistic universals will be uniform. She comments:

> . . . it may be necessary to distinguish between absolute constraints and an overall shaping factor.

But it is not yet clear how such a distinction is to be drawn.

Linguistic universals and L1 transfer

Markedness theory provides a basis for solving some of the problems of the Contrastive Analysis Hypothesis (see Chapter 2). In particular it can help to explain why some differences between the native and the target language lead to learning difficulty, while other differences do not.

Table 8.3 summarizes the various claims that are commonly made regarding the relationship between markedness theory and L1 transfer (see Hyltenstam 1982b).[6] The basic assumption is that unmarked settings of parameters will occur in interlanguage before marked settings, even if the L2 provides evidence of a marked setting (as in case 4). Thus it is predicted that no transfer will take place from native to target language when the L1 has a marked setting (i.e. cases (3) and (4) in Table 8.3). The most obvious case of transfer is (2), where the native language shows an unmarked setting and the target language a marked one. It should be noted, however, that the presence of an unmarked setting in early interlanguage in such a case need not be the result of transfer, as the unmarked setting is predicted to occur in all four cases. In other words, the unmarked setting is the setting that might be expected to take place if the learner was following Universal Grammar. However, as will be argued below, a case can be made for transfer effects in (2) at least.

Native language (L1)	Target language (L2)	Interlanguage
1 unmarked	unmarked	unmarked
2 unmarked	marked	unmarked
3 marked	unmarked	unmarked
4 marked	marked	unmarked

Table 8.3   Markedness theory and L1 transfer

The next section will examine in detail two claims: (1) L1 unmarked forms are transferred into interlanguage, and (2) L1 marked forms are not transferred into interlanguage.

The transfer of L1 unmarked forms

Zobl (1983c, 1984) argues that transfer functions only as an 'auxiliary evaluation measure'. That is, it takes over when the projection device (which constitutes the primary evaluation measure) is unable or finds it difficult to set a particular parameter of grammar. To put it another way, the learner falls back on his L1 knowledge when the L2 rule is obscure. Zobl describes two main ways in which obscurity can arise. The first is when the L2 is typologically inconsistent. In such cases the normal (i.e. 'universal') implicational relationships among rules are not manifest in the L2, with the result that the projection which the learner makes on the basis of his expectancy that the 'universal' implicational patterns will hold is refuted by the L2 data. The learner solves this problem by turning to his L1, particularly if the equivalent L1 rule is unmarked. The second cause of obscurity that Zobl describes is typological indeterminacy. This arises when the setting of a particular parameter is idiosyncratic, that is it varies across languages so that there are a large number of possible settings. An example is the position of adverbs, which is highly variable in different languages. Again the learner is likely to resort to his L1 to solve the learnability problem. For Zobl, then, L1 influence will be felt only in peripheral rules where there are no universals, or only very weak tendencies.

Viewing the L1 as an auxiliary evaluation measure assigns only a very limited role to transfer in SLA. Transfer is most likely to occur when the L1 construction is unmarked, but Zobl's theory also allows for the transfer of marked forms. That is, if a particular L2 rule is obscure (i.e. marked), so that it cannot be easily derived by means of the learner's projection device, the learner falls back on his L1 and may be prepared to transfer even a marked rule to solve his learnability problem. The condition for transfer to take place is not whether the L1 has a marked construction, but whether the L2 has.

Eckman (1977), however, argues that transfer effects are most in evidence when the L1 setting is unmarked and the L2 setting marked (i.e. case (2) in Table 8.3). He develops what he calls the Markedness Differential Hypothesis. This states that the areas of the target language which will be difficult are those areas which are both different from the L1 and relatively more marked than the L1. He illustrates this with reference to the distribution of voice contrast in pairs such as /t/ and /d/ in English and German. In English this contrast can be observed word-initially (e.g. 'tin'—'din'), word-medially (e.g. 'betting'—'bedding'), and word-finally (e.g. 'bet'—'bed'). In German the contrast occurs only in initial and medial positions but not in final position. Traditional Contrastive Analysis would predict that English-speaking learners of German would have more difficulty than German-speaking learners of English with regard to this contrast. However, Eckman shows the opposite to be true. This can be explained if it is assumed that voice contrast is marked in final position in comparison to the other two positions. English learners of German (case (3) in Table 8.3) have no difficulty in mastering the unmarked form in final position, but German learners of English (case (2) in Table 8.3) do experience problems in mastering the marked target language contrast.

There is another possibility to consider with regard to the putative transfer of an unmarked L1 form. Kellerman (1984) proposes that where the L1 pattern corresponds with a universal developmental stage in SLA, the learner may proceed to that stage faster than learners whose L1s do not have the pattern. He cites Hammarberg (1979), who suggests that English learners of L2 Swedish are likely to miss out the early pre-verbal negation stage because their L1 does not contain this pattern. Thus, as Kellerman puts it, learners can get a 'leg up' the developmental ladder with the help of their L1. The opposite is also possible. If the L1 contains an unnatural pattern that corresponds to an early developmental pattern, progress may be slowed down. Such is the case with Spanish learners of L2 English, who can get stuck on pre-verbal negation because this is the L1 pattern.

The non-transfer of L1 marked forms

There are arguments and evidence to support the non-transfer of L1 marked forms, although they are by no means definitive. Kellerman (1979) suggests that learners tend to avoid one-to-one correspondences between the L1 and L2 when meanings are considered far from prototypical, even though error can result. His work on the semantics of 'break' referred to in a previous section provides a good example. Dutch and English share both transitive and intransitive uses of 'break'. Dutch-speaking learners of L2 English accept both uses in the early stages of development. This might be because they are transferring from Dutch, or it might be because they are responding to evidence of both uses in the L2 data. Later, however, they reject English sentences exemplifying the more marked, intransitive use of 'break', while later still they once again accept both marked and unmarked uses. This leads to what Kellerman calls 'U-shaped behaviour', with error frequency following a low–high–low pattern as development takes place. This study shows that learners may initially transfer both marked and unmarked features, while in more advanced interlanguage they resist transferring marked features. Thus the acceptance or rejection of L1 peripheral features may be complicated by developmental factors.

Less ambiguous evidence for the avoidance of marked forms in L1 transfer is provided by Zobl (1984). He investigated L1 French/L2 English learners' use of 'How many . . .' constructions. French permits extraction of a noun phrase modified by 'combien':

Combien voulez-vous d'oranges?
Combien d'oranges voulez-vous?

whereas English does not:

*How many do you want oranges?
 How many oranges do you want?

Zobl argues that non-extraction represents the unmarked rule, and extraction the marked one. A group of low-level French learners of English showed a strong preference for the non-extracted rule. In other words, they resisted the possibility of transferring the marked L1 rule.

There is also counter-evidence, however. Liceras (1983) investigated preposition stranding (e.g. 'Who did John give the book to?') in English-speaking learners of L2 Spanish. Although preposition stranding is possible in English, it is not possible in Spanish. Liceras found that 43 per cent of her English-speaking subjects accepted stranding in Spanish at the beginner level (i.e. were prepared to transfer a L1 marked form), although at intermediate and advanced levels the marked constructions were generally rejected.

The evidence for the non-transfer of marked forms is mixed. White (1984) argues strongly that learners may have difficulty in 'unsetting' marked parameters in the L1 when they learn a L2. She claims that learners carry over marked constructions from the L1 to the L2. Furthermore, she suggests that once the marked L1 form has been established in interlanguage, it may be difficult to dislodge it, with the result that fossilization occurs.

It often happens that the L1 possesses both an unmarked and a marked setting of the same parameter. 'Combien' extraction in French is a case in point. Kellerman (1979) proposes that in such cases it will be the L1 construction that is most explicit and, therefore, least marked that will be transferred. Zobl's study could be interpreted as illustrating this. Kellerman gives other examples. For instance in pairs like:

17 He claims that he knows it.
18 He claims to know it.

(17) is more explicit than (18), because it contains more grammatical information (i.e. there is a subject and the verb is tensed). A L2 learner with English as his L1 will be more likely to transfer (17). This may occur even if the L2 has only the marked construction.

In conclusion, the theory of markedness offers a number of interesting and plausible hypotheses about the role of transfer in SLA, but there is at the moment no agreement regarding the precise nature of the interaction between L1 and L2 features from the point of view of linguistic universals. The following reflect widely held views, but there are alternative opinions for which at least some evidence can be found.

1 Learners transfer unmarked L1 forms when the corresponding L2 forms are more marked.

2 The effect of the L1 will be observed more strongly where peripheral rules in the L2 are concerned.
3 In general, marked forms are not transferred into interlanguage, particularly when the L1 possesses both marked and unmarked constructions.
4 Marked forms may be transferred in the early stages of SLA.
5 An L1 pattern that corresponds to an interlanguage universal can accelerate or delay SLA, depending on whether the correspondence is with an early- or late-occurring developmental pattern.

Some problems with the Universal Hypothesis

It is intuitively plausible that SLA is at least in part determined by purely linguistic factors to do with the L1 and L2. The Universal Hypothesis is an attempt to explain how these factors operate in interlanguage. It presupposes that there is a relationship between language universals (seen from the point of view either of Universal Grammar or of typological universals) and SLA, such that features that are universal or show a strong tendency to be universal will be easy to learn and so will be learnt early.

So far, however, the application of linguistic universals to SLA has been sparse. It is not possible, therefore, to take the Universal Hypothesis as proven. A number of arguments and some empirical evidence have been advanced in support of it. There are also a number of problems, to which I now turn.

1 Linguistic universals must be seen to have psycholinguistic validity if they are to be treated as a determinant of SLA. That is, it must be assumed that language universals are as they are because of the way the human mind works. It is this assumption that underlies Chomsky's concept of Universal Grammar as an innate faculty in the mind. The problem with an innateness explanation of linguistic universals is that it rules out alternative explanations which may be equally valid. In particular it rules out the kind of pragmatic explanation offered by Halliday (1978). Halliday sees linguistic universals as a manifestation of the types of use to which we put language, while language development (a term that Halliday prefers to language acquisition) is the product of learning how to communicate in face-to-face interaction. In this view of linguistic universals, then, there is no need to treat them as innate. If anything is innate, it is the potential to communicate.

Universal Grammar divorces language from its primary function as communication. As Cook (1985) puts it, Chomsky's innateness theory sets up barriers against the real world:

Competence is separated from performance, grammatical competence from pragmatic competence, acquisition from development, core from peripheral grammar, each abstracting something away from language use.

For many researchers of SLA, this 'abstracting away from language use' is not acceptable.

2 A problem related to (1) concerns the distinction between 'acquisition' and 'development'. There are two points to be made. First, it is not clear how the two can be separated, as there are no reliable means for deciding what aspects of language learning are constrained by the language faculty and what aspects are constrained by cognitive faculties. Second, there seems no obvious reason for preferring to look at 'acquisition' rather than 'development', at least as far as the developmental psycholinguist is concerned. If the aim is to describe and explain SLA, it is important to look at *all* the determinants in order to arrive at a comprehensive picture. To restrict investigation to linguistic universals will be equivalent to agreeing to provide only a part of the total picture.

3 Chomsky's theory of Universal Grammar relies on 'the poverty of the stimulus' argument. To begin with, Chomsky argued that input was degenerate and therefore could not provide an adequate data basis for setting the parameters of a language. This claim has been shown to be empirically unfounded (see Chapter 6). More recently, therefore, Chomsky has argued that data-driven hypotheses cannot explain language acquisition, because of the absence of negative feedback. The learner would have no way of discovering that he had formed a wrong hypothesis. Thus, Chomsky argues that there must be constraints on what hypotheses can be formed, so as to prevent the learner forming hypotheses that would require negative feedback. The problem with this reasoning is the assumption that learners do not produce errors of the kind:

* We explained the girl the answer.

This is an empirical question, but I consider it quite feasible that L2 learners, at least, will produce such errors. It would also be possible (if not very economical) for the learner to disconfirm incorrect hypotheses on the basis of positive evidence alone, provided he was equipped with a device that worked probabilistically; that is, if the learner was prepared to abandon hypotheses after a time when the absence of supporting data suggested that they were improbable. If this argument is accepted, then there is no need to treat the input as impoverished.

4 Kellerman (1984) refers to 'the cavalier attitude to markedness'. Various criteria have been used to explicate markedness—core vs. peripheral, typological frequency, complexity, simplicity, explicitness. It is perhaps not surprising that the same phenomena are classified as

unmarked by one researcher and marked by another. For example White (1984) sees Pro-drop (a rule that specifies that the subject pronoun can be deleted from a sentence) as the marked form, while Hyams (1983) sees it as unmarked. There is also a danger of circularity: an unmarked parameter is one that is fixed early, while a parameter that is fixed early is unmarked. Until reliable and generally accepted means are found for establishing which of two or more forms are marked and unmarked or more or less marked, the whole construct of markedness must be considered of doubtful value for empirical research.

5 The final problem is a methodological one. Chomsky is concerned with describing and explaining *competence*. SLA researchers are, more often than not, concerned with carrying out empirical research, which must necessarily involve them in examining *performance* (see Chapter 1). The question that arises is what type of performance provides the best window for looking at competence. Most of the research reported in the previous section was based on grammaticality judgements. However, as was made clear in Chapter 4, error patterns evident in such tasks are very different from those evident in tasks involving more spontaneous speech. Results are likely to be messy, as a result of different performance styles. This is not a problem, if competence itself is seen as heterogeneous, as suggested by Tarone (1983), but it poses a serious methodological problem if, as Chomsky proposes, competence is viewed as homogeneous.[7] It is not clear what sort of performance best reflects homogeneous competence.

These various criticisms do not invalidate the Universal Hypothesis. They suggest that at the moment its explanatory power may be limited, and they point to methodological difficulties in examining it empirically.

Summary and conclusion

The Universal Hypothesis states that there are linguistic universals which determine the course of SLA as follows:

1 Linguistic universals impose constraints on the form that interlanguages can take.
2 Learners find it easier to acquire patterns that conform to linguistic universals than those that do not. The linguistic markedness of L2 rules explains the developmental route.
3 Where the L1 manifests linguistic universals, it is likely to assist interlanguage development through transfer.

Linguistic universals have been investigated by the in-depth study of a single language. Those working in this tradition argue that there is a Universal Grammar that constrains the kind of hypotheses that the learner can form and that it is innate. An alternative approach to investigating linguistic universals is to study a large number of languages from different language families in order to discover typological universals.[8] A number of possible explanations for universals are entertained by those working in this tradition, including pragmatic explanations.

In both L1 and L2 acquisition the effect of linguistic universals has been investigated primarily in terms of markedness theory. This states that some rules are unmarked or weakly marked and others marked or more strongly marked. Various criteria have been proposed for determining the markedness of a rule. Chomsky proposes that an unmarked rule is one that requires no or minimal 'triggering' from the environment. A typological universal or a strong universal tendency can also be considered as unmarked. There is some evidence to suggest that language acquisition proceeds by mastering the easier unmarked properties before the more difficult marked ones. In SLA there is also some evidence to suggest that when the L2 rule is marked, the learner will turn to his L1, particularly if this has an equivalent unmarked rule.

So far the evidence in support of the Universal Hypothesis is inconclusive. There are a number of theoretical and methodological problems. In particular, the Hypothesis tends to discount pragmatic explanations and ignores variability in interlanguage.

Notes

1 The distinction between absolute universals and tendencies is now also recognized by Chomsky. The distinction, therefore, no longer separates the Greenbergian approach to universals from the Chomskyan approach.

2 The effect of the Minimal Distance Principle has also been investigated in SLA, using the same sentences as in Chomsky's study. Cook (1973) and d'Anglejan and Tucker (1975) found that adult L2 learners also acquired sentences which violated the principle after sentences that conformed to it.

3 Kellerman (1984) provides an excellent review of a number of studies, including that of Gass, which have investigated various aspects of relative clauses. He concludes that the accessibility hierarchy is a good predictor of frequency of relative pronoun functions in SLA.

4 The 'no + V' stage can also be explained in other ways—by vertical construction, for instance. The problems of competing explanations of the same interlanguage phenomena are considered in the Conclusion.

5 There are difficulties in determining markedness relations where lexical or grammatical meaning is concerned, not least because it is difficult to see how they can be determined typologically. The notion

of 'core' meaning that both Kellerman and Gass and Ard invoke appears to be determined intralingually. That is, where two meanings are associated with a single lexical form in a language, one is posited to be 'core' and the other more 'peripheral'. But what is the evidence for this? If the evidence is the learning behaviour of the L2 learners, the argument becomes circular. The 'core' meaning is defined as that meaning that is learned first, but the notion of markedness is then used to explain the learning order.

6 It should be noted that Hyltenstam's summary of the relationship between markedness theory and L1 transfer is based on a binary opposition between marked and unmarked. It may be more accurate, however, to distinguish 'more marked' and 'less marked' on the grounds that markedness operates as a continuum.

7 The distinction between homogeneous and heterogeneous competence is considered in detail in Chapter 4.

8 In order to carry out a cross-linguistic comparison it is, of course, necessary to work on hypothetical assumptions about what the universal categories will be.

Further reading

Relatively little has been published on the Universal Hypothesis in SLA. It may be better, therefore, to start with an account that deals with L1 acquisition. L. White, in 'The responsibility of grammatical theory to acquisitional data', in *Explanation in Linguistics*, edited by N. Hornstein and D. Lightfoot (Longman, 1981), provides a fairly clear statement of the basic Chomskyan position.

B. Comrie, in *Language Universals and Linguistic Typology* (Basil Blackwell, 1981) explains and illustrates typological universals.

There are two overview articles that consider the Universal Hypothesis in relation to SLA. 'Markedness in second language acquisition' by W. Rutherford (*Language Learning* 32/1) looks at various definitions of markedness, and reports on some valuable research. 'Universal Grammar and second language learning' by V. Cook (*Applied Linguistics* 6/1) offers an excellent summary of Chomsky's position and then discusses implications for SLA.

9 The role of formal instruction in Second Language Acquisition

Introduction

This chapter looks at second language acquisition in a classroom setting. It considers whether formal instruction makes a difference to SLA. This is an important issue, because it addresses the question of the role played by environmental factors in SLA. It is also an important educational issue, as language pedagogy has traditionally operated on the assumption that grammar can be taught.

Two broad types of SLA can be identified according to the acquisitional setting: (1) naturalistic SLA, and (2) classroom SLA (see Chapter 1). In Chapter 6 some of the differences in the types of input/interaction associated with these two settings were considered. It was pointed out that classroom discourse can be distorted, in comparison to naturally occurring discourse. An important question, therefore, is in what ways this distortion, which is largely brought about by the attempt to instruct rather than to converse, affects the route and rate of SLA in the classroom. By considering how formal instruction affects SLA, it is possible to address the wider issue of the role of environmental factors.

Language instruction can have many purposes. One of these has traditionally been to teach the learner the formal systems of a L2, in particular grammar, although phonology and lexis are also likely to receive attention. This chapter will be solely concerned with the role of instruction in the acquisition of L2 grammar. It considers *formal* instruction.[1]

In many instructional methods an assumption is made that focusing on linguistic form aids the acquisition of grammatical knowledge, or, to put it another way, that raising the learner's consciousness about the nature of target language rules helps the learner to internalize them. In the case of deductive methods this is self-evidently the case. But it is also true in 'habit forming' methods such as audio-lingualism, as the purpose of the practice provided is to focus on specific linguistic forms, which the learner is encouraged to induce and of which ultimately he will form a more or less conscious mental representation. Of course, the acquisition that results from teaching may not be immediate. Most methods distinguish 'skill getting' and 'skill using' (Rivers and Temperley 1978). Acquisition requires practice of one kind or another.

Another assumption of formal instruction is that the order in which grammatical features are taught will govern the order in which they are learnt. Language syllabuses are organized in such a way as to facilitate the correlation between the teaching order and the learning order. However, both of these assumptions can be questioned in the light of what is known about naturalistic SLA, where learners follow a natural acquisitional route as a result of learning how to communicate in the L2 (see Chapter 3). But although the evidence from naturalistic SLA casts doubt on the assumptions of traditional language pedagogy, it does not refute them. What is needed for a thorough appraisal is evidence about classroom SLA itself.

The investigation of the role of formal instruction can be undertaken in two ways. First, an answer to the question 'Does formal instruction aid SLA?' can be sought. Secondly, the question 'What kinds of formal instruction facilitate SLA the most?' can be tackled. In the first question there is an assumption that all types of formal instruction share certain basic premises and that it is, therefore, possible to talk generically of 'formal instruction'. In the second question there is an assumption that formal instruction in general is facilitative and that the important issue is what distinguishes the more successful from the least successful types.

There can be little doubt that formal instruction can be extremely varied. Ellis (1984a) considers some of the major dimensions of this variance. Consciousness-raising can vary, depending on both the degree of explicitness with which a rule is presented and also the degree of elaboration involved (Sharwood-Smith 1981). The practising of a grammatical structure can also vary according to the intensity of the practice and the particular techniques used. The nature of the target rule is also potentially a significant factor—some rules may be easier than others both to teach and to learn.[2] The instructional goal can be rule internalization or formula memorization, the latter posing a lighter learning burden than the former. But even more important is the learner's perspective; what is intended as an attempt to practise a grammatical rule by the teacher may be seen as a cognitive puzzle by the learner, requiring not language learning strategies, but procedures for getting right answers (see Hosenfeld 1976).[3]

Given the variation that can exist in formal instruction, it is perhaps not surprising that investigations concerning its effects on learning have consisted of comparative studies, aimed at establishing which of several types is most effective. However, as pointed out in Chapter 6, these comparative studies did not succeed in showing that one instructional method was more effective than another. As a result, attention has shifted to the first of the two questions—whether formal instruction *per se* aids SLA. What the different instructional methods had in common was a focus on form, manifested, for instance, in the provision of feedback by the teacher for correcting formal errors (Krashen and

Seliger 1975). Thus, it has been argued not only that it is possible to talk about the role of instruction in general, but that this issue is logically prior to any consideration of whether different types of instruction produce different outcomes. Comparative studies have given way to the investigation of what part formal instruction, viewed generically, plays in classroom SLA.

What then are the criterial attributes of formal instruction? I would like to suggest two (although it is recognized that there may well be others). These are (1) specific grammatical features are selected for the learner's attention, and (2) this attention is manifest in a focus on the formal characteristics of the grammatical features. In terms of these two attributes, formal instruction is taken to include the instruction that results from deductive methods such as cognitive code, inductive methods such as audiolingualism, and, also, instruction based on notional/functional materials where specific linguistic means for realizing various speech acts or semantico-grammatical categories are introduced and practised. It is *not* taken to include instruction where the learner is encouraged to engage in natural communication using whatever linguistic resources he possesses (e.g. as illustrated in the Bangalore Project—see Johnson 1982).[4]

In order to study the effects of instruction it is important to distinguish different aspects of SLA. The role of instruction in SLA must be considered separately in terms of the effect instruction has on the *route* of development (i.e. the general sequence or specific order of acquisition) and the effect instruction has on the *rate* of development (i.e. the speed at which learning takes place) or the *success* of development (i.e. the proficiency level finally achieved). This distinction between route on the one hand and rate and success on the other has also been considered in Chapter 5. It is an important distinction when considering formal instruction because it is possible that instruction may determine both route *and* rate/success, or just one of these.

To summarize, studying the role of formal instruction in SLA is important both for developing a theoretical understanding of SLA and for language pedagogy. In the case of the former, it can shed light on how differences in environmental conditions affect SLA. In the case of the latter, it can help to test basic pedagogic assumptions such as whether the order in which grammatical structures are presented corresponds to the order in which they are learnt. Instruction can take many different forms, but for the purposes of this chapter, the issue to be investigated is not which type of instruction is most effective, but whether formal instruction *per se* has any effect. To this end instruction is taken to imply some form of consciousness-raising, targeted at specific linguistic features. Its effect may be evident on the route of SLA and/or the rate/success of SLA.

This chapter has four sections. The first examines the effect of instruction on the route of SLA. The second examines its effect on the rate/success of SLA. In the third section, explanations of the results reported in the first two sections will be reviewed. Finally, the conclusion briefly considers the implications for both SLA theory and language pedagogy.

The effects of formal instruction on the route of SLA

In Chapter 3 the route of SLA was considered in terms of a general *sequence* of development and the *order* in which specific grammatical features were acquired. The evidence for the reported universality of the sequence and the minor differences in the order came from (1) morpheme studies and (2) longitudinal studies. These studies however were of either pure naturalistic SLA or mixed SLA (i.e. where there was both natural exposure and instruction). This chapter will now consider similar studies of classroom SLA. However, because there have been relatively few such studies, the conclusions that can be drawn must necessarily be tentative. The morpheme and longitudinal studies will again be considered separately.

Morpheme studies of classroom SLA

The morpheme studies can be divided into two groups. In the first group are five studies that investigated *second* language learners. In the other group are four studies that investigated *foreign* language learners.

Three of the studies of second language learners found the same morpheme order in classroom SLA as in naturalistic SLA. Fathman (1975) used an oral production test to assess the grammatical knowledge of two hundred children aged from six to fifteen years, from diverse backgrounds. Some of the children were receiving language instruction, while others were placed in normal classrooms. Fathman found a highly significant correlation between the morpheme orders of the two groups of learners and concluded that the order of acquisition remained constant, irrespective of instruction. Perkins and Larsen-Freeman (1975) investigated the morpheme orders of twelve Venezuelan university students after they had undergone two months of language instruction upon arriving in the United States. They used two tasks to collect data: (1) a translation test, and (2) a description task based on a non-dialogue film. On (1) the morpheme orders before and after instruction differed significantly, but on (2) there was no significant difference. The researchers concluded that where spontaneous speech is concerned, formal instruction does not influence development. Turner (1978) investigated three L2 learners and found that the order of instruction of a set of grammatical morphemes did not correlate very highly with the order of their acquisition. In other words, the teaching and learning orders were different. Taken together, these studies suggest (but do not prove) that formal instruction does not alter the order of acquisition of grammatical morphemes when the learner is engaged in language use and is focused on meaning.

The two other studies of second language learners suggest that instruction can have an effect on morpheme orders, although the effect is relatively minor and not long-lasting. Lightbown *et al.* (1980) investigated the performance of 175 French-speaking students of English on (1) a grammaticality judgement test, and (2) a communication task involving picture description. They found that the scores on (1) improved as a result of the instruction, but that the overall scores fell back later (i.e. when the students were no longer receiving instruction on the grammatical features tested). On (2) they found that the order of various noun and verb morphemes was different from the 'natural' order. This was because the students did worse on the plural than the progressive morpheme, possibly because of the effects of their first language (i.e. in French the '-s' plural ending occurs only in writing). However, when verb and noun morphemes were considered separately, the orders conformed to those occurring naturally.[5] In a later study, Lightbown (1983) found that a similar group of students to those in the first study had 'overlearnt' the progressive '-ing' at one stage of their development. Lightbown suggests that this may have been the result of intensive formal practice of this morpheme at an earlier stage and that highly concentrated practice may have a delayed effect. However, the students did not use '-ing' appropriately, but overextended its use to contexts requiring the third person '-s' morpheme. Later, the frequency of '-ing' declined as the learners began to sort out the respective uses of '-s' and '-ing'. Once again, therefore, the disturbance in the natural order proved to be only temporary.

One of the problems with all the five classroom morpheme studies of second language learners is that the learners were receiving instruction in an environment where it was possible for them to have exposure to the L2 outside the classroom. In other words, the studies may not have tapped the effects of pure classroom learning. Pica (1983), however, mentions a number of studies where such exposure is less likely to have been a confounding variable. Fathman (1978) compared what she calls the 'difficulty order' of learners of English as a foreign language in classes in Germany with that of learners of English as a second language in schools in the United States. In the case of the former, the instruction provided conformed to the two criteria already mentioned: that is, it was structured and required a focus on form. In the case of the latter, little formal instruction was provided. Nevertheless, Fathman reports a positive correlation in the orders produced by the two groups of learners, although she does identify a number of minor differences.

The second study of pure classroom learning that Pica reviews is that by Makino (1979). Makino investigated nine morphemes produced in a writing task by 777 subjects learning English as a foreign language in Japanese secondary schools. The results showed that the resulting morpheme order correlated significantly with the orders reported by Dulay and Burt and by other morpheme researchers (Hakuta 1974 excepted).

The third study that Pica looks at is Sajavaara (1981a). He collected spontaneous speech from Finnish learners of English as a foreign language and found a disturbed order. One of the major differences was in the rank position of the article. Pica notes that both Finnish and Japanese article systems are different from English, but that only the Finnish learners in Sajavaara's study diverge from the natural order.

Pica carried out her own study of the effect of instruction on the morpheme order. She compared six learners of English as a foreign language receiving formal instruction in Mexico City with both a group of naturalistic learners and a mixed group (i.e. one receiving both exposure and instruction) in Philadelphia. Pica looked at eight morphemes and found significant correlations among the three groups and with Krashen's natural order.

The nine morpheme studies referred to are summarized in Table 9.1. What conclusions can be drawn? In general, formal instruction does not appear to have any marked effect on the morpheme order reported for naturalistic or mixed SLA. Only when the data used to compute the morpheme order are heavily monitored (as in the study by Perkins and Larsen-Freeman, for instance) do differences emerge. When data are collected that reflect the communicative uses of the L2 (as in Pica's study, for instance), the morpheme order is either the same as the natural order or differs from it only in the short term and only in one or two features which may have been 'overlearnt'. This general conclusion holds true irrespective of whether the learners are children or adults and, most interestingly, irrespective of whether the learners are in foreign or second language environments. The one exception is Sajavaara's study.

Formal instruction appears, then, to have only a negligible effect on the morpheme order manifest in spontaneous language use. However, as pointed out in Chapter 3, morpheme orders measure accuracy rather than acquisition. In order to obtain a more reliable picture of the effects of instruction on L2 development, it is necessary to turn to the longitudinal studies of transitional structures.

Longitudinal studies of classroom SLA

Allwright (1980: 165) observes:

> Curiously the case-study approach, so central to the methodological baggage of first and second language acquisition researchers, has not, typically, been thought sensible for learners in class.

There are very few longitudinal studies of classroom SLA. The three that will be discussed here are Felix (1981), Ellis (1984a) and Schumann (1978b). The available longitudinal evidence, therefore, is even slighter than that provided by the morpheme studies.

Felix's study is of particular interest, because his subjects were pure classroom learners i.e. they were entirely dependent on formal instruction for L2 input. They were thirty-four German pupils aged ten to eleven years, studying first-year English in a German high school. The general teaching method was a traditional audio-lingual one. The pupils received one forty-five minute period of English teaching for five days a week. In all the study lasted eight months.

The grammatical structures that Felix reports on are negation, interrogation, sentence types, and pronouns. For each structure, parallels were found between tutored and naturalistic SLA. For example, despite daily drilling in negative elliptical sentences (e.g. 'It isn't') during the first few weeks, the pupils were not able to produce correct sentences using 'not' or 'n't', while the few spontaneous negative utterances during this period contained the 'no' operator (e.g. 'It's no my comb'). When main verb negation was introduced (e.g. using 'don't/ doesn't'), many of the children's negative utterances had the negative auxiliary external to the rest of the sentence (e.g. 'Doesn't she eat apples' = She doesn't eat apples). In other words, the children used the highly practised 'don't/doesn't' in an identical way to a naturalistic learner's use of 'no'. Similar examples of forms observed in naturalistic SLA are reported for the other structures investigated by Felix.

Felix concludes that tutored and naturalistic SLA involve the same learning processes and that

> . . . the possibility of manipulating and controlling the students' verbal behaviour in the classroom is in fact quite limited. (Felix 1981:109)

In a classroom where the instruction is very formal, learners are constantly being forced to produce structures they are not ready for. Felix suggests that they solve the problem that this poses for them in one of two ways. Either they select randomly from the structures in their repertoire, irrespective of syntactic or semantic appropriateness, or they follow the same rules that characterize the early stages of naturalistic language acquisition.

Ellis investigated three L2 learners aged ten to thirteen years. They received instruction in a full-time withdrawal situation (i.e. without any exposure to native speaking children). It should be pointed out, however, that English—the L2—was used as a general medium of communication both between the teacher and the pupils and among the pupils themselves. Thus both the classroom and the school environments provided opportunities for the communicative use of English.[6] The language instruction itself was varied, but primarily of the audio-lingual type. The study covered a nine-month period. At the starting point, two of the children were total beginners, while the other was almost so (i.e. he possessed only a few words of English).

Ellis examined negatives, interrogatives, and a number of verb phrase morphemes. All of these structures were formally taught at one time or another during the nine months—some on several occasions. When the communicative speech produced by the learners in the classroom was analysed, it was shown to display a pattern of development more or less identical to that observed in naturalistic SLA. This was true for all the structures investigated. For example, the children's first negative utterances consisted of anaphoric negation (i.e. 'no' by itself or 'no' + a separate statement). External negation followed, first in verbless utterances and later in utterances containing a verb. The gradual replacement of external negation by internally negated utterances took place. Concurrently 'not' replaced 'no' as the principal negator. Ellis, like Felix, concluded that the same processes found in naturalistic SLA were at work. The only difference between naturalistic and classroom SLA that could be observed was that some transitional patterns were prolonged (e.g. the use of uninverted yes/no interrogatives) and some other structures slow to emerge (e.g. past tense forms).[7] Ellis explains this as the result of the distorted pattern of communication which takes place in the classroom. Further evidence for this explanation comes from Long and Sato (1983), who found, for instance, that a characteristic of classroom input is that present temporal reference predominates.

In Schumann's study a deliberate attempt was made to teach an adult L2 learner how to negate. This took place in the context of a longitudinal study of what was otherwise naturalistic SLA. Prior to the instructional experiment the learner's negative utterances were primarily of the 'no + V' type. The instruction covered a seven-month period, during which time both elicited and spontaneous negative utterances were collected. The elicited utterances showed a marked development (64 per cent correct as opposed to 22 per cent before instruction). The spontaneous utterances, however, showed no significant change (20 per cent correct as opposed to 22 per cent before instruction). Schumann concluded that the instruction influenced the learner's production only in test-like situations, while normal communication remained unaffected.

Taking these studies together (they are summarized in Table 9.1), the following can be hypothesized:

1 Instruction does not circumvent the processes responsible for the sequence of development evident in transitional structures such as negatives and interrogatives in naturalistic SLA.
2 When classroom learners are required to produce structures beyond their competence, idiosyncratic forms are likely to result.
3 The distorted input may prolong certain stages of development and slow down the emergence of some grammatical features.
4 Classroom learners are able to make use of knowledge acquired

Type	Study	Type of classroom	Subjects	Proficiency level	Data	Results
Morpheme	Fathman (1975)	ESL United States	260 children aged 6–15 yrs— mixed first language backgrounds	Elementary and intermediate	Oral production test	Morpheme orders of pupils receiving instruction significantly correlated with those pupils not receiving instruction.
Morpheme	Perkins and Larsen-Freeman (1975)	ESL United States	12 university students—recent arrivals—first language Spanish	Intermediate	1 Translation test 2 Spontaneous speech on picture task	Morpheme orders before and after instruction differed on (1) but not on (2).
Morpheme	Turner (1978)	ESL United States	3 students of English as a second language	Elementary	1 Samples of spontaneous speech 2 Diagnostic grammar test	Order of instruction different from morpheme order in spontaneous speech but related to test data.
Morpheme	Lightbown et al. (1980)	ESL Canada	175 Grade 6, 7 and 8 students—first language French	Mixed ability levels— primarily intermediate	1 Grammatical judgement test 2 Spontaneous speech on picture task	Short-term gains observed on (1). Different order on (2) from natural order, but not if verb and noun morphemes are considered separately.
Morpheme	Lightbown (1983)	ESL Canada	75 Grade 6 students (36 of whom studied in Grades 7 and 8 also)	Mainly lower intermediate	Spontaneous speech on picture task	Differences from natural order for a number of morphemes (e.g. '-ing') but disruption only temporary.
Morpheme	Fathman (1978)	EFL Germany	Adolescents receiving grammar lessons, drills, and controlled dialogues	Mixed ability levels	Oral production test	'Difficulty order' of morphemes significantly correlated with order evident in speech of adolescent ESL learners (not receiving instruction) in United States.
Morpheme	Makino (1979)	EFL Japan	777 adolescents and children receiving formal classroom instruction	Mixed ability levels	Written short-answer test	No significant difference between morpheme order of subjects and the natural order reported by Krashen (1977).
Morpheme	Sajavaara (1981)	EFL Finland	Adolescents receiving formal classroom instruction	?	Spontaneous elicitation measure	Natural morpheme order disturbed —in particular, articles ranked lower.
Morpheme	Pica (1983)	EFL Mexico	6 adult native Spanish speakers (18–50 yrs) receiving grammar instruction and communicative language practice	Mixed ability levels	Hour-long audiotaped conversations with researcher	Morpheme order correlated significantly with (1) that of naturalistic group, (2) that of mixed group, and (3) Krashen's natural order.
Longitudinal	Felix (1981)	EFL Germany	34 children aged 10 to 11 years—first language German	Beginners	Classroom speech audio-recorded	Learners (1) selected any structure randomly from repertoire or (2) produced utterances following same rules as naturalistic SLA.
Longitudinal	Ellis (1984a)	ESL Britain	3 children aged 10 to 13 years—first languages Punjabi and Portuguese	Beginners	Communicative classroom speech i.e. where focus was on meaning)	Overall developmental route the same as in naturalistic SLA. Minor differences in order as a result of distorted input.
Longitudinal	Schumann (1978)	ESL United States	1 adult—first language Spanish	Fossilized in early stages	1 Elicitation test 2 Naturally occurring speech	Substantial improvement in overall correctness of negative utterances on (1), but none on (2).

Table 9.1   Empirical studies of the effects of instruction on the route of SLA

through formal instruction when they are focused on form (e.g. in discrete item tests).

However, more research is needed to substantiate these hypotheses.

Summary

Morpheme studies and longitudinal studies of SLA together indicate that although formal instruction may develop L2 knowledge, this knowledge manifests itself in language use only where the learner is attending to form. It does not, therefore, except in relatively minor ways, affect the natural route of SLA which is evident in communicative speech. To use the distinction between *sequence* and *order* of development made in Chapter 3, we can say that the overall sequence of development is not affected by formal instruction, while the order of development is hardly disturbed either. Formal instruction influences knowledge only at the *careful* end of the interlanguage stylistic continuum, not the *vernacular* end (see Chapter 4). These conclusions, however, are necessarily tentative, as there have been few studies of classroom SLA, particularly longitudinal.

The effects of formal instruction on the rate/success of SLA

Studies of the effects of formal instruction on the rate/success of SLA have been more plentiful. Long (1984d), in a thorough review of the relevant research, lists eleven studies. However, all of these studies examined the 'relative utility' of instruction. That is, they were concerned with the overall effects of instruction on L2 proficiency in relation to the effects of simple exposure to the L2 in natural settings. Thus, none of the studies examined the 'absolute effects' of formal instruction, that is, whether instruction could speed up the acquisition of specific grammatical structures. Also, as the studies examined mixed L2 learners (i.e. those who received both exposure and instruction), the studies were not able to say whether formal instruction *per se* was more effective than exposure *per se*, but only whether instruction plus exposure was better than exposure by itself, or whether more instruction plus exposure was better than less instruction and exposure. This is not entirely satisfactory on a number of grounds, which will be considered later. First the studies, however. They will be divided into two groups. The first group consists of the eleven studies considered by Long; these, as noted above, look at relative utility. The next group consists of one study by Ellis (1984a) which looks at absolute effects. All the studies consider the effects on grammatical development only.

The relative utility of formal instruction

Studies of this type can be further divided as follows: (1) those studies that show a positive effect of instruction, (2) those studies that are ambiguous, and (3) those studies that show no effect of instruction.

Long (1983d) discusses six studies that show a positive effect of formal instruction. Two of these compare the effects of different amounts of instruction on students who have received the same amount of exposure. Four others investigate the relationship between different amounts of instruction and exposure and the students' proficiency levels. Altogether the studies cover children and adults, a range of proficiency levels, and different target languages. Also the tests used to measure proficiency levels were both of the discrete point (e.g. multiple choice) and integrative (e.g. cloze) types.

The procedure adopted by Krashen and Seliger (1976) and Krashen, Seliger, and Hartnett (1974) was to match pairs of students who had had the same amount of exposure but different periods of formal instruction (i.e. to hold the exposure factor constant in order to gauge the effects of the instruction factor). Both studies found that those students with more instruction scored higher on proficiency tests than those with less. However, as Long points out, it is not possible to be sure that it is instruction *per se* that is having the effect, as, presumably, those students with more instruction experienced more overall contact with the L2. Thus the results obtained could be explained in terms of the amount of total contact (i.e. total instruction time plus total exposure time). In order to claim a positive effect for formal instruction, it is necessary to show that when students are matched for instruction but differ in exposure (i.e. the instruction factor is held constant in order to investigate the exposure factor), there is no corresponding positive effect for exposure. In both studies this was in fact found to be the case, suggesting that the positive effect observed for instruction was not just the result of more overall contact time. However, a study by Martin (1980) did find a positive effect for exposure when instruction was controlled for.[8] In conclusion, therefore, the studies by Krashen and Seliger (1976) and by Krashen, Seliger, and Hartnett (1974) suggest that instruction is helpful, but the evidence is uncertain.

The procedure used by the other four studies (Krashen *et al.* 1978; Brière 1978; Carroll 1967; Chihara and Oller 1978) that also showed a positive effect for instruction was to measure statistically the degree of fit between the amount of instruction and exposure experienced by different students on the one hand, and proficiency scores on the other. All four studies found a positive relationship between instruction and proficiency, but only three found a similar relationship between exposure and proficiency. Also the strength of the relationship with instruction was stronger in two of the studies, and weaker in only one.

In general, then, instruction was a better predictor of proficiency level than exposure. However, once again it is difficult to separate out the effects of instruction and exposure in this type of study.

Long discusses two studies with ambiguous results (Hale and Budar 1970, and Fathman 1976). In both cases the studies themselves produced results that indicated instruction was not helpful. Hale and Budar, for instance, wrote:

> It appears that those (students) who spent two or three periods of the six period day in special TESOL classes were being more harmed than helped. (Hale and Budar 1970: 297)

They argued that those students who attained the highest proficiency in the shortest possible time were those who underwent total immersion in the English language and culture. Long, however, rightly points out that because of the design of Hale and Budar's study, variables such as instruction, socio-economic background, amount of exposure, and parental attitudes are conflated so that it is not possible to determine reliably which were responsible for the differences in observed proficiency levels. Long also shows that methodological problems cast doubts on Fathman's results.

Three studies (Upshur 1968; Mason 1971; Fathman 1975) show no advantage for instruction. In each case the comparison made was between instruction plus exposure and exposure only, with the total contact time kept equal. Long argues that despite the negative results, there are some indications that instruction helped, although not sufficiently for the results to reach statistical significance.

Taking all these studies together (they are summarized in Table 9.2), Long claims that 'there is considerable evidence to indicate that SL instruction does make a difference' (1983d: 374). He argues that its effects hold (1) for children as well as adults, (2) for intermediate and advanced learners as well as beginners, (3) on integrative as well as discrete point tests, and (4) in acquisition-rich as well as acquisition-poor environments. (3) is significant, because it suggests that instruction aids communicative performance, which integrative tests are supposed to measure, as well as monitored performance of the kind observed in discrete point tests. (4) is a contradiction of a hypothesis put forward by Krashen to the effect that instruction will be of value in acquisition-poor environments, where the learner may not be able to obtain adequate input through exposure, but of no significant value in acquisition-rich environments, where there is plenty of comprehensible input. In Long's assessment of the available research, the effects of formal instruction are comprehensive.

The absolute effects of formal instruction

The kinds of studies reported above do not shed any light on what actually happens when formal instruction takes place. If it does aid SLA, how does it do so? Ellis (1984e) set out to examine this. He measured the effects of three hours of instruction on the form and meaning of WH questions to a group of thirteen elementary L2 learners aged between ten and fifteen years. Two of the subjects were the learners investigated in the longitudinal study discussed earlier. This showed that at the time of the instruction, WH interrogatives had begun to appear in their communicative speech. As these two children were gauged to be slightly below average for the group as a whole, it could be surmised that WH interrogatives were within the subjects' 'zones of proximal development' (Vygotsky 1962); that is, the learners were developmentally 'ready' for WH questions. However, the results showed that for the group as a whole there was no significant increase in the children's ability to use semantically appropriate and grammatically well-formed WH questions as a result of the instruction. Some of the children, though, did show a marked individual improvement. To establish whether this could be put down to the instruction they received, Ellis measured the participation of each pupil in instructional exchanges in one of the lessons. He found that it was the low interactors rather than the high interactors who progressed in ability to use the WH question which was the target of this lesson. Thus active involvement in formal language instruction did not appear to facilitate SLA.

This study cannot claim to show that formal instruction has no absolute effect—many more confirmatory studies would be required to reach such a conclusion—but it does indicate that the relative utility of instruction may not result from the acquisition of those structures that constitute the pedagogic targets of lessons. This point is taken up later.

Discussion

There are a number of problems with the studies reported in this section, which cast doubts on Long's optimistic conclusion regarding the positive effect of formal instruction. As already noted in the six studies which reported that instruction is helpful, there is the problem of determining whether the effects observed were the result of the instruction itself, or simply of more contact opportunity. Also there is the problem of the learner's motivation. This can influence the results in several ways. For instance, learners who are highly motivated are more likely to seek out instruction (or more instruction) than learners who are not so highly motivated. Thus the effects of motivation will be confounded with those of instruction. In some of the studies (e.g. Hale and Budar 1970) the learners were not given any choice about whether

Type	Study	Type of classroom	Subjects	Proficiency	Data	Results
Relative utility	Carroll (1967)	Foreign language learning in United States (exposure abroad)	Adults—first language English	All proficiency levels	Integrative test	Both instruction and exposure help, but exposure helps most.
Relative utility	Chihara and Oller (1978)	EFL in Japan	Adults—first language Japanese	All proficiency levels	1 Discrete point test 2 Integrative test	Instruction helps, but exposure does not.
Relative utility	Krashen, Seliger and Hartnett (1974)	ESL in United States	Adults—mixed first languages	All proficiency levels	Discrete point test	Instruction helps, but exposure does not.
Relative utility	Brière (1978)	Spanish as a second language in Mexico	Children—local Indian language is first language	Beginners	Discrete point test	Both instruction and exposure help, but instruction helps most.
Relative utility	Krashen and Seliger (1976)	ESL in United States	Adults—mixed first languages	Intermediate and advanced	Integrative test	Instruction helps, but exposure does not.
Relative utility	Krashen et al. (1978)	ESL in United States	Adults—mixed first languages	All proficiency levels	1 Discrete point test 2 Integrative test	Both instruction and exposure help, but instruction helps most.
Relative utility	Hale and Budar (1970)	ESL in United States	Adolescents—mixed first languages	All proficiency levels	1 Discrete point test 2 Integrative test	Exposure helps but instruction does not—results doubtful, however.
Relative utility	Fathman (1976)	ESL in United States	Children—mixed first languages	All proficiency levels	Integrative test	Exposure helps but instruction does not—results doubtful, however.
Relative utility	Upshur (1968)	ESL in United States	Adults—mixed first languages	Intermediate and advanced	Discrete point test	Instruction does not help.
Relative utility	Mason (1971)	ESL in United States	Adults—mixed first languages	Intermediate and advanced	1 Discrete point test 2 Integrative test	Instruction does not help.
Relative utility	Fathman (1975)	ESL in United States	Children—mixed first languages	All proficiency levels	Integrative test	Instruction does not help.
Absolute effect	Ellis (1984e)	ESL in Britain	Children—mixed first languages	Post-beginner level	Spontaneous speech from picture task	Instruction had no overall effect on production of WH questions—individual development not related to instructional opportunities.

Table 9.2   Empirical studies of the effects of instruction on the rate/success of SLA

they should receive instruction. In such instances they may have resented the instruction (Hale and Budar report just this), with the result that they were less likely to benefit from it. Finally, it is not clear in what way formal instruction is supposed to aid SLA. With the exception of Ellis's study, there was no account of what went on in the classrooms themselves.

However, to deny that instruction can help learners to acquire a L2 is not only counter-intuitive, but contrary to the personal experience of countless teachers and students. In broad terms, therefore, Long's review of the research only confirms a common-sense assumption. What is of interest, however, is not so much *whether* formal instruction facilitates the rate/success of SLA, but *how*. On this score the studies are not helpful. As a result it is necessary to try to seek a theoretical rather than empirical answer. This is the aim of the following section.

Summary

Studies of the relative utility of formal instruction have produced mixed results, but in general support the hypothesis that instruction aids the rate/success of SLA. It is not clear, however, whether it is instruction *per se* or some associated factor such as motivation which is responsible for the observed effects—both positive and negative. It is also not clear how instruction leads to more rapid development, particularly as there is some evidence to suggest that formal instruction may not have any absolute effect.

Explaining the role of instruction

A review of empirical research into the effects of formal instruction on SLA has indicated that although instruction has no apparent effect on the sequence of development and very little on the order of development, it does have relative utility where the rate/success of SLA is concerned. Any explanation of the role of instruction in SLA will have to account for these results. This section will consider three possible explanations in the light of the empirical research reported in the previous section. These are (1) the non-interface position, (2) the interface position, and (3) the variability position.

The non-interface position

The non-interface position has been advanced most strongly by Krashen (1982). Krashen, it will be recalled, identifies two types of linguistic knowledge in SLA. 'Acquisition' occurs automatically when the learner engages in natural communication where the focus is on meaning and where there is comprehensible input. 'Learning' occurs as a result of formal study where the learner is focused on the formal properties of the L2. 'Acquired' knowledge consists of subconscious L2 rules which the learner can call upon automatically; 'learnt' knowledge consists of metalingual knowledge which can only be used to monitor output generated by means of 'acquired' knowledge. Krashen argues that the two knowledge types are entirely separate and unrelated. In particular he disputes the view that 'learnt' knowledge is converted into 'acquired' knowledge. He writes:

> A very important point that also needs to be stated is that learning does not 'turn into' acquisition. The idea that we first learn a new rule, and eventually, through practice, acquire it, is widespread and may seem to some people to be intuitively obvious . . . Language acquisition . . . happens in one way, when the acquirer understands input containing a structure that the acquirer is 'due' to acquire, a structure at his or her 'i + 1'. (1982: 83–4)

This is the non-interface position.

Krashen advances a number of reasons for the separateness of 'acquired' and 'learnt' knowledge:

1 There are plenty of cases of 'acquisition' where no 'learning' has occurred. These are widely reported in studies of naturalistic SLA.
2 There are cases where 'learning' has taken place but where it has failed to become 'acquisition'. Krashen refers to the case of 'P' (Krashen and Pon 1975), who had 'learnt' rules like the third person singular '-s', but was unable to use them in casual conversation because she had not yet 'acquired' them.
3 Even the best 'learners' can master only a small sub-set of the grammatical rules of the L2. This is because most of the rules are far too difficult for the average 'learner' to follow. Krashen points out that it often takes a linguist years to describe successfully rules that are easily 'acquired'.

Krashen does acknowledge that sometimes a rule can be 'learnt' before it is 'acquired'. However, he argues that this does not establish that 'learning' is a prerequisite of 'acquisition'. In Krashen's view, having 'learnt' a rule does not preclude having to 'acquire' it later on.

Evidence that shows that learners can often articulate formal rules of grammar but cannot use them correctly in spontaneous communication lends some support to the non-interface position. Seliger (1979) carried out an interesting study to investigate whether this was in fact the case. He asked a number of adult classroom learners to describe some pictures and then analysed their use of 'a/an' in the speech they produced. He also asked the learners to state the relevant rule. The results showed clearly that there was no relationship between actual performance and conscious knowledge of the rule. This was so, despite the fact that many learners believed that their knowledge of the rule had guided their performance. One interpretation of Seliger's study is that 'learning' and 'acquisition' are indeed separate, although other explanations are also possible, as will become clearer later.

How does the non-interface position account for the results of the empirical research? It provides a clear explanation of why formal instruction fails to have any substantial effect on the route of SLA. This route is a reflection of 'acquisition' and will become evident only in data taken from spontaneous speech. Formal instruction is directed at consciousness-raising and so, presumably, affects only 'learning'. Thus, although classroom learners may 'learn' rules, they do not manifest them in natural conversation until they have 'acquired' them. By positing that 'acquisition' and 'learning' are completely separate, Krashen is able to explain why formal instruction is apparently powerless to subvert the natural sequence of development. The teacher's syllabus is a 'learning' syllabus; the learner's own in-built syllabus is an 'acquisition' syllabus.

However, it is not immediately so apparent how the non-interface position can explain the positive effect that formal instruction has on the rate/success of SLA. It might be expected that classroom environments will slow down SLA rather than speed it up, given that formal instruction only aids 'learning'. However, Krashen develops arguments to protect his theory against such a criticism.

Krashen (1982), in fact, claims that the classroom can do much better than informal environments, just as the empirical research shows. He argues this is particularly so in the case of the adult beginner. Beginners are likely to experience difficulty in obtaining comprehensible input (the source of 'acquisition') in natural settings, but are much more likely to obtain it in the classroom. Thus although the outside world may supply more input to the learner, the classroom is better equipped to ensure that the right kind of qualitative input needed for 'acquisition' is available. These arguments are a development of Krashen (1976), where a distinction is made between 'exposure-type' and 'intake-type' environments. Many adults are likely to experience only 'exposure-type' environments in a natural setting and thus will not obtain the necessary input adjusted to ensure comprehension. In contrast, classrooms are much more likely to ensure that 'intake-type' environments occur and so meet the conditions by which 'acquisition' can take place. However, the contribution of classroom settings is not so much a product of formal instruction as of the provision of comprehensible input as a result of successful communication taking place. Krashen (1982) summarizes his position with regard to the role in the classroom:

> The value of second language classes, then, lies not only in the grammar instruction, but in the 'teacher talk', the comprehensible

input. It can be an efficient place to achieve at least the intermediate levels rapidly, as long as the focus of the class is on providing input for acquisition. (1982: 59).

What evidence is there that 'acquisition' can take place in the classroom? Terrell *et al.* (1980) carried out a study to investigate whether classroom learners could 'pick up' structures which were not part of the explicit teaching syllabus. They found that junior high school students of Spanish as a L2 successfully acquired question forms without any direct teaching. Terrell *et al.* point out that this result can be explained only by the students having internalized the syntax of Spanish questions as a result of answering the large number of teacher questions used to drill other structures. In other words, the study by Terrell *et al.* shows that the 'acquisition' of one linguistic rule can occur when the instruction is directed at 'learning' other linguistic rules. Their study provides one reason why formal instruction may have only a relative and not an absolute effect. Krashen argues that when instruction is not formal (i.e. is geared to communication), 'acquisition' is even more likely in the classroom.

To summarize, the non-interface position explains the results of the empirical studies which have investigated the effects of formal instruction on SLA by positing that there are two types of linguistic knowledge that are entirely unrelated. Formal instruction does not affect the developmental route, because the 'learning' which it produces is powerless to alter the sequence of development that occurs through 'acquisition'. However, classrooms foster more rapid development because they constitute 'intake environments', whereas for many learners, particularly adults, natural settings only afford 'exposure environments' and thus do not enable 'acquisition' to take place. It is not, however, formal instruction *per se* that enhances development.

Superficially, Krashen's non-interface position appears to account for the results of the empirical research. However, there are a number of problems:

1 The first problem has to do with the fact that the empirical research discussed in the previous sections has presumably examined the effects of classrooms where the bulk of the instruction was formal rather than communicative. This being so, Krashen is in the position of having to argue that the positive effects on rate/success of SLA that were shown to arise have nothing to do with the formal instruction itself, but, as illustrated in the study by Terrell *et al.*, are the incidental results of 'picking up' structures from the classroom input which occurs in the process of the instruction. Krashen claims that instruction which is communicative rather than formal will lead to faster development. However, this can be demonstrated only by comparative and method studies. Krashen reviews a number of

different methods to determine to what extent they are likely to supply comprehensible input, and uses the results of the available empirical research of the comparative effects of different methods (such as Audio-lingualism, Cognitive Code, Total Physical Response, and the Natural Method) to support his argument that it is comprehensible input, rather than formal instruction, that aids development. However, Krashen does not refer to any studies which have directly compared methods based on formal grammar teaching of one kind or another and methods based on providing opportunities for authentic communication. Indeed, the one such study that is mentioned in a footnote in Krashen (1981a)—Palmer (1978)—produced results that do not support Krashen's claim. Until more such studies have been carried out, Krashen's position must be treated as speculative. For many teachers—and researchers—a more intuitively satisfying explanation of the positive effects found for formal instruction will be that it is the focus on form, rather than just the 'intake-environment', that is responsible.

2 Long (1983d) has pointed out that as children are not supposed to 'learn' but only to 'acquire', they ought to benefit less from formal instruction than adults. However, the research indicates that children profit from formal instruction just as much as adults. Once again it might be possible to 'immunize' the non-interface position by claiming (as Krashen does) that the advantages of the classroom environment consist of the provision of opportunities for 'acquisition' rather than 'learning'. But, as children are considered to have fewer problems than adults in obtaining comprehensible input outside the classroom, they should be less reliant on the classroom for 'acquisition', so the research should show a greater effect for instruction on adults than for instruction on children. This prediction, however, is not borne out. Thus, whereas Krashen anticipates that instruction will have a differential effect on adults and children, this does not, in fact, occur.

3 Long (1983d) also notes that instruction ought to show a greater effect on beginners than on advanced learners, as Krashen claims that it is possible to 'learn' only easy grammatical rules. Again, however, the research does not support such a claim; advanced learners also appear to benefit from formal instruction. Where 'acquisition' is concerned, Krashen also argues that classrooms aid the beginner more than the advanced learner, as the latter is in a better position to obtain comprehensible input outside the classroom. But the finding that advanced learners also benefit from instruction, even when acquisition-rich environments are available in natural settings, runs counter to Krashen's prediction.

4 Another point raised by Long is that the effects of classroom 'learning' ought to be observed only on discrete-point tests, but that the research shows that instruction also leads to improved scores on integrative tests, which in Krashen's terms ought to tap 'acquired' knowledge.

These are serious criticisms of the non-interface position. They can be resolved without abandoning the basic position, if, as Long suggests, greater weight is attributed to 'learning' by redefining it as involving more than knowledge of 'easy' rules and accepting that it can aid performance on integrative as well as discrete-point tests. Another solution, however, lies in rejecting the 'acquisition/learning' schism and adopting an interface position.

The interface position

The interface position states that although the learner possesses different kinds of L2 knowledge, these are not entirely separate, with the result that 'seepage' from one knowledge type to the other occurs. It is possible to distinguish a weak and a strong interface position.

A weak interface position has been proposed by Seliger (1979). Seliger argues that the conscious rules which learners 'learn' as a result of formal instruction are anomalous, in that different learners end up with different representations of the rules they have been taught. The rules that are 'learnt' do not describe the internal knowledge that is called upon in natural communication, so, not surprisingly, they cannot be held responsible for actual language behaviour. However, pedagogical rules do serve a purpose. They act as 'acquisition facilitators' by focusing the learner's attention on 'critical attributes of the real language concept that must be induced' (Seliger 1979: 368). Thus they help to make the inductive hypothesis testing process more efficient. Seliger also suggests that pedagogical rules can serve as mnemonics for retrieving features of an internal rule which are rarely used by the learner. In other words, Seliger accepts that the internalization of rules is a different process from that involved in learning pedagogical rules, but believes that knowledge of a pedagogical rule (1) may make the internalization of the rule easier when the learner is 'ready' to undertake this, and (2) may facilitate the use of features which, although 'acquired', are still only 'shallow'. However, Seliger does not propose that 'learnt' knowledge (or pedagogical rules) are converted into 'acquired' (or internalized) knowledge.

In contrast Stevick (1980) develops a model of SLA (which he calls the Levertov Machine) which does allow for a flow of knowledge from 'learning' to 'acquisition' and vice versa. He suggests that 'learning' may relate to secondary memory (which is capable of holding material for longer than two minutes, but from which material is gradually lost unless it is occasionally used), and that 'acquisition' may relate to tertiary memory (which contains material that is never lost, even if it is not used). Stevick, like Krashen, sees 'acquisition' as the product of communicative experience, but argues that this can make use of material that has been recently memorized and is part of secondary memory. When this happens, there is the possibility that the material transfers into tertiary memory, i.e. 'learning' becomes 'acquisition'.

Bialystok (see Bialystok and Fröhlich 1977; Bialystok 1979 and 1981) also develops a model of SLA based on two types of knowledge which can interact. She calls these knowledge types 'implicit' and 'explicit', but it is clear from her description of them that they correspond fairly closely to Krashen's 'acquired/learnt' types. Bialystok suggests that *practice* serves as the mechanism by which explicit knowledge turns into implicit knowledge. Thus implicit knowledge can be built up in two different ways: (1) the primary means is 'unconscious acquisition', and (2) the secondary means is through the automatizing of explicit knowledge by practice.

One way, then, in which 'acquired' and 'learnt' may be connected is in terms of automaticity. This is a view developed by McLaughlin (1978b) in his attack on Krashen's non-interface position. McLaughlin refers to Schneider and Shriffin's (1977) distinction between 'controlled' and 'automatic' processing. Controlled processing requires active attention, so that only a limited number of features can be controlled at a time without interference occurring. 'Automatic' processing takes place without active control or attention. The important point is that 'automatic processes are learned following the earlier use of controlled processes' (McLaughlin 1978b: 319). Thus SLA entails going from the controlled to the automatic mode of operation. It is, therefore, not necessary to presuppose two unconnected knowledge types such as the 'acquired/learnt' distinction.

Sharwood-Smith (1981) builds on the work of Bialystok and McLaughlin and develops a full interface model to account for the role of formal instruction in SLA. He argues that such instruction serves as the means by which consciousness-raising can take place, and the resulting explicit knowledge is practised until it is automatized. He writes:

> Whatever the view of the underlying processes in second language learning . . . it is quite clear and uncontroversial to say that most spontaneous performance is attained by dint of practice. In the course of actually performing in the target language, the learner gains the necessary control over its structures such that he or she can use them quickly without reflection. (1981: 166)

Figure 9.1 reproduces Sharwood-Smith's model. The learner can produce L2 output in three different ways: (1) using just implicit knowledge, (2) using just explicit knowledge, and (3) using both explicit and implicit knowledge. The learner's own utterances constitute part of the input to the learner's language learning mechanisms. The other part of the input is made up by the other speaker's utterances. The total input provides information which can lead the learner to alter the composition of either his implicit or his explicit knowledge, or both. It follows from this model that performance that is planned entirely or partly on the basis of explicit knowledge which is lacking in automaticity can provide feedback into implicit knowledge; if this happens often enough (i.e. through practice), the explicit knowledge can become fully automated as part of implicit knowledge.

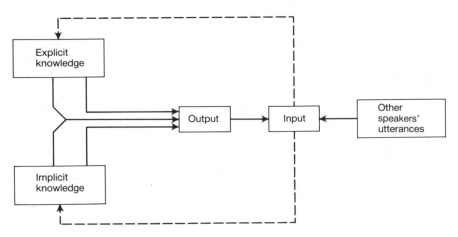

Figure 9.1   Linguistic input and output: three potential sources of feedback (Sharwood-Smith 1981: 166)

How well do the weak and the strong interface positions account for the results of empirical research into the effects of formal instruction? The weak position can comfortably account for both the failure to find any positive effect on the route of SLA and for the finding that formal instruction does influence the rate/success of development. The strong position can account for the rate/success finding, but is less comfortable with the route finding.

The weak position, as advanced by Seliger, acknowledges that pedagogical rules will not alter the sequence in which L2 rules are naturally 'acquired', as their effect will be felt only when the learner is 'ready' to acquire the rules. However, pedagogical rules will enhance the speed of development, because they make the 'acquisitional' process shorter. Because the learner is 'primed' by his knowledge of the pedagogical rule, he takes less time to perceive and internalize the salient features of the rule.

The strong position, advocated by Stevick, Bialystok, McLaughlin, and Sharwood-Smith, provides a convincing explanation of why classroom learners outstrip naturalistic learners, even when the measure of proficiency is one that ought to favour 'acquisition' (i.e. an integrative test). Classroom learners have the advantage that they can augment their implicit or 'acquired' knowledge in two ways: (1) directly, by means of the 'intake environment' supplied by the classroom, and (2) indirectly, by automatizing explicit knowledge through practice. In contrast, naturalistic learners will be almost entirely reliant on (1). It is not so clear, however, how the strong position can explain the absence of any major effect for instruction on the route of SLA. If, as is suggested, explicit knowledge can turn into implicit knowledge when it is automatized, learners who receive formal instruction that practises specific linguistic forms ought to manifest these in the acquisition order, even if they would not 'naturally' occur until later. In other words, teaching grammar ought to subvert the natural order. There is some evidence to suggest that this does in fact take place (recall Lightbown's (1983) observation that 'overlearnt' forms can intrude into the natural order), but only to a very limited extent, nothing like as much as Sharwood-Smith's model seems to predict. The route from explicit to implicit knowledge is a very restricted one.

One of the problems of the interface position is that it still assumes that L2 knowledge can be dichotomized as 'acquired/learnt', or implicit/explicit. It also accepts Krashen's view that 'acquired' knowledge is in some way primary and 'learnt' knowledge secondary. The alternative view is to treat the learner's knowledge as variable. The kind of knowledge which the learner internalizes depends on the nature of the interactional context. Also L2 performance is variable. The kind of knowledge which is employed by the learner depends on the nature of the task. Arguably this perspective is part of the interface position, but it is not highly articulated. For this reason it is convenient to consider a third position—the variability position—as an alternative to the non-interface and interface positions.

The variability position

The variability position has already been described in Chapter 4. To recapitulate briefly, the learner's interlanguage comprises both non-systematic and systematic variability. Systematic variability is the product of both the linguistic and situational contexts. The learner is credited with a number of different styes ranged from the careful to the vernacular. Which style he uses is a function of the amount of attention he is able to pay to his speech (Tarone 1983).

The variability position emphasizes the interrelationship between use and acquisition. The kind of language use that the learner engages in determines the kind of knowledge that he acquires. Similarly, different kinds of knowledge are used in different types of language performance. Thus, acquiring the necessary linguistic knowledge to perform one kind of activity does not guarantee the ability to perform a different kind of activity. For example, the effects of practice may be specific to the kind of activity that is being exercised.

Bialystok (1982, 1984) seeks to account for the learner's variable control of the L2 system by examining the constraints that are imposed by various language situations. To do so, she distinguishes two continua involving an analysed factor and a control factor. The analysed factor 'refers to the extent to which the learner is able to prepresent the structure of knowledge along with its content' (Bialystok 1984). The learner who has gained analysed knowledge is able to operate on it by transforming it, comparing it, and using it for problem solving. Roughly speaking, then, the analysed factor corresponds to the earlier explicit/implicit distinction. The control factor refers to the relative ease of access that the learner has to different items of linguistic knowledge; it relates to automaticity. Bialystok emphasizes that these factors are not dichotomies but continua, that is there are degrees of analycity and automaticity. It is convenient however to identify four basic types of knowledge, as shown in Figure 9.2. Using this framework, Bialystok makes two basic points. (1) Different tasks require different types of knowledge. The most difficult tasks are those requiring knowledge that is marked on both factors (i.e. C in Figure 9.2), the least difficult are those that are unmarked on both factors (i.e. B), while tasks requiring knowledge marked on just one factor but unmarked on the other (i.e. A or D) are intermediate. (2) Different kinds of learners can be identified according to which kind of knowledge they possess. For example, child learners and adult informal learners will be typically characterized by type B knowledge in the early stages, and by type A in the later stages. Formal L2 learners will be typically characterized by type D knowledge

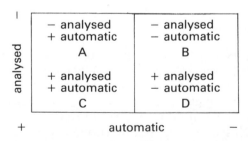

Figure 9.2 Types of knowledge in a variable L2 system
(based on Bialystok 1982)

in the initial stages and type C in the later. Bialystok is careful to state that 'the qualitative differences do not imply value judgement' (Bialystok 1982: 205).

How does a variable position such as that described by Bialystok (1982) or Tarone (1983) account for the results of the empirical studies into the effects of formal instruction? Because the natural sequence of development is a reflection of one particular type of language use—spontaneous communication—it will never change. In Tarone's model the so-called natural route is the product of the learner's vernacular style; in Bialystok's model it is the product of type A knowledge. A different order will emerge only when the learner is confronted with a task which requires a different kind of knowledge. Thus formal instruction, which develops the learner's careful style (or type C knowledge in Figure 9.2), will be powerless to affect the route of SLA as long as this is measured using tasks that call upon the vernacular style. What formal instruction will be able to achieve is to increase the learner's control over the analysed knowledge he has learnt; that is, to automatize it through practice. From the point of view of the variability position, the question of an alternative order of development does not arise, as the so called 'acquisitional' order is only a reflection of a particular type of performance.

The variability position can also explain why classroom learners outperform naturalistic learners on discrete-point tests. Formal instruction presumably develops the type of knowledge (type C in Bialystok's framework) that is required to undertake the kinds of tasks which are posed in these tests. Natural settings presumably do not develop this type of knowledge. It is less clear how the variability position can explain why classroom learners also outperform naturalistic learners on integrative tests. There are a number of possibilities. First, the integrative tests may require analysed rather than unanalysed knowledge; in other words, they call upon more or less the same type of knowledge as discrete-point tests as far as the analysed factor is concerned, differing only with regard to the automatic factor. Second, it is possible that there is movement of knowledge along the stylistic continuum over time, as suggested by Tarone (1983). Dickerson (quoted in Tarone 1982) suggests that the continued advancement in formal styles may have a 'pull effect' on the casual style. One problem with this explanation is that if this were the case, a different natural order ought to result from formal instruction, unless the 'pull effect' is seen as just sensitizing the learner to vernacular forms that are 'ready' to emerge (as suggested by Seliger 1979). Third, it can be hypothesized that formal instruction does more than just develop analysed knowledge for use in the careful style; it also enables unanalysed knowledge to become internalized for use in the vernacular style. This point demands careful explication.

It cannot be assumed that formal instruction contributes only to the learner's careful style. The classroom interaction which forms the matrix of formal instruction may also serve as input to the learner's vernacular style. Evidence for this has already been cited in the study by Terrell *et al.* (1980). In Chapter 6 it was also shown that even a formal classroom is likely to contain a variety of different kinds of interaction, a point made forcibly by Bialystok (1981: 65):

> . . . a formal learning situation encompasses many more features than those which are explicitly designated as the goal of the lesson, such as extraneous conversation, the social context in which the lesson occurs, and so on, and many of these features may be concurrently assimilated into implicit linguistic knowledge.

Ellis (1984e), in the study referred to earlier, also suggests that opportunities for communicative interactions may occur in the context of formal instruction. It will be recalled that Ellis was unable to explain why some pupils benefited from instruction in the use of WH questions while others did not, in terms of how often they participated in instructional exchanges. However, he offers qualitative evidence to suggest that the students who progressed were those who engaged in interactions where some negotiation of meaning took place, either in the classroom itself or in the elicitation sessions where the data for the study were collected. But it is not just the communicative interactions that help to develop the learner's vernacular style. An argument can be offered that interactions where the focus is on form may also help, although not in the way that teachers envisage. Consider, for instance, a lesson which requires students to produce sentences like 'This is a pencil' and 'These are pencils' in order to practise markers of plurality. It is true that such sentences model the grammatical information which is the target of the lesson, but they also contain other grammatical information which is not marked for conscious attention. Students producing and listening to such sentences may focus on the plurality markers, but at the same time they are being exposed to how the copula is used in equational sentences. Drilling the production of such sentences may facilitate the development of analysed knowledge where plurality markers are concerned, but may also incidentally facilitate the development of unanalysed knowledge where the use of the copula is concerned (e.g. it may help the learners to internalize the formula 'This is a . . .'). Thus, even though formal instruction is directed at the mastery of specific L2 forms, it may, for the reasons advanced above, also lead to the mastery of other L2 forms, not designated from the teacher's point of view as the goal of the lesson.

However, even if it is accepted that formal instruction serves as input to a variety of interlanguage styles by fostering L2 knowledge in varying degrees of analycity, it still remains to explain why this input enables classroom learners to develop more rapidly than naturalistic learners. One strong possibility is that the classroom input is richer, in the sense that it stimulates the growth of a variety of knowledge types, whereas naturalistic input serves to stimulate only unanalysed knowledge in the main. The learner who has access to a variety of styles is better equipped to perform successfully on both the discrete-point and integrative tests by which means proficiency is measured. In most cases, learners will benefit from access to both unanalysed and analysed knowledge, because this will enable them to perform a range of different tasks.

Summary

This section has examined three theoretical positions which provide explanations of why formal instruction does not affect the natural sequence of SLA but does facilitate more rapid development. The non-interface position proposed by Krashen claims that 'acquisition' and 'learning' are separate. Because 'acquisition' is responsible for the natural sequence, the 'learning' that results from formal instruction cannot influence it. However, classrooms that provide opportunities for comprehensible input will accelerate 'acquisition'. The interface position also posits two types of L2 knowledge, but argues that they are related, so that 'learning' (or explicit knowledge) can become 'acquisition' (or implicit knowledge) when it is sufficiently practised. A weaker version of this position, however, states that 'learning' does not so much turn into 'acquisition' as facilitate it, when the learner is 'ready'. The variability position differs from the other two positions in that it recognizes a variety of different 'styles', each calling on knowledge types that vary in terms of analycity and automaticity. Different tasks require the utilization of different kinds of knowledge. Formal instruction contributes directly or indirectly to the internalization of these different knowledge types and in so doing enables the classroom learner to perform a wider range of linguistic tasks than the naturalistic learner.

All three positions provide arguments to account for the results of the empirical research into the effects of formal instruction. These have been considered in some detail. At the moment there is insufficient evidence to make a clear choice between them. It is not likely that such evidence will be forthcoming until there are more qualitative studies of the classroom discourse that results from formal instruction and of the linguistic development that such discourse induces.

Conclusion: some implications

This chapter began by asserting that the investigation of the role played by instruction in SLA was of significance for both SLA theory and language pedagogy. In this conclusion I shall briefly consider some of the implications.

SLA theory

Studying the role of instruction can throw light on the contribution of environmental factors in SLA. The classroom environment provides a different kind of input from a natural setting. If environmental factors are important for SLA, it might be predicted that (1) the acquisitional route in the two settings will be different, and (2) the rate/success of SLA in the two settings will also differ. The research reviewed in the earlier sections shows that (1) does not arise, while (2) may. The failure of the classroom setting to influence the route of SLA can be explained in two ways. First, it might be taken to show that the real determinants of SLA are learner-internal rather than environmental factors. That is, despite differences in input, the L2 learner will follow the same route because he is programmed to do so. The second explanation permits a more central role for input/interaction to be maintained. Classroom SLA and naturalistic SLA follow the same developmental path, because, although there are differences in the types of input to be found in each setting, there are also similarities. The natural sequence is the product of one type of language use—spontaneous communication—which, although restricted in classroom contexts, does take place. The first explanation follows a nativist interpretation of SLA, the second follows an interactionist interpretation (see Chapter 6). What is quite clear, whatever interpretation is adopted, is that SLA possesses certain structural properties which are immune to environmental differences inherent in classroom and natural settings. The effect of environmental factors appears to be restricted largely to how quickly and how much of the L2 the learner acquires.

Language pedagogy

Looking at instruction from the viewpoint of the learner rather than the teacher is salutary. It puts into perspective the widely held view that if instruction is based on a sound syllabus and employs motivating techniques, acquisition will result. Unless account is taken of the structural properties of SLA, success is by no means certain.

However, it is not easy to arrive at firm recommendations based on the results of SLA research. As Hughes (1983: 1–2) writes:

> It must be said at the outset that it is not at all certain that at the present time there are any clear implications for language teaching to be drawn from the study of second language learning.

Reticence is in order for two reasons. First, it must be recognized that teaching is not the same as learning. In devising a teaching programme it is clearly desirable to take into consideration how learners learn, but it is also necessary to take into account non-learner factors. Brumfit (1984), for instance, points out that even if learners do follow a fixed route, the

teacher ought not to feel obligated to ensure that his teaching also
follows it, as it is far more important that the teacher works from a
syllabus which he finds logically acceptable. Brumfit argues that
language teaching will be most successful when it follows a well-worked
out plan which directs and organizes what the teacher does. The second
reason for reticence is that, although there is a fair degree of agreement
among SLA researchers concerning *what* happens in SLA, there is far
less agreement about *why* it happens in the way it does. This has been
evident in the different positions which have been adopted to explain the
results of research into the effects of formal instruction. However, while
it is wise to be tentative in seeking implications for language pedagogy
from SLA research, it would be foolish to ignore this research totally. As
Corder (1980: 1) notes, 'we always have an obligation to attempt to
answer practical questions in the light of the best available knowledge'.

Only one issue will be considered here—what Stern (1983) refers to as
the code-communication dilemma in language pedagogy.[9] The key
question is this: to what extent should instruction be directed at raising
learners' consciousness about the formal properties of the L2, as
opposed to providing opportunities for them to engage in natural
communication? This is a controversial issue. On the one hand there are
advocates of what Widdowson (1984: 23) calls 'pure education . . . and
its associated permissive pedagogy of non-intervention'. On the other
hand there are those who argue that teaching learners to be analytical
contributes to development. I shall briefly outline what attitude to the
code-communication dilemma is held by protagonists of each of the
three positions considered in the previous section.

1 The non-interface position
Krashen (1982) pays close attention to the role of grammar teaching
in classroom SLA. He sees only two uses for it. First, it enables the
Monitor to function by providing for 'learning'. However, Monitor
use is restricted to occasions when the learner has time to access his
'learnt' knowledge, and is also restricted by the fact that only a small
sub-section of total rules of a L2 are 'learnable'. The second use of
grammar teaching is to satisfy learners' curiosity about the nature of
the L2 grammatical system—'grammar appreciation', as Krashen
calls it. Krashen (1982) concludes:

> The use of conscious grammar is limited. Not everyone Monitors.
> Those who do only Monitor some of the time and use the Monitor
> for only a sub-part of the grammar . . . the effect of self-correction
> on accuracy is modest. Second language performers can typically
> self-correct only a small percentage of their errors, even when
> deliberately focused on form . . . and even when we only consider
> the easiest aspects of grammar. (1982: 112)

Krashen, therefore, believes that the role of teaching is to afford opportunities for communication, rather than to draw attention to the L2 code. Krashen (1981b) lists the defining characteristics of what he considers an effective pedagogical programme: (1) the classroom input must be comprehensible; (2) the programme must consist of 'communicative activities', as only these will ensure that the input is interesting and relevant; (3) there should be no attempt to follow a grammatically sequenced programme; and (4) the input must be of sufficient quantity (hence the importance of extensive reading). Krashen and Terrell (1983) outline a programme that conforms to these principles, calling it 'the natural approach'.

2 The interface position
Whereas the non-interface position emphasizes the importance of communication and minimizes the importance of the code, the interface position asserts the contribution of the code. Sharwood-Smith (1981) sees grammar teaching as a short cut to communicative ability. That is, the adult learner who has his attention drawn to features of the code can practise these, both in and out of the classroom, until he can use them subconsciously in fluent communicative speech. Sharwood-Smith emphasizes that grammar teaching (or 'consciousness-raising', as he calls it) can take many different forms. He distinguishes two basic dimensions: elaborateness (i.e. whether the teaching offers only brief descriptions or highly structured explanations), and explicitness (i.e. indirect clues or standard pedagogical rules). Consciousness-raising, therefore, does not require that the learner is able to verbalize the rules he has learnt. For Sharwood-Smith, then, the important issue is not whether the code should be taught, but in what way it should be taught.

3 The variability position
The variability position stresses the importance of matching the learning process with the type of instruction. Bialystok (1982: 205) comments:

> . . . instruction must consider the specific goals of the learner and attempt to provide the appropriate form of knowledge to achieve those goals.

The 'goals' refer to the type of language use that the learner needs (or wants) to engage in. If the goal is to participate in natural conversation, the learner will need to develop his vernacular style by acquiring L2 knowledge that is automatic but unanalysed. This can be achieved directly by means of instruction that emphasizes communication in the classroom. It may also be achieved indirectly by teaching that focuses on the code, if there are also sufficient practice opportunities to trigger the passage of knowledge from the careful to the vernacular style. If the learner's goal is to participate in discourse that requires careful, conscious planning, he will need to develop a careful style by acquiring L2 knowledge that is automatic and analysed. This can best be accomplished by formal instruction that focuses on the L2 code.

Just as it was not possible to make a definite choice as to which position offered the best explanation of the results of empirical research into classroom SLA, so it would be premature to lay down a solution to the code-communication dilemma in language pedagogy. However, one effect of SLA studies in general has been to suggest that teaching the code may play a smaller part than has been previously thought. As Corder (1980) points out, this suggestion is in accord with current teaching directions. SLA research, therefore, may be seen as reinforcing existing trends, rather than arguing for radically new approaches.

Summary

In order to investigate the role of instruction in SLA, it is necessary to separate out the effects that formal instruction has on the route of SLA and on the rate/success of SLA. Where the route is concerned, formal instruction appears to have no major effect. The overall sequence of development associated with natural communicative language use does not change, while only a few minor and temporary differences in the acquisition of specific grammatical features have been observed. Thus classroom SLA appears to involve the same processing strategies as naturalistic SLA. Where the rate/success is concerned, instruction is facilitative, although only in terms of relative utility, not in terms of absolute effects. These results must be treated tentatively, as there has been little empirical research.

Three different positions have been advanced to explain classroom SLA. The non-interface position, associated with Krashen (1982), distinguishes 'acquired' and 'learnt' knowledge and argues that they are separate. This position offers a convincing explanation of why formal instruction fails to influence the natural route of SLA, as this is a reflection of 'acquisition'. The explanation it gives for why formal instruction aids the rate/success of SLA is less clear, however. The interface position, associated with Stevick (1980) and Sharwood-Smith (1981) among others, claims that 'learnt' or explicit knowledge can turn into 'acquired' or implicit knowledge if there is enough practice. This position offers an explanation for the rate/success finding, but is less convincing about the route finding. The variability position, associated with Tarone (1983) and Bialystok (1982), sees acquisition and language use closely linked, such that different types of knowledge arise from and are required for the performance of different language tasks. This position deals comfortably with the route finding (which occurs in a particular kind of performance) and can explain the rate/success finding if it is assumed that a learner who has access to a variety of different knowledge types will outperform one who is more reliant on a single kind of knowledge. However, it is premature to choose from among these positions.

The study of the role of instruction in SLA has implications for both SLA theory and language pedagogy. In the case of the former, it stresses the importance of acknowledging the structural properties of SLA which are relatively immune to environmental differences. Where language pedagogy is concerned, it sheds light on the code-communication dilemma, although once again it would be premature to come to any firm conclusions about the effectiveness of formal grammar teaching.

Notes

1 The teaching of grammar can be direct and concerned only with formal features (as in audiolingual drills), or it can be indirect and related to language function (as in situational drills or drills based on a notional/functional syllabus).

2 Krashen (1982) makes much of the difference between 'easy' rules such as the third person singular '-s', and 'difficult' rules such as subject–verb inversion in WH questions. He claims that only 'easy' rules can be learnt.

3 Hosenfeld (1976) investigated the kinds of strategies used by learners to complete standard language teaching exercises. The conclusion was that such exercises may help to develop the strategies needed to obtain correct answers, rather than the target structures they were designed to practise.

4 The Bangalore project consists of a teaching programme in which no attempt is made to follow a linguistically organized syllabus. Instead there are a number of graded activities (e.g. map making) which are carried out in the classroom. The teacher teaches only that language which is required to undertake each activity.

5 Lightbown's (1983) finding supports the criticism of morpheme studies made in Chapter 3 to the effect that it does not make sense to compare the acquisition of radically different grammatical features.

6 The three learners in Ellis's (1984a) study may have been exposed to English outside the classroom, although as far as could be told this was not the case with two of them. These lived exclusively in a Punjabi-speaking community and had zero contact with native English speakers. They even watched Punjabi videos on television!

7 The three learners continued to produce large numbers of uninverted intonation questions throughout the period of Ellis's study. Thus this developmentally early interrogative form did not substantially change.

One explanation for this is that in a classroom environment, procedural questions (i.e. requests for confirmation and clarification), which are typically realized by means of intonation questions, were very frequent, because of the pupils' need to establish the tasks they were required to undertake. Similarly, the almost complete absence of past forms from the speech of the learners can be explained by the fact that past time reference is not required very much in communicative classroom speech.

8 Long (1983d) attempts to explain the difference between Martin's (1980) results and those of the other studies by suggesting that exposure may be important in the early stages of SLA (Martin's subjects were beginners), but not in more advanced stages.

9 The code-communication contrast has been referred to in various ways. For instance, Brumfit (1979) distinguishes 'accuracy' and 'fluency', suggesting that different traditional pedagogic practices have focused on one or the other.

Further reading

Classroom SLA has received little attention. Most of the available research is summarized in 'Does second language instruction make a difference?' by M. Long, in *TESOL Quarterly* 17/3, and in *Classroom Second Language Development* by R. Ellis (Pergamon, 1984) (see in particular chapters 2–4).

S. D. Krashen, in *Principles and Practice in Second Language Acquisition* (Pergamon, 1982), considers classroom SLA from the point of view of his general acquisition theory, and also looks in detail at the role of the grammar. Chapter V provides a review of the comparative method studies which have been mentioned only briefly in this chapter.

It is important to read 'Consciousness-raising and the second language learner', by M. Sharwood-Smith (*Applied Linguistics* II/2: 159–68), as this offers a strongly argued alternative to Krashen's position.

'Second language acquisition research and the teaching of grammar', by S. P. Corder (*BAAL Newsletter* 10), considers the implications of SLA studies for teaching.

10 Theories of Second Language Acquisition

Introduction

There has been no shortage of theorizing about second language acquisition (SLA). The research literature abounds in approaches, theories, models, laws, and principles. It is arguable that there has been a superfluity of theorizing. Schouten (1979:4), for instance, claims:

> . . . in second language learning, too many models have been built and taken for granted too soon, and this has stifled relevant research.

He believes that theorizing should only follow extensive and rigorous empirical research. However, it might also be argued that theorizing should precede and, therefore, inform empirical study, guiding the specific hypotheses it seeks to examine. Irrespective of these methodological issues, SLA research has gone ahead and spawned a plethora of theories.

The main aim of this chapter is to review a number of theories of SLA. The ones that have been selected for discussion have assumed a central place in SLA research. They reflect the variety of perspectives evident in SLA studies. They are:

1 The Acculturation Model (and closely associated with it, the Nativization Model)
2 Accommodation Theory
3 Discourse Theory
4 The Monitor Model[1]
5 The Variable Competence Model
6 The Universal Hypothesis
7 A Neurofunctional Theory

The discussion of each theory will take the form of an account of its central premises, followed by a critical evaluation. The discussions will reflect the issues which have been considered in detail in the previous chapters.

The role of theory in SLA research

What is the role of theory in SLA research? Hakuta (1981: 1) sees the main goal of SLA research as follows:

> The game of language acquisition research can be described as the search for an appropriate level of description for the learner's system of rules.

In other words, the main goal of a theory of SLA is *description*—the characterization of the nature of the linguistic categories which constitute the learner's interlanguage at any point in development. However, most other researchers have aimed at more than just description. They have tried to discover why the learner develops the particular linguistic categories that he does. As Rutherford (1982: 85) puts it:

> We wish to know *what* it is that is acquired, *how* it is acquired and *when* it is acquired. But were we to have the answers even to these questions, we would still want to know *why* . . .

In other words, theory building is concerned with *explanation* as well as with description.

But the term 'explanation' is ambiguous. Firstly, it can refer to the way in which the learner works on samples of the input data, converting them into intake and then using his knowledge to produce output. Explanation in this sense covers the acquisition sequence and order and the processes responsible for it. Secondly, the term 'explanation' can also refer to what motivates the learner to learn and what causes him to cease learning (i.e. fossilize). Schumann (1976) distinguishes these two types of explanation, which he refers to respectively as 'cognitive processes' responsible for *how* SLA takes place and 'initiating factors' responsible for *why* SLA takes place. Ellis (1984a) refers to the two types as 'assembly mechanisms' and 'power mechanisms'. The distinction is an important one where SLA theorizing is concerned, because, as will be shown, whereas some theories focus on the *how*, others focus on the *why*. The kind of explanation they offer, therefore, is of a different order. A comprehensive theory of SLA will need to explain both assembly and power mechanism.

How do researchers set about building an explanation of how and why SLA takes place? Long (1983e), drawing on the work of Reynolds (1971), distinguishes two approaches to theory building: the *theory-then-research* approach and the *research-then-theory* approach. These will be discussed briefly.

The theory-then-research approach involves five stages:

1 Develop an explicit theory.
2 Derive a testable prediction from the theory.
3 Conduct research to test the prediction.
4 Modify (or abandon) the theory if the prediction is disconfirmed.
5 Test a new prediction if the first prediction is confirmed.

The starting point of this approach is to invent a theory using hunches and relevant research. The theory constitutes what Popper (1976) calls 'dogmatic thinking'. It is important that the theory is presented in such a way that it is falsifiable. That is, the researcher must not be able to interpret any conceivable event as verification of the theory, or, as Popper puts it, it must exclude some 'immunizations'. The strength of the theory rests both in its ability to 'cover' what is already known about the phenomenon under investigation and also to predict what will be observed in future. The prediction is a test of the theory. The process of testing and amending the theory is a continuous one that, in Popper's view, never ends. Thus it is possible to talk about a comprehensive theory which accounts for all the available facts, but it is not possible to talk about a true theory, as any theory must remain open to modification.

The research-then-theory approach has four stages:

1 Select a phenomenon for investigation.
2 Measure its characteristics.
3 Collect data and look for systematic patterns.
4 Formalize significant patterns as rules describing natural events.

The starting point of this approach is not a theory but a 'research question'—an area of interest into which the researcher wants to enquire. This area is likely to have been decided on as a result of hunches or reading the relevant research, but the research question is not formulated in such a way as to provide a testable prediction. The research-then-theory approach need never lead to a comprehensive theory—it can produce a 'bits-and-pieces' view of SLA, a series of insights into what motivates behaviour.

The study of SLA has involved both approaches. The experimental studies of the effects of motivation and attitudes undertaken by Canadian researchers (e.g. Gardner and Lambert 1972) are examples of a theory-then-research approach. The experimental studies examining the universal hypothesis discussed in the last chapter might also be seen as examples of this approach. In contrast, the longitudinal studies of individual L2 learners considered in Chapters 3 and 9 follow a research-then-theory approach. Their aim is not so much to build a comprehensive theory as to examine specific aspects of SLA in detail.

As Long points out, both approaches have their strengths and weaknesses. The theory-then-research approach provides an approximate answer and a basis for systematically testing aspects of the overall theory. But researchers are not always prepared to abandon a theory even in the face of substantial disconfirmatory evidence. The research-then-theory approach means that the researcher is less likely to be 'wrong' at any time and can provide valuable insights into selected aspects of the whole process being investigated. But the claims that derive from this approach are necessarily limited, and it is not always clear how one claim relates to another.

Long argues that the theory-then-research approach leads to more efficient research because:

> ... the theory governing the research at any point in time tells the investigator what the relevant data are, which is the crucial experiment to run. (1983e: 22).

The study of SLA, however, needs both approaches. First, there is no agreed initial theory to motivate an experimental hypothesis-testing approach, and it is doubtful whether there will be in the near future. The insights provided by a research-then-theory approach provide a basis for theory building. Second, there is a recognized need to construct theories in order to provide a general explanation of SLA. The fact that different researchers have used different approaches may, as Long suggests, be a reflection of their different personalities, but it probably also reflects the recognition that the field of SLA requires different research perspectives.

The subsequent sections of this chapter review a number of theories of SLA. They differ in what they seek to explain—the 'assembly mechanisms' that govern how SLA takes place or the 'power mechanisms' that explain why it takes place, or both. They also differ in how they have been arrived at. Some are the result of a theory-then-research approach, while others owe more to a research-then-theory approach. The reader who seeks a tidy and exhaustive account of SLA is likely to be disappointed. The theories offer 'complementary alternatives', as Selinker and Lamendella (1978b: 168) put it; 'each perspective has advantages other lack, while at the same time embodying disadvantages'.

Seven theories of SLA

1 The Acculturation Model

Acculturation is defined by Brown (1980a: 129) as 'the process of becoming adapted to a new culture'. It is seen as an important aspect of SLA, because language is one of the most observable expressions of culture and because in second (as opposed to foreign) language settings the acquisition of a new language is seen as tied to the way in which the learner's community and the target language community view each other. One view of how acculturation affects SLA has already been described (see Chapter 5). The account that follows is based on the work of John Schumann (see Schumann 1978a; 1978b; 1978c). In addition, an elaborated version of Schumann's model—the Nativization Model—is discussed, with reference to Andersen (1980; 1981; 1983b).

The central premise of the Acculturation Model is:

> ... second language acquisition is just one aspect of acculturation and the degree to which a learner acculturates to the target language group will control the degree to which he acquires the second language. (Schumann 1978c: 34)

Acculturation, and hence SLA, is determined by the degree of *social* and *psychological distance* between the learner and the target language culture. Social distance is the result of a number of factors which affect the learner as a member of a social group in contact with the target language group. Psychological distance is the result of various affective factors which concern the learner as an individual. The social factors are primary. The psychological factors come into play in cases where the social distance is indeterminant (i.e. where social factors constitute neither a clearly positive nor a clearly negative influence on acculturation), although they can also modify the modal level of learning associated with a particular social situation.

Schumann (1978b) lists the various factors which determine social and psychological distance. The social variables govern whether the overall learning situation is 'good' or 'bad'. An example of a 'good' learning situation is when (1) the target language and L2 groups view each other as socially equal; (2) the target language and L2 groups are both desirous that the L2 group will assimilate; (3) both the target language and L2 groups expect the L2 group to share social facilities with the target language group (i.e. there is low enclosure); (4) the L2 group is small and not very cohesive; (5) the L2 group's culture is congruent with that of the target language group; (6) both groups have positive attitudes to each other; and (7) the L2 group envisages staying in the target language area for an extended period. An example of a 'bad' learning situation is when the conditions are opposite to the ones described above.[2] It is, of course, possible to have varying degrees of social distance.

The psychological factors are affective in nature. They include (1) language shock (i.e. the learner experiences doubt and possible confusion when using the L2); (2) culture shock (i.e. the learner experiences disorientation, stress, fear, etc. as a result of differences between his or her own culture and that of the target language community); (3) motivation; and (4) ego boundaries (see Chapter 5).

Social and psychological distance influence SLA by determining the amount of contact with the target language that the learner experiences, and also the degree to which the learner is open to that input which is available. Thus in 'bad' learning situations the learner will receive very little L2 input. Also, when the psychological distance is great, the learner will fail to convert available input into intake.

Schumann also describes the kind of learning which takes place. He suggests that the early stages of SLA are characterized by the same processes that are responsible for the formation of pidgin languages. When social and/or psychological distances are great, the learner fails to progress beyond the early stages, with the result that his language is pidginized. Schumann refers to this account of SLA as the *pidginization hypothesis*. He documents in detail the pidginization that characterizes one adult Spanish speaker's acquisition of L2 English in the United States. The learner, Alberto, was subject to a high degree of social distance and failed to progress very far in learning English. His English was characterized by many of the forms observed in pidgins, e.g. 'no + V' negatives, uninverted interrogatives, the absence of possessive and plural inflections, and a restricted verb morphology. Schumann suggests 'pidginization may characterize all early second language acquisition and . . . under conditions of social and psychological distance it persists' (1978a: 110). When pidginization persists the learner fossilizes. That is, he no longer revises his interlanguage system in the direction of the target language. Thus early fossilization and pidginization are identical processes.[3]

Thus continued pidginization is the result of social and psychological distance. The degree of acculturation leads to pidgin-like language in two ways. First, as suggested above, it controls the level of input that the learner receives. Second, it reflects the function which the learner wishes to use the L2 for. Following Smith (1972), Schumann distinguishes three broad functions of language: (1) the communicative function, which concerns the transmission of purely referential, denotative information; (2) the integrative function, which involves the use of language to mark the speaker as a member of a particular social group; and (3) the expressive function, which consists of the use of language to display linguistic virtuosity (e.g. in literary uses). Initially L2 learners will seek to use the L2 for the communicative function. Pidgins and interlanguages which fossilize in the early stages of development remain restricted to the communicative function. Native speakers of the target language use it for both the communicative and integrative functions, as will those L2 learners who do not fossilize early on, but many native speakers and L2 learners will never aspire to master the expressive uses of language.

The Nativization Model

Andersen builds on Schumann's Acculturation Model, in particular by providing a cognitive dimension which Schumann does not consider. For Schumann, SLA can be explained simply in terms of input and the general function the learner wants to use the L2 for. He is not concerned with the learner's internal processing mechanisms. Andersen, to a much greater extent, is concerned with learning processes.

Andersen sees SLA as the result of two general forces, which he labels *nativization* and *denativization*. Nativization consists of assimilation; the learner makes the input conform to his own internalized view of what constitutes the L2 system. In terms of the typology of learner strategies described in Chapter 7, the learner simplifies the learning task by building hypotheses based on the knowledge he already possesses (e.g. knowledge of his first language; knowledge of the world). In this sense, then, he attends to an 'internal norm'. Nativization is apparent in pidginization and the early stages of both first and second language acquisition. Denativization involves accommodation (in the Piagetian sense); the learner adjusts his internalized system to make it fit the input. In terms of the terminology used in Chapter 7, the learner makes use of inferencing strategies which enable him to remodel his interlanguage system in accordance with the 'external norm' (i.e. the linguistic features represented in the input language). Denativization is apparent in depidginization (i.e. the elaboration of a pidgin language which occurs through the gradual incorporation of forms from an external language source) and also in later first and second language acquisition. Figure 10.1 summarizes Andersen's Nativization Model.

Nativization	**Denativization**
	Accommodation
Growth independent	— — — — — — →Growth towards an
of the external norm ←Assimilation	external norm
Restricted access to input	Adequate access to input
Pidginization Creation of a unique first/second language acquisition	Depidginization First/second language as increasing approximation towards external 'target' norm

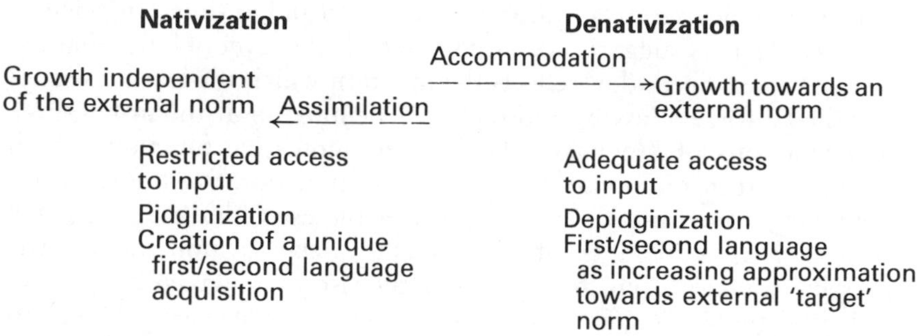

Figure 10.1   Andersen's Nativization Model (slightly simplified from Andersen 1983b: 11)

Evaluation

The Acculturation and Nativist models focus on the power mechanisms of SLA. They provide explanations of why L2 learners, unlike first language learners, often fail to achieve a native-like competence. L2 learners may be cut off from the necessary input as a result of social distance, or they may fail to attend to it as a result of psychological distance. These models also indicate that SLA involves processes of a very general kind, which are also found in the formation and elaboration of pidgin languages. The notions of 'internal' and 'external norms' are elegant devices for explaining why early and late interlanguage systems are so very different. Characterizing SLA as the gradual transition of attention from an internal to an external norm explains the developmental sequence which has been observed in SLA (see Chapter 3), and the switch that learners make from reliance on simplifying to reliance on inferencing strategies (see Chapter 7).

Neither model sheds light on how L2 knowledge is internalized and used. In other words, there is no specification of the learner's assembly mechanisms. This is quite evident in the Acculturation model. It is also true of the Nativization model. Although this model does consider internal factors (in the form of the assimilation/accommodation distinction), there is no discussion of how these operate. The relationship between primary linguistic data and internal processing is an intricate one, requiring a detailed account of how learner strategies operate on input and produce output. Thus, while accepting that in the final analysis SLA is dependent on input and on a preparedness of the learner to convert input into intake, a comprehensive theory of SLA will also need to consider *how* input becomes intake and *how* this is integrated into the existing interlanguage system. In particular it will need to consider whether intake is controlled by the way the input is shaped in interaction involving the learner and other speakers or whether it is controlled by the structure of the internal processing mechanisms themselves—the differential contribution of environment and 'black box'. Andersen's 'internal' and 'external norms' suggest that the internal mechanisms play a crucial part, but this is not elaborated upon. And neither Andersen nor Schumann pays attention to the potentially facilitating effects of input/interaction, as described in the work of Hatch and Long (see Chapter 6). In short, what is missing from these models is an account of the role of the interaction between situation and learner.

The Acculturation and Nativization Models address naturalistic SLA, where the L2 learner has contact with the target language community. It is not clear whether the models are also applicable to classroom SLA (i.e. foreign language instruction), where no such contact is possible. Presumably the factors responsible for social distance are not relevant in foreign language learning, although those responsible for psychological distance may be.[4]

2 Accommodation Theory

Accommodation Theory derives from the research of Giles and associates into the intergroup uses of language in multilingual communities such as Britain. Giles operates within a socio-psychological framework, drawing on the work of Lambert and Gardner in the Canadian context. His primary concern is to investigate how intergroup uses of language reflect basic social and psychological attitudes in inter-ethnic communication. As an offshoot of this, he has also considered SLA from an intergroup stance (see Giles and Byrne 1982) and it is the resulting view of SLA which has become known as Accommodation Theory.

The Accommodation Theory shares certain premises with the Acculturation Model, but it also differs from it in a number of significant ways. Like Schumann, Giles is concerned to account for successful language acquisition. Both seek the answer in the relationships that hold between the learner's social group (termed the 'ingroup') and the target language community (termed the 'outgroup'). However, whereas Schumann explains these relationships in terms of variables that create *actual* social distance, Giles does so in terms of *perceived* social distance.[5] Giles argues that it is how the ingroup defines itself in relationship to the outgroup that is important for SLA. Also, where Schumann appears to treat social and psychological distance as absolute phenomena that determine the level of interaction between the learner and native speakers, Giles sees intergroup relationships as subject to constant negotiation during the course of each interaction. Thus, whereas for Schumann social and psychological distance are static (or at least change only slowly over time), for Giles intergroup relationships are dynamic and fluctuate in accordance with the shifting views of identity held by each group *vis-à-vis* the other. As will be discussed later, this enables Accommodation Theory to take account of the variability inherent in language-learner language and, also, the native speaker's input.

Giles agrees with Gardner (1979) that motivation is the primary determinant of L2 proficiency. He considers the level of motivation to be a reflex of how individual learners define themselves in ethnic terms. This, in turn, is governed by a number of key variables:

1 Identification of the individual learner with his ethnic ingroup:
   the extent to which the learner sees himself as a member of a specific ingroup, separate from the outgroup.

2 Inter-ethnic comparison:
   whether the learner makes favourable or unfavourable comparisons between his own ingroup and the outgroup. This will be influenced by the learner's awareness of 'cognitive alternatives' regarding the status of his own group's position, for instance when he perceives the intergroup situation as unfair.

3 Perception of ethno-linguistic vitality:
   whether the learner sees his ingroup as holding a low or high status and as sharing or excluded from institutional power.

4 Perception of ingroup boundaries:
   whether the learner sees his ingroup as culturally and linguistically separate from the outgroup (= hard boundaries) or as culturally and linguistically related (= soft boundaries).

5 Identification with other ingroup social categories:
   whether the learner identifies with few or several other ingroup social categories (e.g. occupational, religious, gender) and as a consequence whether he holds adequate or inadequate status within his ingroup.

Column A in Table 10.1 shows when the individual learner is likely to be highly motivated to learn the L2 and hence acquire a high level of proficiency. Conversely, column B shows when he is likely to be unmotivated and so achieve only a low level of proficiency. Where the motivation is high as a result of favourable socio-psychological attitudes (as described in column A in Table 10.1), the learner will not only benefit from formal instruction in the L2, but is also likely to avail himself of the opportunities for informal acquisition (in Seliger's (1977) terms, high input generators in the classroom are likely to also obtain a high level of exposure outside). In contrast, when motivation is low as a consequence of unfavourable socio-psychological attitudes (as described in column B of Table 10.1), whether the learner succeeds in formal language contexts will depend instead on intelligence and aptitude, because he is less likely to take advantage of informal acquisition contexts.

Key variables	**A** high motivation, high level of proficiency	**B** low motivation, low level of proficiency
1 Identification with ingroup	weak identification	strong identification
2 Inter-ethnic comparison	makes favourable or no comparison, i.e. ingroup not seen as inferior	makes negative comparison, i.e. ingroup seen as inferior
3 Perception of ethno-linguistic vitality	low perception	high perception
4 Perception of ingroup boundaries	soft and open	hard and closed
5 Identification with other social categories	strong identification —satisfactory ingroup status	weak identification —inadequate group status

Table 10.1   Determinants of successful and unsuccessful learning according to Accommodation Theory

In addition to determining the overall level of proficiency achieved in SLA, Accommodation Theory also accounts for the learner's variable linguistic output. Giles *et al.* (1977) write:

> . . . people are continually modifying their speech with others so as to reduce or accentuate the linguistic (and hence) social differences between them depending on their perceptions of the interactive situation.

Giles (1979) distinguishes two types of change which occur in the L2 speaker's use of 'ethnic speech markers' (i.e. linguistic features which mark the ingroup membership of the speaker).[6] *Upward convergence* involves the attenuation of ingroup speech markers. It occurs when the learner is positively motivated towards the outgroup community (i.e. when his socio-psychological set is favourable). *Downward divergence* involves the accentuation of ethnic speech markers. It occurs when the learner is not positively motivated towards the outgroup (i.e. when his socio-psychological set is unfavourable). In language *use* the occurrence of upward convergence or downward divergence can fluctuate as a result of the L2 speaker's ongoing assessment of himself *vis-à-vis* his own group and the outgroup community. It follows, therefore, that the learner possesses a stylistic repertoire from which he selects in accordance with his shifting socio-psychological set, and that in any one situation the learner may employ different linguistic forms according to the extent to which he chooses to mark his speech as that of the ingroup. In language *acquisition*, progress takes place when the overall predisposition of the learner is towards upward convergence, although this need not be evident in every instance of use. Conversely, fossilization occurs when the overall predisposition of the learner is towards downward divergence.

Evaluation

Accommodation Theory, like the Acculturation Model, does not explain assembly mechanisms. It does not account for the developmental sequence. It is another 'black box' model in this respect. The strength of Accommodation Theory is that it encompasses language acquisition and language use within a single framework. It also relates the acquisition of a new dialect or accent to the acquisition of a L2, as both are seen as a reflection of the learner's perception of himself with regard to his own social group and the target language/dialect group.

Accommodation Theory provides an explanation of language-learner language variability. Variable language use is the result of conflicting socio-psychological attitudes in different situations. Variability of use is related to acquisition, in the sense that the same set of factors is responsible for both. This explanation of variability is compatible with that outlined in Chapter 4 with reference to the work of Tarone. Tarone accounts for variability in terms of varying degrees of attention to form, but she does not address what motivates this. Attention to form can be seen as a consequence of the kind of factors that Giles considers. That is, the learner's perception of himself *vis-à-vis* the target-language community in face-to-face interaction governs when he attends to form. Upward convergence will be characterized by attention to form and to the use of the careful style. Downward divergence will be characterized by an absence of attention to form and a reliance on the vernacular style, through which the learner displays his ingroup membership. Thus diverging or converging may represent aspects of style-shifting involving the vernacular–careful style continuum. However, it is doubtful whether Accommodation Theory can be applied to foreign language learning, when intergroup relationships are not an obvious issue. Foreign language learners also style-shift. This suggests that although ethnic identity is an important aspect of variability in SLA, it does not account for total variability.

3 Discourse Theory

It follows from a theory of language use, in which communication is treated as the matrix of linguistic knowledge (as proposed for instance in Hymes's description of communicative competence), that language development should be considered in terms of how the learner discovers the meaning potential of language by participating in communication. This is how Halliday (1975) views first language acquisition. In a study of how his own child acquired language, Halliday shows that the development of the formal linguistic devices for realizing basic language function grows out of the interpersonal uses to which language is put. Because the structure of language is itself a reflection of the functions it serves, it can be learnt through learning to communicate. As Cherry (1979: 122) puts it:

> Through communicating with other people, children accomplish actions in the world and develop the rules of language structure and use.

It is because the L2 learner is similarly motivated to 'accomplish actions' (at least in informal SLA) that a parallel can be drawn between first and second language acquisition. In SLA this view of how development takes place has become known as the Discourse Theory.

The Discourse Theory, proposed by Hatch (1978c; 1978d) has already been described in some detail in Chapter 6. Only its main principles are considered here:

1 SLA follows a 'natural' route in syntactical development.
2 Native speakers adjust their speech in order to negotiate meaning with non-native speakers.
3 The conversational strategies used to negotiate meaning, and the resulting adjusted input, influence the rate and route of SLA in a number of ways:
   (a) the learner learns the grammar of the L2 in the same order as the frequency order of the various features in the input;
   (b) the learner acquires commonly occurring formulas and then later analyses these into their component parts;

(c) the learner is helped to construct sentences vertically; vertical structures are the precursors of horizontal structures.
4 Thus, the 'natural' route is the result of learning how to hold conversations.

Evaluation

Whereas Schumann and Giles are interested in explaining the rate of SLA and the level of proficiency achieved, Hatch is interested in explaining *how* SLA takes place. As Hatch says:

> The basic question that second language acquisition research addresses is: how can we describe the *process* of second language acquisition. (Hatch 1980: 177—my italics)

Hatch tries to provide an answer to this question by qualitative analyses of face-to-face interactions involving L2 learners. The route of development is explained in terms of the properties of these interactions. The strength of Hatch's approach lies in the detailed insights it provides into how the process of constructing discourse contributes to the process of building an interlanguage.

It is arguable, however, that notwithstanding these insights, Hatch has not been able to demonstrate conclusively that negotiation of input is the necessary and sufficient condition of SLA. Hatch herself notes:

> We have not been able (nor have we tried) to show how, or if, making messages simpler or more transparent promotes language learning. (1980: 181)

Hatch is only too aware of the huge leap that is made from 'low-inference descriptions' to 'high-inference explanations'. The relationship between negotiated input and SLA is, therefore, likely but not substantiated. SLA research still needs to carry out the kind of empirical studies which have taken place in first language acquisition research and which demonstrate that where rate of development is concerned, at least some discourse features are facilitative (e.g. Cross 1978; Ellis and Wells 1980). Moreover, the Discourse Theory needs to accommodate the fact that, as Larsen-Freeman (1983a) has observed, successful SLA can take place even when there is no negotiated input (e.g. in self-study).

The Discourse Theory, like the two preceding theories, does not address the nature of the learner strategies responsible for SLA. When Hatch talks of *processes*, she means external processes—those which can be observed in face-to-face interaction—not internal processes, those that can only be inferred by observing how learners perform. Hatch does not look at the cognitive processes that control how the learner (and native speaker) construct discourse, or how data made available through discourse are sifted and internalized. There is no specification of the relationship between external and internal processing. In fairness, though, it should be noted that Hatch does not intend to dismiss the cognitive side of SLA. Hatch writes:

> While social interaction may give the learner the 'best' data to work with, the brain in turn must work out a fitting and relevant model of that input. (1983a: 186)

The Discourse Theory, however, is not concerned with what this model consists of.

4 The Monitor Model

Krashen's Monitor Model has enjoyed considerable prominence in SLA research. In so far as it is probably the most comprehensive of existing theories, this is justified. However, as I shall attempt to show later, the theory is seriously flawed in a number of respects, in particular in its treatment of language-learner variability.

The Monitor Model consists of five central hypotheses. In addition, it makes reference to a number of other factors which influence SLA and which relate to the central hypotheses. Each hypothesis is briefly summarized below. Krashen's views on the different causative variables of SLA are also considered. A full account of the Monitor Model is available in Krashen (1981a; 1982), and in Krashen and Terrell (1983).

The five hypotheses

1 The acquisition learning hypothesis
The 'acquisition–learning' distinction has already been considered in Chapter 9. The distinction lies at the heart of Krashen's theory. It is applicable to the process of internalizing new L2 knowledge, to storing this knowledge, and also to using it in actual performance. 'Acquisition' occurs subconsciously as a result of participating in natural communication where the focus is on meaning. 'Learning' occurs as a result of conscious study of the formal properties of the language. In storage, 'acquired' knowledge is located in the left hemisphere of the brain (in most users) in the language areas; it is available for automatic processing. 'Learnt' knowledge is meta-linguistic in nature. It is also stored in the left hemisphere, but not necessarily in the language areas; it is available only for controlled processing. Thus, 'acquired' and 'learnt' knowledge are stored separately. In performance, 'acquired' knowledge serves as the major source for initiating both the comprehension and production of utterances. 'Learnt' knowledge is available for use only by the Monitor (see Hypothesis (3) below).

2 The natural order hypothesis

The natural order hypothesis draws on the SLA research literature that indicates that learners may follow a more or less invariant order in the acquisition of formal grammatical features (see Chapter 3). The hypothesis affirms that grammatical structures are 'acquired' in a predictable order. Thus when the learner is engaged in natural communication tasks, he will manifest the standard order. But when he is engaged in tasks that require or permit the use of metalinguistic knowledge, a different order will emerge.

3 The Monitor hypothesis

The Monitor is the device that learners use to edit their language performance. It utilizes 'learnt' knowledge by acting upon and modifying utterances generated from 'acquired' knowledge. This can occur either before the utterance is uttered or after (see Figure 10.2). In either case its use is optional. Krashen argues that Monitoring has an extremely limited function in language performance, even where adults are concerned. He gives three conditions for its use: (1) there must be sufficient time; (2) the focus must be on form and not meaning; and (3) the user must know the rule (see Chapter 9 for a fuller discussion). Krashen recognizes that editing can also take place using 'acquired' competence. He refers to this as editing by 'feel'. However, this aspect of L2 performance is not developed. Figure 10.2, for instance, does not show how editing by 'feel' takes place.

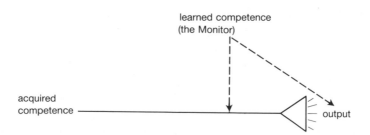

*Figure 10.2   A model of adult second language performance
(Krashen and Terrell 1983: 30)*

4 The input hypothesis

This has already been discussed at some length in Chapter 6. It states that 'acquisition' takes place as a result of the learner having understood input that is a little beyond the current level of his competence (i.e. the i + 1 level). Input that is comprehensible to the learner will automatically be at the right level.

5 The affective filter hypothesis
  This deals with how affective factors relate to SLA, and covers the
  ground of the Acculturation Model. Krashen incorporates the notion
  of the Affective Filter as proposed by Dulay and Burt (1977). The
  filter controls how much input the learner comes into contact with,
  and how much input is converted into intake. It is 'affective' because
  the factors which determine its strength have to do with the learner's
  motivation, self-confidence, or anxiety state. Learners with high
  motivation and self-confidence and with low anxiety have low filters
  and so obtain and let in plenty of input. Learners with low
  motivation, little self-confidence, and high anxiety have high filters
  and so receive little input and allow even less in. The Affective Filter
  influences the rate of development, but it does not affect the route.

Causative variables taken into account in the Monitor Model

Krashen also discusses a number of other factors, each of which figures
conspicuously in the SLA research literature.

1 Aptitude
  Krashen argues that aptitude only relates to 'learning'. That is, the
  learner's aptitude predicts how well he will perform on grammar-type
  tests that provide the right conditions for the operation of the
  Monitor. In contrast, attitude is related to 'acquisition' (see Hypothesis
  (5) above).

2 Role of the first language
  Krashen rejects the view that the first language interferes with SLA.
  Rather, he sees the use of the first language as a performance strategy.
  The learner falls back on his first language when he lacks a rule in the
  L2. He initiates an utterance using his first language (instead of
  'acquired' L2 knowledge) and then substitutes L2 lexical items, also
  making small repairs to the resulting string by means of the Monitor.

3 Routines and patterns (see the section on formulaic speech in Chapter
  7)
  Krashen rejects the view that formulaic speech (consisting of routines
  and patterns) contributes to 'acquisition'. In his opinion, formulas
  play a performance role only by helping the learner to 'outperform his
  competence'. They are not broken down, and their separate parts are
  not, therefore, incorporated into the learner's creative rule system.
  Rather 'acquisition' catches up with the routines and patterns; that is,
  the structural knowledge contained in the formulas is developed
  separately.

4 Individual differences
  Krashen claims that 'acquisition' follows a natural route (Hypothesis
  (2)). Thus there is no individual variation in the acquisition process

itself. However, there is variation in the rate and the extent of acquisition as a result of the amount of comprehensible input received, and the strength of the Affective Filter. There is also variation in performance, brought about by the extent of the learner's reliance on 'learnt' knowledge. Krashen indicates three types of Monitor Users: (1) over-users, (2) under-users, and (3) optimal users (i.e. those who apply conscious knowledge when it is appropriate).

5 Age
Age influences SLA in a number of ways. It affects the amount of comprehensible input that is obtained; younger learners may get more than older learners. Age also affects 'learning'; older learners are better suited to study language form and also to use 'learnt' knowledge in monitoring. Finally, age influences the affective state of the learner; after puberty the Affective Filter is likely to increase in strength.

Evaluation

Perhaps as a result of its prominence in SLA research, the Monitor Model has also attracted a lot of criticism. I shall select three central issues for detailed consideration. These are the 'acquisition–learning' distinction, the Monitor, and Krashen's treatment of variability. A fourth issue—Krashen's conceptualization of the role of input—has already been examined (see Chapter 6) and, will therefore, not be treated here.

The 'acquisition–learning' distinction　The 'acquisition–learning' distinction has been called 'theological', in that it has been formulated in order to confirm a specific goal, namely that successful SLA is the result of 'acquisition' (James 1980). McLaughlin (1978b) argues that the Monitor Model is unreliable, because the 'acquisition–learning' distinction is defined in terms of 'subconscious' and 'conscious' processes, which are not open to inspection. The first criticism, then, is a methodological one. The 'acquisition–learning' hypothesis is not acceptable, because it cannot be tested in empirical investigation.

A further objection concerns Krashen's claims that 'acquisition' and 'learning' are entirely separate, and that 'acquired' knowledge cannot turn into 'learnt' knowledge. Krashen refers to this as *the non-interface position*, which has been considered in some detail in Chapter 9. McLaughlin (1978b), Rivers (1980), Stevick (1980), Sharwood-Smith (1981), and Gregg (1984) have all challenged this position on the basis that when 'learnt' knowledge is automatized through practice it becomes 'acquired' i.e. available for use in spontaneous conversation.

Irrespective of whether the 'acquisition–learning' distinction is valid or not, it can also be criticized on the grounds that Krashen does not really explicate the cognitive processes that are responsible either for 'acquisition' or 'learning'. As Larsen-Freeman (1983b) observes, Krashen does not explain what the learner does with input. If the 'acquisition–learning' distinction is to have any power, it is surely necessary to specify in what way the processes responsible for each knowledge type are different from each other. This Krashen does not do. Thus, despite its comprehensiveness, the Monitor Model is still a 'black box' theory.

Monitoring　There are several difficulties with Krashen's account of Monitoring. One of these is again methodological. The only evidence for Monitoring lies in the language user's own account of trying to apply explicit rules (e.g. Cohen and Robbins 1976). But both McLaughlin (1978b) and Rivers (1980) point to the difficulty of distinguishing introspectively 'rule' application (as in Monitoring) and 'feel' (the implicit use of 'acquired' knowledge to judge or modify an utterance). Editing by 'feel' (or 'monitoring' with a small 'm') subsumes Monitoring (with a big 'M'). Both can be seen as aspects of what Morrison and Low (1983) refer to as the 'critical faculty'. This enables us to become critically aware of what we have created and hence allows us to control it. We are able to attend to the form of our utterances without using conscious rules, and without being able to make explicit how modifications in the initial output have been effected. This happens all the time in writing when we seek to conform to the conventions of the written medium, and it also happens in speech.

　　Morrison and Low offer a number of other criticisms of Monitoring. They point out that Monitoring does not account for the reception of utterances (i.e. as explained by Krashen, it refers only to production). They also note that Monitoring is limited to syntax, but in fact learners and users have the ability to edit their pronunciation, lexis, and, perhaps most important of all, their discourse. Krashen does not give any consideration to Monitoring as a collaborative activity involving both the learner and his interlocutor. To this list, I would also draw attention to the fact that Krashen tends to conflate Monitoring and 'learning', although the former refers to performance and the latter to rule internalization. As commented on above, there is no detailed discussion of how 'learning' takes place.

Variability　The Monitor Model is a 'dual competence' theory of SLA. That is, it proposes that the learner's knowledge of the L2, which is reflected in variable performance, is best characterized in terms of two separate competences, which Krashen labels 'acquisition' and 'learning'. The alternative position is to build a variable competence model (see next section), in which the learner's variable performance is seen as a reflection of a stylistic continuum. Which model—the Monitor Model or a variable competence model—best fits the known facts about SLA?

The available evidence indicates that learners produce utterances which are formally different even when it is evident that they are focused on meaning. Chapter 4 considered two utterances from Ellis (1984b) produced by one classroom learner within seconds of each other, each performing the same communicative function:

No look my card.   (instruction to another pupil during a
Don't look at my card.   word bingo game)

Data such as these, which are common in SLA research literature (see the case studies in Hatch, 1978a, for instance), demonstrate that even what Krashen calls 'acquired' knowledge is not homogeneous. But once claims about the homogeneity or 'acquired' knowledge are seen to be ill-founded, it makes little sense to maintain a dual competence explanation. The kinds of performance that result from focusing on meaning and on form are best treated as aspects of a single but variable competence which contains alternative rules for realizing the same meanings, in much the same way as does the native speaker's competence.

In summary, despite the comprehensiveness of the Monitor Model, it poses serious theoretical problems regarding the validity of the 'acquisition–learning' distinction, the operation of Monitoring, and the explanation of variability in language-learner language. Also the input hypothesis does not account for the fact that acquisition can take place without two-way negotiation of meaning, nor does it recognize that output also plays an important role.

5 The Variable Competence Model

The case for viewing the learner's knowledge of the L2 in terms of variable competence has already been made in Chapter 4. Here I shall summarize the Variable Competence theory proposed by Ellis (1984a). This draws on and extends the work of Tarone (1982; 1983), Widdowson (1979; 1984), and Bialystok (1982).

The Model is based on two distinctions—one of which refers to the process of language use, and the other to the product. The theory also proposes to account for SLA within a framework of language use. In other words, it claims that the way a language is learnt is a reflection of the way it is used.

The *product* of language use comprises a continuum of discourse types ranged from entirely unplanned to entirely planned. The planned–unplanned continuum has already been discussed in Chapter 4. To summarize briefly, unplanned discourse is discourse that lacks fore-thought and preparation. It is associated with spontaneous communication, e.g. everyday conversation or brainstorming in writing. Planned discourse is discourse that is thought out prior to expression. It requires conscious thought and the opportunity to work out content and expression. Examples are a prepared lecture or careful writing.

The *process* of language use is to be understood in terms of the distinction between linguistic knowledge (or *rules*) and the ability to make use of this knowledge (*procedures*). Widdowson (1984) refers to a knowledge of rules as *competence* and to a knowledge of the procedures involved in using rules to construct discourse as *capacity*. Widdowson points out that the narrow concept of linguistic competence has been widened to include appropriate use as well as correct use (i.e. communicative competence). But he argues that even this broader view of competence does not account for the language user's ability 'to create meanings by exploiting the potential inherent in the language for continual modification. . .' (Widdowson 1984: 8). It is for this reason that he adds the term *capacity*. The language user possesses procedures for realizing the meaning potential of rules in context. In other words, the language user makes his knowledge of linguistic rules work by exploiting them in relationship to both the situational and linguistic context. He actualizes his abstract knowledge of sentences to create utterances in discourse.

It follows from this view of the process of language use that the product (i.e. the different types of discourse) is the result of either or both of the following:

1 a variable competence, i.e. the user possesses a heterogeneous rule system;
2 variable application of procedures for actualizing knowledge in discourse.

The Variable Competence Model of SLA claims that both (1) and (2) occur. Furthermore, it claims that they are related.

The variability of the learner's rule system is described with reference to Bialystok's (1982) dual distinction between automatic/non-automatic and analytic/unanalytic (see Chapter 9). The first distinction concerns the relative access that the learner has to L2 knowledge. Knowledge that can be retrieved easily and quickly is automatic. Knowledge that takes time and effort to retrieve is non-automatic. The second distinction concerns the extent to which the learner possesses a 'propositional mental representation which makes clear the structure of the knowledge and its relationship to other aspects of knowledge' (op. cit., 183). Bialystok points out that unanalysed knowledge is the general form in which we know most things, in that we are usually not aware of the way in which our knowledge is structured. Both the automatic/non-automatic and the analysed/unanalysed distinctions represent continua rather than dichotomies. There are degrees of automatic and analysed knowledge.

Procedures for actualizing knowledge are of two types, which Ellis (1984a) refers to as primary and secondary processes.[7] Each set of processes has an external and internal representation, referred to as discourse and cognitive processes respectively. Primary processes are responsible for engaging in unplanned discourse. They draw on knowledge that is relatively unanalysed and automatic. Secondary processes come into play in planned discourse and draw on knowledge towards the analysed end of the continuum. An example of a primary process is *semantic simplification* (i.e. the omission of elements from a proposition in production). An example of a secondary process is *monitoring* (i.e. the editing of language performance). As an example of what is meant by discourse and cognitive processes, semantic simplification can be accounted for as follows:

Discourse process:
  Simplify the semantic structure of a message by omitting meaning elements that are communicatively redundant or that can be realized by a non-verbal device (e.g. mime)

Cognitive process:
  (a) Construct an underlying conceptual structure of a message.
  (b) Compare this structure with the frame of reference shared with an interlocutor.
  (c) Eliminate redundant elements and elements for which no lexical item is available.

Primary and secondary processes account for how L2 learners actualize their linguistic knowledge in discourse. They account for the variability of language-learner language by positing that both different types of knowledge and different procedures are involved in the construction of different discourse types. They also account for acquisition. To explain how, it is necessary to return to what Widdowson has to say about rules and procedures.

Widdowson argues that through using procedures, not only does the language user utilize his existing linguistic knowledge but he also, potentially at least, creates new linguistic rules. As Widdowson (1979: 62) puts it:

  We draw upon our knowledge of rules to *make sense*. We do not simply measure discourse up against our knowledge of pre-existing rules, we create discourse and commonly bring new rules into existence by so doing. All competence is transitional in this sense.

In other words, language acquisition is the result of our capacity to make sense. New rules are created when we endeavour to use existing knowledge in relation to the linguistic and situational context in order to create shared frames of reference. A theory of language use is the matrix of a theory of language acquisition.

Ellis (1984a) goes one step further and suggests that SLA follows the sequence that it does because the processes that the learner calls on to participate in discourse are themselves developmental. That is, their prominence in SLA coincides with different stages of development.

Thus, for instance, early SLA is characterized by the heavy use of semantic simplification, because this is a procedure that requires little L2 knowledge. Later procedures, such as those used to reduce reliance on shared knowledge and non-verbal devices, by making explicit the relationship between one proposition and another and between each proposition and its situational context (see Widdowson (1984: 67ff), are characteristic of later SLA. Also knowledge that to begin with is available only for use via secondary processes (because it exists only in analysed form) can eventually be accessed by means of primary processes and so used in unplanned as well as planned discourse.

To summarize, the Variable Competence Model proposes:

1 There is a single knowledge store containing variable interlanguage rules according to how automatic and how analysed the rules are.
2 The learner possesses a capacity for language use which consists of primary and secondary discourse and cognitive processes.
3 L2 performance is variable as a result of whether primary processes employing unanalysed L2 rules are utilized in unplanned discourse, or secondary processes employing analysed L2 rules are utilized in planned discourse.
4 Development occurs as a result of
   (a) acquisition of new L2 rules through participation in various types of discourse (i.e. new rules originate in the application of procedural knowledge);
   (b) activation of L2 rules which initially exist in either a non-automatic unanalysed form or in an analysed form so they can be used in unplanned discourse.

These proposals are shown in Figure 10.3.

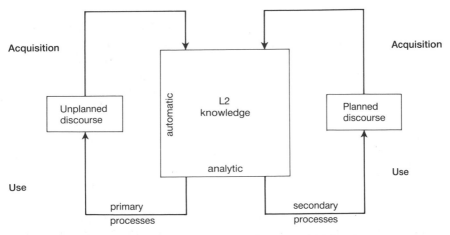

Figure 10.3   Variable Competence Model of SLA

Evaluation

The Variable Competence Model of SLA attempts to account for (1) the variability of language-learner language, and (2) the external and internal processes responsible for SLA. It incorporates within the same framework a theory of language use and a theory of SLA. As it stands at the moment, the Model is in need of development in two directions. First it needs to provide a more detailed analysis of the primary and secondary processes responsible for use and acquisition. Second, it needs to incorporate the role of input into the overall framework. Learners do not construct discourse in isolation (at least not in face-to-face interaction), so how input is negotiated must be considered. SLA is the result of the exchange of linguistic information which occurs in the process of discourse construction involving both the learner and an interlocutor.

6 The Universal Hypothesis

An adequate summary of the Universal Hypothesis can be found in Chapter 8, so it will not be recapitulated here. A few evaluative comments, however, will be added.

Evaluation

The Universal Hypothesis provides an interesting account of how the linguistic properties of the target language and the learner's first language may influence the course of development. It constitutes an attempt to explain SLA in terms of an independent language faculty, rather than in more general cognitive terms. One advantage of this is that it brings SLA studies into line with current linguistic research that follows the Chomskyan tradition. It also avoids the quagmire of explanations based on learner strategies.

The value of the Universal Hypothesis for SLA theory is twofold: (1) it focuses attention on the nature of the target language itself, lending support to Wode's (1980b: 136/7) claim that 'the linguistic devices used in a given language are the major variable(s) determining . . . linguistic sequences'; and (2) it provides a subtle and persuasive reconsideration of transfer as an important factor in SLA.

One of the major problems of the Universal Hypothesis lies in the difficulty in defining the markedness construct. Various criteria have been used to explicate it—core vs peripheral grammar, complexity and explicitness. Moreover, it is not clear whether markedness is to be seen as just a linguistic construct or whether it has psycholinguistic validity.

Even if linguistic markedness is a major determinant of SLA (and this is not yet proven, as it is possible that many of the facts explained in terms of markedness theory might also be explained by other factors, such as the frequency of occurrence of different structures in the input), it is unlikely that it will be able to explain the complexity of SLA by itself. In addition, the Universal Hypothesis operates on the assumption that linguistic knowledge is homogeneous, and, therefore, ignores variability.

7 A neurofunctional theory

Whereas all the previous models discussed have attempted to explain SLA in linguistic or *psycholinguistic* terms, the theory considered in this section draws on *neurolinguistic* research. It constitutes, therefore, a different type of explanation. Lamendella (1979: 5/6) defines the scope of a neurofunctional approach as follows:

> A neurofunctional perspective on language attempts to characterize the neurolinguistic information processing systems responsible for the development and use of language.

The account of a neurofunctional theory of SLA that follows draws primarily on the work of Lamendella (1977; 1979; Selinker and Lamendella 1978b).

The basic premise of a neurofunctional view of SLA is that there is a connection between language function and the neural anatomy. It is important, however, to recognize that, as Hatch (1983a: 213) puts it, 'there is no single "black box" for language in the brain'. It is not possible to identify precisely which areas of the brain are associated with language functioning. Therefore it is better to speak of 'the relative contribution of some areas more than others under certain conditions' (Seliger 1982: 309). The adult's brain never entirely loses the plasticity of the new-born baby's brain, with the result that in cases of damage to specific areas of neural tissue (as in aphasia), the functions associated with those areas need not be completely lost, but transferred to other areas.

Neurofunctional accounts of SLA have considered the contribution of two areas of the brain: (1) the right (as opposed to the left) hemisphere, and (2) the areas of the left hemisphere (in particular those known as Wernicke's and Broca's areas), which clinical studies have shown to be closely associated with the comprehension and production of language. Neurofunctional accounts have also tended to focus on specific aspects of SLA: (1) age differences, (2) formulaic speech, (3) fossilization, and (4) pattern practice in classroom SLA. The relationship between the maturation of neural mechanisms and SLA has already been considered (see Chapter 5) and so will not be dealt with again here. The other issues are considered briefly below in a discussion of the two areas of the brain that research has focused on.

Right hemisphere functioning

Right hemisphere functioning is generally associated with holistic processing, as opposed to serial or analytic processing, which occurs in the left hemisphere. Not surprisingly, therefore, it has been suggested (e.g. by Obler 1981; Krashen 1981a) that the right hemisphere is responsible for the storing and processing of formulaic speech. The routines and patterns which comprise formulaic speech are unanalysed wholes and as such belong to the 'gestalt' perception of the right hemisphere. It has also been suggested that right hemisphere involvement in L2 processing will be more evident in the early, non-proficient stages than in later, more advanced stages of SLA. This hypothesis is compatible with the link between the right hemisphere and formulaic speech, as the early stages of SLA are more likely to be characterized by heavy use of formulaic speech. However, Genesee (1982), reviewing this hypothesis, found conflicting evidence. Out of the thirteen studies he examined, three provided positive support, six found comparable patterns of left hemisphere involvement, and four were opposed to the stage hypothesis. Genesee concluded that the stage hypothesis has received insufficient support. He found greater support for another hypothesis concerning right hemisphere involvement, namely that it is associated to a greater extent with informal than formal language acquisition. This hypothesis is also compatible with the right hemisphere connection with formulaic speech, which is generally considered to be more prominent in settings where natural language use is common. It seems, therefore, that there is considerable evidence to associate the acquisition and use of formulaic speech with the right hemisphere.

The right hemisphere may also be involved in pattern practice in classroom SLA. Seliger (1982) suggests that the right hemisphere may act as an initial staging mechanism for handling patterns which can then be re-examined later in left hemisphere functioning. Pattern practice and minimal pair drills may utilize right hemisphere abilities in the adult learner and so contribute to what Seliger calls 'primitive hypotheses'. If subsequent analysis by the left hemisphere does not take place, the learner will not be able to utilize the language forms that have been drilled in the construction of spontaneous, creative speech. This offers an interesting neurolinguistic explanation of why formal language practice does not appear to facilitate natural language use immediately (see Chapter 9).

Left hemisphere functioning

Where the left hemisphere is concerned, there is less clarity regarding the location of specific language functions. In general the left hemisphere is associated with creative language use, including syntactic and semantic processing and the motor operations involved in speaking and writing.

However the extent to which these different functions can be localized is not clear (see Hatch 1983a for a detailed review of this issue). Walsh and Diller (1981) distinguish two broad types of functioning: (1) lower order functioning and (2) higher order functioning. The former, associated with Wernicke's and Broca's area, involves basic grammatical processing, together with the motor operations. The latter, associated with a different area of the cerebral cortex, involves semantic processing and verbal cognition. Walsh and Diller suggest that lower-order processing is a function of early maturing, while higher-order processing depends on late developing neural circuitry. Thus whereas younger learners rely primarily on lower-order processing, older learners make use of higher-order processing. There have also been suggestions that different levels of language processing (e.g. pronunciation vs. syntax) are linked to different neural mechanisms. The fact that different aspects of language fossilize at different times (e.g. learners with native-like syntax but non-native pronunciation are not uncommon) is evidence of this. Seliger (1978) develops an interesting argument based on neurolinguistic evidence to support a differential fossilization hypothesis. In general, though, claims about localized functions need to be treated circumspectly.

These various observations do not amount to a theory of SLA. However, Lamendella has attempted to formulate a neurofunctional theory of SLA. This is described below.

Lamendella's Neurofunctional Theory

Lamendella distinguishes two basic types of language acquisition: (1) Primary Language Acquisition and (2) Secondary Language Acquisition. (1) is found in the child's acquisition of one or more languages from 2 to 5 years. (2) is subdivided into (a) foreign language learning (i.e. the formal classroom learning of a L2), and (b) second language acquisition (i.e. the natural acquisition of a L2 after the age of five).

Linked to these two types of language acquisition are different neurofunctional systems, each of which consists of a hierarchy of functions. Each system has a different overall role in information processing. Lamendella pinpoints two systems as particularly important for language functioning:

1 The communication hierarchy: this has responsibility for language and other forms of interpersonal communication.
2 The cognitive hierarchy: this controls a variety of cognitive information processing activities that are also part of language use.

Primary language acquisition and also second language acquisition (i.e. (2b)) are marked by the use of the communication hierarchy, whereas foreign language acquisition, i.e. (2a), is marked by the use of the cognitive hierarchy. Pattern practice drills are likely to involve the cognitive hierarchy and hence material learnt in this way is not available in language behaviour that draws on the communicative hierarchy. As Lamendella puts it:

> . . . the executive functions of the communication hierarchy do not seem to have the capacity to call up automated subroutines whose construction was directed by the cognitive hierarchy. (1979: 17)

Thus the theory posits a different neurolinguistic base for the kind of acquisition and language use typically found in natural SLA and tutored SLA. The distinction between the communicative and cognitive hierarchies seems to parallel the psycholinguistic distinction between 'acquisition' and 'learning' in the Monitor Model.

Each neurofunctional system is composed of different levels, ranged from higher to lower order, and each associated with different levels of neural organization (which Lamendella does not specify). The different levels can be interconnected, but they can also be disassociated. Thus, for instance, it is possible to engage what Lamendella calls 'copying circuits' in order to repeat what someone has said, without engaging other circuits that are responsible for language comprehension or formulation (e.g. a typist can type out a letter without bothering to understand its content). Furthermore, L2 forms acquired by means of higher-level systems can be stored as automatic sub-routines at lower levels of the communication hierarchy. In language performance, lower-level sub-routines can be accessed without calling upon higher levels within the same hierarchy.

Lamendella sums up the task facing the language learner:

> When first confronted with the need to acquire new information structures . . . a learner must identify the functional hierarchy best suited to this learning, then establish the appropriate level and subsystems within the hierarchy with which to begin the learning process. (1979: 15)

In other words, Lamendella claims that SLA can be explained neurofunctionally with reference to (1) which neurofunctional system is used—the communication or the cognitive—and (2) which level within the chosen neurofunctional system is engaged.

Evaluation

Neurofunctional explanations of SLA are based on the premise that it is possible to trace the neurolinguistic correlates of specific language functions. However, there is still considerable uncertainty regarding the identification of specific neurofunctions and their neurolinguistic correlates. The evidence from clinical studies (see Genesee 1982) is conflicting. Also it is not clear to what extent studies of language *processing* based on tests where linguistic stimuli are presented separately to the left and right ear (i.e. dichotic listening tests) or studies of aphasia, which together serve as the major sources of information about neurofunctioning, provide reliable insights into the neurolinguistic bases of language *acquisition.*

Lamendella's neurofunctional theory offers an interesting account of a number of facts about SLA (e.g. the inutility of material learnt through pattern practice in spontaneous communication). But there are many facts which it does not explain (or even seek to). In particular it is not clear how it can account for the natural sequence of development. Also the distinction between foreign and second language learning is a simplification. As discussed in Chapters 6 and 9, it is not so much the type of setting which is important, as the type of interaction which occurs in these settings. Thus natural communication in a L2 is quite possible in a foreign language classroom.

Neurolinguistic and neurofunctional explanations are perhaps best treated as affording additional understanding about SLA, rather than an explanation of it. However, in the long run it will be useful if psycholinguistic constructs used to explain SLA can be matched up with neurofunctional mechanisms.

Conclusion: towards a composite picture

What aspects of SLA must a theory of SLA cover in order to provide a composite picture? To answer this question I shall return to the framework outlined in Chapter 1. This will serve as a basis for summarizing the first six theories discussed in the previous section (the neurofunctional perspective is excluded, as this constitutes a different kind of account of SLA). I shall then use the framework to present what I see as the key issues in SLA in the form of a number of hypotheses. These will draw on many of the constructs to be found in the six theories and also on the different aspects of SLA which have been considered in the previous chapters. The statement of the key issues is an attempt to summarize the major variables involved in SLA.

The framework for investigating SLA reconsidered

In Chapter 1 a number of components of SLA were considered. These were (1) situational factors, (2) the linguistic input, (3) learner differences, (4) learner processes, and (5) linguistic output. Figure 10.4 below shows the interrelationship between these components. Situational factors influence input (e.g. input in a classroom setting is likely to differ from that in a natural setting) and also the use of learner processes (e.g. communication strategies). Learner differences on such variables as motivation and personality help to determine the quantity and quality of the input and also affect the operation of learner strategies (e.g. the use of metalingual strategies). Input comprises (1) the inherent properties of the target language system, and (2) the formally and interactionally adjusted features found in foreigner and teacher talk. Input constitutes the data upon which the learner strategies work, but also the input is itself in part determined by the learner's use of communication strategies. Thus the relationship between input and learner processes is an interactive one. The learner's strategies (composed of learning, production, and communication strategies) produce a variable L2 output. This in turn is part of the input. Thus the framework is cyclical. Table 10.2 summarizes the main premises of the six theories of SLA. It shows that none of the theories covers all the slots of the framework, although taken together they do so.

A theory, of course, does not stand by its exhaustiveness. Equally, if not more important, is whether the premises upon which a theory rests are valid (i.e. consistent with the known facts) and internally consistent (i.e. non-contradictory). The evaluation of the six theories indicates that in some cases there are grounds for disputing the validity of the premises.

I turn now to a consideration of the basic issues which a theory of SLA will need to consider. These are presented as a series of hypotheses.

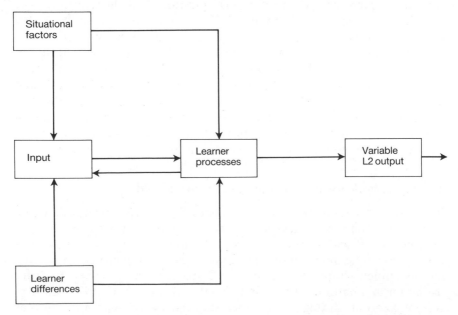

Figure 10.4   A framework for examining the components of SLA

SLA theory	Situational factors	Input (1) Target language features	Input (2) Adjusted input features	Learner differences	Learner strategies (1) Learning	Learner strategies (2) Production	Learner strategies (3) Communication	Variable L2 output
Acculturation theory/Nativization Theory	Considers only naturalistic SLA. Within this, distinguishes different settings.			These are treated in terms of socio-psychological variables affecting social and psychological distance.	Initially the learner assimilates to an internal norm; later he accommodates to an external norm.			
Accommodation Theory	Considers only naturalistic SLA. Within this, distinguishes different settings.	Target language represents a shifting target as a result of NS's upward divergence.		These are treated in terms of socio-psychological variables affecting the learner's perception of his ethnic ingroup and the L2 outgroup.				Learner makes variable use of L2 depending on use of ethnic speech markers to converge or diverge.
Discourse Theory	Considers only naturalistic SLA. Focuses on one-to-one conversations between NSs and NNSs.		Input features are adjusted formally and interactionally in the negotiation of meaning.	Learners differ in terms of the conversational strategies they employ. A major factor is age.				Learners make use of (1) formulaic speech; (2) vertical structures; (3) creative rules.
Monitor Model	Considers both classroom and naturalistic SLA.		Comprehensible input consists of 'i + 1'.	Learners differ in terms of (1) socio-affective variables which determine strength of filter, (2) level of Monitoring.	One set of mechanisms for 'acquisition', another for 'learning'.		Monitoring functions as production strategy.	Variability is a product of application of Monitor.
Variable Competence Model	Considers both classroom and naturalistic SLA.		Input differs in terms of level of planning of discourse.	Learners differ in their preference for planned or unplanned discourse.	Two sets of processes for engaging in planned and unplanned discourse also govern internalization of L2 knowledge.			Variability is product of use of primary or secondary processes or mixture.
Markedness Theory	Treats SLA as a uniform phenomenon.	Features of target language seen as 'core' (unmarked) or 'peripheral' (degrees of markedness).			Assumes learner selects less complex data for attention before more complex.			

Table 10.2. A summary of the scope of six theories of SLA

Eleven hypotheses about SLA

The hypotheses are organized in sections corresponding to the components of SLA identified in Figure 10.4. In addition there are two general hypotheses. Each hypothesis will be presented with a brief discussion where necessary, together with cross-references to relevant chapters.

General

Hypothesis 1 SLA follows a natural *sequence* of development, but there will be minor variations in the *order* of development and more major variations in the *rate* of development and in the *level of proficiency* achieved.

The sequence refers to the general stages of development which characterize SLA, and the order to the development of specific grammatical features. This distinction, together with the evidence for it, is considered in Chapter 3. Variations in the rate and success of SLA are examined in Chapter 5.

Hypothesis 2 At any one stage of development, the learner's *interlanguage* comprises a system of *variable rules*.

Whereas Hypothesis (1) refers to vertical variability, this hypothesis acknowledges horizontal variability. The two are closely related, in that horizontal variability is the mirror of vertical variability. This relationship is examined in Chapter 4.

Situation

Hypothesis 3 Situational factors are indirect determinants of the rate of SLA and also of the level of proficiency achieved, but they do not influence the sequence of development, and affect the order of development only in minor and temporary ways.

It follows from this hypothesis that classroom and naturalistic SLA will follow the same developmental route (see Chapter 9). It also follows that differences in specific settings (e.g. in terms of the level of formality) will not influence the developmental route. This would appear to contradict the important role played by situational factors in language-learner variability. But it should be remembered that the notions of sequence and order of SLA apply to the learner's vernacular style, which has been taken to be primary (see Chapter 4). Situational factors do not affect the route of development evident in the vernacular style.

Hypothesis 4 Situational factors are the primary causes of variability in language-learner language.

Situational factors (i.e. who is addressing whom, when, about what, and where) govern the learner's variable use of his interlanguage in the same way as they govern the native speaker's use of his mother tongue. This hypothesis is considered in Chapter 4.

Input

Hypothesis 5   Input that is interactionally (but not necessarily formally) adjusted as a result of the negotiation of meaning in two-way discourse between the learner and another speaker functions as a determinant (but not the sole determinant) of the sequence of development, the order of development, and the rate of development.

This hypothesis draws on the Discourse Theory in allocating a constitutive role for adjusted input in SLA. It recognizes, however, that adjusted input cannot alone explain SLA. Chapter 6 considers the role of input.

Learner differences

Hypothesis 6   Affective learner differences (e.g. those relating to motivation and personality) determine the rate of SLA and the level of proficiency achieved, but not the sequence or order of development.

The contribution of individual learner differences is considered in Chapter 5.

Hypothesis 7   The learner's first language influences the order of development (although not in major ways), but it does not affect the sequence of development.

While behaviourist accounts of the role of the first language have not proved durable, more cognitive explanations of transfer show that the first language is still an important factor in SLA (see Chapter 2). It is doubtful, however, if the sequence of development is affected by the first language. It is more likely that the appearance of specific grammatical features in the order of development of different learners can be traced to their first language, perhaps as a result of the degree of markedness of the same features in the first language (see Chapter 8).

Learner processes

Hypothesis 8   Interlanguage development occurs as a product of the learner's use of procedural knowledge to construct discourse.

The centrality of procedural knowledge (or capacity) in the process of using and building an interlanguage has been discussed in this chapter (see the account of the Variable Competence Model.). The nature of the learner's procedural knowledge was described in Chapter 7. This identified three kinds of learner strategies. The following three corollaries of hypothesis 9 are based on this classification:

Corollary 1: The processes of hypothesis testing, hypothesis formation, and automatization account for how the learner operates on input data, and determine the sequence and order of development.

Corollary 2: Performance strategies (such as semantic simplification) account for the variable use of the learner's interlanguage system in different contexts of use.

Corollary 3: Communication strategies enable the learner to obtain comprehensible input, and also contribute to the variability of language-learner language performance.

Hypothesis 9 Interlanguage development occurs as the product of the learner's universal grammar, which makes some rules easier to learn than others.

This hypothesis can be seen as an alternative to hypothesis (8) in that it seeks to explain the learner's 'black box' in terms of an independent linguistic faculty. However, hypotheses (8) and (9) are not mutually incompatible. It is conceivable that some features of SLA are the result of linguistic processing and reflect 'acquisition', and others the result of more general cognitive factors and reflect 'development'. The evidence for the Universal Hypothesis was considered in Chapter 8.

Linguistic output

Hypothesis 10 Language-learner language consists of (1) formulaic speech, and (2) utterances constructed creatively.

This hypothesis gives recognition to a basic difference in the linguistic output. The evidence for it is discussed in Chapter 7. Formulaic speech may play a part in interlanguage development—a possibility accounted for by Corollary (1) of hypothesis (9), in that processes of hypothesis testing, etc. can operate on formulas in the same way as they operate on input.

Hypothesis 11 Language learner language is variable, dynamic, but also systematic.

These characteristics of the linguistic output—which constitute the primary evidence for the preceding hypotheses—were examined in Chapters 3 and 4.

It is unlikely that all SLA researchers would agree with all eleven of these hypotheses, and they might well want to phrase some in rather different ways, or attribute a different emphasis to them. However, they reflect the basic issues which have directed SLA enquiry and which will need to be considered in any composite picture of SLA.

Notes

1 Krashen's Monitor Model and Dulay and Burt's Creative Construction Theory are closely related, sharing many premises. The former is considered in this chapter, as a recognition of the considerable interest is has aroused in SLA research.
2 More than one type of 'bad' learning situation is possible, as many of the variables permit three-way alternatives. For instance, a 'bad' situation arises when the target language group sees itself as either dominant *or* subordinate.
3 Schumann's (1978a) study of Alberto lasted ten months. This is perhaps too short a period to conclude that fossilization has taken place. Ellis (1984a) observed little syntactical development in three classroom learners over a similar period, but another twelve months showed evidence of considerable development.
4 To the best of my knowledge, neither Schumann and Andersen has discussed the application of their theories to classroom SLA. The psychological factors which Schumann considers are likely to be relevant to the classroom, as Gardner and Lambert's (1972) work on motivation and attitude has shown (see Chapter 6).
5 Brown (1980a) has in fact criticized Schumann's theory on the grounds that there is no objective means of measuring actual social distance. He points out that it is how the learner views his own culture in relation to the culture of the target language community that affects SLA.
6 Giles also identifies a third type of speech marker—*upward divergence*—which occurs when an outgroup speaker accentuates speech markers that distinguish him from the ingroup speaker. In so doing the outgroup speaker may deviate from the standard forms of his language. Thus the L2 learner may find the prestige dialect 'an ever-moving target' (Giles and Byrne 1982: 22).
7 The terms 'primary' and 'secondary processes' are chosen to reflect the primacy of unplanned discourse. It is not intended to suggest that 'primary processes' are more important than 'secondary processes', only that they are responsible for the style associated with spontaneous face-to-face communication.

Further reading

'Second language acquisition: getting the whole picture' by D. Larsen-Freeman in *Second Language Acquisition Studies*, edited by K. Bailey, M. Long, and S. Peck (Newbury House, 1983), provides an overview of a number of SLA theories, together with some interesting comments about the nature of theory building in SLA research.

Schumann's Acculturation Model receives a full treatment in *The Pidginization Hypothesis: A Model for Second Language Acquisition* by J. Schumann (Newbury House, 1978). R. Andersen's Introduction to *Pidginization and Creolization as Language Acquisition*, edited by R. Andersen (Newbury House, 1983), reviews the analogy between pidginization/depidginization and SLA.

A full account of the Accommodation Model as it applies to SLA can be found in 'An intergroup approach to second language acquisition' by H. Giles and J. Byrne (*Journal of Multilingual and Multicultural Development* 3/1).

'A look at process in child second language acquisition' by E. Hatch, S. Peck, and J. Wagner-Gough in *Developmental Pragmatics* edited by E. Ochs and B. Schieffelin (Academic Press, 1979), discusses the main features of the Discourse Theory.

There are innumerable statements of the Monitor Model. For the reader who wants a detailed account, S. Krashen's *Second Language Acquisition and Second Language Learning* (Pergamon, 1981) is recommended. There are also many critiques. 'Krashen's Monitor Model and Occam's razor' by K. Gregg (*Applied Linguistics* 5/2) is one of the most recent.

For the Variable Competence Model see *Classroom Second Language Development* by R. Ellis (Pergamon, 1984) (Chapter 7).

'Two perspectives on fossilization in interlanguage' by L. Selinker and J. Lamendella (*Interlanguage Studies Bulletin* 3) is perhaps the best account of Lamendella's Neurofunctional Theory.

Conclusion

The purpose of this chapter is to step back and take a look at second language acquisition (SLA) research in order to assess what has been achieved and what still needs to be done. In attempting this, I shall offer a more personal view than in the other chapters.

The field of SLA research is scarcely more than fifteen years old. Before 1970 there was only a handful of empirical studies of SLA. Before 1967, when Corder published his seminal paper 'The significance of learners' errors', there was also little theoretical enquiry. As discussed in Chapter 2, there was an assumption that SLA could be accounted for by extrapolating from general learning theory. The 1970s saw a growing body of empirical studies of SLA. These were both cross-sectional (e.g. the morpheme studies) and longitudinal (e.g. Cazden *et al*. 1975). At the same time, theorizing about SLA flourished, both stimulating and stimulated by the empirical research. Currently SLA publications appear at a rate that researchers struggle to keep up with, and the field has sub-divided into fairly recognizable areas of interest—creolinguistics, input/ interaction, learner strategies, classroom SLA, universal grammar, etc.

This startling growth of interest in SLA prompts a number of questions. What has stimulated the growth? How much have we actually found out about SLA? What are the outstanding problems? I shall take a brief look at each of these questions and then conclude with a set of questions which have motivated SLA research in the past and are likely to continue to do so in the future.

Factors stimulating SLA research

In order to understand the surge of interest in SLA, it is useful to distinguish what motivated it and what made research possible.

The chief motivation was undoubtedly the paradigm shift brought about in linguistics and related fields by Chomsky's theory of grammar. Behaviourist accounts of L1 learning were discredited (see Chapter 3), and the focus of attention shifted from learner-external to learner-internal factors. The child was seen as an active contributor to the learning process. This paradigm shift provided the theoretical impetus to challenge the prevailing theory of L2 learning (i.e. the Contrastive Analysis Hypothesis). It is perhaps a puzzling irony that when the prevailing theory emphasized environmental factors, there were no actual studies of what happened during SLA, and that it took a theory that stressed innate mental factors before such studies got underway. The reason, of course, was the desire to test empirically the rival claims of competing theories.

SLA studies have from the outset owed a great deal to the methodology and theory of L1 acquisition research. The methodology of the morpheme studies was a direct borrowing of the analytical techniques developed by Brown (1973) and de Villiers and de Villiers (1973) for L1 acquisition. The case studies have also adopted the techniques used by L1 researchers. The theoretical focus of SLA enquiry has shifted in accordance with the changes of direction in L1 acquisition research. For instance, the resurgence of interest in input/interaction is directly traceable to the studies of motherese. It is not surprising, therefore, that one of the abiding issues in SLA research has been the L2 = L1 hypothesis. SLA researchers have always felt free (if not obligated) to make reference to L1 acquisition, but it is interesting to note that this attention is not often repaid by L1 researchers. SLA continues to feed methodologically and theoretically off L1 acquisition research, but not vice versa.

If L1 acquisition research has provided many of the tools of SLA research, the language teaching profession has helped to pay for them. In the United States, funding has been (and still is) made available by the Department of Health, Education, and Welfare. In Canada, the bilingual education studies which have provided a wealth of information about SLA have also been publicly funded to a large extent. In both these countries the public concern for the education of ethnic-minority children and the recognition that language learning is a crucial issue in the planning and implementing of educational programmes have led to finance being made available to carry out research projects. It is not chance, therefore, that the bulk of the research has taken place in North America. It is only recently that a major publicly-funded European initiative—The European Science Foundation Project on Second Language Acquisition by Adult Immigrants—has got under way.

The potential importance of SLA research for the language teaching profession has not only ensured that funding is available, it has also led to much of the research having an 'applied' perspective. Language teachers want to know how SLA research can help them to make language learning more effective in the classroom. To this end it has been customary for research reports to conclude with a brief section devoted to 'implications', where a number of suggestions, usually of a general nature, are made concerning what or how teachers should teach. Much of the earlier research, however, investigated naturalistic (or mixed) SLA, motivated by the felt need to discover how informal learning takes place. More recently, attention has been focused on the direct study of classroom SLA.

Not all SLA research has been 'applied' in orientation. There has also been a lot of 'pure' research. As knowledge of the field has grown, research questions and hypotheses have been generated and investigated without reference to whether they are relevant or not to the classroom. It is my opinion that 'pure' SLA research is becoming more common as time passes, although there are still many researchers for whom the classroom remains the focal issue. There is, of course, no reason why SLA research should not help to inform other areas of human enquiry. Lightbown (1984) shows how the fields of linguistics, social psychology, sociolinguistics, neurolinguistics, and psychology have contributed to SLA research. The contribution can be two-way.

Understanding SLA

The second question I want to address is 'How much do we know about SLA?' This is the question that has guided this whole book, and the preceding chapters have been an attempt to provide an answer. I shall not attempt a summary (this has already been done in Chapter 10). Instead I want to consider briefly our understanding of SLA in general terms with regard to our ability to describe SLA and to explain it.

We now know quite a lot about what SLA consists of. There is considerable evidence to suggest that learners of a particular L2 follow a fairly well-defined sequence of development, and that even the order in which specific morphemes are acquired is subject to only minor modifications as a result of the learner's L1 or the environmental setting. The investigation of transitional structures such as negatives and interrogatives also shows that there is a clear developmental route. The interim rules which learners build in acquiring these structures may even hold across acquisitional types (Wode 1984). In addition, we know quite a lot about the nature of the input that L2 learners receive both inside and outside the classroom. These descriptive studies have built up a picture of how learners assemble a knowledge of a L2. Lightbown (1984) concludes:

> We have now scores of descriptive studies covering many odds and ends, bits and pieces of learner's language chosen for analysis because they caught the researcher's eye, seemed to exhibit some systematicity, or confirmed some intuition one had about SLA. Such research has, in fact, confirmed that there are patterns of regularity in learner's developing interlanguage.

In other words, descriptive studies of SLA have dominated the field.

Just how 'universal' the course of development is, however, remains a matter of some disagreement. Lightbown goes on to point out that for every descriptive study that demonstrates the existence of a universal pattern, there is another that provides counter-evidence. The influence of the L1, variation in input, and even the degree of social integration of the learner into the target language community have been shown to have some influence on the acquisition route. This raises the important question of how to interpret the descriptive studies. How much weight should be attached to the claims about a universal pattern? It is not surprising that different researchers give different answers. On the one hand there are those, who, like Krashen, take the natural order as proven, while on the other hand there are those like Lightbown, who, while recognizing the existence of 'regularity', remain sceptical about universality. In Chapter 3 I suggested that while there is a natural *sequence* which specifies the general outline of development, there will be differences in the *order* of development of specific features. It is, perhaps, inevitable that there should be both counterfactual evidence and opposing interpretations, given the large number of variables which studies of SLA have to grapple with. However, until some means of reconciling these differences can be agreed upon, it must be acknowledged that, despite our increasing knowledge of what takes place in SLA, we are not yet able to produce a description that is both generalizable and reliable.

When it comes to *explaining* SLA, the differences among researchers are much greater. Consider, for instance, the alternative explanations of negative utterances where the negator is external to the rest of the utterance:

No speak Portuguese.
No finish book.
No like beer.

This regularity has received considerable attention from researchers, and a number of different explanations have been offered:

1 *Transfer strategy*
Spanish and Portuguese learners have pre-verbal negation in their L1s (which also permit subject pronoun deletion). Therefore, when such learners produce utterances displaying external negation, they may simply be using the negative pattern of their L1s.

2 *Production strategy*
A second possibility is that such utterances are the product of a general process of simplification, which is evident in all L2 production. If the learner is credited with 'knowing' that negation in English is internal as in:

I no speak Portuguese, etc.

the occurrence of what is apparently external negation can be explained as the result of a pro-drop rule (i.e. a production rule which states that pronouns can be deleted from sentences). This production strategy will, of course, be evident in both positive and negative utterances.

3 *Acquisition strategy*
It is also possible that 'no X' utterances reflect the natural language processing mechanisms of the brain. In this view, external negation is not the result of restrictive simplification, but of an acquisition strategy which governs how learners handle negation in all languages. Wode (1984), for instance, points out that the 'neg X' structure is not counter to the universal constraints on the structural options available in natural languages. An extension of this explanation is to argue that 'no X' is an 'unmarked' structure in comparison to internal negation (Felix 1984).

4 *Interactional strategy*
Yet another possibility is that 'no X' is the result of an interactional strategy. That is, the learner borrows a chunk from the previous discourse and then attaches the negator to the front of it:

A. Do you like beer?
B. No like beer.

The learner may then memorize the pattern which he has constructed as a vertical structure and later may use it to initiate his own negative utterances.

My purpose is not to argue that one explanation is better than another. Rather, I wish to use the 'neg X' pattern as an example of a general issue in SLA studies, namely that a generally acknowledged descriptive feature of SLA can be accounted for in very different ways. The same phenomena can be used to justify opposing theories of SLA.

It is likely that we will be in a better position to choose among competing explanations as our understanding of SLA increases. Already, for instance, we have enough evidence to reject (1) above. But it is not at all clear whether we will be able to arrive at a final unambiguous interpretation. In order to explain SLA, it is necessary to probe the internal mechanisms that are responsible for processing input data. The evidence available will always be indirect (i.e. the utterances that comprise the learner's output or introspective observations). It is likely, therefore, that there will always be room for multiple explanations.

In reviewing what we understand about SLA, I have sought to be cautionary. There is an abundance of descriptive evidence, but no unanimity about what this tells us. It will take time and much research slowly to eliminate inappropriate explanations. It is also possible that a single phenomenon is the result of more than one cause.

Problems in SLA research

Four principal issues will be considered here: (1) the centrality of morphosyntax; (2) the failure to consider function as well as form; (3) the piecemeal approach to describing interlanguage; and (4) methodology. Each issue is problematic in one way or another.

As was made clear in Chapter 1 the study of L2 learner-language has been almost entirely taken up with investigating how learners develop grammatical knowledge. This book has reflected this preoccupation. The centrality of grammar in linguistics has been echoed in SLA studies. Acquiring a L2 has meant acquiring the grammar of the L2. There have been a few studies of interlanguage phonology (e.g. Dickerson 1975; Tarone 1978), but hardly any of vocabulary (see Meara 1980 for a review) or of pragmatic development (although see a recent collection of articles by Wolfson and Judd (1983)). Our understanding of SLA, is therefore, very lop-sided. Moreover, the priority given to grammar is not likely to correspond to the learner's approach. Informal learners, at least, are more concerned with communicating than with acquiring grammatical rules. To this end, their focus is likely to be on developing lexical resources and pragmatic skills. SLA research needs to redress the present imbalance by paying more attention to these other aspects of language.

There is another reason for extending the range of SLA enquiry beyond grammar. The acquisition of one linguistic level is unlikely to proceed in total independence of other levels. Hatch (1983a) suggests that L2 learners' preference for post-verb relative clauses (i.e. those modifying objects rather than subjects in the main clause) can be explained at the discourse level. Generally speaking, in narrative it is the entities and people that are affected by the major character's actions that require identification. The protagonist is likely to be defined in an initial equational sentence. Long and Sato (1984) provide other examples of the interdependence of linguistic levels in SLA, for example the delayed acquisition of the English past tense inflection by Vietnamese learners may be the result of syllable structure transfer from the L1. They conclude:

> It should be clear that broadening the scope of IL (interlanguage) analysis to include, simultaneously or sequentially, more than one level of analysis, helps to integrate heretofore discrete, apparently unrelated levels of development. Further, and crucially, multilevel analyses have greater potential explanatory power for phenomena within single linguistic levels and for IL development in general.

Not only has SLA research been preoccupied with morpho-syntax, but also it has been narrowly concerned with formal aspects. The functions realized by the grammatical forms have been largely ignored. But to talk about the acquisition of a specific form without reference to its language functions is meaningless. A learner cannot be said to have acquired a form until he is able to use it to express those functions, and only those functions which it serves in the target language. It follows that what is needed are both form → function analyses (i.e. studies of the functions realized by particular forms) and function → form analyses (i.e. studies of how particular functions are\ realized by different forms). These analyses will have to take account of learner variability, as form–function relationships are kaleidoscopic and shift over time (see Chapter 4).

Even if the narrow morpho-syntactic confines of SLA research prevail, there is still another problem. To date, attention has been focused on the description of isolated features of the total grammatical system, rather than on the grammatical system as a whole. For example, the morpheme studies have examined an odd assortment of grammatical features, while longitudinal studies have plotted the separate development of particular sub-systems such as pronouns, negatives, interrogatives, and relative clauses. However, learners do not develop each area of grammar separately; rather they work simultaneously on a whole range of features. This is one reason why the acquisition of any specific feature is so gradual; the learner's attention is divided. In order to understand the processes of acquisition, it is important to obtain an overall picture of the learner's developing grammar. We need to know, for instance, in what way the development of negatives is correlated with that of relative clauses (see Schumann 1980). This poses a considerable descriptive burden on the SLA researcher, but it is necessary to look at the whole picture if we are to advance our understanding of the morpho-syntactical level of interlanguage.

Finally, there are methodological problems. One set has to do with the way in which data are collected. Another set concerns the overall direction which SLA research should follow.

A recurring issue in SLA research is the validity of different data types (see, for instance, Naiman 1974, Adams 1978, Burt and Dulay 1980 and Wode *et al.* 1979). The principal point is that different tasks elicit different kinds of performance—grammaticality judgement tasks, discrete-point tests, integrative tests, imitation tasks, picture describing tasks, and free conversation are likely to reveal different patterns of language use. Thus research that makes use of elicited speech using pictures (e.g. the morpheme studies) cannot claim that the corpus obtained constitutes natural speech. Furthermore, different data collection instruments may have differential effects according to the individual characteristics of the learner who is being investigated. The same procedure can tap different things in adults and children, for instance. Great care, therefore, needs to be taken in generalizing the results of a study based on one specific data type. SLA is not a monolithic process and we would be better advised not to talk of a 'natural' acquisition order, but of a regular pattern of development in the context of a particular type of language use. We should be wary of assuming that one type of language use is inherently more important than any other type, as what is important for one learner may not be so for another. It may be that for most learners the vernacular style is primary, but there will always be some who are more intent on developing a careful style. In order to solve the methodological problems associated with data collection, it is necessary to accept the variable nature of the learner's interlanguage system. In this way it will be possible to work towards an integrated theory of language learning and language use.

There is no consensus about the overall direction that SLA research should follow. On the one hand there are researchers who view SLA as amenable to the same methods of enquiry as a natural science. On the other hand there are those who treat it as a highly complex subject more akin to literature than to science. The former are likely to insist on a 'scientific' approach; that is, they identify specific hypotheses and then set about testing them in a systematic way, usually with the help of quantitative procedures. Progress is viewed as the steady accretion of 'proven' hypotheses. The latter are more inclined to the 'data-then-theory' approach. They engage in imaginative speculation based on existing empirical research or on the qualitative analysis of selected gobbets of L2 learner-language. This contrast in approaches is healthy. The danger lies in the tendency to project the 'scientific' approach as the only legitimate way of advancing, and to insist on a single conventional formula according to which all research should be conducted. As Lightbown (1984) argues, there is a place for both hypothesis-testing and hypothesis-generating research and, I would add, for research that attempts both.

Some key questions

Hatch (1978b) began her review of SLA research with ten questions. I conclude with a set of questions. They are not new ones. The main purpose of this book has been to clarify the questions that need to be asked and to suggest some answers to them. The prospect is that SLA research will continue to investigate these questions.

1 Assuming that there is regularity in the way learners acquire the grammatical knowledge needed to participate in spontaneous conversation, how can this regularity be best described? In particular how can form–function relationships be taken into account, and how can a 'whole picture' be provided?
2 How does the regularity referred to in (1) relate to other kinds of grammatical knowledge that are required to perform tasks which do not lead to spontaneous conversation?

3 What constraints are there on the regularity referred to in (1)? To what extent and in what ways do the learner's L1, the acquisitional setting, and, perhaps, individual learner differences affect the pattern of regularity observed?

4 To what extent can regularity be observed in other linguistic systems? Is there a natural sequence of development for vocabulary and pragmatic knowledge?

5 To what extent is the regularity observed in (1) similar to or different from the regularities which have been found to exist in other learner languages (e.g. L1 acquisition and pidgins)?

6 How can the regularity referred to in (1) be explained? How can a principled selection between competing explanations be made?

7 Why do some learners learn more rapidly and carry on learning for longer than other learners? Is it possible to influence the speed of learning by manipulating environmental factors?

8 How can a style of SLA research be developed that is of maximum relevance to pedagogic issues? To what extent is it possible to 'apply' the results of 'pure' SLA research?

Glossary

acculturation

Acculturation is the process of adapting to a new culture. This involves developing an understanding of the systems of thought, beliefs, and emotions of the new culture as well as its system of communication. Acculturation is an important concept for understanding SLA because, it has been hypothesized, successful language learning is more likely when learners succeed in acculturating.

accuracy order

Learners produce L2 morphemes such as the third person -*s* or the articles, *a* and *the*, with varying levels of accuracy at different stages of development. Accuracy orders can be obtained by ranking a number of morphemes according to their accuracy level. Some SLA researchers (e.g. Dulay and Burt) have hypothesized that the accuracy order corresponds to the acquisition order.

acquisition

Acquisition can be broadly defined as the internalization of rules and formulas which are then used to communicate in the L2. In this sense the term 'acquisition' is synonymous with the term 'learning'. However, Krashen (1981) uses these terms with different meanings. 'Aquisition', for Krashen, consists of the spontaneous process of rule internalization that results from natural language use, while 'learning' consists of the development of conscious L2 knowledge through formal study.

acquisition device

Nativist theories of language acquisition emphasize the importance of the innate capacity of the language learner at the expense of environmental factors. Each learner is credited with an 'acquisition device' which directs the process of acquisition. This device contains information about the possible form that the grammar of any language can take. (See *Universal Grammar*.)

approximative system

This is the term used by Nemser (1981) to refer to the deviant linguistic system which the learner employs when trying to use the target language. The learner passes through a number of 'approximative systems' on the way to acquiring full target-language proficiency. The term is almost identical in meaning with 'interlanguage' and 'transitional competence'.

aptitude

Aptitude refers to the specific ability a learner has for learning a second language. This is hypothesized to be separate from the general ability to master academic skills, which is referred to as 'intelligence'.

attitudes

Learners possess sets of beliefs about such factors as the target language culture, their own culture and, in the case of classroom learning, of their teacher and the learning tasks they are given. These beliefs are referred to as 'attitudes'. They influence language learning in a number of ways. (See also *motivation*.)

avoidance

Avoidance is said to take place when specific target language structures are under-represented in the learner's production in comparison to native-speaker production. Learners are likely to avoid structures they find difficult. One cause of this difficulty may be a lack of correspondence between the target language and mother tongue structures. In this respect, 'avoidance' is a reflection of language transfer.

backsliding

L2 learners are likely to manifest correct target language forms on some occasions but deviant forms on other occasions. When this happens they are said to 'backslide'. Backsliding involves the use of a rule belonging to some earlier stage of development. It occurs when learners are under some pressure, as, for instance, when they have to express difficult subject matter or are feeling anxious (see Selinker 1972).

behaviourist learning theory

Behaviourist learning theory is a general theory of learning (i.e. it applies to all kinds of learning, not just language learning). It views learning as the formation of habits. These arise when the learner is confronted with specific stimuli which lead to specific responses, which are, in turn, reinforced by rewards. Behaviourist learning theory emphasizes environmental factors as opposed to internal, mental factors.

careful style

When language users are able to attend closely to the form of the language they produce, they call upon their 'careful style' (Tarone 1983). This contrasts with 'vernacular style'. A 'careful style' is evident in formal language tasks such as reading pairs of words, or doing a grammar test.

channel capacity

Channel capacity refers to the language learner's ability to process utterances. Processing language in both comprehension and production involves more than just knowing the rules of the language. It also involves being able to recover the rules from memory and to use them easily and spontaneously. Learners in the early stages of development are likely to experience difficulty in accessing and using their knowledge, with the result that they have limited channel capacity.

cognitive organizer

This term is used by Dulay and Burt (1977) to refer to that part of the learner's internal processing system that is responsible for organizing the input into a system. Thus the internal organizer is responsible for the transitional stages through which the learner passes. The cognitive organizer operates subconsciously.

communication strategies

These are strategies for using L2 knowledge. They are employed when learners are faced with the task of communicating meanings for which they lack the requisite linguistic knowledge (e.g. when they have to refer to some object without knowing the L2 word). Typical communication strategies are paraphrase and mime. Communication strategies contrast with 'learning strategies' and 'production strategies'.

competence

When learners acquire a L2, they internalize rules which are then organized into a system. This constitutes their 'competence'. The actual use of this system to comprehend and produce utterances is referred to as 'performance'. Researchers (and linguists) disagree about the exact nature of 'competence'. Some (e.g. Chomsky) view competence as entirely linguistic, while others (e.g. Hymes) view it as communicative (i.e. 'communicative competence' consists of both knowledge of linguistic rules *and* knowledge of how these rules are used to communicate meanings). Another difference is whether competence is to be treated as homogeneous (a single set of rules) or variable (alternative sets of rules which are drawn upon differently in different situations).

comprehensible input

The 'input' refers to the language which learners are exposed to. This can be 'comprehensible' (i.e. input that they can understand) or 'incomprehensible' (i.e. input that they cannot understand). When native speakers speak to L2 learners, they frequently adjust their speech to make it more comprehensible (see *foreigner talk*). Access to comprehensible input may be a necessary condition for acquisition to take place.

comprehensible output

The 'output' is the language produced by the learner. This can be comprehensible or incomprehensible. The efforts that learners make to be comprehensible may also play a part in acquisition, as they may force them to revise their internalized rule systems.

context

The 'context' of an utterance can mean two different things. (1) It can refer to the situation in which the utterance is produced; this is the 'situational context'. (2) It can refer to the linguistic environment — the surrounding language; this is the 'linguistic context'. Both types of context influence the choice of language forms and therefore have an effect on output.

Contrastive Analysis Hypothesis

According to the Contrastive Analysis Hypothesis, L2 errors are the result of differences between the learner's first language and the target language. The strong form of the hypothesis claims that these differences can be used to *predict* all errors that will occur. The weak form of the hypothesis claims that these differences can be used only to *identify* some out of the total of errors that actually arise.

contrastive pragmatics

A contrastive analysis of two languages is usually carried out on the grammatical systems of the two languages. However, it can also be carried out with reference to how language uses differ in the two languages (e.g. how the two languages handle a language function such as 'apology'). This kind of analysis is called contrastive pragmatics.

creative construction

Dulay *et al.* (1982: 276) define 'creative construction' as 'the subconscious process by which language learners gradually organize the language they hear, according to the rules they construct to understand and generate sentences.'

critical period hypothesis

This states that there is a period when language acquisition can take place naturally and effortlessly, but that after a certain age the brain is no longer able to process language input in this way. Researchers differ over when the critical period comes to an end.

development

The term 'development' is often used as a synonym for 'acquisition' or 'learning'. Chomsky, however, makes a distinction between 'development' and 'acquisition'. The former is real-time learning that is affected by language processing abilities, while the latter is 'pure' learning that is dependent entirely on the learner's 'acquisition device'. Thus 'development' is a reflection of both general cognitive abilities and the acquisition device.

diffusion model

The diffusion model was designed by Gatbonton (1979) to account for the way that learners develop and change their internal rules, gradually sorting out how to use forms correctly.

error analysis

Error analysis is a procedure used by both researchers and teachers. It involves collecting samples of learner language, identifying the errors in the sample, describing these errors, classifying them according to their hypothesized causes, and evaluating their seriousness.

feedback

This is the response to efforts by the learner to communicate. Feedback can involve such functions as correction, acknowledgement, requests for clarification, and backchannel cues such as 'Mmm'. It has been suggested that feedback plays a major role in helping learners to test hypotheses they have formed about the rule system of the target language.

field dependence/independence

Language learners differ in the manner in which they perceive, conceptualize, organize, and recall information. 'Field dependents' operate holistically (i.e. they see the field as a whole), whereas 'field independents' operate analytically (i.e. they perceive the field in terms of its component parts). The distinction may be important for understanding how learners acquire a second language.

filter

Learners do not necessarily attend to all the input they are exposed to. Rather they attend to some features, but 'filter' others out. Dulay *et al.*

(1982) suggest that the use of the filter depends upon affective factors such as the learner's motives, attitudes, and emotions.

foreigner talk

When native speakers address learners, they adjust their normal speech in order to facilitate understanding. These adjustments, which involve both language form and language function, constitute 'foreigner talk'. Foreigner talk may aid acquisition by ensuring that the learner obtains comprehensible input.

formal instruction

Formal instruction occurs in classrooms when attempts are made to raise the learners' consciousness about the nature of target language rules in order to aid learning. Formal instruction can take place deductively (e.g. the learners are told the rules) or inductively (i.e. learners carry out language tasks designed to develop a knowledge of specific rules).

formulaic speech

Formulaic speech consists of 'expressions which are learned as unanalysable wholes and employed on particular occasions. . .' (Lyons 1968: 177). (See also *routines* and *patterns*.)

fossilization

Selinker (1972) noted that most L2 learners fail to reach target language competence. That is, they stop learning when their internalized rule system contains rules different from those of the target language. This is referred to as 'fossilization'.

frequency

The language to which the learner is exposed contains a range of linguistic forms which occur with varying frequency. Similarly, the learner's output contains a range of linguistic forms used with varying frequency. The notion of frequency is important, because there is evidence to show that input frequency matches output frequency.

hypothesis formation

It has been suggested that during SLA, the learner forms hypotheses about the nature of the target-language rules and then tests them out. A hypothesis in this sense is an internalized rule which is used in L2 communication.

hypothesis testing

Once a learner has formed a hypothesis about a target-language language rule, he or she can test it out in a variety of ways in order to confirm or reject it. Rejection leads to a revision of the rule system as a new hypothesis is formed to replace the old one. Hypothesis testing can take place consciously or subconsciously.

implicational analysis/scaling

Implicational scaling is a technique used by SLA researchers (e.g. Dittmar 1980) to represent variation in L2 performance. It rests on the notion that the presence of one linguistic form in learner language occurs only if one or more other forms are also present. Thus one form 'implicates' other forms.

implicational universals

Linguistic universals are features which occur in all or a large number of the world's languages (see *typological universals*). Implicational universals relate the presence of one linguistic feature to the presence of other linguistic features. Thus, if feature x is present in a given language, it can be assumed that features y, z,. . . .n are also present.

inferencing

Inferencing is the means by which the learner forms hypotheses by attending to input. It involves forming hypotheses about the target language, either by attending to specific features in the input, or by using the context of situation to interpret the input.

input

The input constitutes the language to which the learner is exposed. It can be spoken or written. Input serves as the data which the learner must use to determine the rules of the target language.

interaction analysis

Interaction analysis is a research procedure used to investigate classroom communication. It involves the use of a system of categories to record and analyse the different ways in which teachers and students use language.

interactionist learning theory

Interactionist learning theory emphasizes the joint contributions of the linguistic environment and the learner's internal mechanisms in language development. Learning results from an interaction between the learner's mental abilities and the linguistic input.

interface position

Theories of SLA which emphasize the distinctness of 'acquired' and 'learnt' knowledge (see *acquisition* and *learning*) can maintain either that they are completely separate, or that each knowledge type 'leaks', so that acquired knowledge can become learnt knowledge and vice-versa. The latter is referred to as the 'interface position.'

interference

According to behaviourist learning theory, old habits get in the way of learning new habits. Thus in SLA, the patterns of the learner's mother tongue get in the way of learning the patterns of the L2. This is referred to as 'interference'.

interlanguage

Interlanguage is the term coined by Selinker (1972) to refer to the systematic knowledge of a second language which is independent of both the learner's first language and the target language. The term has come to be used with different but related meanings: (1) to refer to the series of interlocking systems which characterize acquisition, (2) to refer to the system that is observed at a single stage of development (i.e. 'an interlanguage'), and (3) to refer to particular mother tongue/target language combinations (e.g. French mother tongue/English target language vs German mother tongue/English target language).

latent language structure

This is a term used by Lenneberg (1967) to refer to the child's innate capacity to learn language. It corresponds closely to *acquisition device*.

learning

Learning can be broadly defined as the internalization of rules and formulas which are then used to communicate in the L2. In this sense it is synonymous with 'acquisition'. However, Krashen (1981) uses the term to refer to the process of developing conscious or metalingual knowledge through formal study. (See *acquisition*.)

learning strategies

Learning strategies account for how learners accumulate new L2 rules and how they automatize existing ones. They include the strategies involved in the general processes of hypothesis formation and testing.

These can be conscious or subconscious. Learning strategies contrast with both communication strategies and production strategies, which account for how the learners *use* their rule systems, rather than how they acquire them.

markedness

Linguists working in the Chomskyan school suggests that linguistic rules can either be part of the core grammar (i.e. the universal rules) or be part of the periphery (i.e. are specific to particular languages). Core rules are considered to be unmarked and therefore easily acquired. Periphery rules are considered to be marked and therefore difficult to learn.

mentalism

Mentalist theories of language learning emphasize the learner's innate mental capacities for acquiring a language, and minimize the contribution of the linguistic environment. (See also *acquisition device*.)

monitoring

Both language learners and native speakers typically try to correct any errors in what they have just said. This is referred to as 'monitoring'. The learner can monitor vocabulary, grammar, phonology, or discourse. Krashen (1981) uses the term 'Monitoring' (with a big 'M') to refer to the way the learner uses 'learnt' knowledge to improve utterances generated by means of 'acquired' knowledge.

motherese

When mothers speak to their children they typically simplify their speech and make efforts to sustain communication. The formal and interactional characteristics of this kind of speech are referred to as 'motherese'. They may help the child to learn the language.

motivation

Motivation in language learning can be defined in terms of the learner's overall goal or orientation. Gardner and Lambert (1982) distinguish 'instrumental motivation', which occurs when the learner's goal is functional (e.g. to get a job or pass an examination), and 'integrative motivation', which occurs when the learner wishes to identify with the culture of the L2 group. Another kind of motivation is 'task motivation' — the interest felt by the learner in performing different learning tasks.

nativism

(see *mentalism*.)

negotiation of meaning

When learners interact with native speakers or other learners, they often experience considerable difficulty in communicating. This leads to substantial interactional efforts by the conversational partners to secure mutual understanding. This work is often called the 'negotiation of meaning'. It contributes to SLA in a number of ways.

non-interface position

Theories of SLA which emphasize the distinctness of 'acquired' and 'learnt' knowledge (see *acquisition* and *learning*) can maintain either that they are completely separate or that one type of knowledge can turn into the other. The former is referred to as the 'non-interface position'.

obligatory occasions

When the linguistic context necessitates the use of a particular morpheme, it is said to constitute an 'obligatory occasion'. For example the context created by 'There are two _____ playing in the garden' requires the use of a plural morpheme. The first step in establishing the accuracy level of individual morphemes is to identify all obligatory occasions for the morphemes in the data. (See also *accuracy order*.)

operating principles

Slobin (1973) coined the term 'operating principles' to describe the various strategies used by children in acquiring their mother tongue. Examples are 'Pay attention to the ends of words' and 'Avoid exceptions'. Similar strategies are used in SLA.

order of development

In this book a distinction has been drawn between 'order' and 'sequence' of development. The term 'order of development' is used to refer to the order in which specific grammatical features are acquired in SLA. These vary according to such factors as the learner's L1 background and the learning context.

over-generalization

Language learners in both first and second language acquisition have been observed to produce errors like 'comed' which can be explained as extensions of some general rule to items not covered by this rule in the target language. This process is referred to as 'over-generalization'.

patterns

Patterns are one type of formulaic speech. They are unanalysed units which have one or more open slots e.g. 'Can I have a—?' (See also *formulaic speech* and *routines*.)

primary levels of language

Neufeld (1978) distinguishes 'primary' and 'secondary' levels of language. Primary levels include a reasonably large functional vocabulary and basic mastery of pronunciation and grammar rules. Neufeld suggests that all learners have an innate ability to acquire these primary levels.

proactive inhibition

Proactive inhibition is the way in which previous learning prevents or inhibits the learning of new habits. L2 learners are hypothesized to experience difficulty in acquiring target language forms that are different from first language forms. (See also *interference*.)

production strategies

Production strategies refer to utilization of linguistic knowledge in communication. They differ from 'communication strategies' in that they do not imply any communication problem, and in that they operate largely subconsciously.

proficiency

Proficiency consists of the learner's knowledge of the target language; it can be considered synonomous with 'competence'. 'Proficiency' can be viewed as linguistic competence or communicative competence. L2 proficiency is usually measured in relation to native speaker proficiency.

projection device

Zobl (1984) has suggested that one component of the 'acquisition device' is a 'projection device'. This acts as a trigger, enabling the learner to acquire any rule or rules that are implicated by the prior acquisition of another rule. (See also *implicational universals*.)

psychological distance

'Psychological distance' is the term used by Schumann (1978a) to refer to the learner's overall psychological set with regard to the target language and its community. It is determined by a cluster of factors such as language shock and motivation.

rate of acquisition

This is the speed at which the learner develops L2 proficiency. It contrasts with 'route of acquisition'.

recreation continuum

Interlanguage is viewed as a continuum (i.e. a series of stages). One possible starting point for this continuum is 'some basic simple grammar' (Corder, 1981: 150) which is recalled from an early stage of first language acquisition. The 'recreation continuum' consists of the gradual complexification of this simple grammar.

restructuring continuum

Interlanguage is viewed as a continuum (i.e. a series of stages). One possible starting point is the learner's first language. The 'restructuring continuum' consists of the gradual replacement of L1-based rules with L2-based rules.

route of development

L2 learners go through a number of transitional states en route to acquiring the target language rules. This is referred to as the 'route of development'. In this book 'route' is intended to be neutral regarding whether it is universal or subject to variation. (See also *order of development* and *sequence of development*.)

routines

Routines are one type of formulaic speech. They are units that are totally unanalysed and are learnt as wholes. A common routine is 'I don't know'. (See also *formulaic speech* and *patterns*.)

scripts

Scripts can also be considered a type of formulaic speech. They are memorized sequences of utterances which are more or less fixed and predictable. An example is a greeting sequence.

secondary levels of language

Neufeld (1978) distinguishes 'primary' and 'secondary' levels of language. Secondary levels include the ability to handle complex grammatical structures and different language styles. Not all L2 learners succeed in mastering the secondary levels of language.

semantic simplification

Semantic simplification occurs when learners simplify the utterances they intend to produce by leaving out propositional elements that would occur in native speaker speech. For example, a learner might say 'Hitting' when he means 'He is hitting me'.

sequence of development

In this book a distinction is drawn between 'order' and 'sequence' of development. The term 'sequence of development' is used to refer to the overall profile of development of SLA which is held to be universal and, thus, not subject to variation as a result of L1 background or other factors.

simplification

Simplification refers to the way in which learners seek to ease the burden of learning or using a second language by controlling the number of hypotheses they try to form at any one stage of development, or by omitting grammatical and/or propositional elements in production.

social distance

'Social distance' is the term used by Schumann (1978a) to refer to the position of the learner *vis-à-vis* the target language community. It is determined by a cluster of factors to do with the relationship between the learner's social group and the target language community.

success of acquisition

This has to do with the level of proficiency that the learner finally achieves. (See *fossilization*.)

target language

The target language is the language that the learner is attempting to learn. It comprises the native speaker's grammar.

teacher talk

Teachers address classroom language learners differently from the way they address other kinds of classroom learners. They make adjustments to both language form and language function in order to facilitate communication. These adjustments are referred to as 'teacher talk'. (See also *foreigner talk*.)

transfer

Transfer is the process of using knowledge of the first language in learning a second language. Transfer can be positive, when a first-language pattern identical with a target-language pattern is transferred, or it can be negative, when a first-language pattern different from the target-language pattern is transferred. In the latter case. L1-induced errors occur.

transitional competence

This is the term used by Corder (1967) to refer to interim rule systems that learners develop in the process of SLA. (See also *approximative systems* and *interlanguage*.)

transitional constructions

Dulay *et al.* (1982: 281) define 'transitional constructions' as 'the interim language forms that learners use while they are still learning the grammar of a language'. For example, before learners master the rule for English negatives, they operate with interim rules (e.g. 'no' + Verb).

typological universals

Typological universals are identified by examining a representative sample of natural languages in order to identify features that are common to all or most of these languages. Typological universals can consist of absolutes (which occur in all languages) or tendencies (which occur in a large number of languages).

universal grammar

Cook (1985) summarizing the Chomskyan position, defines 'universal grammar' as 'the properties inherent in the human mind'. Universal grammar consists of a set of general principles that apply to all languages rather than a set of particular rules. (See also *acquisition device*.)

universal hypothesis

The 'universal hypothesis' states that language acquisition is governed by the way in which natural languages are organized. That is, certain universal linguistic properties influence the order in which the rules of a specific language are acquired. According to the universal hypothesis, then, it is linguistic rather than general cognitive factors that determine acquisition.

variability

Language users (including language learners) vary in the use they make of their linguistic knowledge. This variability can be unsystematic (i.e.

haphazard) or systematic (i.e. two or more linguistic forms function as variants, which are used predictably according to the context).

variable rules

When variability is systematic, it can be described by means of variable rules which indicate the likelihood of alternative forms occurring in different contexts.

vernacular style

When language users are attending to *what* they wish to communicate rather than to *how*, and when they are performing spontaneously, they call upon their 'vernacular style'. A vernacular style is evident in everyday conversation.

vertical structures

Vertical structures are learner utterances which are constructed by borrowing chunks from the preceding discourse and then adding to these from the learner's own resources. For example, a learner utterance like 'No come here' could be constructed by taking 'Come here' from a previous utterance and adding 'no'.

References

Adams, M. 1978. 'Methodology for examining second language acquisition' in Hatch (ed.) 1978a.

Adjemian, C. 1976. 'On the nature of interlanguage systems. *Language Learning* 26: 297–320.

Allwright, R. 1975. 'Problems in the study of the language teacher's treatment of learner error' in M. Burt and H. Dulay (eds.). *On TESOL 1975*. Washington D.C.: TESOL.

Allwright, R. 1980. 'Turns, topics and tasks: patterns of participation in language learning and teaching' in Larsen-Freeman (ed.) 1980.

Allwright, R. 1983. 'Classroom-centred research on language teaching and learning: a brief historical overview.' *TESOL Quarterly* 17: 191–204.

Andersen, R. 1980. 'The role of creolization in Schumann's Pidginization Hypothesis for second language acquisition' in Scarcella and Krashen (eds.) 1980.

Andersen, R. (ed.). 1981. *New Dimensions in Second Language Acquisition Research*. Rowley, Mass.: Newbury House.

Andersen, R. (ed.). 1983a. *Pidginization and Creolization as Language Acquisition*. Rowley, Mass.: Newbury House.

Andersen, R. 1983b. 'Introduction: A language acquisition interpretation of pidginization and creolization' in Andersen (ed.) 1983a.

d'Anglejan, A. 1978. 'Language learning in and out of classrooms' in Richards (ed.) 1978.

d'Anglejan, A. and G. Tucker. 1975. 'The acquisition of complex English structures by adult learners.' **Language Learning** 25/2.

Arthur, B., R. Weiner, M. Culver, J. L. Young, and D. Thomas. 1980. 'The register of impersonal discourse to foreigners: verbal adjustments to foreign accent' in Larsen-Freeman (ed.) 1980.

Asher, J. 1977. *Learning Another Language Through Actions: The Complete Teacher's Guidebook*. Los Gatos, CA: Sky Oak Productions.

Bailey, K. 1980. 'An introspective analysis of an individual's language learning experience' in Scarcella and Krashen (eds.) 1980.

Bailey, K. 1983. 'Competitiveness and anxiety in adult second language learning: looking *at* and *through* the diary studies' in Seliger and Long (eds.) 1983.

Bailey, K., M. Long, and S. Peck (eds.). 1983. *Second Language Acquisition Research*. Rowley, Mass.: Newbury House.

Bailey, N., C. Madden, and S. Krashen. 1974. 'Is there a "natural sequence" in adult second language learning?' *Language Learning* 24: 235–44.

Barnes, D. 1976. *From Communication to Curriculum*. Harmondsworth: Penguin.

Barnes, S., M. Gutfreund, S. Satterly, and G. Wells. 1983. 'Characteristics of adult speech which predict children's language development.' *Journal of Child Language* 10/1: 65–84.

Beebe, L. 1980. 'Sociolinguistic variation and style shifting in second language acquisition'. *Language Learning* 30/1: 433–47.

Bertkau, J. 1974. 'Comprehension and production of relative clauses in adult second language and child first language acquisition.' *Language Learning* 24: 279–86.

Bialystok, E. 1979. 'An analytical view of second language competence: a model and some evidence.' *The Modern Language Journal* LXIII: 257–62.

Bialystok, E. 1981. 'Some evidence for the integrity and interaction of two knowledge sources' in Andersen (ed.) 1981.

Bialystok, E. 1982. 'On the relationship between knowing and using forms.' *Applied Linguistics* III: 181–206.

Bialystok, E. 1983a. 'Inferencing: testing the "hypothesis-testing" hypothesis' in Seliger and Long (eds.) 1983.

Bialystok, E. 1983b. 'Some factors in the selection and implementation of communication strategies' in Faerch and Kasper (eds.) 1983a.

Bialystok, E. 1984. 'Strategies in interlanguage learning and performance' in Davies and Criper (eds.) 1984.

Bialystok, E. and M. Fröhlich. 1977. 'Aspects of second language learning in classroom setting.' *Working Papers on Bilingualism* 13: 2–26.

Bickerton, D. 1975. *Dynamics of a Creole System*. Cambridge: Cambridge University Press.

Blank, M., S. Rose and L. Berlin. 1978. *The Language of Learning: The Preschool Years*. New York: Grune and Stratton.

Bloomfield, L. 1933. *Language*. New York: Holt.

Blum-Kulka, S. and E. Levenston. 1978. 'Universals of lexical simplification.' *Language Learning* 28: 399–415. Also in Faerch and Kasper (eds.) 1983a.

Brière, E. 1978. 'Variables affecting native Mexican children's learning Spanish as a second language.' *Language Learning* 28: 159–74.

Bright, J. and G. McGregor. 1970. *Teaching English as a Second Language: Theory and Techniques for the Secondary Stage*. London: Longman.

Brooks, N. 1960. *Language and Language Learning*. New York: Harcourt Brace and World.

Brown, H. 1980a. *Principles of Language Learning and Teaching*. Englewood Cliffs, N.J.: Prentice-Hall.

Brown, H. 1980b. 'The optimal distance model of second language acquisition.' *TESOL Quarterly* 14: 157–64.

Brown, H. 1981. 'Affective factors in second language learning' in J. Alatis, H. Altman, and P. Alatis (eds.). *The Second Language Classroom: Directions for the 1980s*. New York: Oxford University Press.

Brown, R. 1973. *A First Language: The Early Stages*. Cambridge, Mass.: Harvard University Press.

Brown, R. 1977. 'Introduction' in Snow and Ferguson (eds.) 1977.

Brumfit, C. J. 1979. 'Accuracy and fluency as polarities in foreign language teaching materials and methodology.' *Bulletin CILA* 29: 89–99.

Brumfit, C. J. 1984. 'Theoretical implications of interlanguage studies for language teaching' in Davies and Criper (eds.) 1984.

van Buren, P. 1974. 'Contrastive analysis' in J. Allen and S. Corder (eds.). *The Edinburgh Course in Applied Linguistics Vol. 3: Techniques in Applied Linguistics*. London: Oxford University Press.

Burmeister, H. and D. Ufert. 1980. 'Strategy switching' in Felix (ed.) 1980a.

Burstall, C. 1975. 'Factors affecting foreign-language learning: a consideration of some relevant research findings.' *Language Teaching and Linguistics Abstracts* 8: 5–125.

Burt, M. and H. Dulay. 1980. 'On acquisition orders' in Felix (ed.) 1980a.

Burt M., H. Dulay, and E. Hernandez. 1973. *Bilingual Syntax Measure*. New York: Harcourt Brace Jovanovich.

Burton, D. 1981. 'Analysing spoken discourse' in Coulthard and Montgomery (eds.) 1981.

Butterworth, B. 1980. 'Introduction: A brief review of methods of studying language production' in B. Butterworth (ed.). *Language Production*, Vol. 1. New York: Academic Press.

Butterworth, G. and E. Hatch. 1978. 'A Spanish-speaking adolescent's acquisition of English syntax' in Hatch (ed.) 1978a.

Canale, M. and M. Swain. 1980. 'Theoretical bases of communicative approaches to second language teaching and testing.' *Applied Linguistics* I: 1–47.

Carroll, J. 1967. 'Foreign language proficiency levels attained by language majors near graduation from college.' *Foreign Language Annals* 1: 131–51.

Carroll, J. and S. Sapon. 1959. *Modern Language Aptitude Test (MLAT)*. New York: Psychological Corporation.

Carton, A. 1971. 'Inferencing: a process in using and learning language' in Pimsleur and Quinn (eds.) 1971.

Cattell, R. 1970. *Handbook for the 16 Personality Factor Questionnaire*. Champaign, Ill.: Institute for Personality and Ability Testing.

Cazden, C. 1972. *Child Language and Education.* New York, Holt Rinehart & Winston.

Cazden, C., H. Cancino, E. Rosansky, and J. Schumann. 1975. *Second Language Acquisition Sequences in Children, Adolescents and Adults.* Final Report, US Department of Health, Education, and Welfare.

Chastain, K. 1969. 'The audiolingual habit theory versus cognitive code-learning theory: some theoretical considerations.' *International Review of Applied Linguistics* VII: 97–106.

Chastain, K. 1975. 'Affective and ability factors in second language acquisition.' *Language Learning* 25: 153–61.

Chaudron, C. 1983a. 'Foreigner-talk in the classroom—an aid to learning?' in Seliger and Long (eds.) 1983.

Chaudron, C. 1983b. 'Research on metalinguistic judgements: a review of theory, methods and results.' *Language Learning* 33: 343–78.

Cherry, L. 1979. 'A sociolinguistic approach to language development and its implications for education' in O. Garnica and M. King (eds.). *Language, Children, and Society.* Oxford: Pergamon.

Chihara, T. and J. Oller. 1978. 'Attitudes and attained proficiency in EFL: a sociolinguistic study of adult Japanese speakers.' *Language Learning* 28: 55–68.

Chomsky, C. 1969. *The Acquisition of Syntax in Children from Five to Ten.* Cambridge, Mass.: MIT Press.

Chomsky, N. 1957. *Syntactic Structures.* The Hague: Mouton.

Chomsky, N. 1959. Review of *Verbal Behaviour* by B. F. Skinner. *Language* 35: 26–58.

Chomsky, N. 1965. *Aspects of the Theory of Syntax.* Cambridge, Mass.: MIT Press.

Chomsky, N. 1966. *Topics in the Theory of Generative Grammar.* The Hague: Mouton.

Chomsky, N. 1980. 'On cognitive structures and their development: a reply to Piaget' in M. Piatelli-Palmarini (ed.). *Language and Learning.* London: Routledge and Kegan Paul.

Chomsky, N. 1981. 'Principles and parameters in syntactic theory' in Hornstein and Lightfoot (eds.) 1981.

Cicourel, A., K. Jennings, S. Jennings, K. Leiter, R. Mackay, H. Mehan, and D. Roth. 1974. *Language Use and School Performance.* New York: Academic Press.

Clark, R. 1974. 'Performing without competence.' *Journal of Child Language* 1: 1–10.

Clark, H. and E. Clark. 1977. *Psychology and Language: An Introduction to Psycholinguistics.* New York: Harcourt Brace Jovanovich.

Cohen, A. and M. Robbins. 1976. 'Toward assessing interlanguage performance: the relationship between selected errors, learners' characteristics and learners' explanations.' *Language Learning* 26: 45–66.

Comrie, B. 1981. *Language Universals and Linguistic Typology.* Oxford: Basil Blackwell.

Comrie, B. and E. Keenan. 1978. 'Noun phrase accessibility revisited.' *Language* 55: 649–64.

Cook, V. 1971. 'The analogy between first and second language learning' in R. Lugton (ed.). *Toward a Cognitive Approach to Second Language Acquisition.* Philadelphia, Penn.: Center for Curriculum Development.

Cook, V. 1973. 'The comparison of language development in native children and foreign adults.' *International Review of Applied Linguistics* XI: 13–28.

Cook, V. 1975. 'Strategies in the comprehension of relative clauses.' *Language and Speech* 18: 204–12.

Cook, V. 1977. 'Cognitive processes in second language learning.' *International Review of Applied Linguistics* XV: 1–20.

Cook, V. 1978. 'Second-language learning: a psycholinguistic perspective.' *Language Teaching and Linguistics: Abstracts* 2: 73–89.

Cook, V. 1985. 'Universal Grammar and second language learning.' *Applied Linguistics* 6/1: 2–18.

Corder, S. 1967. 'The significance of learners' errors.' *International Review of Applied Linguistics* V: 161–9.

Corder, S. 1971. 'Idiosyncratic dialects and error analysis.' *International Review of Applied Linguistics* IX: 149–59.

Corder, S. 1974. 'Error analysis' in J. Allen and S. Corder (eds.). *The Edinburgh Course in Applied Linguistics*, Vol. 3. Oxford: Oxford University Press.

Corder, S. 1976. 'The study of interlanguage' in *Proceedings of the Fourth International Congress in Applied Linguistics*. Munich: Hochschulverlag. Also in Corder 1981.

Corder, S. 1978a. 'Language-learner language' in Richards (ed.) 1978.

Corder, S. 1978b. 'Language distance and the magnitude of the learning task.' *Studies in Second Language Acquisition* 2/1. Also in Corder 1981a.

Corder, S. 1978c. 'Strategies of communication.' *AFinLa* 23. Also in Corder 1981.

Corder, S. 1980. 'Second language acquisition research and the teaching of grammar.' Plenary address at 1980 Annual BAAL Conference. Also in *BAAL Newsletter 10*.

Corder, S. 1981a. *Error Analysis and Interlanguage*. Oxford: Oxford University Press.

Corder, S. 1981b. 'Formal simplicity and functional simplification in second language acquisition' in Andersen (ed.) 1981.

Coulthard, M. and M. Montgomery. 1981. *Studies in Discourse Analysis*. London: Routledge and Kegan Paul.

Cross, T. 1977. 'Mothers' speech adjustments: the contribution of selected child listener variables' in Snow and Ferguson (eds.) 1977.

Cross, T. 1978. 'Mothers' speech and its association with rate of linguistic development in young children' in Waterson and Snow (eds.) 1978.

Crystal, D. 1976. *Child Language Learning and Linguistics: An Overview for the Teaching and Therapeutic Professions*. London: Edward Arnold.

Cummins, J. 1979. 'Cognitive/academic language proficiency, linguistic interdependence, the optimal age question and some other matters.' *Working Papers on Bilingualism* 19: 197–205.

Dahl, O. 1979. 'Typology of sentence negation.' *Linguistics* 17: 79–106.

Davies, A., C. Criper, and A.P.R. Howatt, (eds.). 1984. *Interlanguage: Proceedings of the Seminar in Honour of Pit Corder*. Edinburgh: Edinburgh University Press.

Decamp, D. 1971. 'Implicational scales and sociolinguistic linearity.' *Linguistics* 13: 30–43.

Dickerson, L. 1975. 'Interlanguage as a system of variable rules.' *TESOL Quarterly* 9: 401–7.

Diller, K. (ed.). 1981. *Universals in Language Learning Aptitude*. Rowley, Mass.: Newbury House.

Dittmar, N. 1976. *Sociolinguistics*. London: Edward Arnold.

Dittmar, N. 1980. 'Ordering adult learners according to language abilities' in Felix (ed.) 1980a.

Dulay, H. and M. Burt. 1973. 'Should we teach children syntax?' *Language Learning* 23: 245–58.

Dulay, H. and M. Burt. 1974a. 'You can't learn without goofing' in Richards (ed.) 1974.

Dulay, H. and M. Burt. 1974b. 'Natural sequences in child second language acquisition.' *Language Learning* 24: 37–53.

Dulay, H. and M. Burt. 1975. 'Creative construction in second language learning' in M. Burt and H. Dulay (eds.). *New Directions in Second Language Learning, Teaching and Bilingual Education*. Washington D.C.: TESOL.

Dulay, H. and M. Burt. 1977. 'Remarks on creativity in language acquisition' in M. Burt, H. Dulay, and M. Finocchiaro (eds.). *Viewpoints on English as a Second Language*. New York: Regents.

Dulay, H., M. Burt, and S. Krashen. 1982. *Language Two*. New York: Oxford University Press.

Eckman, F. 1977. 'Markedness and the Contrastive Analysis Hypothesis.' *Language Learning* 27: 315–30.

Eisenstein, M., N. Bailey, and C. Madden. 1982. 'It takes two: contrasting tasks and contrasting structures.' *TESOL Quarterly* 16/3.

Ekstrand, L. 1975. 'Age and length of residence as variables related to the adjustment of migrant children with special reference to second language learning.' Paper presented at AILA, Stuttgart. Also in Krashen, Scarcella, and Long (eds.) 1982.

Ekstrand, L. 1977. 'Social and individual frame factors in second language learning: comparative aspects' in T. Skutnabb-Kangas (ed.). *Papers from the First Nordic Conference on Bilingualism*. Helsingsfors Universitat.

Ellis, R. 1980. 'Classroom interaction and its relation to second language learning.' *RELC Journal* 11/2: 29–48.

Ellis, R. 1982a. 'The origins of interlanguage.' *Applied Linguistics* III: 207–23.

Ellis, R. 1982b. 'Discourse Processes in Classroom Second Language Development.' PhD thesis, University of London.

Ellis, R. 1983. 'Teacher–pupil interaction in second language development.' Paper presented at the Tenth University of Michigan Conference on Applied Linguistics, Ann Arbor.

Ellis, R. 1984a. *Classroom Second Language Development*. Oxford: Pergamon.

Ellis, R. 1984b. 'Sources of Variability in Interlanguage.' Paper presented at the Interlanguage Seminar in Honour of Pit Corder, Edinburgh.

Ellis, R. 1984c. 'Formulaic speech in early classroom second language development' in J. Handscombe, R. Orem and B. Taylor (eds.), *On TESOL '83: The Question of Control*. Washington, D.C.: TESOL.

Ellis, R. 1984d. 'Communication strategies and the evaluation of communicative performance.' *ELT Journal* 38/1: 39–44.

Ellis, R. 1984e. 'Can syntax be taught? A study of the effects of formal instruction on the acquisition of WH questions by children.' *Applied Linguistics* 5/2: 138–55.

Ellis, R. and G. Wells. 1980. 'Enabling factors in adult–child discourse.' *First Language* 1: 46–82.

Ervin, S. 1964. 'Imitation and structural change in children's language' in E. Lenneberg (ed.). *New Directions in the Study of Language*. Cambridge, Mass.: MIT Press.

Ervin-Tripp, S. 1974. 'Is second language learning like the first?' *TESOL Quarterly* 8: 111–27.

Eysenck, H. 1964. *Manual for the Eysenck Personality Elementary*. London: London University Press.

Faerch, C. 1984. 'Strategies of production and reception' in Davies and Criper (eds.) 1984.

Faerch, C. and G. Kasper. 1980. 'Processes in foreign language learning and communication.' *Interlanguage Studies Bulletin* 5: 47–118. Also in Faerch and Kasper (eds.) 1983a.

Faerch, C. and Kasper, G. (eds.). 1983a. *Strategies in Interlanguage Communication*. London: Longman.

Faerch, C. and Kasper, G. 1983b. 'Procedural knowledge as a component of foreign language learners' communicative competence' in H. Boete and W. Herrlitz (eds.) *Kommunikation im (Sprach-)Unterricht*. Utrecht.

Faerch, C. and G. Kasper. 1983c. 'On identifying communication strategies' in Faerch and Kasper (eds.) 1983a.

Faerch, C. and G. Kasper. 1984. 'Two ways of defining communication strategies.' *Language Learning* 34/1.

Fanselow, J. 1977. 'Beyond Rashoman—conceptualising and describing the teaching act.' *TESOL Quarterly* 11: 17–39.

Fathman, A. 1975. 'The relationship between age and second language productive ability.' *Language Learning* 25: 245–53. Also in Krashen, Scarcella, and Long (eds.) 1982.

Fathman, A. 1976. 'Variables affecting the successful learning of English as a second language.' *TESOL Quarterly* 10: 433–41.

Fathman, A. 1978. 'ESL and EFL learning: similar or dissimilar?' in C. Blatchford and J. Schachter (eds.). *On TESOL '78: EFL Policies, Programs, Practices*. Washington D.C.: TESOL.

Felix, S. 1978. 'Some differences between first and second language acquisition' in Waterson and Snow (eds.) 1978.

Felix, S. (ed.) 1980a. *Second Language Development*. Tübingen: Gunther Narr.

Felix, S. 1980b. 'Interference, interlanguage and related issues' in Felix (ed.) 1980a.

Felix, S. 1981. 'The effect of formal instruction on second language acquisition.' *Language Learning* 31: 87–112.

Felix, S. 1984. 'Two problems of language acquisition: the relevance of grammatical studies in the theory of interlanguage' in Davies and Criper (eds.) 1984.

Ferguson, C. 1977. 'Baby talk as a simplified register' in Snow and Ferguson (eds.) 1977.

Ferguson, C. and C. Debose. 1977. 'Simplified registers, broken languages and pidginization' in A. Valdman (ed.). *Pidgin and Creole*. Indiana University Press.

Ferrier, L. 1978. 'Some observations of error in context' in Waterson and Snow (eds.) 1978.

Fillmore, C. 1968. 'The case for case' in E. Bach and R. Harms (eds.). *Universals of Linguistic Theory*. New York: Holt Rinehart and Winston.

Fillmore, W. 1976. 'The Second Time Around: Cognitive and Social Strategies in Second Language Acquisition.' PhD thesis, Stanford University.

Fillmore, W. 1979. 'Individual differences in second language acquisition' in C. Fillmore, D. Kempler, and W. Wang (eds.) *Individual Differences in Language Ability and Language Behavior*. New York: Academic Press.

Fillmore, W. 1980. 'Cultural perspectives on second language learning.' *TESL Reporter* 14: 23–31.

Fillmore, W. 1982. 'Instructional language as linguistic input: second language learning in classrooms' in L. Wilkinson (ed.). *Communicating in the Classroom*. New York: Academic Press.

Fisiak, J. (ed.). 1981. *Contrastive Linguistics and the Language Teacher*. Oxford: Pergamon.

Fitzgerald, M. 1978. 'Factors influencing ELT policies in England with particular reference to children from Pakistan, India and Bangladesh.' *ELT Journal* 33/1: 13–21.

Flanders, N. 1970. *Analyzing Teacher Behavior*. Reading, Mass.: Addison-Wesley.

Flick, W. 1980. 'Error types in adult English as a second language' in B. Ketterman, and R. St. Clair (eds.). *New Approaches to Language Acquisition*. Heidelberg: Julius Groos.

Freed, B. 1980. 'Talking to foreigners versus talking to children: similarities and differences' in Scarcella and Krashen (eds.) 1980.

French, F. 1949. *Common Errors in English*. London: Oxford University Press.

Fries, C. 1952. *The Structure of English: An Introduction to the Construction of English Sentences*. New York: Harcourt Brace.

Furrow, D., K. Nelson, and H. Benedict. 1979. 'Mothers' speech to children and syntactic relationships.' *Journal of Child Language* 6: 423–42.

Gaies, S. 1977. 'The nature of linguistic input in formal second language learning: linguistic and communicative strategies' in H. Brown, C. Yorio and R. Crymes (eds.). *On TESOL '77*. Washington D.C.: TESOL.

Gaies, S. 1979. 'Linguistic input in first and second language learning' in F. Eckman and A. Hastings (eds.). *Studies in First and Second Language Acquisition*. Rowley, Mass.: Newbury House.

Gaies, S. 1983. 'The investigation of language classroom processes.' *TESOL Quarterly* 17: 205–18.

Gardner, R. 1979. 'Social psychological aspects of second language acquisition' in H. Giles and R. St. Clair (eds.). *Language and Social Psychology*. Oxford: Basil Blackwell.

Gardner, R. 1980. 'On the validity of affective variables in second language acquisition: conceptual, contextual and statistical considerations.' *Language Learning* 30: 255–70.

Gardner, R. and W. Lambert. 1972. *Attitudes and Motivation in Second Language Learning*. Rowley, Mass.: Newbury House.

Gardner, R., P. Smythe, and R. Clement. 1979. 'Intensive second language study in a bicultural milieu: an investigation of attitudes, motivation and language proficiency.' *Language Learning* 29/2.

Gass, S. 1979. 'Language transfer and universal grammatical relations.' *Language Learning* 29: 327–44.

Gass, S. 1980. 'An investigation of syntactic transfer in adult second language learners' in Scarcella and Krashen (eds.) 1980.

Gass, S. 1982. 'From theory to practice' in W. Rutherford and M. Hines (eds.). *On TESOL '81*. Washington D.C.: TESOL.

Gass, S. 1984. 'The empirical basis for the universal hypothesis in interlanguage studies' in Davies and Criper (eds.) 1984.

Gass, S. and J. Ard. 1980. 'L2 data: their relevance for language universals.' *TESOL Quarterly* 16: 443–52.

Gass, S. and J. Ard. 1984. 'Second language acquisition and the ontology of language universals' in W. Rutherford (ed.). *Second Language Acquisition and Language Universals*. Amsterdam: John Benjamins.

Gass, S. and L. Selinker (eds.). 1983. *Language Transfer in Language Learning*. Rowley, Mass.: Newbury House.

Gatbonton, E. 1978. 'Patterned phonetic variability in second language speech: a gradual diffusion model.' *Canadian Modern Language Review* 34: 335–47.

Genesee, F. 1976. 'The role of intelligence in second language learning.' *Language Learning* 26: 267–80.

Genesee, F. 1982. 'Experimental neuropsychological research on second language processing.' *TESOL Quarterly* 16: 315–24.

George, H. 1972. *Common Errors in Language Learning: Insights from English*. Rowley, Mass.: Newbury House.

Giles, H. 1979. 'Ethnicity markers in speech' in K. Scherer and H. Giles (eds.). *Social Markers in Speech*. Cambridge: Cambridge University Press.

Giles, H., R. Bourhis, and D. Taylor. 1977. 'Toward a theory of language in ethnic group relations' in H. Giles (ed.). *Language Ethnicity and Intergroup Relations*. New York: Academic Press.

Giles, H. and J. Byrne. 1982. 'An intergroup approach to second language acquisition.' *Journal of Multilingual and Multicultural Development* 3: 17–40.

Gillis, M. and R. Weber. 1976. 'The emergence of sentence modalities in the English of Japanese-speaking children.' *Language Learning* 26: 77–94.

Gleason, J. and S. Weintraub. 1978. 'Input language and the acquisition of communicative competence' in K. Nelson (ed.). *Children's Language*, Vol. 1. New York: Gardner's Press.

Gleitman, L., E. Newport and H. Gleitman. 1984. 'The current status of the motherese hypothesis.' *Journal of Child Language* 11: 43–79.

Grauberg, W. 1971. 'An error analysis in the German of first-year university students' in Perren and Trim (eds.) 1971.

Greenberg, J. 1966. *Universals of Language* (2nd edition). Cambridge, Mass.: MIT Press.

Gregg, K. 1984. 'Krashen's Monitor and Occam's razor.' *Applied Linguistics* 5: 79–100.

Gremmo, M., H. Holec, and P. Riley. 1978. 'Taking the initiative: some pedagogical applications of discourse analysis.' *Mélanges Pedagogiques*, University of Nancy: CRAPEL.

Guiora, A., B. Beit-Hallahmi, R. Brannon, and C. Dull. 1972a. 'The effects of experimentally induced changes in ego status on pronunciation ability in a second language: an exploratory study.' *Comprehensive Psychiatry* 13: 421–8.

Guiora, A., R. Brannon, and C. Dull. 1972b. 'Empathy and second language learning.' *Language Learning* 22: 111–30.

Haastrup, K. and R. Phillipson. 1983. 'Achievement strategies in learner/native speaker interaction' in Faerch and Kasper (eds.) 1983a.

Hakuta, K. 1974. 'A preliminary report of the development of grammatical morphemes in a Japanese girl learning English as a second language.' *Working Papers on Bilingualism* 3: 18–43.

Hakuta, K. 1981. 'Some common goals for second and first language acquisition research' in Andersen (ed.) 1983a.

Hale, T. and E. Budar. 1970. 'Are TESOL classes the only answer?' *Modern Language Journal* 54: 487–92.

Halliday, M. 1973. *Explorations in the Functions of Language*. London: Edward Arnold.

Halliday, M. 1975. *Learning How to Mean*. London: Edward Arnold.

Halliday, M. 1978. *Language as a Social Semiotic*. London: Edward Arnold.

Hamayan, E. and G. Tucker. 1980. 'Language input in the bilingual classroom and its relationship to second language achievement.' *TESOL Quarterly* 14: 453–68.

Hammarberg, B. 1979. 'On Intralingual, Interlingual and Developmental Solutions in Interlanguage.' Paper presented at the Fifth Scandinavian Conference of Linguistics, Frostvallen.

Hansen, J. and C. Stansfield. 1981. 'The relationship of field dependent–independent cognitive styles to foreign language achievement.' *Language Learning* 31: 349–67.

Harder, P. 1980. 'Discourse as self-expression—on the reduced personality of the second language learner.' *Applied Linguistics* I/3: 262–70.

Hatch, E. 1974. 'Second language learning—universals.' *Working Papers on Bilingualism* 3: 1–18.

Hatch, E. (ed.). 1978a. *Second Language Acquisition*. Rowley, Mass.: Newbury House.

Hatch, E. 1978b. 'Acquisition of syntax in a second language' in Richards (ed.) 1978.

Hatch, E. 1978c. 'Discourse analysis and second language acquisition' in Hatch (ed.) 1978a.

Hatch, E. 1978d. 'Discourse analysis, speech acts and second language acquisition' in Ritchie (ed.) 1978.

Hatch, E. 1980. 'Second language acquisition—avoiding the question' in Felix (ed.) 1980a.

Hatch, E. 1983a. *Psycholinguistics: a Second Language Perspective*. Rowley, Mass.: Newbury House.

Hatch, E. 1983b. 'Simplified input and second language acquisition' in Andersen (ed.) 1983a.

Hatch, E. and H. Farhady. 1982. *Research Design and Statistics for Applied Linguistics*. Rowley, Mass.: Newbury House.

Hatch, E., S. Peck and J. Wagner-Gough. 1979. 'A look at process in child second language acquisition' in E. Ochs and B. Schieffelin (eds.). *Developmental Pragmatics*. New York: Academic Press.

Hatch, E., R. Shapira, and J. Gough. 1978. '"Foreigner-talk" discourse.' *ITL: Review of Applied Linguistics* 39–40: 39–59.

Hatch, E. and J. Wagner-Gough. 1975. 'Explaining sequence and variation in second language acquisition' in H. Brown (ed.). *Papers in Second Language Acquisition*. Ann Arbor, Michigan: Language Learning.

Hawkey, R. 1982. 'An Investigation of Inter-Relationships Between Cognitive/Affective and Social Factors and Language Learning.' PhD thesis, University of London.

Hellwig, L. 1983. 'A Prefabricated Pattern as a Communication Strategy.' Paper given at BAAL Annual Conference, Leicester.

Henzl, V. 1979. 'Foreigner talk in the classroom.' *International Review of Applied Linguistics* XVII: 159–65.

Hornstein, N. and D. Lightfoot (eds.). 1981. *Explanation in Linguistics: The Logical Problem of Language Acquisition*. London: Longman.

Hosenfeld, C. 1976. 'Learning about language: discovering our students' strategies.' *Foreign Language Annals* 9: 117–29.

Huang, J. and F. Hatch. 1978. 'A Chinese child's acquisition of English' in Hatch 1978a.

Huebner, T. 1979. 'Order-of-acquisition vs. dynamic paradigm: a comparison of method in interlanguage research.' *TESOL Quarterly* 13: 21–8.

Huebner, T. 1981. 'Creative construction and the case of the misguided pattern' in J. Fisher, M. Clarke, and J. Schachter (eds.). *On TESOL '80: Building Bridges*. Washington D.C.: TESOL.

Hughes, A. 1983. 'Second language learning and communicative language teaching' in K. Johnson and D. Porter (eds.). *Perspectives in Communicative Teaching*. New York: Academic Press.

Hyams, N. 1983. 'The pro-drop parameter in child grammars' in D. Flickinger (ed.). *Proceedings of WCCFL II*. Stanford, CA.: Stanford Linguistics Association.

Hyltenstam, K. 1982. 'Language, Typology, Language Universals, Markedness and Second Language Acquisition.' Paper presented at the Second European–North American Workshop of Second Language Acquisition Research, Göhrde, Germany.

Hymes, D. 1971. *On Communicative Competence*. Philadelphia, PA.: University of Pennsylvania Press.

Ioup, G. 1983. 'Acquiring complex sentences in ESL' in Bailey *et al*. 1983.

Itoh, H. and E. Hatch. 1978. 'Second language acquisition: a case study' in Hatch (ed.) 1978a.

Jackson, H. 1981. 'Contrastive analysis as a predictor of errors, with reference to Punjabi learners of English' in Fisiak (ed.) 1981.

Jackson, K. and R. Whitnam. 1971. *Evaluation of the Predictive Power of Contrastive Analyses of Japanese and English*. Final Report; Contract No. CEC-0-70-5046 (-823), US Office of Health, Education and Welfare.

Jakobovits, L. 1970. *Foreign Language Learning: a Psycholinguistic Analysis of the Issue*. Rowley, Mass.: Newbury House.

James, C. 1980. *Contrastive Analysis*. London: Longman.

James, C. 1981. 'The transfer of communicative competence' in Fisiak (ed.) 1981.

James, J. 1980. 'Learner variation: the monitor model and language learning.' *Interlanguage Studies Bulletin* 2: 99–111.

Johnson, K. 1982. *Communicative Syllabus Design*. Oxford: Pergamon.

Kasper, G. 1979. 'Communication strategies: modality reduction.' *Interlanguage Studies Bulletin* 4: 266–81.

Keenan, E. 1974. 'Conversational competence in children.' *Journal of Child Language* 1: 163–83.

Kellerman, E. 1979. 'Transfer and non-transfer: where are we now?' *Studies in Second Language Acquisition* 2: 37–57.

Kellerman, E. 1984. 'The empirical evidence for the influence of the L1 in interlanguage' in Davies and Criper (eds.) 1984.

Kleinmann, H. 1978. 'The strategy of avoidance in adult second language acquisition' in Ritchie (ed.) 1978.

Klima, E., and V. Bellugi. 1966. 'Syntactic regularities in the speech of children' in J. Lyons and R. Wales (eds.). *Psycholinguistic Papers*. Edinburgh: Edinburgh University Press.

Krashen, S. 1976. 'Formal and informal linguistic environments in language acquisition and language learning.' *TESOL Quarterly* 10: 157–68.

Krashen, S. 1977. 'Some issues relating to the monitor model' in H. Brown, C. Yorio, and R. Crymes (eds.). *On TESOL '77*. Washington, D.C.: TESOL.

Krashen, S. 1981a. *Second Language Acquisition and Second Language Learning*. Oxford: Pergamon.

Krashen, S. 1981b. 'Effective second language acquisition: insights from research' in J. Alatis, H. Altman and P. Alatis (eds.). *The Second Language Classroom: Directions for the 1980s*. New York: Oxford University Press.

Krashen, S. 1982. *Principles and Practice in Second Language Acquisition*. Oxford: Pergamon.

Krashen, S., J. Butler, R. Birnbaum, and J. Robertson. 1978. 'Two studies in language acquisition and language learning.' *ITL: Review of Applied Linguistics* 39–40: 73–92.

Krashen, S., C. Jones, S. Zelinski, and C. Usprich. 1978. 'How important is instruction?' *ELT Journal* XXXII: 257–61.

Krashen, S., M. Long, and R. Scarcella. 1979. 'Age, rate and eventual attainment in second language acquisition.' *TESOL Quarterly* 13: 573–82.

Krashen, S. and P. Pon. 1975. 'An error analysis of an advanced ESL learner: the importance of the Monitor.' *Working Papers on Bilingualism* 7: 125–9.

Krashen, S. and R. Scarcella. 1978. 'On routines and patterns in language acquisition and performance.' *Language Learning* 28: 283–300.

Krashen, S., R. Scarcella, and M. Long (eds.). 1982. *Child–Adult Differences in Second Language Acquisition*. Rowley, Mass.: Newbury House.

Krashen, S. and H. Seliger. 1975. 'The essential characteristics of formal instruction.' *TESOL Quarterly* 9: 173–83.

Krashen, S. and H. Seliger. 1976. 'The role of formal and informal linguistic environments in adult second language learning.' *International Journal of Psycholinguistics* 3: 15–21.

Krashen, S., H. Seliger, and D. Hartnett. 1974. 'Two studies in adult second language learning.' *Kritikon Litterarum* 3: 220–8.

Krashen, S. and T. Terrell. 1983. *The Natural Approach: Language Acquisition in the Classroom.* Oxford: Pergamon.

Labov, W. 1970. 'The study of language in its social context.' *Studium Generale* 23: 30–87.

Labov, W. 1972. *Sociolinguistic Patterns.* Oxford: Basil Blackwell.

Lado, R. 1957. *Linguistics Across Cultures: Applied Linguistics for Language Teachers.* Ann Arbor, Michigan: University of Michigan.

Lado, R. 1964. *Language Teaching: A Scientific Approach.* New York: McGraw Hill.

Lamendella, J. 1977. 'General principles of neurofunctional organization and their manifestations in primary and non-primary acquisition.' *Language Learning* 27: 155–96.

Lamendella, J. 1979. 'The neurofunctional basis of pattern practice.' *TESOL Quarterly* 13: 5–19.

Larsen-Freeman, D. 1978. 'Evidence of the need for a second language acquisition index of development' in Ritchie (ed.) 1978.

Larsen-Freeman, D. (ed.). 1980. *Discourse Analysis in Second Language Research.* Rowley, Mass.: Newbury House.

Larsen-Freeman, D. 1983a. 'The importance of input in second language acquisition' in Andersen (ed.) 1983a.

Larsen-Freeman, D. 1983b. 'Second language acquisition: getting the whole picture' in Bailey *et al.* (eds.) 1983.

Lee, W. 1968. 'Thoughts on contrastive linguistics in the context of language teaching' in J. Alatis (ed.). *Contrastive Linguistics and its Pedagogical Implications.* Washington, D.C.: Georgetown University.

Lenneberg, E. 1967. *Biological Foundations of Language.* New York: Wiley and Sons.

Liceras, J. 1983. 'The Role of Intake in the Determination of Learners' Competence.' Paper presented at the Tenth University of Michigan Conference on Applied Linguistics.

Lightbown, P. 1983. 'Exploring relationships between developmental and instructional sequences in L2 acquisition' in Seliger and Long (eds.) 1983.

Lightbown, P. 1984. 'The relationship between theory and method in second language acquisition research' in Davies and Criper (eds.) 1984.

Lightbown, P., N. Spada, and R. Wallace. 1980. 'Some effects of instruction on child and adolescent ESL learners' in Scarcella and Krashen (eds.) 1980.

Littlewood, W. 1979. 'Communicative performance in language developmental contexts.' *International Review of Applied Linguistics* XVII: 123–38.

Littlewood, W. 1981. 'Language variation and second language acquisition.' *Applied Linguistics* II/1: 150–8.

Lococo, V. 1976. 'A comparison of three methods for the collection of L2 data: free composition, translation and picture description.' *Working Papers on Bilingualism* 8: 59–86.

Long, M. 1977. 'Teacher feedback on learner error: mapping cognitions' in H. Brown, C. Yorio, and R. Crymes (eds.). *On TESOL '77.* Washington D.C.: TESOL.

Long, M. 1980. 'Inside the "black box": methodological issues in classroom research on language learning.' *Language Learning* 30: 1–42. Also in Seliger and Long (eds.) 1983.

Long, M. 1981a. 'Input, Interaction and Second Language Acquisition.' Paper presented at the New York Academy of Sciences Conference on Native and Foreign Language Acquisition.

Long, M. 1981b. 'Questions in foreigner talk discourse.' *Language Learning* 31: 135–57.

Long, M. 1983a. 'Native speaker/non-native speaker conversation and the negotiation of comprehensible input.' *Applied Linguistics* 4/2: 126–41.

Long, M. 1983b. 'Native speaker/non-native speaker conversation in the second language classroom' in M. Clarke and J. Handscombe (eds.). *On TESOL '82: Pacific Perspectives on Language Learning and Teaching. Washington D.C.: TESOL.*

Long, M. 1983c. 'Input and Second Language Acquisition Theory.' Paper presented at the Tenth University of Michigan Conference on Applied Linguistics.

Long, M. 1983d. 'Does second language instruction makes a difference? A review of the research.' *TESOL Quarterly* 17: 359–82.

Long, M. and C. Sato. 1983. 'Classroom foreigner talk discourse: forms and functions of teachers' questions' in Seliger and Long (eds.) 1983.

Long, M. and C. Sato. 1984. 'Methodological issues in interlanguage studies: an interactionist perspective' in Davies and Criper (eds.) 1984.

Lott, D. 1983. 'Analysing and counteracting interference errors.' *ELT Journal* 37/3: 256–61.

Lukmani, Y. 1972. 'Motivation to learn and language proficiency.' *Language Learning* 22: 261–73.

Lyons, J. 1968. *Introduction to Theoretical Linguistics.* Cambridge: Cambridge University Press.

McDonough, S. 1978. 'The foreign language learning process: introspection and generalisation' in Pickett 1978.

McDonough, S. 1981. *Psychology in Foreign Language Teaching.* London: Allen and Unwin.

McLaughlin, B. 1978a. *Second Language Acquisition in Childhood.* New York: Lawrence Erlbaum.

McLaughlin, B. 1978b. 'The Monitor Model: some methodological considerations.' *Language Learning* 28: 309–32.

MacNamara, J. 1972. 'The cognitive basis of language learning in infants.' *Psychological Review* 19: 1–13.

MacNamara, J. 1973. 'Nurseries, streets and classrooms: some comparisons and deductions.' *Modern Language Journal* 57: 250–4.

McNeill, D. 1966. 'Developmental psycholinguistics' in F. Smith and G. Miller (eds.). *The Genesis of Language: a Psycholinguistic Approach.* Cambridge, Mass.: MIT Press.

McNeill, D. 1970. *The Acquisition of Language.* New York: Harper Row.

McTear, M. 1975. 'Structure and categories of foreign language teaching sequences' in R. Allwright (ed.). *Working Papers: Language Teaching Classroom Research.* University of Essex, Department of Language and Linguistics.

Makino, T. 1979. 'English morpheme acquisition order of Japanese secondary school students.' Abstract of PhD Dissertation, *TESOL Quarterly* 13: 428.

Martin, G. 1980. 'English language acquisition: the effects of living with an American family.' *TESOL Quarterly* 14: 388–90.

Marton, W. 1981. 'Contrastive analysis in the classroom' in Fisiak (ed.) 1981.

Mason, C. 1971. 'The relevance of intensive training in English as a foreign language for university students.' *Language Learning* 21: 197–204.

Meara, P. 1980. 'Vocabulary acquisition: a neglected aspect of language learning.' *Language Teaching and Linguistics: Abstracts* 13: 221–46.

Meisel, J. 1980. 'Linguistic simplification' in Felix (ed.) 1980a.

Meisel, J. 1983. 'Strategies of second language acquisition: more than one kind of simplification' in Andersen (ed.) 1983a.

Milon, J. 1974. 'The development of negation in English by a second language learner.' *TESOL Quarterly* 8: 137–43.

Morrison, D. and G. Low. 1983. 'Monitoring and the second language learner' in J. Richards and R. Schmidt (eds.). *Language and Communication.* London: Longman.

Moskowitz, G. 1971. 'Interaction analysis—a new modern language for supervisors.' *Foreign Language Annals* 5: 211–21.

Mowrer, O. 1960. *Learning Theory and Symbolic Processes.* New York: John Wiley and Sons.

Mukattash, L. 1977. 'Problematic areas in English syntax for Jordanian students.' University of Amman, Jordan.

Naiman, N. 1974. 'The use of elicited imitation in second language acquisition research.' *Working Papers on Bilingualism* 2: 137.

Naiman, N., M. Frohlich, H. Stern, and A. Todesco. 1978. *The Good Language Learner. Research in Education No. 7.* Toronto: Ontario Institute for Studies in Education.

Naro, A. 1983. 'Comments on "Simplified Input and Second Language Acquisition"' in Andersen (ed.) 1983a.

Nemser, W. 1971. 'Approximate systems of foreign language learners.' *International Review of Applied Linguistics* IX: 115–23.

Neufeld, G. 1978. 'A theoretical perspective on the nature of linguistic aptitude.' *International Review of Applied Linguistics* XVI: 15–26.

Newport, E., H. Gleitman, and L. Gleitman. 1977. '"Mother, I'd rather do it myself": some effects and non-effects of maternal speech styles' in Snow and Ferguson (eds.) 1977.

Obler, L. 1981. 'Right hemisphere participation in second language acquisition' in Diller (ed.) 1981.

Ochs, E. 1979. 'Planned and unplanned discourse' in T. Givón (ed.). *Syntax and Semantics Vol. 12: Discourse and Semantics.* New York: Academic Press.

Oller, J. 1980. 'Communicative competence: can it be tested?' in Scarcella and Krashen (eds.) 1980.

Oller, J. and K. Perkins. 1978. 'A further comment on language proficiency as a source of variance in certain affective measures.' *Language Learning* 28: 417–23.

Oyama, S. 1976. 'A sensitive period in the acquisition of a non-native phonological system.' *Journal of Psycholinguistic Research* 5: 261–85. Also in Krashen, Scarcella, and Long (eds.) 1982.

Palmer, A. 1978. 'Measures of Achievement, Communication, Incorporation and Integration for Two Classes of Formal ESL Learners.' Paper presented at Fifth International Conference of Applied Linguistics, Montreal, Canada.

Paribakht, T. 1982. 'The Relationship Between the Use of Communication Strategies and Aspects of Target Language Proficiency: A Study of Persian ESL Students.' PhD thesis, University of Toronto.

Peck, S. 1978. 'Child–child discourse in second language acquisition' in Hatch (ed.) 1978a.

Peck, S. 1980. 'Language play in child second language acquisition' in Larsen-Freeman (ed.) 1980.

Penfield, W. and L. Roberts. 1959. *Speech and Brain Mechanisms.* New York: Atheneum Press.

Perkins, K. and D. Larsen-Freeman. 1975. 'The effect of formal language instruction on the order of morpheme acquisition.' *Language Learning* 25: 237–43.

Perren, G. and J. Trim (eds.). 1971. *Applications of Linguistics.* Cambridge: Cambridge University Press.

Pica, T. 1983. 'Adult acquisition of English as a second language under different conditions of exposure.' *Language Learning* 33: 465–97.

Pickett, G. 1978. *The Foreign Language Learning Process.* London: The British Council.

Pimsleur, P. 1966. *Pimsleur Language Aptitude Battery (PLAB).* New York: Harcourt Brace Jovanovich.

Pimsleur, P. and T. Quinn (eds.). 1971. *The Psychology of Second Language Learning.* Cambridge: Cambridge University Press.

Piranian, D. 1979. 'Communication Strategies of Foreign Language Learners: A Pilot Study.' Unpublished manuscript, Department of Slavic Linguistics, University of Washington.

Popper, K. 1976. *Unended Quest.* London: Fontana Collins.

Porter, R. 1977. 'A cross-sectional study of morpheme acquisition in first language learners.' *Language Learning* 27: 47–62.

Prator, C. 1967. 'Hierarchy of Difficulty.' Unpublished classroom lecture, University of California, Los Angeles. Cited in H. Brown 1980a.

Ravem, R. 1968. 'Language acquisition in a second language environment.' *International Review of Applied Linguistics* VI: 175–85.

Ravem, R. 1974. 'The development of WH-questions in first and second language learners' in Richards (ed.) 1974a.

Reynolds, P. 1971. *A Primer in Theory Construction*. Indianapolis: Bobbs-Merrill.

Richards, J. (ed.). 1974a. *Error Analysis*. London: Longman.

Richards, J. 1974b. 'A non-contrastive approach to error analysis' in Richards (ed.) 1974a.

Richards, J. (ed.). 1978. *Understanding Second and Foreign Language Learning*. Rowley, Mass.: Newbury House.

Richards, J. and G. Kennedy. 1977. 'Interlanguage: a review and a preview.' *RELC Journal* 8/1.

Riley, P. 1977. 'Discourse networks in classroom interaction: some problems in communicative language teaching.' *Mélanges Pedagogiques*. University of Nancy: CRAPEL.

Riley, P. 1981. 'Towards a contrastive pragmalinguistics' in Fisiak (ed.) 1981.

Ritchie, W. (ed.). 1978. *Second Language Acquisition Research*. New York: Academic Press.

Rivers, W. 1971. 'Linguistic and psychological factors in speech perception and their implications for teaching materials' in Pimsleur and Quinn (eds.) 1971.

Rivers, W. 1980. 'Foreign language acquisition: where the real problems lie.' *Applied Linguistics* I/1: 48–59.

Rivers, W. and M. Temperley. 1978. *A Practical Guide to the Teaching of English*. New York: Oxford University Press.

Robinett, B. and J. Schachter (eds.). 1983. *Second Language Learning*. University of Michigan.

Rosansky, E. 1975. 'The critical period for the acquisition of language: some cognitive developmental considerations.' *Working Papers on Bilingualism* 6: 92–102.

Rosansky, E. 1976. 'Methods and morphemes in second language acquisition research.' *Language Learning* 26: 409–25.

Rossier, R. 1976. 'Extroversion–Introversion as a Significant Variable in the Learning of Oral English as a Second Language.' PhD dissertation, University of Southern California.

Rubin, J. 1975. 'What the "Good Language Learner" can teach us.' *TESOL Quarterly* 9/1.

Rutherford, W. 1982. 'Markedness in second language acquisition.' *Language Learning* 32: 85–107.

Sachs, J. 1977. 'The adaptive significance of linguistic input to prelinguistic infants' in Snow and Ferguson (eds.) 1977.

Sajavaara, K. 1981a. 'The Nature of First Language Transfer: English as L2 in a Foreign Language Setting.' Paper presented at the first European–North American Workshop in Second Language Acquisition Research, Lake Arrowhead, California.

Sajavaara, K. 1981b. 'Contrastive linguistics past and present and a communicative approach' in Fisiak (ed.) 1981.

Sanders, C. 1981. 'Recent developments in contrastive analysis and their relevance to teachers' in Fisiak (ed.) 1981.

Savignon, S. 1976. 'On the other side of the desk: a look at teacher attitudes and motivation in second language learning.' *Canadian Modern Language Review* 76, 32.

Scarcella, R. and C. Higa. 1981. 'Input, negotiation and age differences in second language acquisition.' *Language Learning* 31: 409–37.

Scarcella, R. and S. Krashen (eds.). 1980. *Research in Second Language Acquisition*. Rowley, Mass.: Newbury House.

Schachter, J. 1974. 'An error in error analysis.' *Language Learning* 24: 205–14.

Schachter, J. and E. Kimmell. 1983. 'An Experiment with Input.' Paper given at the Seventeenth Annual TESOL Convention, Toronto.

Schachter, J. and W. Rutherford, 1979. 'Discourse function and language transfer.' *Working Papers on Bilingualism* 19: 3–12.

Scherer, A. and M. Wertheimer. 1964. *A Psycholinguistic Experiment in Foreign Language Teaching*. New York: McGraw Hill.

Schmidt, M. 1980. 'Coordinate structures and language universals in interlanguage.' *Language Learning* 30: 397–416.

Schmidt, R. 1977. 'Sociolinguistic variation and language transfer in phonology.' *Working Papers on Bilingualism* 12: 79–95.

Schneider, W. and **R. Shriffen.** 1977. 'Controlled and automatic human information processing: in detection, search and attention.' *Psychological Review* 84: 1–66.

Schouten, M. 1979. 'The missing data in second language learning research.' *Interlanguage Studies Bulletin* 4: 3–14.

Schumann, F. 1980. 'Diary of a language learner. A further analysis' in Scarcella and Krashen (eds.) 1980.

Schumann, F. and **J. Schumann.** 1977. 'Diary of a language learner: an introspective study of second language learning' in H. Brown, C. Yorio, and R. Crymes (eds.) *On TESOL '77.* Washington D.C.: TESOL.

Schumann, J. 1976. 'Second language acquisition research: getting a more global look at the learner' in H. Brown (ed.). *Papers in Second Language Acquisition. Language Learning* Special Issue 4.

Schumann, J. 1978a. *The Pidginization Process: A Model for Second Language Acquisition.* Rowley, Mass.: Newbury House.

Schumann, J. 1978b. 'Second language acquisition: the pidginization hypothesis' in Hatch (ed.) 1978a.

Schumann, J. 1978c. 'The acculturation model for second language acquisition' in R. Gingras (ed.). *Second Language Acquisition and Foreign Language Teaching.* Arlington, VA.: Center for Applied Linguistics.

Schumann, J. 1979. 'The acquisition of English negation by speakers of Spanish: a review of the literature' in Andersen, R. (ed.). *The Acquisition and Use of Spanish and English as First and Second Languages.* Washington. D.C.: TESOL.

Schumann, J. 1980. 'The acquisition of English relative clauses by second language learners' in Scarcella and Krashen (eds.) 1980.

Schwartz, J. 1980. 'The negotiation for meaning: repair in conversations between second language learners of English' in Larsen-Freeman (ed.) 1980.

Scollon, R. 1976. *Conversations with a One Year Old.* Honolulu: University of Hawaii.

Seliger, H. 1977. 'Does practice make perfect? A study of interaction patterns and L2 competence.' *Language Learning* 27: 263–75. Also in Seliger and Long (eds.) 1983.

Seliger, H. 1978. 'Implications of a multiple critical periods hypothesis for second language learning' in Ritchie (ed.) 1978.

Seliger, H. 1979. 'On the nature and function of language rules in language teaching.' *TESOL Quarterly* 13: 359–69.

Seliger, H. 1980. 'Utterance planning and correction behaviour: its function in the grammar construction process for second language learners' in H. Dechert, and M. Raupach (eds.). *Temporal Variables of Speech: Studies in Honor of Frieda Goldman-Eisler.* The Hague: Mouton.

Seliger, H. 1982. 'On the possible role of the right hemisphere in second language acquisition.' *TESOL Quarterly* 16: 307–14.

Seliger, H. and **M. Long** (eds.). 1983. *Classroom Oriented Research in Second Language Acquisition.* Rowley, Mass.: Newbury House.

Selinker, L. 1972. 'Interlanguage.' *International Review of Applied Linguistics* X: 209–30.

Selinker, L. and **J. Lamendella.** 1978a. 'Fossilization in interlanguage' in C. Blatchford and J. Schachter (eds.). *On TESOL '78: EFL Policies, Programs, Practices.* Washington D.C.: TESOL.

Selinker, L. and **J. Lamendella.** 1978b. 'Two perspectives on fossilization in interlanguage learning.' *Interlanguage Studies Bulletin* 3: 143–91.

Shapira, R. 1978. 'The non-learning of English: case study of an adult' in Hatch (ed.) 1978a.

Sharwood-Smith, M. 1981. 'Consciousness-raising and the second language learner.' *Applied Linguistics* II: 159–69.

Sinclair, J. and D. Brazil. 1982. *Teacher Talk*. Oxford: Oxford University Press.

Sinclair, J. and M. Coulthard. 1975. *Towards an Analysis of Discourse*. Oxford: Oxford University Press.

Skinner, B. 1957. *Verbal Behavior*. New York: Appleton Century Crofts.

Slobin, D. 1973. 'Cognitive prerequisites for the development of grammar' in C. Ferguson and D. Slobin (eds.). *Studies of Child Language Development*. New York: Holt Rinehart and Winston.

Smith, D. 1972. 'Some implications for the social status of pidgin languages' in D. Smith and R. Shuy (eds.). *Sociolinguistics in Cross-Cultural Analysis*. Washington D.C.: Georgetown University Press.

Smith, P. (Jr.). 1970. *A Comparison of the Cognitive and Audiolingual Approaches to Foreign Language Instruction: the Pennsylvania Foreign Language Project*. Philadelphia, PA.: Center for Curriculum Development.

Snow, C. 1976. 'The language of the mother–child relationship' in S. Rogers (ed.). *They Don't Speak Our Language*. London: Edward Arnold.

Snow, C. and C. Ferguson (eds.). 1977. *Talking to Children*. Cambridge: Cambridge University Press.

Snow, C. and M. Hoefnagel-Höhle. 1978. 'Age differences in second language acquisition' in Hatch (ed.) 1978a.

Snow, C. and M. Hoefnagel-Höhle. 1982. 'School-age second language learners' access to simplified linguistic input.' *Language Learning* 32: 411–30.

Sridhar, S. 1981. 'Contrastive analysis, error analysis and interlanguage' in Fisiak (ed.) 1981.

Stern, H. 1983. *Fundamental Concepts of Language Teaching*. Oxford: Oxford University Press.

Stevick, E. 1980. *Teaching Languages: A Way and Ways*. Rowley, Mass.: Newbury House.

Stockwell, R. and J. Bowen. 1965. *The Sounds of English and Spanish*. Chicago: Chicago University Press.

Stockwell, R., J. Bowen and J. Martin. 1965. *The Grammatical Structures of English and Spanish*. Chicago: Chicago University Press.

Strong, M. 1983. 'Social styles and second language acquisition of Spanish-speaking kindergartners.' *TESOL Quarterly* 17: 241–58.

Swain, M. 1983. 'Understanding Input Through Output.' Paper presented at the Tenth University of Michigan Conference on Applied Linguistics.

Swain, M. and B. Burnaby. 1976. 'Personality characteristics and second language learning in young children: a pilot study.' *Working Papers on Bilingualism* 11: 76–90.

Tarone, E. 1977. 'Conscious communication strategies in interlanguage: a progress report' in H. Brown, C. Yorio, and R. Crymes (eds.). *On TESOL '77*. Washington D.C.: TESOL.

Tarone, E. 1978. 'The phonology of interlanguage' in Richards (ed.) 1978.

Tarone, E. 1980. 'Communication strategies, foreigner talk and repair in interlanguage.' *Language Learning* 30: 417–31.

Tarone, E. 1981. 'Some thoughts on the notion of communicative strategy.' *TESOL Quarterly* 15: 285–95.

Tarone, E. 1982. 'Systematicity and attention in interlanguage.' *Language Learning* 32: 69–82.

Tarone, E. 1983. 'On the variability of interlanguage systems.' *Applied Linguistics* 4/2: 143–63.

Tarone, E., A. Cohen, and G. Dumas. 1976. 'A closer look at some interlanguage terminology: a framework for communication strategies.' *Working Papers on Bilingualism* 9: 76–90.

Taylor, B. 1975. 'Adult language learning strategies and their pedagogical implications.' *TESOL Quarterly* 9: 391–9.

Terrell, T., E. Gomez, and J. Mariscal. 1980. 'Can acquisition take place in the language classroom?' in Scarcella and Krashen (eds.) 1980.

Tran-Chi-Chau. 1975. 'Error analysis, contrastive analysis and students' perception: a study of difficulty in second language learning.' *International Review of Applied Linguistics* XIII: 119–43.

Tucker, G., E. Hamayan, and **F. Genesee.** 1976. 'Affective, cognitive and social factors in second language acquisition.' *Canadian Modern Language Review* 23: 214–26.

Turner, D. 1978. 'The Effect of Instruction on Second Language Learning and Second Language Acquisition.' Paper presented at the Twelfth Annual TESOL Convention, Mexico City.

Upshur, J. 1968. 'Four experiments on the relation between foreign language teaching and learning.' *Language Learning* 18: 111–24.

Varadi, T. 1973. 'Strategies of Target Language Learner Communication: Message Adjustment.' Paper presented at the Sixth Conference of the Romanian–English Linguistic Project in Timisoara.

Varonis, E. and **S. Gass.** 1983. 'Target Language Input from Non-native Speakers.' Paper given at TESOL Seventeenth Annual Convention, Toronto.

de Villiers, J. and **P. de Villiers.** 1973. 'A cross-sectional study of the acquisition of grammatical morphemes in child speech.' *Journal of Psycholinguistic Research* 2: 267–78.

Vygotsky, L. 1962. *Thought and Language.* Cambridge, Mass.: MIT Press.

Wagner-Gough, J. 1975. 'Comparative Studies in Second Language Learning.' MA thesis, UCLA, California. Also in Hatch (ed.) 1978a.

Walsh, T. and **K. Diller** (eds.). 1981. 'Neurolinguistic considerations on the optimum age for second language learning' in Diller (ed.) 1981.

Wardhaugh, R. 1970. 'The contrastive analysis hypothesis.' *TESOL Quarterly* 4: 123–30.

Waterson, N. and **C. Snow** (eds.). 1978. *The Development of Communication.* New York: John Wiley and Sons.

Watson, J. 1924. *Behaviourism.* New York: Norton.

Wells, G. 1981. 'Becoming a communicator' in G. Wells. *Learning Through Interaction.* Cambridge: Cambridge University Press.

Wells, G., M. Montgomery, and **M. McLure.** 1979. 'The development of discourse: a report on work in progress.' *Journal of Pragmatics* 3: 337–80.

Wesche, W. and **D. Ready.** 1983. 'Foreigner-Talk Discourse in the University Classroom.' Paper presented at the Tenth University of Michigan Conference on Applied Linguistics.

White, L. 1981. 'The responsibility of grammatical theory to acquisitional data' in Hornstein and Lightfoot (eds.) 1981.

White, L. 1984. 'Markedness and Parameter Setting: Some Implications for a Theory of Adult Second Language Acquisition.' Mimeograph, McGill University.

Widdowson, H. 1975a. 'EST in theory and practice.' *English for Academic Study.* ETIC Occasional Paper. London: The British Council.

Widdowson, H. 1975b. 'The significance of simplification.' *Studies in Second Language Acquisition* 1/1.

Widdowson, H. 1979. 'Rules and procedures in discourse analysis' in T. Myers (ed.). *The Development of Conversation and Discourse.* Edinburgh: Edinburgh University Press.

Widdowson, H. 1984. *Learning Purpose and Language Use.* Oxford: Oxford University Press.

Witkin, H., P. Oltman, E. Raskin, and **S. Karp.** 1971. *A Manual for the Embedded Figures Test.* Palo Alto, California: Consulting Psychologists Press.

Wode, H. 1976. 'Developmental sequences in naturalistic L2 acquisition.' *Working Papers on Bilingualism* 11: 1–13.

Wode, H. 1978. 'The L1 vs. L2 acquisition of English interrogation.' *Working Papers on Bilingualism* 15: 37–57.

Wode, H. 1980a. *Learning a Second Language 1: An Integrated View of Language Acquisition.* Tübingen: Gunter Narr.

Wode, H. 1980b. 'Operating principies and "universals" in L1, L2 and FLT' in D. Nehls (ed.). *Studies in Language Acquisition.* Heidelberg: Julius Groos.

Wode, H. 1984. 'Some theoretical implications of L2 acquisition research and the grammar of interlanguages' in Davies and Criper (eds.) 1984.

Wode, H., J. Bahns, and W. Frank. 1979. 'Developmental sequence: an alternative approach to morpheme order.' *Linguistische Berichte* 64: 55–104.

Wolfson, N. and E. Judd. 1983. *Sociolinguistics and Second Language Acquisition*. Rowley, Mass.: Newbury House.

Zobl, H. 1983a. 'Contact-induced language change, learner language and the potentials of a modified contrastive analysis' in Bailey, Long, and Peck (eds.) 1983.

Zobl, H. 1983b. 'Grammars in Search of Input and Intake.' Paper presented at the Tenth University of Michigan Conference on Applied Linguistics.

Zobl. H. 1983c. 'Markedness and the projection problem.' *Language Learning* 33: 293–313.

Zobl, H. 1984. 'Cross-language generalisations and the contrastive dimension of the interlanguage hypothesis' in Davies and Criper (eds.) 1984.

Index